CSR, Sustainability, Ethics & Governance

Series Editors
Samuel O. Idowu, London Metropolitan University, Calcutta House, London, UK
René Schmidpeter, Cologne Business School, Cologne, Germany

In recent years the discussion concerning the relation between business and society has made immense strides. This has in turn led to a broad academic and practical discussion on innovative management concepts, such as Corporate Social Responsibility, Corporate Governance and Sustainability Management. This series offers a comprehensive overview of the latest theoretical and empirical research and provides sound concepts for sustainable business strategies. In order to do so, it combines the insights of leading researchers and thinkers in the fields of management theory and the social sciences – and from all over the world, thus contributing to the interdisciplinary and intercultural discussion on the role of business in society. The underlying intention of this series is to help solve the world's most challenging problems by developing new management concepts that create value for business and society alike. In order to support those managers, researchers and students who are pursuing sustainable business approaches for our common future, the series offers them access to cutting-edge management approaches.

CSR, Sustainability, Ethics & Governance is accepted by the Norwegian Register for Scientific Journals, Series and Publishers, maintained and operated by the Norwegian Social Science Data Services (NSD)

Uwe G. Schulte

Sustainable Business

Executive Insights on Shaping Sustainable Corporate Practices

Uwe G. Schulte
Harsefeld, Germany

ISSN 2196-7075 ISSN 2196-7083 (electronic)
CSR, Sustainability, Ethics & Governance
ISBN 978-3-031-58595-1 ISBN 978-3-031-58596-8 (eBook)
https://doi.org/10.1007/978-3-031-58596-8

© The Editor(s) (if applicable) and The Author(s), under exclusive license to Springer Nature Switzerland AG 2024

This work is subject to copyright. All rights are solely and exclusively licensed by the Publisher, whether the whole or part of the material is concerned, specifically the rights of translation, reprinting, reuse of illustrations, recitation, broadcasting, reproduction on microfilms or in any other physical way, and transmission or information storage and retrieval, electronic adaptation, computer software, or by similar or dissimilar methodology now known or hereafter developed.

The use of general descriptive names, registered names, trademarks, service marks, etc. in this publication does not imply, even in the absence of a specific statement, that such names are exempt from the relevant protective laws and regulations and therefore free for general use.

The publisher, the authors and the editors are safe to assume that the advice and information in this book are believed to be true and accurate at the date of publication. Neither the publisher nor the authors or the editors give a warranty, expressed or implied, with respect to the material contained herein or for any errors or omissions that may have been made. The publisher remains neutral with regard to jurisdictional claims in published maps and institutional affiliations.

This Springer imprint is published by the registered company Springer Nature Switzerland AG
The registered company address is: Gewerbestrasse 11, 6330 Cham, Switzerland

If disposing of this product, please recycle the paper.

*In grateful memory of Prof. Robert U. Ayres,
the father of Industrial Ecology*

Acknowledgements

The Conference Board (TCB) kindly permitted to use the content of the Podcast series 'Let's Talk Sustainable Business' as the basis for this book. The book covers the content of the series for the 2 years the author had the privilege to prepare and host all the podcast episodes. The success of the podcast would not have been possible without the able support from the TCB podcast team at the time: Margaret Murphy, Marie-Jeanne Merillet, and Derek Servais.

Anke Schrader, Inga Schuster, Frauke Schulte and my wife Barbara gave valuable feedback. Lucy Goudsouzian helped with editing the raw transcripts and sorting out the publishing rights of the many graphs and pictures.

I would also like to thank my interview partners for their support and mention with gratitude their able assistants smoothing the communications, arranging recording dates and locations.

Introduction

Between May 2019 and November 2022, the author engaged in dialogues with Sustainability Experts and Senior Executives representing major multinational corporations, overseeing their corporate sustainability endeavours. The resultant podcast episodes, recorded and broadcasted during the prevailing COVID pandemic, featured the pandemic as a recurring contextual backdrop, albeit not the primary focus of these deliberations. The orchestration of the podcast series was facilitated by The Conference Board, a non-profit global think tank specialising in corporate executive peer exchange.

This podcast series garnered a diverse audience globally, as evidenced by feedback from students, executives, academics, consultants, and individuals with a general interest in sustainability. Each episode embarked upon a dual exploration, initially acquainting the audience with the interviewee and their personal sustainability journey, followed by an examination of how sustainability considerations permeate and shape their company's strategic framework. The thematic spectrum of these conversations encompassed diverse topics such as The United Nations Sustainable Development Goals, Water-stressed Regions, Ocean Plastic, Chemical Recycling, Renewable Energy, Sustainable Tourism, and the Just Transition, among others, with each episode concentrating on a singular subject.

Recognising the potential insights encapsulated in these conversations, a project was conceived to transcribe and edit the podcast episodes. This undertaking sought to enrich the transcripts with scholarly references and illustrative materials, thereby augmenting the overall reader experience. The edited text aims to preserve the conversational tone while enhancing readability. The amalgamation of experiences from these experts as presented in this book aims to provide a comprehensive overview of corporate sustainability efforts. Notably, the narrative refrains from passing judgments, affording readers the autonomy to form their own perspectives on the various approaches delineated. Supplementary references and links are provided for readers inclined to delve deeper into specific subjects. It is acknowledged that the one-hour duration of each conversation limits coverage of the multifaceted sustainability performance of each company.

Gratitude is extended to The Conference Board for their support of this project, and sincere appreciation is extended to all conversation partners who generously granted permission for the publication of their transcripts and provided valuable editorial insights.

Hamburg, Spring 2024

Contents

A Brief History of Corporate Sustainability: A Conversation with John Elkington 1

The United Nations Sustainable Development Goals 21

Human Rights in the Supply Chain 41

Sustainable Business Transformation: A Renewable Energy Example... 61

Water the New Oil.. 77

A Global Company with a Purpose................................. 95

Sustainable Tourism and Corporate Governance in Asia 109

Business Integration of Sustainability: The Customer Perspective 127

Chemical Recycling... 143

Sustainability and Science: For Impact and Value Chain Resilience..... 165

Business Success with Purpose 181

Social Innovation... 201

Energy Transition Scenarios 217

Ocean Plastics 237

Sustainable Packaging 257

Sustainable Procurement 279

Sustainable Mining and the Biodiversity Challenge 297

Decarbonising Container Shipping................................. 315

Just Transition... 333

Epilogue: Net Positive... 351

List of Figures

Fig. 1	Gro Harlem Brundtland, former Prime Minister of Norway, Chair of the Brundtland Commission on Sustainable Development. Photo: Harry Wad. Source: Wikipedia, CC BY 2.5 DEED, Attribution 2.5 Generic	2
Fig. 2	Global Reporting Initiative (GRI) history timeline. Source: Global Reporting Initiative, https://www.globalreporting.org/about-gri/mission-history/	6
Fig. 3	James Lovelock Centenary. Source: James Vine/University of Exeter	7
Fig. 4	Green Swans by Elkington. Source: John Elkington	10
Fig. 5	Fooled by Randomness by Nassim Nicolas Taleb. Source: Penguin Random House LLC, Nassim Nicolas Taleb	12
Fig. 6	The Power of Unreasonable People by Elkington/Hartigan. Source: John Elkington/Pamela Hartigan, https://en.wikipedia.org/wiki/File:The_Power_of_Unreasonable_People.jpg	15
Fig. 7	Regeneration of grasslands. Source: Savory Institute, https://web.archive.org/web/20230104015802/https:/savory.global/	16
Fig. 8	Future Fit Business Benchmark. Source: https://futurefitbusiness.org/, CC BY-SA 4.0 DEED Attribution-ShareAlike 4.0 International	19
Fig. 9	Plimsoll Line. Source: Wikipedia, public domain, Author: Wualex, Source: own work	19
Fig. 1	Benjamin Franklin House London. Source: Benjamin Franklin House, https://www.historichouses.org/house/benjamin-franklin-house/visit/	23
Fig. 2	Ex-UN General Secretary Kofi Annan, Photo: Wikipedia. Source: Wikipedia, public domain, Author: US Mission in Geneva, https://www.flickr.com/photos/us-mission/7474208582	23
Fig. 3	Millenium Development Goals Achievements 2015. Source: From "Millenium Goals Indicators", by Clarence Lio, UNSD, ©2023 United Nations. Reprinted with the permission of the United Nations. https://www.un.org/millenniumgoals/2015_	

	MDG_Report/pdf/MDG%202015%20PC%20final.pdf, downloaded 10/2023	24
Fig. 4	United Nations Sustainable Development Goals. Source: https://www.un.org/sustainabledevelopment/. The content of this publication has not been approved by the United Nations and does not reflect the views of the United Nations or its officials or Member States	25
Fig. 5	UN SDGs goal 15 Life on Land 2022 status. Source: From "The Sustainable Development Goals Report 2022", by Lois Jensen, ©2022 United Nations. Reprinted with the permission of the United Nations. https://unstats.un.org/sdgs/report/2022/The-Sustainable-Development-Goals-Report-2022.pdf, downloaded 2023, page 22. Design of Overview infographics on pages 8–25: Dewi Glanville, using icons from thenounproject.com under a NounPro licence	28
Fig. 6	RELX SDG Resource Centre. Source: RELX SDG Resource Centre	31
Fig. 7	The Responsibility100 Index, Tortoise media, 2022. Source: Tortoise Media 2022, https://www.tortoisemedia.com/	33
Fig. 8	RELX SDG resources per SDG. Source: RELX SDG Resource Centre	34
Fig. 9	RELX SDG Inspiration Days. Source: RELX SDG Resource Centre	37
Fig. 1	Declaration of Human Rights 1948. Source: Wikipedia, public domain, Author: UN, Source: United Nations Department of Public Information	43
Fig. 2	Workers' needs by Impactt. Source: Impactt Limited, https://www.workerswelfare.qa/sites/default/files/reports_item/field_document/impactt-ltd-compliance-report-en-2017.pdf	45
Fig. 3	Forced labour abuse worldwide by the RESPECT initiative. Source: *ILO* (International Labour Organization), 2012	48
Fig. 4	Textile workers Bangladesh, Photo: Impactt. Source: Impactt Limited 2013, Author: Rosey Hurst, https://impacttlimited.com/docs/2013/Report170x240v4-1.pdf	50
Fig. 5	Force majeure. Source: Wikipedia, Creative Commons Attribution-ShareAlike License 4.0	51
Fig. 6	Guiding Principles on Business and Human Rights (UN). Source: From "Guiding Principles on Business and Human Rights: Implementing the United Nations 'Protect, Respect and Remedy' Framework", by Office of the High Commissioner for Human Rights, © 2011 United Nations. Reprinted with the permission of the United Nations	53
Fig. 7	Modern slavery. Source: *ILO* (International Labour Organization), 2021	56
Fig. 8	Bangladesh exports by product group. Source: public domain, CC BY 4.0 DEED, Attribution 4.0 International, UNIDO - United Nations Industrial Development Organization, Investment and	

List of Figures   xv

	Technology Promotion Office Tokyo, 2015, http://www.unido.or.jp/en/news/1650/	57
Fig. 9	Top 10% national income share, World Inequality Database. Source: World Inequality Lab, wid.world (2023), CC BY 4.0 DEED Attribution 4.0 International	59
Fig. 1	From DONG to Ørsted. Source: Ørsted A/S, https://orsted.dk/	62
Fig. 2	Off-shore wind capacity density. Source: Deutsche WindGuard GmbH, Capacity Densities of European Offshore Wind Farms, Report conducted by Deutsche WindGuard Gmbh, 2018, https://vasab.org/wp-content/uploads/2018/06/BalticLINes_CapacityDensityStudy_June2018-1.pdf	67
Fig. 3	Floating wind turbine. Source: Ørsted A/S, https://orsted.dk/	68
Fig. 4	Off-shore wind cost decline based on IRENA 2022. Source: Uwe G. Schulte	69
Fig. 5	Fraunhofer levelized cost of electricity 2021. Source: Fraunhofer ISE, 2021, https://www.ise.fraunhofer.de/en/press-media/press-releases/2021/levelized-cost-of-electricity-renewables-clearly-superior-to-conventional-power-plants-due-to-rising-co2-prices.html	71
Fig. 6	Green hydrogen production. Source: Wikipedia, CC BY-SA 3.0 DEED, Attribution-ShareAlike 3.0 Unported, Author: Davidlfritz, Source: own work	72
Fig. 7	Irena cost reduction potential green hydrogen. Source: IRENA (2021), Making the breakthrough: Green hydrogen policies and technology costs, International Renewable Energy Agency Abu Dhabi	73
Fig. 8	Global energy consumption by source. Source: Wikipedia, CC BY-SA 3.0 DEED, Attribution-ShareAlike 3.0 Unported, Author: Our World in Data, Source: Our World in Data, https://ourworldindata.org/grapher/energy-consumption-by-source-and-region	74
Fig. 1	Earth Water. Source: Wikipedia, public domain in the United States, Author: USGS, Source: https://water.usgs.gov/edu/gallery/watercyclekids/earth-water-distribution.html, traced and redrawn from file: Earth's water distribution.gif	80
Fig. 2	Global Water Intelligence. Source: Global Water Intelligence, https://www.globalwaterintel.com/global-water-intelligence-magazine/24/2	81
Fig. 3	Smart Water Navigator. Source: Ecolab, Smart Water Navigator, https://www.smartwaternavigator.com/	82
Fig. 4	Water stress map. Source: World Resources Institute/Aqueduct, https://www.wri.org/insights/highest-water-stressed-countries	82
Fig. 5	Industrial water usage. Data source: Food and Agriculture Organization of the United Nations (via World Bank), OurWorldInData.org/water-use-stress, CC BY 4.0 DEED Attribution 4.0 International	84

Fig. 6	Water treatment percentage in 2015, unwater.org. Source: UN Habitat and WHO (2021). Progress on Wastewater Treatment: Global status and acceleration needs for SDG indicator 6.3.1., https://www.unwater.org/publications/progress-on-wastewater-treatment-631-2021-update/	85
Fig. 7	GreenBiz State of Green Business 2020. Source: GreenBiz Group Inc., https://www.greenbiz.com/report/2020-state-green-business-report	88
Fig. 8	The five steps of the Alliance for Water Stewardship (AWS) Standard V.2.0. Source: a4ws.org	90
Fig. 1	Natura Reason for Being. Source: Natura & Co, https://www.naturabrasil.com/pages/about-us	97
Fig. 2	B Corp Certification, photo: Jurre Rompa & B Lab Europe, 2019	102
Fig. 3	Natura Sustainability Vision 2030. Source: Natura & Co, https://www.naturabrasil.fr/en-us/	103
Fig. 4	Nagoya Protocol. Source: 2011 by the Secretariat of the Convention on Biological Diversity, https://www.cbd.int/abs/doc/protocol/nagoya-protocol-en.pdf	105
Fig. 1	Banyan Tree Resort, Phuket. Source: Banyan Tree Hotels & Resorts, https://www.banyantree.com/thailand/phuket/gallery	110
Fig. 2	Kosmos Journal Regenerative Capitalism. Source: Bill Reed, Regenesis	112
Fig. 3	Banyan Tree Island Farm–to–Table. Source: Banyan Tree Hotels & Resorts, https://www.banyantree.com/article/island-farm-to-table-ori9in-phuket	115
Fig. 4	Chinese characters (trad. and simplified) wēijī. Source: Wikipedia, public domain, CC0 1.0 Universal Public Domain Dedication, Author: Tomchen1989, Source: own work	118
Fig. 5	Lee Kuan Yew, Singapore's 1st Prime Minister. Source: Wikipedia, this image is a work of a U.S. military or Department of Defense employee, taken or made as part of that person's official duties. As a work of the U.S. federal government, the image is in the public domain in the United States. Author: Robert D. Ward	120
Fig. 6	Corruption Perceptions Index. Source: Wikipedia, CC BY-SA 4.0 DEED, Attribution-ShareAlike 4.0 International, Author: ConnerMiner, Source: Template used: https://commons.wikimedia.org/wiki/File:BlankMap-World.svg, Data from: https://www.transparency.org/en/cpi/2022	122
Fig. 1	Carbon Disclosure Project (CDP). Source: www.cdp.net/en/	131
Fig. 2	SAP Purpose Statement. Source: www.sap.com	132
Fig. 3	Dow Jones sustainability ranking software sector. Source: S&P Global, https://www.spglobal.com/esg/csa/yearbook/2023/ranking/	133
Fig. 4	CDP climate change 2022 company rating. Source: www.cdp.net/en/	133

List of Figures   xvii

Fig. 5	Pathfinder project. Source: public domain, The Pathfinder Framework, https://www.wbcsd.org/Programs/Climate-and-Energy/Climate/SOS-1.5/Resources/Pathfinder-Framework-Version-2.0	134
Fig. 6	SAP Sustainability Control Tower. Source: www.sap.com, https://blogs.sap.com/2021/12/14/getting-esg-reporting-and-performance-management-under-control-with-the-sap-sustainability-control-tower/	138
Fig. 7	Value Balancing Alliance impact approach. Source: CC BY-ND 4.0 DEED, Attribution-NoDerivs 4.0 International	140
Fig. 1	Plastic polymers. Source: Wikipedia, https://upload.wikimedia.org/wikipedia/commons/5/5f/Plastics_Summary.svg, CC0 1.0 DEED, CC0 1.0 Universal, Author: Orion Lawlor, Source: own work	145
Fig. 2	Pyrolysis oil from Pyrum. Source: www.basf.com	146
Fig. 3	Global plastic recycling rates. Source: Uwe G. Schulte	147
Fig. 4	Plastic types. Source: Plastics for Change, https://www.plastics-forchange.org/blog/different-types-of-plastic (right part), Uwe G. Schulte (left part)	147
Fig. 5	BASF ChemCycling project. Source: BASF, https://www.basf.com/at/de/who-we-are/sustainability/whats-new/sustainability-news/2021/BASF-quantafuel-and-remondis-want-to-cooperate-on-chemical-recycling-of-plastic-waste.html	149
Fig. 6	Plastic packaging recycling rates 2018 Europe. Source: Eurostat, https://ec.europa.eu/eurostat/de/web/products-eurostat-news/-/ddn-20210113-1, modifications: UK data deleted as per https://ec.europa.eu/eurostat/web/main/about-us/policies/copyright	150
Fig. 7	Sphera life cycle assessment of chemical recycling vs incineration. Source: BASF, https://www.basf.com/global/de.html	151
Fig. 8	Plastic garbage landfill, Vietnam. Source: Böll Foundation. Photo: Lê Đình Tuyến	152
Fig. 9	Mass balance approach. Source: Circularise, https://www.circularise.com/blogs/mass-balance-approach-for-the-sustainable-chemicals-transition	156
Fig. 10	Steamcracking process by ChemistryViews. Source: Wiley-VCH GmbH, a Wiley Company, V. Koester, Steamcracker, ChemistryViews 2019, https://doi.org/10.1002/chemv.201900023; reproduced with permission	158
Fig. 11	Chemical recycling outlook. Source: Plastics Europe, https://plasticseurope.org/	162
Fig. 1	3M State of Science survey. Source: 3M State of Science Index, 2022, https://www.3m.com/	167
Fig. 2	3M technical forum session in the early 1950s. Source: 3M, https://multimedia.3m.com/mws/media/1712400/3m-century-of-innovation-book.pdf	169

Fig. 3	3M sustainability commitment. Source: 3M, https://multimedia.3m.com/mws/media/2292786O/3m-2023-global-impact-report.pdf	172
Fig. 4	Earthworm Foundation. Source: Earthworm Foundation (EF)	176
Fig. 1	First Dutch state mine Wilhelmina 1906. Source: dsm-firmenich, https://www.dsm-firmenich.com/corporate/home.html	184
Fig. 2	DSM share development 2010–2021. Source: dsm-firmenich, https://www.dsm.com/corporate/investors/shares/share-performance.html	185
Fig. 3	Salmon farming with algae feed. Source: dsm-firmenich, https://www.dsm.com/corporate/markets/animal-feed/replacing-fish-with-algae-with-veramaris.html	190
Fig. 4	UN Sustainable Development Goal 2. Source: https://www.un.org/sustainabledevelopment/. The content of this publication has not been approved by the United Nations and does not reflect the views of the United Nations or its officials or Member States	192
Fig. 5	UN Sustainable Development Goal 3. Source: https://www.un.org/sustainabledevelopment/. The content of this publication has not been approved by the United Nations and does not reflect the views of the United Nations or its officials or Member States	192
Fig. 6	UN Sustainable Development Goal 12. Source: https://www.un.org/sustainabledevelopment/. The content of this publication has not been approved by the United Nations and does not reflect the views of the United Nations or its officials or Member States	192
Fig. 7	UN Sustainable Development Goal 13. Source: https://www.un.org/sustainabledevelopment/. The content of this publication has not been approved by the United Nations and does not reflect the views of the United Nations or its officials or Member States	193
Fig. 8	Effects of malnutrition on children. Source: Uwe G. Schulte, Source: Unicef	195
Fig. 9	Prevalence of children under five who are not growing well (stunted, wasted, or overweight), 2018. Source: Uwe G. Schulte, Source: Unicef	196
Fig. 10	Africa Improved Foods (AIF). Source: Africa Improved Foods, https://africaimprovedfoods.com/	197
Fig. 1	Steelcase Camp Ignite 2019. Source: Steelcase Inc., https://www.steelcase.com/eu-en/research/articles/topics/social-impact/camp-ignite-sparks-equitable-opportunities/	206
Fig. 2	From input to impact. Source: Uwe G. Schulte, Source: https://www.oecd.org/dac/results-development/what-are-results.htm	207
Fig. 3	Steelcase SDG priority goals 4,10, and 11. Source: https://www.un.org/sustainabledevelopment/. The content of this publication has not been approved by the United Nations and does not reflect the views of the United Nations or its officials or Member States	208

List of Figures   xix

Fig. 4	Steelcase core values. Source: Steelcase Inc., https://www.steelcase.com/	212
Fig. 5	Global Initiative for Inclusive Information and Communication Technology. Source: G3ict, https://g3ict.org/	213
Fig. 1	Putting the Genie Back, book by D. Hone. Source: Shell International Ltd., https://blogs.shell.com/category/sea-level/	219
Fig. 2	Shell global warming scenarios. Source: Shell International Ltd., https://blogs.shell.com/2021/02/10/exploring-the-energy-future/	222
Fig. 3	Shell's world energy model. Source: Shell International Ltd., https://www.shell.com/news-and-insights/scenarios/what-scenario-planning-models-does-shell-use/worldenergy-model/_jcr_content/root/main/section/simple/call_to_action/links/item0.stream/1651505502658/2ee82a9c68cd84e572c9db09cc43d7ec3e3fafe7/shell-worldenergy-model.pdf	223
Fig. 4	Shell 1.5 degree Sky scenario. Source: Shell International Ltd., https://aperc.or.jp/file/2021/5/21/S2-1+Powell.pdf	227
Fig. 5	Shell 2.5 degrees Islands scenario. Source: Shell International Ltd., https://www.shell.com/news-and-insights/scenarios/what-are-the-previous-shellscenarios/_jcr_content/root/main/section_1789847828/promo_copy_142460259/links/item0.stream/1652119830834/fba2959d9759c5ae806a03acfb187f1c33409a91/energytransformation-scenarios.pdf	228
Fig. 6	Overview Shell Sky, Waves, Islands. Source: Shell International Ltd., https://blogs.shell.com/2021/02/10/exploring-the-energy-future/	230
Fig. 7	Green hydrogen steel process. Source: Uwe G. Schulte	233
Fig. 8	IEA: green hydrogen cost. Source: IEA - International Energy Agency, https://www.iea.org/reports/the-future-of-hydrogen, Creative Commons Attribution 4.0 licence (CC BY 4.0)	233
Fig. 9	Bloomberg top 10 global electrolysers. Source: BloombergNEF	234
Fig. 1	Ocean acidification, Scripps Institution of Oceanography. Source: Sky Smith, California Sea Grant	239
Fig. 2	Sustainable fishery. Source: Wikipedia, CC BY-SA 4.0 DEED, Attribution-ShareAlike 4.0 International, Author: Hannah Ritchie and Max Roser, Source: https://ourworldindata.org/fish-and-overfishing	241
Fig. 3	The POSEIDON model of ocean fisheries. Source: Springer Nature	242
Fig. 4	Data from Ocean Conservancy's 2019 International Coastal Cleanup®. Source: Ocean Conservancy, https://oceanconservancy.org/wp-content/uploads/2020/10/FINAL_2020ICC_Report.pdf	243
Fig. 5	Abandoned fishing gear. Source: Joel Baziuk, Global Ghost Gear Initiative	246

Fig. 6	Trash trapper, Centre for Marinelife Conservation and Community Development. Source: Ocean Conservancy, https://oceanconservancy.org/blog/2021/01/06/cleaning-arteries-vietnam/	248
Fig. 1	Example shelf-ready packaging. Source: Smurfit Kappa, https://www.smurfitkappa.com/de/products-and-services/packaging/shelf-ready-packaging	260
Fig. 2	Roermond Circular Paper Mill. Source: Smurfit Kappa, https://www.smurfitkappa.com/de/sustainability/approach/our-circular-business/roermond-case-study	261
Fig. 3	Sankey diagram wood biomass EU 2017. Source: European Union, 2022, Sankey diagrams of woody biomass flows in the EU, Release 2021, Years 2009–2017, https://knowledge4policy.ec.europa.eu/sites/default/files/Sankey_diagrams.pdf	264
Fig. 4	Carbon storage by tree age. Source: NCASI 2021, https://www.ncasi.org/wp-content/uploads/2021/01/NCASI22_Forest_Carbon_YoungVsOld_print.pdf	265
Fig. 5	Smurfit Kappa recycling process. Source: Smurfit Kappa, https://www.smurfitkappa.com/-/m/files/publications%2D%2D-global/sustainability-reports/smurfit_kappa_sustainable_development_report_2022.pdf?rev=e2161db1df74451ca8dfc031214638d4	267
Fig. 6	Thermo box. Source: Smurfit Kappa, https://www.smurfitkappa.com/de/products-and-services/packaging/thermobox	272
Fig. 7	Honeycomb packaging. Source: Smurfit Kappa, https://www.smurfitkappa.com/products-and-services/packaging/hexacomb-packaging	274
Fig. 8	Detergent box with child safety closure. Source: Smurfit Kappa, https://www.smurfitkappa.com/products-and-services/packaging/toplock-detergent-box	275
Fig. 9	Graduates of Smurfit Kappa's Back to School Programme. Source: Smurfit Kappa, https://www.smurfitkappa.com/-/m/files/publications%2D%2D-global/sustainability-reports/our-open-community-2021.pdf?rev=3ebc3d758d444c3ba5258e7d7781dbee	277
Fig. 1	World population projections. Source: Wikipedia, CC BY 3.0 IGO DEED, Attribution 3.0 Intergovernmental Organization, Author: United Nations, DESA, Population Division, Source: https://population.un.org/wpp/Graphs/Probabilistic/POP/TOT/900	282
Fig. 2	Global agricultural land (% of land areas), World Bank Data. Source: CC BY 4.0 DEED, Attribution 4.0 International, The World Bank, https://data.worldbank.org/indicator/AG.LND.AGRI.K2?end=2021&start=1961	283
Fig. 3	TfS member companies. Source: Together For Sustainability, TfS Membership – status June 2022, www.tfs-initiative.com	286
Fig. 4	Example child labour incidence monitoring. Source: Bayer AG, Sustainability Report	289

Fig. 5	Development of hunger—FAO Report 2022. Source: Food and Agriculture Organization of the United Nations. Reproduced with permission	290
Fig. 6	Sustainable Procurement Pledge logo. Source: Sustainable Procurement Pledge, https://spp.earth/	292
Fig. 1	French National Museum of Natural History. Source: Wikipedia, Creative Commons Attribution-Share Alike 3.0 Unported, 2.5 Generic, 2.0 Generic and 1.0 Generic, Author: Spiridon MANOLIU, Source: own work	302
Fig. 2	NZ North Island brown kiwi. Source: Wikipedia, public domain worldwide, Author: Maungatautari Ecological Island Trust, Source: https://www.sanctuarymountain.co.nz/	304
Fig. 3	Act4nature partners. Source: act4nature international, https://www.act4nature.com/	305
Fig. 4	Barrikote waterproofing paperboard. Source: Imerys S. A., https://www.imerys.com/product-ranges/barrikote-systems	306
Fig. 5	Barrikote food tray. Source: Imerys S. A., https://www.imerys.com/product-ranges/barrikote-systems	306
Fig. 6	Lithium-ion battery. Source: VectorMine, https://vectormine.com/	308
Fig. 7	Graphite. Source: Wikipedia, CC BY-SA 2.5 DEED, Attribution-ShareAlike 2.5 Generic, Author: Intercalactionrp.png: Anton, derivative work: Mattman723 (talk), Source: Intercalactionrp.png	309
Fig. 8	Imerys life-cycle analysis method. Source: Imerys S. A., https://www.imerys.com/sustainability	310
Fig. 9	Imerys Pioneer label. Source: Imerys S. A., https://www.imerys.com/sustainability	310
Fig. 1	Allen, Cecil J. (1928), The Steel Highway. Source: Wikipedia, public domain, Author: Andy Dingley (scanner), Source: Scan from Allen, Cecil J. (1928), The Steel Highway, London: Longmans, Green & Co., pp. facing page. (II) 108	317
Fig. 2	Maersk assessment of social and environmental materiality. Source: A.P. Moller—Maersk, 2021 Sustainability Report, https://www.maersk.com/	321
Fig. 3	Maersk roadmap to net zero. Source: A.P. Moller—Maersk, https://www.maersk.com/news/articles/2022/01/12/apmm-accelerates-net-zero-emission-targets-to-2040-and-sets-milestone-2030-targets	323
Fig. 4	Green methanol production process from different renewable feedstocks. Source: The Methanol Institute, https://www.methanol.org/wp-content/uploads/2020/01/Methanol-Emerging-Global-Energy-Markets-energy-industry-forum.pdf	324
Fig. 5	Projected renewable methanol production capacity. Source: The Methanol Institute, https://www.methanol.org/renewable/	328
Fig. 1	Fischer–Tropsch synthesis—ACS Publications. Source: Reprinted with permission from ACS Catal. 2022, 12, 19,	

	12092–12112 Publication Date: September 21, 2022, https://doi.org/10.1021/acscatal.2c03404, Copyright © 2022 American Chemical Society	335
Fig. 2	Green hydrogen production. Source: CIC energiGUNE, https://cicenergigune.com/en/blog/electrolysis-water-sustainable-produce-green-hydrogen	338
Fig. 3	UN Sustainable Development Goal 17. Source: https://www.un.org/sustainabledevelopment/. The content of this publication has not been approved by the United Nations and does not reflect the views of the United Nations or its officials or Member States	339
Fig. 4	Sasol GHG reduction roadmap. Source: Sasol—used with permission, https://www.sasol.com/sites/default/files/2022-11/SASOL_CC%20Report%202022%20%202_2.pdf	340
Fig. 1	Polman/Winston, Net Positive. Source: Paul Polman, Andrew Winston, https://netpositive.world/book/	352
Fig. 2	Lifebuoy soap brand. Source: Reproduced with kind permission of Unilever PLC and group companies	356
Fig. 3	Doughnut Economics. Source: Wikipedia, CC BY-SA 4.0 DEED, Attribution-ShareAlike 4.0 International, Author: DoughnutEconomics, Source: own work	359

A Brief History of Corporate Sustainability: A Conversation with John Elkington

Recorded April 2020

Uwe Schulte
Today I will be talking to John Elkington from Volans about the journey of corporate sustainability from the 70s of the last century until now. Let me introduce our guests to you. John is an author, advisor, and serial entrepreneur. He is a world authority on corporate sustainability and sustainable development. He has written and co-authored 20 books including 'Green Consumer Guide—Challenge', '10 ways to Connect tomorrow's profits with tomorrow's bottom line'. His latest book, 'Green Swans', was published in 2020, with his 21st due out in September. John is a founder and chief pollinator at Volans. He also co-founded Environmental Data Services (ENDS) and SustainAbility. He is a member of the World Wildlife Fund Council of Ambassadors and a visiting professor at Cranfield University School of Management, Imperial College and UCL in London. He is a member of over 20 boards and advisory boards and over the time he has been in more than 80 boards and advisory boards. A very warm welcome to you, John.

John Elkington

Thank you, Uwe. And thank you to the Conference Board for offering me the platform today.

Uwe Schulte

This is an absolute pleasure for us, and we are looking forward to the conversation and let us get started by talking about sustainability in general. The word has been used in various ways, and I like the definition from the 1987 UN Brundtland report most.[1] Where it says that it is: development that meets the needs of the present without compromising the ability of future generations to meet their own needs. How do you see it, John (Fig. 1)?

John Elkington

That Brundtland Commission definition was clear and has stood the test of time. Still, the intergenerational part of the change agenda is often overlooked. To a degree, that element of the challenge was spotlighted during the Coronavirus crisis, where we were trying to protect older people in the population, me included. Such tensions between the interests of older people and younger people and those not yet born are absolutely central to the sustainability agenda, at least as I understand it.

Uwe Schulte

You are pointing out a key point, but before we get into that, let us mentally step back to the 70s. At that time, corporations did not have a clear concept of sustainability. During my years at university, the chemical disaster in Seveso, Italy happened. It was 1976. The environmental impact of chemicals became much more prominent and problematic in the eyes of the public. Eight years later, the even

Fig. 1 Gro Harlem Brundtland, former Prime Minister of Norway, Chair of the Brundtland Commission on Sustainable Development. Photo: Harry Wad. Source: Wikipedia, CC BY 2.5 DEED, Attribution 2.5 Generic

---

[1] https://sustainabledevelopment.un.org/content/documents/5987our-common-future.pdf

bigger tragedy in Bhopal occurred with Union Carbide, today a Dow plant. The 70s and 80s were the time when corporations started to take Environmental Protection much more seriously. But then you consider Rachel Carson: she published 'Silent Spring', I think in the late 50s or early 60s. That was the start of the environmental movement, and it still took such a long time to catch on. Do you see it the same way?

John Elkington

Yes, I do. Rachel Carson's "Silent Spring"[2] came out in 1962 from memory. And as you say, that really was a seed crystal around which the global environmental movement built. And it is interesting that this year, 2020, will mark on April the 22nd the 50th anniversary of Earth Day. So that started in the United States in 1970. Something over 20 million Americans got involved. That was about 10% of the US population at that stage and launched a whole series of new regulations. Rachel Carson's book was a catalyst for much of that. But over time the environmental movement has been a bit like a snowball. It has pulled up one issue after another and sort of incorporated it—and that complexity sometimes can be a bit of a problem. But I think the 50th anniversary is a good chance not only to look back, but to look forward.

Uwe Schulte

That is what is of course required. I would like to get a sense of how this corporate sustainability has developed because I think this is important. Because we are standing at the brink of a new stage, and it is always good to look back in history. I am sometimes an impatient guy. And, when we are talking about the 60s and 70s, John, you, and I might be sounding to our audience as old men, which we are. But on the other hand, we have seen it coming along. And I think we should talk about it. I will share something: when I was a product developer at Unilever in Germany, even in the 90s, I was scolded by a senior executive from the Unilever Board for collaborating with NGOs for allowing a joint evaluation of critical recipe components. What a long way Unilever has come since then, hasn't it?

John Elkington

It has. Firstly, to the old men, old people point, I was 70 last year in June. At a time when some of my baby boomer colleagues and friends are getting to retirement, the challenge we face is that we are only just beginning to understand the system change agenda. The way I see it, the next 10–15 years are likely to be the most exciting and challenging and, in some ways, politically dangerous period of my entire working life.

But to go back to your question, early on we looked at major projects, in the early 1970s. Back then I would work on environmental impact assessments, for proposed oil refineries, airports, motorways, and so on. Then it moved from those major projects to production facilities and products, precisely what you were dealing with at Unilever. Next, we got into life cycle assessment and the complexities around that.

---

[2] https://www.rachelcarson.org/silent-spring

You mentioned kindly The Green Consumer Guide[3] that came out in 1988; it sold around one million copies, in just over 18 months. It happened to coincide with a period where people were increasingly concerned about a range of issues relating back to products. They would focus on lead, mercury, chlorine, CFCs: a whole range of substances.

You mentioned NGOs and I remember Greenpeace at that time saying to me that they had just discovered the power of brands, the leverage that they could have if they attacked brands—and they just described it as a bit like discovering gunpowder. We went from major projects and products and processes right into the heart of corporate capitalism, driven by this focus on brands and corporate reputation. That was a major shift and drove much of what then happened from the early 90s on.

Uwe Schulte
I was on the other side. I remember it well. When you were in corporate development you saw both sides in a way you have of course to look after the interests of your company but at the same time these guys raised questions that were relevant, and we were struggling for quite a while. What was the right way of engaging with NGOs at that time? And I guess that gradually changed, and those people who scolded me in the beginning for having collaborated with NGOs, those were then really getting the gist of it. And you are right, the brands were an easy lever and I guess that is why the fast-moving consumer goods were one of the first ones to go beyond that reactive way of dealing with things.

John Elkington
Well, it's funny to recall, but in the late 80s, I worked with the chairmen of Unilever in Switzerland and Italy, before the Green Consumer Guide came out. He, like you, already saw the need to engage NGOs at that time. The board of Unilever, though, could not yet see it. So, in the end, we ended up working with Procter and Gamble. But change happened pretty quickly. And one critical driver was the emergence into positions of influence and power in business of a younger generation people who no longer saw this as somebody else's agenda, something imposed on them, something getting in the way of what they were meant to be doing. The question now was how do we do it to the best effect—and, in the process, make commercial sense of it?

Uwe Schulte
In the late 90s and in the turn of the century, we went through a transition where suddenly words like corporate social responsibility emerged. Not lot of people were really very clear what it meant, and a lot of incarnations emerged. I remember that I had very interesting debates about what is more important—should we look after some externalities or should we take care of our shareholder and create value for them and everything else will fall in line.

---

[3] https://www.amazon.com/Green-Consumer-John-Elkington/dp/0140127089

John Elkington

Around the world, the agenda was expressed in different terms, and rooted in different ways. For example, in the United States, corporate citizenship largely meant volunteering. I also worked in Japan for 25 years. There you would find Japanese corporations thinking about global citizenship primarily in terms of the natural environment. Human rights, for example, really wasn't part of their thinking. And in Europe, it fitted into a different cultural concept context yet again, so we saw the region incubating terms like CSR and ESG. But most companies, most industries got stranded there. They thought about how could they be nicer? How could they be a bit better? How could they offer poorer people access to some of their products and services. They were not thinking about system change, at least not then.

Uwe Schulte

No, and it was too early. A decade in the twenty-first century was one of glossy wonderful reports with wonderful stories which were disconnected with the rest of the business and that of course then caused a lot of criticism, greenwashing, and what have you. But you were right. It opened gradually, the visibility of social aspects beyond just environmental and product safety aspects, didn't it?

John Elkington

Yes, it did. It is easy now to look back and criticise corporate reporting in its various versions and forms. But think back to what the world was like when organisations like the Global Reporting Initiative were founded. I was part of the founding group and then on the board for a while. When such initiatives started to evolve, most companies really did not want to talk about this stuff. They did not know how to, and yet they soon found that the reporting process enabled them to begin to identify their priorities, and begin to engage the wider world, including activists and campaigning NGOs (Fig. 2).

Looking back, it was a very, very important part of the opening up process, but over time it lost momentum. But again, recall what the world was like before all of this. I remember a senior executive in Shell, for example, telling me in the 1980s that they would never report. Because their business was too big and too complicated. Well, I worked on the first sustainability report that Shell did, in 1997, which helped introduce my concept of the triple bottom line 'people, planet, profit' to the wider world. Things were changing—and it is easy to forget how much they did change.

Uwe Schulte

You are right, it is easy to criticise in hindsight. We achieved a lot of things in these periods as well. Think about the ozone layer[4] which really improved through these processes. Lead disappeared from gasoline. So yes, things have improved, and people started to have a wider range of visibility and I think that is when the word sustainability came into it more and, the Millennium Goals that have been criticised a

---

[4] https://earth.esa.int/eogateway/news/satellites-track-the-health-of-the-ozone-layer/heritage-missions-track-the-antarctic-ozone-hole

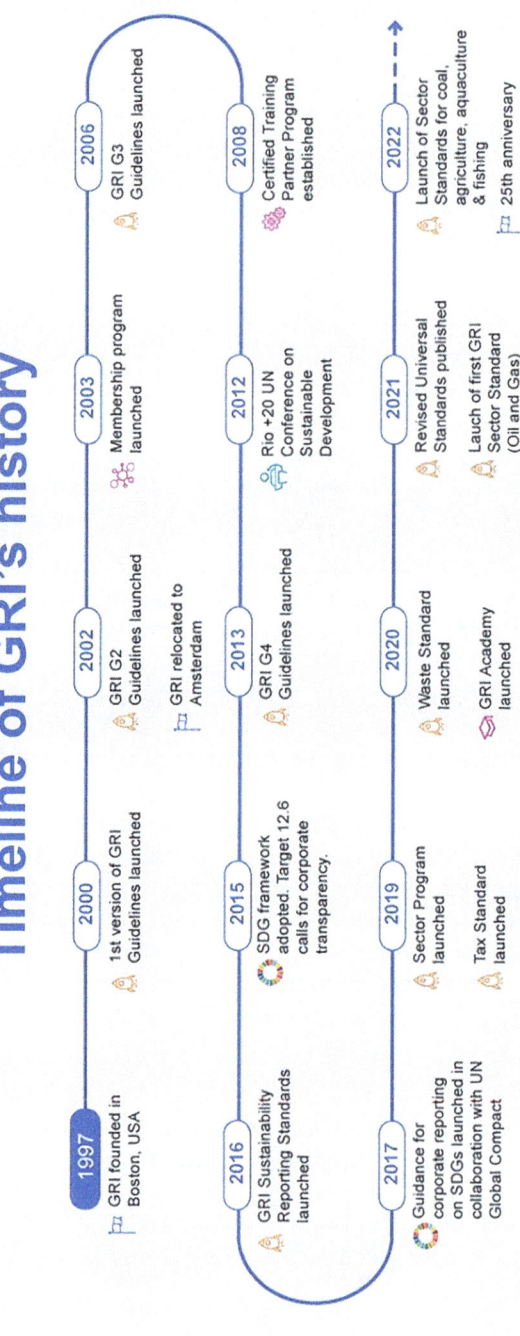

Fig. 2 Global Reporting Initiative (GRI) history timeline. Source: Global Reporting Initiative, https://www.globalreporting.org/about-gri/mission-history/

Fig. 3 James Lovelock Centenary. Source: James Vine/University of Exeter

lot for not having achieved exactly what they were aiming for, but these ambitious goals have also managed to get a lot more things going. Even so, I think with the Millennium Goals differently to the United Nations Sustainable Development Goals the part corporations can play and should play was not as clear as it is now, don't you think?

John Elkington

Well, business still seemed to be, if not the enemy, certainly a complicating factor. So, when the Millennium Development Goals came along, they were shaped largely by the public sector and government. As you say, with the Sustainable Development Goals it was very, very different in the sense that businesspeople were now involved from the very outset.

I just want to offer one tiny little reflection—which is that we tend to forget what was behind some of these big changes. Last year I went to a 100th birthday party of James Lovelock, who I am sure you will know of. But what people do not remember is that Rachel Carson's book Silent Spring was based on work that Lovelock did from the late 50s, which was then picked up by Shell's labs at Sittingbourne. Then came his work on CFCs,[5] which again disrupted the global chemical industry. Then he came up with the idea of Gaia (Fig. 3).

That was a very early, scientifically based effort to address system change issues. It has taken the rest of us a little while to catch up with all of this. But now I think we are on a very strongly accelerative curve where people are suddenly starting to demand: Why didn't you tell us about this before? Why didn't you tell us how to do it? As a result, as the agenda mainstreams, it will be a very challenging moment in our political history.

---

[5] https://en.wikipedia.org/wiki/Chlorofluorocarbon

Uwe Schulte

I like your optimism about the next 15 years. Just let us talk a little bit about Gaia, because I am not sure whether everybody is aware of Mother Earth in that sense.

John Elkington

Well, I should declare an interest, which is that our oldest daughter, now 42, is called Gaia. And that was because I first came across Jim Lovelock's work back in the 1970s. The simple idea behind Gaia was that the entire planet can be seen as working very much like a single organism. In the same way that the body has hormones, there are certain chemicals in the atmosphere which have a quite disproportionate impact on weather and climatic patterns. They may come from seaweed; they may come from elsewhere.

At the time, Jim's thinking was dismissed out of hand by many people. In mainstream science, over time, some people have started to use different phraseology. They talk about global system science, for example, rather than Gaia—but the central concept is that the world is much, much more linked than we originally imagined. So many scientists now talk about the Anthropocene, the first period in this planet's history where one species—our own—has an impact akin to geological forces. We have yet to wake up to that fact—and to its consequences.

Uwe Schulte

This is a very, very powerful concept and even though it took a very long time to catch on, we still should relate back to it. I was not aware of the 100th[6] birthday celebration. That is a great idea. What you were saying resonates with me as well because after the financial crisis in 2008 and 2009, I saw a gradual shift which is now accelerating over the last 2 years. Suddenly people in the financial community are starting to realise that the old idea that sustainability is something companies do when they have time to do it is not enough. The engagement around the sustainability agenda is now a relevant factor to evaluate the solidity, agility—and to use a recently become popular word—resilience of a company.

John Elkington

The current sustainability agenda for business has largely been defined by business, often with clear self-interest, largely as a responsibility agenda. How do you become a bit more transparent? How do you report successfully? How can you be a bit more accountable? How can you get stakeholders engaged? This is the responsibility stakeholder model, which people like the Business Roundtable are now coming round to talking about, once again. But, exactly as you described it, we are in a moment in history where that responsibility paradigm or framing is no longer remotely enough.

Yes, it is a good foundation. But some of the big challenges we have been talking about for an exceedingly long time, most obviously the climate emergency, are now starting to get their claws into supply chains, into urban economies, and so on.

---

[6] https://lovelockcentenary.info/

The whole issue of resilience is now front and centre, a term I first heard businesspeople discussing about 12–15 years ago on the front lawn of the World Economic Forum outside Geneva. That agenda is really coming up the curve. But the only way to ensure the longer-term resilience of complex systems is to regenerate the health of those systems.

Meanwhile, what we have been doing very actively, without thinking about it, is degenerating our economies, degenerating our societies, and degenerating, most critically, the biosphere. Most businesspeople have not yet gone up that learning curve, but by God, I think they will have to in the next few years.

Uwe Schulte
Can we just go back to the situation we are currently in and there are people who look at the COVID-19 crisis and they are wondering how this will affect the corporate sustainability agenda. Is pessimism the right way of looking at this? Will we be just wanting to reboot economies or are we going to reconsider and rethink?

John Elkington
I am not a biblical person, but bits of the Bible still stick in my mind. The writing on the wall was one of those moments where powerful people were suddenly warned about the nature of the world that they were moving into. And I think COVID-19 and its impact around the world is one of those moments where it is becoming very much clearer even to ordinary people.

The way that we have been doing business, the way we have been understanding growth and GDP, these sorts of things really are not fit for purpose in what is to come. Things are going to get a good deal blacker, bleaker. I think the economic and then social repercussions of what has just happened, and is continuing to happen, will play through for not just years, but decades.

And the impact on younger people is something that we are going to have to think about very much more seriously. But I am an optimist. When our species gets backed into a corner or backs itself into a corner as it is now doing, some of our best work can be done. I expect a period of intense innovation at every level in our economies and societies and I am very excited to think that you and I and others may well be part of all of that. The real test will be whether we still have something useful to contribute.

Uwe Schulte
That indeed will be the test. Let us talk about sustainable development, as you have outlined in your new book 'Green Swans'.[7] Do you want to say just a couple of words about the book and what motivated you to write it? (Fig. 4)

John Elkington
Happily. I mean, some people will know that over 25 years ago, I produced the concept of the triple bottom line. I still think the concept was a good one, but in 2018 I launched the first-ever product recall of a management concept. Not because

---

[7] https://volans.com/project/green-swans/

Fig. 4 Green Swans by Elkington. Source: John Elkington

I thought the triple bottom line was a bad idea, but because it was being misunderstood and mis-applied. We were focusing too much on incremental change, too little on systemic change.

Since Covid, however, people have been talking about system change left, right, and centre. Nassim Nicholas Taleb talked about Black Swans, trends and events that take us exponentially in unexpected directions. We are now at one of those points in history where Black Swans are crowding in, whether we predicted them or not. But, in the new book, my question is whether we can ensure that Green Swan change trajectories, involving positive exponentials, can be triggered.

Uwe Schulte

These are challenging times, and it is interesting that your book, even so you wrote it before the Covid crisis broke out, has so much meaning for it. Let us explore that a little bit, but before we do this: You made a very brave, or should I put it, strange move. You just mentioned your concept of triple bottom line. It has been adopted by many people, by many companies, including your own and it is now almost 2 years ago you publicly withdrew and made a public recall. Can you explain that?

John Elkington

Well, you cannot recall an idea. Instead, it was a provocation. The Harvard Business Review, which ran the recall article, told me that it was the first time they knew of where anyone had ever recalled a management concept. The reason I did it was simple. The triple bottom line works perfectly well if used in the right way. But just as car companies sometimes recall vehicles because there is some defect, I felt it was time to do the same here. The defect with the triple bottom line has been that people basically understood this to be about being more responsible, whereas for me it was that, but it was also about how do you make the system more sustainable—not just individual companies, not just their supply chains, but the economic system as a whole. Broadly people were very supportive. I had very positive feedback, but then the question was: OK, what's next?

Uwe Schulte

And that is what we are going to talk about now. And for that you have assembled a whole flock of birds: grey, black, green, even blue, and ugly ducklings. I think we should get started with, at least for me, the least likable variety of Swans, the black ones. Black Swans events were discussed by Nassim Nicholas Taleb in his 2004 Book 'Fooled by Randomness'.[8] And there he only talked about finance. And later, few years later, he extended this metaphor to events beyond the financial markets. And I think you have built on that concept. Explain where you are coming from by using black Swans and we will get back to the green ones, the more hopeful ones a little bit later (Fig. 5).

John Elkington

I have always admired Nassim Nicholas Taleb's work. When he came up with his book 'The Black Swan', it was just before the 2007–2009 crash. People saw him as prophetic. The problem at the time was a financial system issue, rather than something much broader, as with the climate and biodiversity emergencies.

Still, I was struck by Taleb's idea that there are these moments in our history where, out of the blue, a major crisis evolves. They can then have a massive impact, way beyond anything that people expected. Then, unfortunately, and this was the third point that Taleb made about Black Swans, we fail to properly understand what has just happened to us—and set ourselves up for failure next time around.

When he spoke of Black Swans, he was often referring to bad things. But I have chosen to take black swans as largely things that take us exponentially in directions we do not want to travel, while Green Swans are market, special, or political trajectories and dynamics that potentially at least take us in directions we really need to travel and want to travel—particularly in areas such as those flagged by the Sustainable Development Goals.

Uwe Schulte

You described in your book, and I had not come across that expression—I must admit—'wicked' and 'super wicked' problems. Can you explain that a little bit and maybe you give an example in the context of the Black Swan scenarios?

---

[8] https://www.fooledbyrandomness.com/

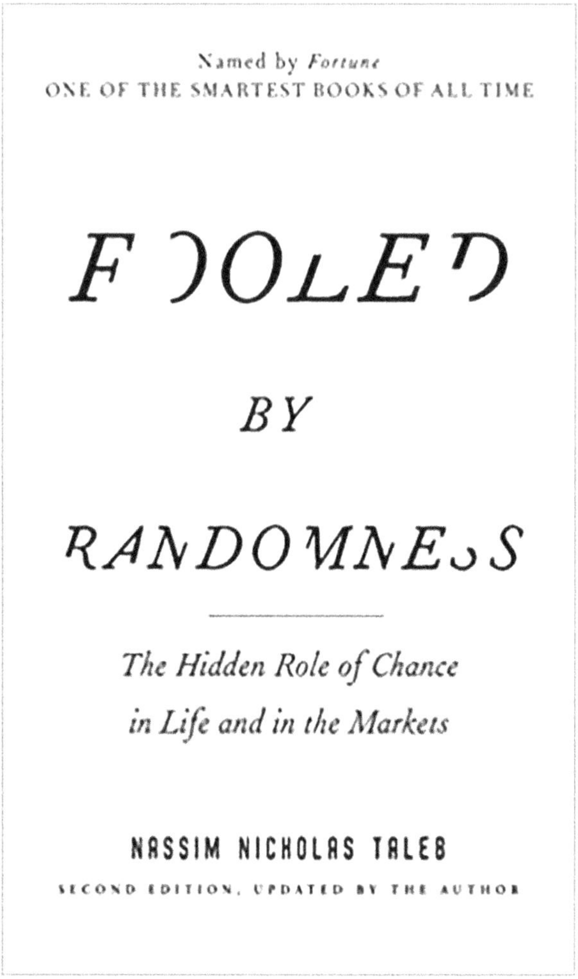

Fig. 5 Fooled by Randomness by Nassim Nicolas Taleb. Source: Penguin Random House LLC, Nassim Nicolas Taleb

John Elkington
Yes, I still remember the first time I heard the phrase 'a wicked problem', and that was in the boardroom of Ford Motor Company outside Detroit, in Dearborn, at the beginning of this century. It struck me as not terribly helpful as a term, but I have changed my mind, as one does, and come to the realisation that wicked problems as a category of challenge are distinctive in the sense that they defy attempts to solve them.

In fact, some people now talk about 'super wicked' problems—and in that category I would put the climate and biodiversity emergencies. These are furiously complex and still-evolving challenges. They defy the ability or the intent of individual actors like companies, or whatever. They can also resist the efforts of individual governments to address them. And yet we increasingly face these sorts of problems.

To your question, Uwe, if I had to pick a couple of examples, one would be plastics in the ocean. No one in the plastics industry intended to plasticise the oceans, but that is what we have collectively done. Antibiotic resistance is another. Even Alexander Fleming, one of the pioneers of antibiotic production, said that if we overuse these things, we will see growing microbial resistance to these extraordinary, miraculous products. Why did we not listen to him?

Well, typically as a species, we do not listen to people who can see the future if the future they see is challenging. And I refer in the book to other examples, ranging from obesity and chronic diseases like diabetes through to space debris. There are a range of these complex issues now, and the question is, how do we best tackle them?

Uwe Schulte
And see, what we humans are struggling with: these things usually start small and suddenly develop with huge speed, and this exponential growth, which we now very vividly lived through with the pandemic, is something that we seem not to be able to put our mind around.

John Elkington
Well, that is intrinsic to the human brain. It is just not wired to track things that are incremental; it is poorly equipped to understand exponentials. I started to understand that when in 2005, I went to California to see one of the founding editors of 'Wired Magazine',[9] Kevin Kelly. He was early into this space of exponential technology and the law of increasing returns, not decreasing returns. Since then, I have been to California to see people like the X Prize Foundation,[10] Singularity University,[11] the Google X facility.[12] I also saw people like DeepMind[13] in London, working at the cutting edge of artificial intelligence (AI).

Indeed, one of my frustrations with the sustainability industry, an industry that I have helped to create, is that it is largely focused on things that build relatively slowly. As a result, the solutions that it is developing are largely non-exponential. But now with things like renewable energy technology you suddenly see some of these technologies business models going exponential.

Uwe Schulte
One of the major theses in your book is you must fight negative exponential things with positive exponential things, and I think that's what you call a Green Swan?

---

[9] https://www.wired.com/magazine/
[10] https://www.xprize.org/
[11] https://www.su.org/
[12] https://x.company/
[13] https://www.deepmind.com/

John Elkington

Well, it is going to be interesting because when I came up with earlier terms like Green Consumer and Triple Bottom Line, some people have then wanted to slap those terms on anything that moved in markets. I think the danger now is that the same will happen with Green Swans, but for me what the concept means is a solution to a systemic challenge. It could be an initiative, it could be a technology, it could be an industry which has got the potential to scale exponentially to address problems that are themselves exponential. It needs a hugely different mindset to engage with both those challenges and potentially those solutions. One of the things I am kicking myself for is that when I was 14, I gave up most forms of science and mathematics. I should have studied calculus because that is what I am going to and people like we are going to need next.

Uwe Schulte

When I was reading your book, I realised that whilst a lot of people are talking about growth as bad and arguing that we should go to a zero-growth economy, what you are saying is that if I want to combat the big, and we call them super wicked problems that we are facing, we must have solutions that can grow fast and vigorously to combat these things, and there is no harm in doing that as long as, and we talked about this earlier, Gaia, Earth, is not suffering from it.

John Elkington

I have great respect for people who argue for no growth or zero growth, but I do not believe for a moment that such an agenda can inspire normal people to do the extraordinary things we now need them to do. That said, we are going to have to kill off certain parts of the industrial spectrum. We are going to have to get rid of fossil fuels in the same way we did with lead, CFCs, or asbestos.

But if you are going to do that, then you really have got to build the future extremely fast as well. We need exponential decay in some of those old unsustainable industries and we need exponential growth at least for a period in some of the new more sustainable industry sectors. I would put renewable energy in that space, and I would put autonomous vehicles potentially in that space.

Uwe Schulte

You expressed or you called one of your chapters 'be a leader, not an algorithm'. When I am a leader in a corporation, what does that new requirement that you be putting out there to nurture Green Swans mean for corporate leaders?

John Elkington

Many years ago, in 2008, I co-authored a previous book called 'The Power of Unreasonable People' with Pamela Hartigan, who then worked with the World Economic Forum, and went on to run the Skoll Centre for Social Entrepreneurship at the Saïd Business School at Oxford University. One thing she would often say, and at the time I thought it was exaggerated, was that MBA students are not well

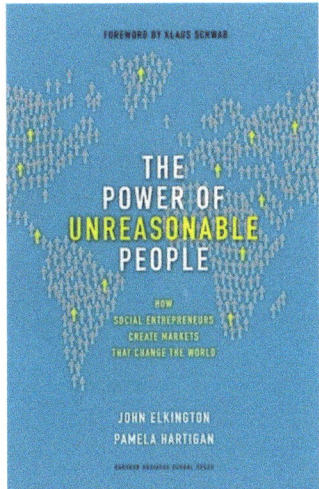

Fig. 6 The Power of Unreasonable People by Elkington/Hartigan. Source: John Elkington/Pamela Hartigan, https://en.wikipedia.org/wiki/File:The_Power_of_Unreasonable_People.jpg

equipped either by their nature, or by their training, to be social entrepreneurs. I think it's true (Fig. 6).

Business and capitalism have been remarkably effective in pushing towards efficiency, squeezing out waste in our economies and in our supply chains. By contrast, many of the things that directly contribute to resilience and directly contribute to the regeneration of critical systems are not particularly efficient. Unless and until business schools for example—I have nothing against business schools—but unless and until they start to embrace this sort of change agenda, I think they are going to continue to churn out people who are not fit for purpose.

Uwe Schulte
That raises a sore point with me where I had some interesting skirmishes with some business school professors recently. I mean it is just 8 years ago that they were still pushing for shareholder value and the main criteria for success of a Business School was entry salary versus exit salary.

John Elkington
We are all interested to see the Business Roundtable in the United States in raising stakeholder capitalism and saying this is the Big New Thing to follow shareholder capitalism. But I am sceptical of that in the sense that I think business and capitalism are still very much configured around ensuring a return to investors, to shareholders. Language is important and if we simply say capitalism now must roll over and be nice to people, I doubt very much that that is going to change the world.

Uwe Schulte
You talk about 3 Rs in your book. Responsibility, Resilience and then most importantly Regeneration. How does that fit with what we have just discussed about shareholder versus stakeholder and long term versus short term?

Fig. 7 Regeneration of grasslands. Source: Savory Institute, https://web.archive.org/web/20230104015802/https:/savory.global/

John Elkington

The regeneration element is not uniquely ours. It is an agenda which has been building in places like people working on soil health. The Allan Savory Institute[14] and even people like Walmart and McDonald's are now looking at how you manage soils sustainably (Fig. 7).

The regeneration agenda has been around for a long time with urban regeneration. In fact, I was originally trained in the early 70s to be a city planner, and my focus at the time was on urban regeneration, so in some ways there is nothing new about this.

The danger is if we expect companies to move directly from responsibility to resilience and regeneration and deliver system level change of that sort. This is because most companies are not designed to do that. They are not rewarded to do that.

That is increasingly a public policy and governmental challenge. And it is a political challenge. What we need to see increasingly is business leaders standing up and calling for system change, not pretending that they can deliver it exclusively on their own with their brand, with their particular organisation. They cannot, they will not. They need sustained government help to do that.

Uwe Schulte

But do they also need alliances within business?

John Elkington

Totally. And I think one of the great achievements of the last 30-plus years has been the evolution of business-to-business platforms like a World Business Council for

---

[14] https://savory.global/

Sustainable Development, the UN Global Compact,[15] the B Team, and so on, popping up. What is interesting is to see someone like Paul Polman, a former CEO of Unilever, serving as chair of the World Economic Forum, WBCSD, the Global Compact, and now the International Chamber of Commerce (ICC). Whereas most other B2B platforms have a few 100s of members, or a few 1000s, the ICC has 45 million. We are getting to the point where all of this could potentially go into the mainstream. Whether COVID-19 and the shocks that come with that will actually help or end up distracting us, I do not want to predict, but I think we can use those shocks in a constructive way if we go at this with a will.

Uwe Schulte

In your book, you are using as guidance for corporate leaders the future fit approach. Can you explain a little bit what is behind that thinking?

John Elkington

Yes, of course. The Future Fit Foundation and the Future Fit Business Benchmark[16] have been embraced by a growing number of pioneering companies from Novo Nordisk in Denmark to De Beers. The idea is that instead of simply looking at yourself as a company and reporting out on what you do, you are looking at the context within which you operate. This is not the first time people have championed this particular approach, but unless we do this and we do it effectively, a lot of what passes for corporate responsibility is really nice to have, but it is not really going to push the levers of change, and it certainly is not going to deliver system change. The Future Fit Team have a wonderful diagram and I reproduced it in the book. At the same time, I should declare an interest. I have been on their Advisory Board since they started. And they do see the triple bottom line as central to what they do. Their diagram starts with an illustration of three unrelated balls or circles. There is business and the economy, there is society, and there is environment. Then they have their version of the triple bottom line where these things progressively overlap, with the final one showing the economy comes right to the centre. Society is wrapped around that, then the environment is wrapped around that. All these things are intrinsically interlinked and must be addressed as an interconnected system. The future fit approach is potentially very powerful, and I hope that once these pioneering companies have co-evolved the approach, it could then spread much more widely[17] (Fig. 8).

Uwe Schulte

That brings me back to the point you made earlier that corporations on their own cannot do it. But I understood in your book you make the point that corporations must play a bigger role in this process towards Green Swans. But it requires

---

[15] https://www.unglobalcompact.org/news/4515-01-13-2020

[16] https://futurefitbusiness.org/wp-content/uploads/2019/04/FFBB-Methodology-Guide-R2.1.pdf

[17] The Future-Fit Foundation was hard-hit by Covid-19 and has gone into stasis for the moment.

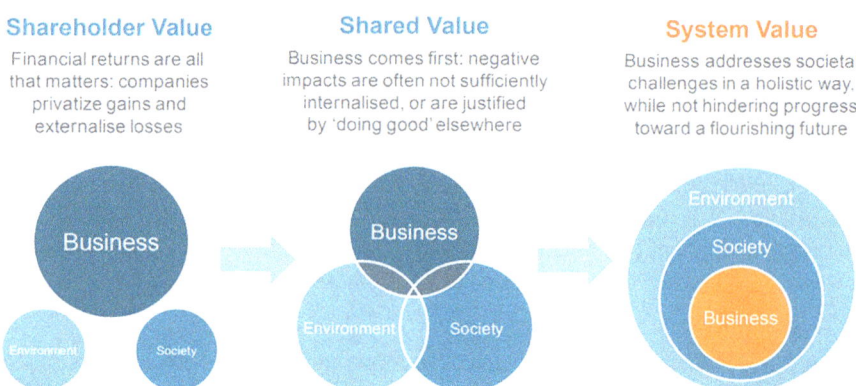

Fig. 8 Future Fit Business Benchmark. Source: https://futurefitbusiness.org/, CC BY-SA 4.0 DEED Attribution-ShareAlike 4.0 International

Fig. 9 Plimsoll Line. Source: Wikipedia, public domain, Author: Wualex, Source: own work

political change, and you even talk about rebooting democracy—that is a bold statement. How would that come about?

John Elkington

Well, entrepreneurs and changemakers, troublemakers, if you like, have throughout history protested about the dysfunctions of democracy or capitalism or whatever it was. And over time, and with the abolition of slavery or the painting of the so-called Plimsoll line on cargo ships,[18] it took decades even generations for these changes to come through. We do not have those sorts of timescales at our disposal now (Fig. 9).

I am not saying companies do not act. I am looking around the world, and seeing companies, most conspicuously in recent years, Tesla, with Elon Musk at its helm, acting as disruptors in the automotive industry, and other sectors.

---

[18] https://commons.wikimedia.org/wiki/File:Freibordmarke.jpg

These things are already happening, and as I once heard somebody say: Something is probably not impossible if it already exists. Part of our challenge now is to just show where these things do exist and are operating, albeit so far on too small a scale. Also, when you have got these potentially disruptive trends, there will always be people who have a vested interest in stopping them. This is going to get a lot more political.

Uwe Schulte
What you are saying is these disruptive entrepreneurs must drive the agenda and we have seen with these ideas of factor 10-X. With 100-X, there are ways of doing that and you just gave an example. That is how we can also move the political systems because we see that all your green swans could have black feathers. We must be aware of that.

John Elkington
Black Swans can also have green feathers. Look at this COVID-19 catastrophe. At the same time, however, you have seen urban air clearing. In India, for example, they can now see the Himalayas in ways that they have not been able to do for decades.

As for Green Swans with black feathers, if you take the case of renewable energy and windmills, we are now finding that we do not know what the hell to do with the windmill rotors, the propellers, when they come to their end of their useful life. These things are piling up now in landfill sites. We really should have thought earlier about how to adopt circular models in such areas, closing the loop on all critical components. We leave it until we are forced to do it. My hope is that as a species, over time, we can become very much better at thinking in circularity terms, in sustainability terms. But by God, it's taking quite a while to get there.

The wider world is starting to signal that it is make or break—that we must do this in very short order now. In effect, it is now a truly existential crisis for our civilisation.

Uwe Schulte
Thank you. That is a great summary. And I must say for me your book, even though you did not write with COVID-19 in mind, there is that light at the end of the tunnel with the pandemic. It suggests a way forward, and perhaps a model for tackling other super wicked problems of our time. It is really encouraging both of us are around 70 now and you wrote in your book you are looking forward to the next 15 years as the most exciting times in your life and big changes ahead. Thank you very much for sharing these engaging perspectives. We were only able to scratch the surface of your book. I strongly recommend reading it, it is full of examples and references, and it even has a guide how to spot Green Swans.

Thank you, John, so much.

John Elkington
And thank you, Uwe, and again, thank you to the Conference Board for making this possible.

The United Nations Sustainable Development Goals

Recorded May 2020

Uwe Schulte
Today I will be talking to Dr Márcia Balisciano from RELX about the United Nations Sustainable Development Goals. Before we do that, I would like to mention that we are recording this podcast during the COVID-19 crisis. Our heart goes to all out there suffering. We believe achieving the ambitious targets of the United Nations Sustainability Development Goals will not prevent pandemics but make outbreaks less likely and will help minimise severe consequences. More about this during the podcast. So first, let me introduce our guest to you. Márcia is the global head of corporate responsibility at RELX. Previously in parts known as Reed Elsevier. And today, this company is much more than a publishing house. It is a provider of global information-based analytics. Marcia, besides her role in RELX, is the chair of the UN Global Compact in the UK and a board member of the Ban Ki Moon Centre for Global Citizen. Márcia is also the founding director of the Benjamin Franklin House in London. For this huge accomplishment, she received the MBE (Member of the British Empire awarded by the Crown) in 2007. Before we dive into specific sustainability matters, Márcia, please tell us about yourself, how sustainability became an important part of your personal life, and a little bit about the Benjamin Franklin House in London. Over to you, Márcia.

Márcia Balisciano

It is great to participate. Thank you for inviting me. My interest in sustainability and the responsibility of all people to society started from my mother. I was raised by an amazing single mother who instilled those values from a very early age. I have had the good fortune of being the founding head of corporate responsibility at RELX and I know we are going to talk a bit about our journey within the company. It has been an interesting vantage point to see our transition over the last 15 years plus from a traditional print-based publisher when I joined the business to a digital company today. Of course, we all have other talents and other interests. And I have a great love for history and have been incredibly lucky to be the founding director of Benjamin Franklin House in London. It is the only house still standing where Benjamin Franklin lived and worked, and in 2006, on Franklin's 300th birthday, we opened to the public as a dynamic museum and an educational facility.[1] As you mentioned, we are recording this while so many of us around the world are in lockdown. And at Benjamin Franklin House, for the first time in our history we have closed, but we have been focusing on what we can deliver digitally to a wider public and are giving lectures and talks and educational activities online, which I'm sure would have interested Benjamin Franklin, who said he was born 200 years too soon (he was born in Boston, Massachusetts in 1706). He would have wanted to see what would become of his great passion for technology and innovation. We are reaping the rewards today of being able to communicate remotely and even record a podcast like today (Fig. 1).

Uwe Schulte

Having had the privilege of a tour to the Benjamin Franklin House, where the historic scenes being enacted was spectacular, and if any of our listeners are going to be in London, hopefully when the lockdown is over, you should consider spending an hour there. It is only fifty or so yards away from Trafalgar Square. As it might be very tempting for you and for me to talk about this pearl of conservation, we should now focus on the United Nations Sustainable Development Goals.[2]

---

[1] https://www.historichouses.org/house/benjamin-franklin-house/visit/

[2] https://sdgs.un.org/goals

Fig. 1 Benjamin Franklin House London. Source: Benjamin Franklin House, https://www.historichouses.org/house/benjamin-franklin-house/visit/

Fig. 2 Ex-UN General Secretary Kofi Annan, Photo: Wikipedia. Source: Wikipedia, public domain, Author: US Mission in Geneva, https://www.flickr.com/photos/us-mission/7474208582

We should call them for brevity the UN SDGs as known in the trade. Over the last few years, the UN SDGs have gained more prominence, which is no doubt good, but nevertheless it would be worth our while to talk a little bit about what they are, how they came about. Márcia, should we start with the Millennium Development Goals (MDGs)?.

Márcia Balisciano
That is a good idea. And maybe just before we change gears, I can say that any listeners who want to take a virtual tour of Benjamin Franklin House can just visit our website: https://benjaminfranklinhouse.org/

Indeed, the precursor to the SDGs were the MDGs coinciding with the year 2000 and the dawn of a new Millennium. Under the leadership of Kofi Annan, who sadly passed away in 2019, the 7th UN Secretary General, 189 countries came together to mark the new Millennium and to introduce a set of goals (Fig. 2).

The idea was that all the nations of the world and the different stakeholders needed to support aiding the world's poorest people over a 15-year period across eight goals such as eradicating extreme poverty and hunger, achieving universal primary education, promoting gender equality, and empowering women, reducing child mortality, improving maternal health, combating HIV, AIDS, and malaria, ensuring environmental sustainability and global partnership for development. These were eight incredibly important goals, and a lot was achieved.[3]

The number of people living in extreme poverty declined by more than half, according to the UN's MDG report, released in 2015. And the number of out-of-school children of primary school age worldwide fell by almost half to an estimated fifty-seven million in 2015, down from one hundred million in 2000. But despite successes, as the MDGs ended, there was a recognition there was still so much yet to be done. Progress across regions and countries was uneven and there was still persistent gender inequality, rise in global emissions of carbon dioxide, which increased by over 50% between 1990 and 2015, with conflict one of the biggest threats to human development. There were still many issues the world, and the world's poorest people, were facing which still needed to be addressed. There was work by different nation states to consider how to follow on from the MDGs and in September 2015, the SDGs were unanimously adopted by all 193 states of the UN under the leadership of the 8th Secretary General of the United Nations, Ban Ki Moon. Where the MDGs were for the world's poorest nations, the SDGs are for all countries. It is for the global North as well as the global South. Expanding them to a wider set of issues, there is an interconnectivity between these seventeen goals (Fig. 3).

Uwe Schulte
I am extremely glad that you talked about what was achieved with the Millennium Goals. Because a lot of people—when the UN SDGS came out—were arguing 'we had the Millennium Goals and not a lot was achieved so why are we now having another set of even more ambitious and wider scoped goals'. What you just pointed out was clear: there are many of the Millennium Goals that achieved a lot, but they were very much focused around poor countries. And the picture people paint of the UN as a toothless tiger is not correct. And the interesting aspect of the UN SDGs was also the process by which they were agreed upon. Can you just say a couple of words about that because not everybody is aware that this was a very wide consultation (Fig. 4).

Márcia Balisciano
Among the different countries that comprise the UN, there was a lot of engagement about what these follow-on goals should be, and a lot of work across the different UN agencies within various Member States, as well as different international institutions that had a say in how they should be formulated and what they should include. There are 169 targets which sit behind the seventeen goals and each target

---
[3] https://www.un.org/millenniumgoals/2015_MDG_Report/pdf/MDG%202015%20rev%20(July%201).pdf

Goals and Targets	Africa		Asia					Oceania	Latin America and the Caribbean	Caucasus and Central Asia
	Northern	Sub-Saharan	Eastern	South-Eastern	Southern	Western				
GOAL 1 ǀ Eradicate extreme poverty and hunger										
Reduce extreme poverty by half	low poverty	very high poverty	low poverty	moderate poverty	high poverty	low poverty		—	low poverty	low poverty
Productive and decent employment	large deficit	very large deficit	moderate deficit	large deficit	large deficit	large deficit		very large deficit	moderate deficit	small deficit
Reduce hunger by half	low hunger	high hunger	moderate hunger	moderate hunger	high hunger	moderate hunger		moderate hunger	moderate hunger	moderate hunger
GOAL 2 ǀ Achieve universal primary education										
Universal primary schooling	high enrolment	moderate enrolment	high enrolment	high enrolment	high enrolment	high enrolment		high enrolment	high enrolment	high enrolment
GOAL 3 ǀ Promote gender equality and empower women										
Equal girls' enrolment in primary school	close to parity	close to parity	parity	parity	parity	close to parity		close to parity	parity	parity
Women's share of paid employment	low share	medium share	high share	medium share	low share	low share		medium share	high share	high share
Women's equal representation in national parliaments	moderate representation	moderate representation	moderate representation	low representation	low representation	low representation		very low representation	moderate representation	low representation

Fig. 3 Millenium Development Goals Achievements 2015. Source: From "Millenium Goals Indicators", by Clarence Lio, UNSD, ©2023 United Nations. Reprinted with the permission of the United Nations. https://www.un.org/millenniumgoals/2015_MDG_Report/pdf/MDG%202015%20PC%20final.pdf, downloaded 10/2023

Fig. 4 United Nations Sustainable Development Goals. Source: https://www.un.org/sustainabledevelopment/. The content of this publication has not been approved by the United Nations and does not reflect the views of the United Nations or its officials or Member States

has between one and three indicators that are used to measure progress towards reaching the targets. We have done work at RELX to review these targets and our corporate responsibility reports examine which of these targets can be business indicators. Some are the responsibility of nation states, but we know all actors have a role to play, including business because of its ability to influence a range of stakeholders including employees, investors, customers, and the communities in which they operate. Business needed to be brought into the picture. The United Nations Global Compact has worked on this, and we indicate our disclosures relative to the SDG targets. Really digging in to see which targets related to business provide a great framework for looking at what you are currently doing and what you could be doing to advance the targets.

Uwe Schulte
That is exactly one of the reasons why they have now gotten so wide attention because they have been developed in a very concise process and all the nations have signed up for it. It is particularly important that you mentioned that it is not just the nations' responsibility. Business must look at them and decide how to deal with it. We will talk about that later in more depth. What would you say? Some people say seventeen goals is way too much with all these targets underneath.

Márcia Balisciano
It is a fair point. Even those of us that are quite engaged with the terminology of the SDGs might struggle to match each area with each number. If I cite SDG 15, can you say quickly that that is 'life on land' or if it is number 9, do you know

immediately that that is 'industry innovation and infrastructure'? For me, it is less important that we are aware of each number, but instead understand it is a kind of interlocking agenda. It is a framework for assessing your corporate action. The complexity was needed to make sure that the SDGs touch all aspects of people, planet, and prosperity. The goals marry up to one of those pillars. This holistic look at the issues we face ensures we can look across the piste for the impact we can have. Children cannot have a quality education, SDG 4, if they do not have sufficient food and are hungry, SDG 2. And tying the SDGs together you need SDG 17, 'partnerships for the goals'. The SDGs really are working together (Fig. 5).

But even if you cannot name particular SDGs, there is an ethos. You might use other words, but the essence remains the same. We need to consider what is happening in our cities (SDG 11), what is happening in our oceans (SDG 14). We must all focus on climate (SDG 13). And the biggest challenge which we face globally at the time of our recording is health, given the COVID-19 crisis (SDG 3). These issues are interlocking. Companies may not have a connection to every SDG, but the SDGs provide a framework for looking at global challenges from a broad perspective.

Uwe Schulte
I could not agree more. For me, it feels like we have finally found a common language. What sustainability means. It is defining the scope of what people must be looking at and the interconnectivity of all these various aspects. Part of the success that so many people are relating to the UN SDGs now, is that it is a common framework, which is a globally agreed common language. You are right and we will talk about how to approach that from a corporate perspective, but before we do that I made a very bold statement at the beginning that the UN SDG could help, once they have been achieved, combatting pandemics and I thought you and I should just look at two of the goals and talk a little bit about why this could be the case, and let me suggest the one that you just mentioned: Sustainable Development Goal 15 life on land.[4] It says protect, restore, and promote sustainable use of terrestrial ecosystems, sustainably managed forest, combat desertification and hold and reverse land degradation and halt biodiversity loss. It has many targets, but I will just cite two and then let us see how you feel about how that relates to COVID-19. It says take urgent and significant action to reduce the degradation of natural habitats, hold the loss of biodiversity and, by 2020, protect and prevent the extinction of threatened species. And target seven of goal fifteen is: take urgent actions to end poaching and trafficking of protected species of flora and fauna, addressing both demand and supply of illegal wildlife products. That resonates, doesn't it?

Márcia Balisciano
It sure does. I am not an expert, but just looking at the loss of biodiversity, it makes zoonotic transmission from animal to human more likely. In the case of bats, they have had in the past robust immune systems and better habitats for breeding. When you take land away, you put stress on their immune system. You make it more

---

[4] https://unstats.un.org/sdgs/report/2022/The-Sustainable-Development-Goals-Report-2022.pdf

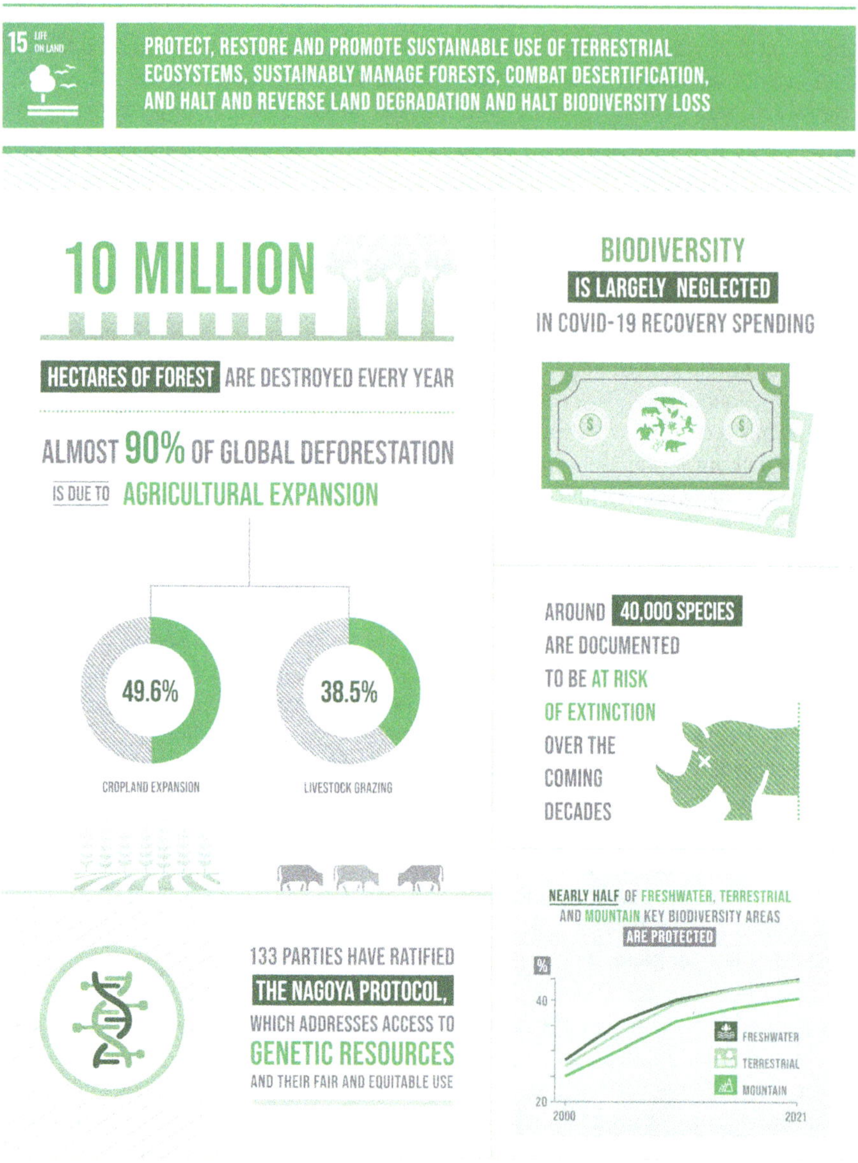

Fig. 5 UN SDGs goal 15 Life on Land 2022 status. Source: From "The Sustainable Development Goals Report 2022", by Lois Jensen, ©2022 United Nations. Reprinted with the permission of the United Nations. https://unstats.un.org/sdgs/report/2022/The-Sustainable-Development-Goals-Report-2022.pdf, downloaded 2023, page 22. Design of Overview infographics on pages 8–25: Dewi Glanville, using icons from thenounproject.com under a NounPro licence

difficult for them to fight infections, that they might have more easily managed before. When humans come in closer contact with animals there is a risk of this kind of transmission. On the one side, it is amazing how interconnected we all are, that you can be in a very rural place or in a jungle one day and a major metropolis the next. But in the past, if there was a zoonotic-transmitted infection, the spread would have been slowed or more naturally contained. With us all so highly interconnected, travelling globally—now reduced with a reduction in carbon emissions which is a good thing—there is more likely to be an uptick in the spread of virus as we have seen. One of the best things we could do to make sure this kind of event does not happen in the future is indeed protecting our species. The animals of our world are innocent; they must deal with the challenges of our human activity. Increasing biodiversity, ensuring that we are reversing deforestation, is one of the best things we can do for so many reasons, not only for flora and fauna, but for combating climate change, so there is a real interconnection.

Uwe Schulte
I agree and I find it interesting, when you talk about biodiversity some people say: 'What does that have to do with me'? And when we have some projects and then environmentalists and people say that you should not do this because you destroy a biodiverse habitat and then people say: 'Are animals suddenly more important than human beings'? We now see that we all live together, and we must be in a reasonable balance, otherwise we face very severe problems as we currently do. And that brings me to goal #3 'good health and well-being', ensures healthy lives and promotes well-being for all at all ages. Target 3.8 is achieving universal health coverage, including financial risk protection, access to quality essential health care services and access to safe, effective, quality, and affordable essential medicines and vaccines for all. Sounds also quite relevant, doesn't it?

Márcia Balisciano
Yes, incredibly relevant. Looking at how the Coronavirus has put the spotlight on the essential nature of health, you cannot pursue other things in life without health. The impact across developed nations has been immense but the challenge for less developed countries is staggering. Our focus at RELX is on sharing information. This includes research and science as our operating business Elsevier is one of the world's largest scientific information providers. It is incredibly important to foster an environment which is not only supporting research from the most developed countries, but from those on the frontline of so many of the issues embodied by the SDGs. In fact, one of our goals at RELX this year is to produce an SDG graphic, as we call it, for every SDG looking at the state of knowledge underpinning the SDGs: which countries are producing content; how good is it using different measures; how often is it cited; and what share of the output of research for that country represents a collaboration between the global north and south. We produced an SDG graphic, for example, on SDG 6, 'clean water and sanitation', and one for SDG 11 'sustainable cities and communities'. We found only 1% of the output came from the least developed countries. That is simply not good enough. With our analytical tools, we can identify the problem, but we also need to be part of the solution. To

that end, we support a programme called 'Research Without Borders' with several partners where pre-Covid we took our experts and brought them to places in Africa, for example, to support the output of indigenous research. We also helped them with the sustainability of their own journals, teaching about open access publishing models and other things that can be helpful to increase their research output.

Uwe Schulte

This is very encouraging, and I have seen some of the things you have been doing and that leads us to the discussion around the business context of the UN SDGs. You have already mentioned of course, the SDGs were developed and written for nations to make a commitment towards the SDGs and therefore they do not lend themselves automatically to targets from companies, but there are clear links, and we will explore that now.

Back in 2015, the SDGs were published and as we already discussed, they were designed with a view to national targets for states. I observed that companies were struggling how to define the meaning for their own business, and they quite often have had the reflex to just look at their existing activities and map them against the SDGs. Márcia, did you have the same impression?

Márcia Balisciano

To look at where your business aligns with the seventeen goals is a suitable place to begin, but you cannot stop there. There must be the will to doing something additional because business as usual is not going to cut it. These are extremely ambitious goals. We have a tight time limit and in fact, as we are recording this in 2020, we have 10 years, and we know that we are behind on so many of the measures. We must be looking at what it is going to take to make real progress, and how we as businesses can contribute to raise our game.

Uwe Schulte

You are right. But I am sometimes thinking when looking at the ambitious targets the nations have agreed to, to do only part will require huge investments and initiatives. Companies could participate in these initiatives and grow their business and contribute at the same time to the achievement of the goals. But the question is then of course, how to do that?

Márcia Balisciano

A key point is the funding gap for the SDGs. The UN has cited an approximate $2.5 trillion annual financing gap for the SDGs. Governments are going to have to step up and put more money on the table to really see progress and that effort needs to be mirrored by investments from companies where relevant. You mentioned the launch of the SDGs in 2015. On that day when nation states were meeting at the UN, colleagues and I were across the street at one UN Plaza because RELX introduced a free report called 'Sustainability Science and Global Research Landscape'. We did not know a lot of detail about the SDGs at that early stage, but we had an overall sense of what they would entail. We wanted to look at the state of science and knowledge that would be needed to drive the SDGs forward. So given the nature of what we do at RELX, this was a starting point. When I was sitting in the audience listening to my colleague Richard Horton, Editor of The Lancet, who presented the findings of the report, I found myself thinking: this is a beginning but now the clock is ticking. What are we going to do about this agenda and what is relevant for our business? In 2017, we launched the RELX SDG Resource Centre. We are curating content from across our business. We have Elsevier focused on science; LexisNexis Risk Solutions, focused on fighting fraud and other crime with the aim to protect society; we have LexisNexis Legal and Professional, focused on the rule of law and access to justice and RX, which fosters communities through its events business. We will have products and services linked to the SDGs in each one of these areas, and that was the basis for launching the free for the world, RELX SDG Resource Centre (Fig. 6).

The site features our content as well as content from various partners, the majority of which are from within the UN system like the UN Global Compact, the business arm, if you will, of the UN. Given what we do, this has been where we have focused our energies. In addition, each year we set public objectives that we put in the public domain and have longer run aspirations like to the 2030 timeline.

Uwe Schulte

You mentioned in the beginning the relevance of the SDGs for your business. And this is a key point because in the beginning there seemed to have been a competition between some people in companies trying to map as many things as possible, all seventeen goals. You should think about where you are going to contribute, where you will have the largest impact and that focus will help to make a true impact. And from your side, it is your capabilities around information and research that will

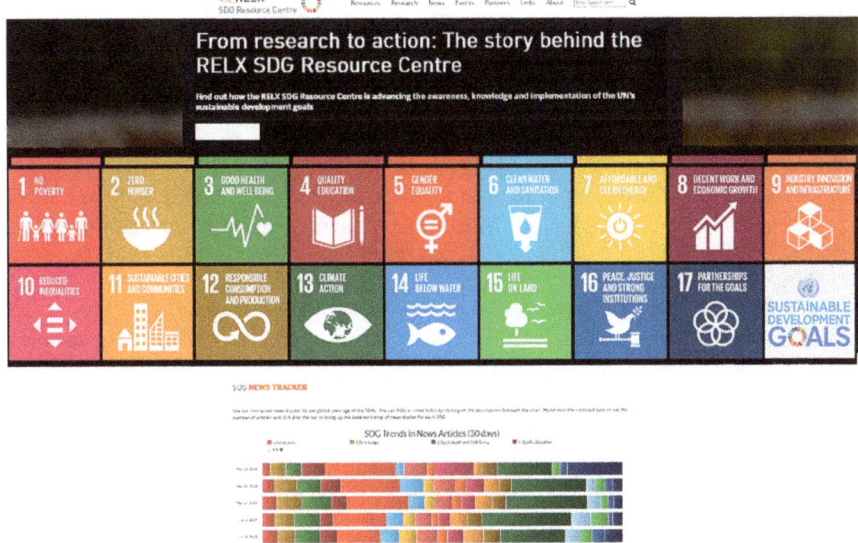

Fig. 6 RELX SDG Resource Centre. Source: RELX SDG Resource Centre

provide exactly that. Isn't that a learning that other companies can take on board as well? Look at your capabilities, look for what is material and focus on that.

Márcia Balisciano

Yes, there has been a lot of talk in recent years as more stakeholders, including investors, are prioritising ESG, environmental, social and governance criteria, as they look at both the financial and the long-term sustainability of a company. Investors are asking companies to share what they are doing and, as you say, it is incumbent on businesses to home in on material issues. It is not just doing what you always have done and then showing how that marries up to a particular SDG. Instead, we need to really think about where we can set impactful goals on the SDGs. There is a lot of good that can come out of that effort.

There is also an opportunity to talk with your customers. For example, we have an SDG working group where we bring together various colleagues, including those that are customer facing. We want to help them not only talk about why a particular product of ours is great but also talk about who we are as a business—why this SDG agenda matters to us. Here is what we are doing about it and tell us what you are doing. In many instances, our customers are very sophisticated in their work on the SDGs, but in some instances they may not be. It creates an opportunity for shared dialogue. You can get closer to your customers. You can also ingratiate the business with investors and analysts prioritising ESG. For example, in the United Kingdom where we are listed on the FTSE share index, the 'Responsibility 100 Index',[5] was released in 2019 to rank the FTSE on their SDG performance. It is something investors will look at and our customers. It is a fantastic way to engage our employees, both prospective and existing, who want to work for a good company. And being able to articulate about the SDGs and get buy-in for this agenda is a wonderful opportunity in terms of having a license to operate with our communities. It can be a fantastic way to crystallise action around corporate purpose (Fig. 7).

Uwe Schulte

You just described that the SDGs are not a side issue which you just talk about, but one that is integrated into your business activities, and you describe this extremely well. I would like to hear a little bit more about your resource set. Because that is not just a nice demonstration of that integration, but it is also something that a lot of our listeners could use and benefit from. What is there, how you can access it?

Márcia Balisciano

We are interested in illuminating the SDGs for everyone through the free RELX SDG Resource Centre. It is a wonderful way for us to curate leading edge articles, reports, tools, events, videos, legal practical guidance from across RELX to advance awareness and understanding on the SDGs. We keep coming back to that point that companies need to figure out what they are good at, and for us, this interplay with information is critical. For example, you can find the SDGs News Tracker on the homepage, which our colleagues at LexisNexis Legal and Professional built for us.

---

[5] https://www.tortoisemedia.com/2022/11/17/the-responsibility100-index-the-findings/

Fig. 7 The Responsibility100 Index, Tortoise media, 2022. Source: Tortoise Media 2022, https://www.tortoisemedia.com/

You can get news on the SDGs searching millions of articles published daily across more than 75,000 news sources in all the UN languages (Fig. 8).

And Uwe, you will be pleased to know, it is also in German. It is a way for us to display knowledge that can be useful to anyone, be they students conducting research, or if you just want to understand what the latest is on a particular topic. You can search the SDG News Tracker by keyword, or you can also search by SDG or geography. You can get up-to-the-minute news as well as over the last 30 days. It is something that we want to make sure gets wider take up. We really are also interested in growing the amount of content on the site. We have a publicly stated goal this year to go from about one thousand content sources and increase it by 25% at least by the close of 2020. We are working behind the scenes to do that because the more content, the richer the site is. We are also introducing podcasts and more. Among a recent one, we recorded is with a colleague who is the founding editor of The Lancet Infectious Diseases, John McConnell. It was fascinating to have a conversation with him about what he sees as the challenges in addressing the pandemic. We keep doing things like this because it is our sweet spot as a knowledge company; we need to make knowledge available.

Uwe Schulte
Now you make me curious when I listen to this. This is a spectacular tool, and a lot of work has gone into it and continues to go into it. How did you convince, for example, your Chief Financial Officer that you would do something like that and not generate revenue from it?

Márcia Balisciano
It does not break the bank. We are a commercial enterprise, as all companies are, and we need to be responsive to our stakeholders, including our investors, and it is a wonderful shop window for RELX. When we originally went to senior leadership and said we would like build something like this, they might not have fully understood what we were creating. But we have kept our senior leadership involved and our board engaged as well. It has been positively received because our senior

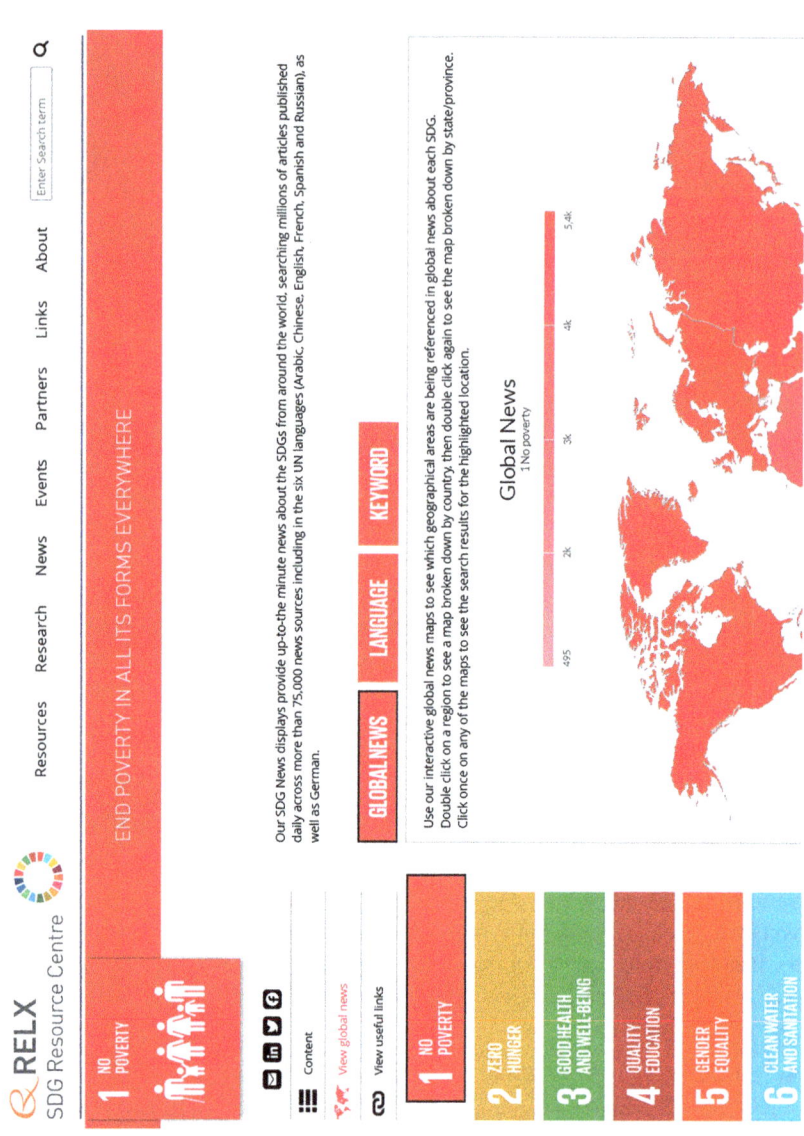

Fig. 8 RELX SDG resources per SDG. Source: RELX SDG Resource Centre

leaders also want to work for a good company and there is a growing recognition that if you want to be around in 2030 and 2050 and beyond, you really need to think about your impact on society. That underpins the things we decide to engage in. For example, I mentioned earlier that we have transitioned to being a digital business. Back in 2000 it was already probably quite 'edgy' that about 22% of our turnover came from online, but last year it was 75%. This is a trend that accelerates. The current crisis highlights just how important technology is to us. But increasingly we use things like machine learning and AI to inform customer decisions. We are creating tools that enable them to make better decisions. One of the things that we are working on right now is a good AI policy, a responsible AI policy. These are the kinds of things relevant to our business and which our leaders understand and support.

Uwe Schulte

I understand. Let me express what I hear you imply. Instead of spending a lot of money on some sort of promotional videos showing your capabilities, by doing something extremely useful like the RELX SDG Resource Centre, you demonstrate to your customers and your potential customers, the capabilities you have. This is bringing your capabilities to bear and having a benefit for their own companies as well, is that a way to express it?

Márcia Balisciano

I think so. We are primarily serving professional customers across every industry you can think of. Within RELX something that is a bit more consumer facing. In Comic Con which is a show, but also a kind of global phenomenon where people from all walks of life in different geographies meet around their passion for characters from film and comic books, etc. Being able to create a portal where we can showcase these various aspects of the company has been incredibly good. There is a win–win in terms of being able to show that we are serious about the SDGs, that we really want to do our part. And it is a fantastic opportunity if somebody can see something from one of our products like The Lancet and then wants to dig a bit further and become a customer of The Lancet. That would be fabulous, and we hope it will work that way. Overall, it is part of the contribution we need to make.

Uwe Schulte

I get that. You also do something else, which you call the Inspiration Days. Can you talk about that as well?

Márcia Balisciano

Absolutely, we launched the RELX SDG Resource Centre at the first Inspiration Day in 2017 which we held in London. The idea was to use our convening power as a business to reach out to a range of stakeholders: business, government, investors, academia, youth, NGOs to look at issues around advancing the SDGs. It was a kind of general one showcasing the launch of the Resource Centre. In 2018 in Silicon Valley, we looked at technology and the role it plays in advancing the SDGs (Fig. 9).

Then we looked at partnerships for the SDGs in Amsterdam that year. In 2019, we were in Delhi and our theme was around sustainable cities and communities where we looked at the interconnection with the other 16 SDGs, including good health and well-being and the rule of law. Being in India was immensely powerful. It was a great learning opportunity because we heard about the issues relevant in that jurisdiction and we were able to engage a wide range of partners because the idea is about inspiring action. It is not so much about educating the uninformed about the SDGs but mobilising the choir. We all need to take some time out and refresh from time to time. I was talking with someone a few days ago who said they recently transitioned to another role where they are trying to embed the SDGs in their work; they said they were used to talking to people who get this agenda but where they have moved, they must do a lot of soul winning. But even the soul winners need some inspiration, and that is the idea. Can we make introductions and create engagement that can help to inspire business action on the SDGs? That is the goal.

Uwe Schulte

Sounds to me like you are really engaging towards the goal 17, the networking.

Márcia Balisciano

Yes, that is certainly it while digging in and looking in more detail. RELX is interested in all the SDGs. The ones most relevant for us include SDG 3, 'good health and well-being' and SDG 16 which focuses on the rule of law and again, we are setting publicly stated objectives linked to these various SDGs. But by looking at SDGs that we are not as familiar with, we learn too and widen our network. The goal for this year is to look at SDG 12 'responsible consumption and production'. We were hoping to go to South Africa and explore what this means in that context, but given the current situation, we may be needing to do this virtually and if that is the case, it will create new opportunities. There will still be an opportunity for us to hear from a wide range of people who can give participants and us an interesting perspective to see where those shared interests lie and where we can scale engagement together.

Uwe Schulte

Doing it is of course a hurdle, but it might even broaden the audience. Always where there is a hurdle, there is also an opportunity. Thank you, Márcia, for illuminating for us how to apply the UN SDGs to your business. When you are outside a business like yours, it does not lend itself easily to understand what the SDGs mean for you and you made it really tangible. Thank you for that. We have been talking already on how the SDGs can have a big relevance in learning about and trying to prevent pandemics. Let us spend a couple of minutes on what companies can do in this context in the COVID-19 crisis. What are your thoughts?

Márcia Balisciano

When you look at the efforts that companies, both multinationals and SMEs, are making, it is very inspiring. By that same process of understanding what you are good at and, seeing how what you are good at can be mobilised to provide value in the coronavirus crisis, is the key step. Just as we were saying in our discussion so far in terms of contributing to the SDGs it is about understanding where the expertise lies, where is that contribution to society that a business can make and then

RELX Group SDG Inspiration Days: videos from Amsterdam and Silicon Valley

RELX, November 28, 2018

Topic:
Goal 9: Industry, innovation and infrastructure
Goal 11: Sustainable cities and communities
Goal 17: Partnership for the goals

Tags:
Multi-stakeholder partnerships; Technology;
Global

In 2018, RELX Group hosted two SDG Inspiration Days to inspire scalable, collaborative action on the 17 SDGs, with particular emphasis on disruptive technology at Silicon Valley and on partnerships at Amsterdam. Watch videos of the speakers from the two days.

Fig. 9 RELX SDG Inspiration Days. Source: RELX SDG Resource Centre

maximising it beyond a current level of activity. We have been using the RELX SDG Resource Centre. I mentioned about the podcast series we launched, and we will be adding to that. Yesterday I interviewed the head of the Global Partnership for Sustainable Development Data looking at the role technology and data can play in not only addressing the crisis now, but in advancing the SDGs more generally. We have also launched several Coronavirus Resource Centres, with links from the RELX SDG Resource Centre. There is one from The Lancet (one of the publications within Elsevier), with the latest scientific knowledge, and one from Elsevier more generally where we have made all relevant content, we can find freely available. Across other parts of our business, colleagues at LexisNexis Legal and Professional have created the Coronavirus Media and News Tracker which is amazing for the latest news and interactive charts on the way coronavirus is developing across the global media landscape in real time. Colleagues within one of our LexisNexis Risk Solutions businesses, Cirium, for the global aviation industry, have been looking at the impact of the crisis making information available. Colleagues within that business unit from ICIS are looking at the effect on markets and commodities pricing. One of the key ICIS analysts who came was featured in Forbes and Bloomberg this week showing that greenhouse gas emissions in Europe will drop about 24.5 % by 2020 due to the lockdown, mirroring a 25% drop for China. That is expertise and knowledge that we have and are making available. At our RX, I was struck by how our colleagues in Austria are working with the City of Vienna to transform an exhibition space into a hospital. There is a lot happening across our business as our colleagues are thinking about: 'What do we do? How can we use that to make a positive impact in this crucial time'?

Uwe Schulte
That is really, really encouraging. There are so many examples of companies that have engaged and found ways of helping to combat the crisis. It is amazing. And it is not only large companies. I've seen here in Germany, a very small business, it's only 5 people, and they were doing work around acrylic glass and they have just completely changed their production and all they make now is stand up shields for supermarkets, banks, and surgeries so that when people talk to the staff there, there is this shield against transmission by droplets. That is extremely encouraging but let us just spend a last minute on any concluding thoughts from you about the new normal, once we will hopefully sooner rather than later, exit this crisis.

Márcia Balisciano
There is certainly thinking around how some of the trends we are seeing will play out past the crisis we are in now. When we are all freely able to move around again, even if there is social distancing over a period of months ahead, will we see people continuing to work remotely, for example, using technology to engage? Will that mean people will not be travelling as much as they used to and will that have a positive impact on, for example, carbon? Hopefully, we will see some of the positives come together. Across geographies and across different segments of society, we are all in this together and we have seen amazing examples of goodwill and the best of humankind. But the fact that we have transitioned so quickly, if we take that will and

impetus and apply it to the SDGs, it shows what can be done; if we really want to make an impact on achieving this very important agenda for the world, for our future, for our children and their offspring, it can be done. And I hope this incredible effort—seeing what can be achieved in a small amount of time—will persist and that we will apply that capability to achieving the 17 SDGs.

Uwe Schulte

Thank you so much, Marcia, for an inspiring hour about the SDGs and business relevance. I think you have helped our listeners to find their own way to engage and work on these longer-term goals. Thank you very, very much indeed. And hope to see you soon in person again.

Human Rights in the Supply Chain

Recorded June 2020

Uwe Schulte

Today I will be talking with Rosey Hurst from Impactt about securing human rights in supply chains. First let me introduce our guest to you. Rosey Hurst is the founder and director of Impactt, a consultancy with a mission of improving the lives and livelihoods of workers worldwide by using the positive power of global supply chains. Rosey founded SEDEX and the local resources network. She worked with the Awaj Foundation, building workers negotiations capabilities, and using techniques derived from social psychology to re-humanise relations in the workplace. Rosey is working with many leading companies and organisations on their human rights programmes. She served on the EcoVadis Technical Committee and is a member of the Responsible Investment Advisory Council at Columbia Threadneedle, and Chair of the UK Modern Slavery charity Unseen. Hello Rosey, please tell us a little bit about yourself.

Rosey Hurst

Well, that is a very open question Uwe, but yes, I first started thinking about workers and supply chains about 25 years ago. It was the mid-90s and I was living in India at just about the time when the economy was opening to foreign direct investment. It was an exciting time, and as trade with the outside world started to increase it became clear that jobs in global supply chains could really help lift Indian workers out of poverty, but it also was very clear that there was a risk not enough money and not enough attention would get through to workers at the bottom. That got me thinking about how to make global trade work for workers and work for business. What I did first, Uwe? My thought was I'll go and do a master's in development studies to learn more. So, I enrolled at the School of Oriental and African Studies at the University of London. But at that time, the syllabus had almost nothing on trade and on supply chains. So, I decided to do my dissertation on this topic. But I am ashamed to say that I have never finished my dissertation. What was meant to be field work for a dissertation turned into paid consultancy and the rest is history. So that is how Impactt started. And many apologies for not having a master's in development studies.

Uwe Schulte
Let us talk a little bit about human rights. We always use that expression and it relates back to the Universal Declaration of Human Rights of 1948.[1] At the time, it was adopted by a vast majority of UN member states. And I think the whole thing got so much traction because people were still in a state of shock and dismay about the atrocities of the German Nazi regime. But even then, already different views about the topic were emerging, and so, for example, South Africa did not sign. Not very surprising because apartheid was still in full swing and Saudi Arabia did not sign because they did not approve of freedom of religion and the Soviet bloc abstained. I am not quite sure why that was the case, but probably for similar reasons. So even then, things were not quite as one would like. How do you see this developing?

Rosey Hurst
Yes, this question about whether human rights are truly universal, or whether they are some sort of Western liberal concept is something that we get thrown back at us quite often, as we work on farms, factories, construction projects, and dockyards around the world. Whilst the normative framework is extremely useful, I think it is extremely important to come down from that high theoretical level and just think about people. The experience of people is really what we are talking about when we think about human rights. It is about the rights of individuals and the responsibilities of individuals. We specialise in human rights in the workplace, and the key to understanding this is to think about what workers themselves want. What is the deal from the workers perspective? What would a decent job look like? We have spoken to tens of thousands of workers over the last 25 years and funnily enough, they all have very similar answers to these questions. They answer them just as you or I would because the answer is about being a human being (Fig. 1).

---

[1] https://en.wikipedia.org/wiki/Universal_Declaration_of_Human_Rights

Fig. 1 Declaration of Human Rights 1948. Source: Wikipedia, public domain, Author: UN, Source: United Nations Department of Public Information

In general, people want three things from their job. They want money, of course, but interestingly it is much less about the quantum of money even amongst very poor people, it is much more about regularity and predictability. So, like all of us, workers want to be able to plan. And they want to be able to plan their lives according to their budget. So, the first thing is money and regularity.

The second thing is respect. Now respect, in a way that sounds like a slightly amorphous concept. But when you talk to workers, it is very clear what they actually mean by this. They mean two things; first, to be respected at work. That is about not being shouted at, being spat at, that kind of thing. But it is also about being respected for the job you do. And those of us who work in the professional arena are very familiar with this. When you go to a social event and explain what you do for a living, people are very interested, and that adds to your social capital. It is just the same for workers. They want to be able to improve their social capital with their family, with their communities because of the job they do. So that means working for a respectable employer and not being despised for the job that you do. If you work for a respectable employer, it is likely that you will be able to get credit from a shopkeeper until the end of the month or be able to get a loan from the bank. That is how a good job gets you respect and social capital.

The third thing is: Does a job help a person to give a better life to their family? Now that is something we all recognise. We all want to be in a job that is going to help us to reach our life goals and help our families and children to have a brighter future. If you ask workers what they think about human rights, they may not have that much to say, but if you ask them what is important to them, you get those three things. If we can make all the jobs in the world perform better in these 3 areas, we almost automatically improve their human rights performance. Why? Because by giving workers the agency to tell us what they want, according to them the dignity necessary to take on board this idea of money, respect, and better life for children, means that we are automatically thinking of those workers as people, as humans, with rights. And once we do that, we are compelled to think about what types of job, what sort of treatment, what terms and conditions will deliver those three important things. But there is also another upside. Thinking about what workers want, and working out how to give it to them has another benefit. It helps to create a workforce that is motivated. If people have jobs which give them what they want, where they feel respected, etc., they are much more likely to be productive, to stay, and to bring their brain to work as well as their hands and feet. So, not quite the answer perhaps you had intended, but I hope that it helps the conversation along.

Uwe Schulte

It very much does—it raises several points, and you make things a lot more tangible, at least in my mind, compared to a questionnaire with a few boxes to tick. Let us get to that.

If I am responsible for a supply chain in a company, what would you say? Taking your concept, what should I be watching and monitoring to secure the adherence to human rights in my supply chain?

Human Rights in the Supply Chain

Rosey Hurst

This is the very, very big question and of course over the last 20 years a lot of sterling and a highly technical work has been done looking at standards, what those standards might mean in practice, how to assess against those standards, whether that is a desk-based questionnaire assessment or whether that is through auditing. But the sad fact is that this has not proven a very good way of the bad practices and the bad actors in global supply chains. To take a step back from all of this, I think the idea of these questionnaires and audit is based on the fallacy that the vast majority of the global supply chain is completely fine, and what we need to do is have a few tripwire questions which enable us to pick out the rotten apples from the barrel. The truth of the matter is, because of power dynamics, differential social and economic development, local practices, because of ingrained societal discrimination, because of poverty and because of migration there are extremely widespread systemic and sever labour rights abuses. These are the norm, not the exception.

And any company that suddenly finds itself in the headlines with a scandal knows this feeling very, very well. The company will say, 'but we checked, we checked, and we didn't find this'. 'We've got an audit that shows it's all fine'. But when you look at the situation with fresh eyes, you find that the journalist, or the campaigners are probably, on average, about 95% correct. And you may find that things are in fact worse than the newspaper story (Fig. 2).

Fig. 2 Workers' needs by Impactt. Source: Impactt Limited, https://www.workerswelfare.qa/sites/default/files/reports_item/field_document/impactt-ltd-compliance-report-en-2017.pdf

The way that we at Impactt[2] try to shift companies' perspectives is to move away from managerialist thinking and to put the worker perspective, the worker experience, at the centre. Very, very many of the human rights problems we find, are issues which are completely normalised in the local context. This normalisation is made possible by dehumanisation, that is, management not viewing workers as like themselves, fully human. Whenever a factory manager says things like, 'Well, you don't understand, it's much, much better here than it is in these people's homes; they don't have bathrooms at home, they make the place very dirty. They are dirty'. Or: 'these people, they can't learn, they are not intelligent', this is a real sign of dehumanisation, and it is something we hear again and again.

And of course, the moment you can think that somebody is dirty, or somebody cannot learn it is second nature then to start managing them in a way that does not deliver money, respect, or indeed better life for their children. One of the key things we do is to helping companies to develop a nose for dehumanisation, to spot these behaviours and identify risk. This means, for example, any context where there are migrant workers is likely to be at very high risk of reasonably serious labour rights abuses because, as we all know, the position of migrants in all societies tends to be a difficult one, and dehumanisation is never far away. Society tends to accept and even approve of different standards being applied when it comes to managing or governing migrants. Our advice is look at the macro risk because it is most unlikely that your suppliers will magically happen not to be engaging in those macro risk behaviours. There are some companies which have thought that, because of the power of their brand name or of the power their own ethics, somehow their supply chain is immune from these societal issues, and it tends to be that blind spot which causes embarrassment in the end. Does that help? Does that go a little tiny way to answering your million-dollar question?

Uwe Schulte
It does not. Let me try to explain why. You know a lot of people in supply chains rely on 3rd party audits. They say this is fine and before they do an audit, they usually do a self-assessment questionnaire with the supplier, and they try to spot risk areas and so on and so forth. Prior to that, they probably have identified areas of high risk. And what you are basically saying is that this does not give you what you want. And what I am hearing you say, and tell me whether I get this right, is you say, don't just check certain boxes are ticked, find the root causes. The box ticking prevents your three elements of paying adequately and regularly, giving people respect and giving them a perspective for their family and their children. Please give me a real example how I would do that if I were in charge of my supply chain.

Rosey Hurst
Well, I think the first thing is, as you say, to look at that macro risk. And for me, that means having a strong understanding of who the workers are in those supply chains. Are they migrants? Are they people from disadvantaged groups? This is the first risk

---

[2] https://impacttlimited.com/docs/2005/ImpacttOvertimeReport-1.pdf

factor. Once one has understood that the next move is to delve in a little bit more deeply. One of the keys here is, rather than asking a question, like 'do you pay the minimum wage'? is to find out how much workers are actually taking home. In other words, rather than saying 'do you meet this standard'?, understand how much people are earning, including overtime, with some background knowledge how much people need to get by and then look at whether wages vary significantly by month. This will give you an idea about whether those jobs are meeting workers' needs on that first category (money and the predictability of income). A standard audit goes out and looks at: 'are you complying with minimum wage legislation'? Tick! You are compliant. 'Do you have a policy on discrimination'? Tick, etc. That does not break through into workers' experience and does not help you understand whether the job is decent. What I think needs to be done is the sort of investigation that puts the worker experience at the centre.

So, let us go back to root causes. A business which employs many, many people and pays them very, very little, a business that works on labour arbitrage as a central tenet of its business model—always looking for the lowest cost of labour—is likely to not to be meeting the human rights standards that you would like to see. So immediately one looks at that. Again, in a way, this kind of thinking really helps sourcing people and procurement people because it is much more about understanding the business model of your supply base. Are we talking labour intensive? Have we moved production to this new place simply because wages are cheaper? Is that company hiring people in from overseas as migrants to do jobs for less because wages in that country have got too expensive? Those are the risk factors. Those are the root causes of the abuses, and those should be the questions in your initial risk assessment.

Then I would suggest a different sort of audit, which puts worker experience at the centre. Let us take forced labour,[3] an issue which is exercising a lot of people now. This is the worst human rights abuse in the labour space and standard audits famously fail to pick up on forced labour. This is because to have a finding of forced labour, an auditor must triangulate evidence. This means the auditor must find people saying, 'I am in a condition of forced labour', and nobody ever says that because it is a very humiliating thing to have to admit, and, certainly no one ever says it to an auditor. The auditor must then find the documentary proof—so a list of forced labourers (which never exists). To be super sure of raising a non-compliance, management also have to say to the auditor, 'Oh yes, we use forced labour'. It is a very, very high burden of proof, a higher burden of proof than we need criminal court. So how can you spot it? You can spot it by understanding if, for example, you have a vulnerable workforce, I said if you have a migrant workforce, understanding, for example, how they were recruited, did they know what sort of job they were going to, did they get into debt in order to be able to get the job, and their wages are sufficient for them to be able, for example, to pay back any debt? We must turn the cart around and make sure the horses are at the front (Fig. 3).

---

[3] https://respect.international/statistics-on-forced-labour-modern-slavery-and-human-trafficking/

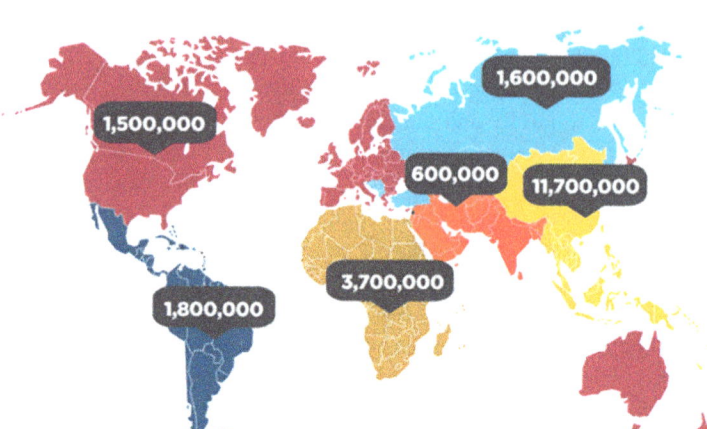

Fig. 3 Forced labour abuse worldwide by the RESPECT initiative. Source: *ILO* (International Labour Organization), 2012

Uwe Schulte

I get that. What made me think when you talked about fulfilling your three conditions that people become more productive, isn't that part of root cause and driving things? Because I remember this challenge in some countries of working hours, and that people work a lot longer than they should. And the question of course is why are they doing that?

Rosey Hurst

The answer is usually money, it is never because they really want to work those very long hours. The clearest example I ever had of that was about 12 years ago now in Bangladesh. In Bangladesh in the garment industry: famously low wages, famously long working hours—the classic sweatshop environment. We were working with this factory to try to limit the working hours, and we realised that workers were actually incentivised to work very long hours because in the first eight hours of the day they earned y-amount, but in any subsequent hours, they earned 2 x y. Obviously, a sensible person would work nice and slowly for the 1st 8 hours and then nice and slowly for the next few hours to double their wage. We got hold of one production line, one whole line of workers, around 60 people. We got them in a room, and we said, 'Could you, if the materials were available, make what you currently make in 12 hours in 10 hours, if you were paid the same amount of money'? And they said yes, and they went off and they did it the next day and they did every subsequent day. What was fascinating was they then became much more demanding of the management because they said, 'Well, listen, we cannot make it if the material is not coming through quickly enough from the previous department'. They became much more demanding of each other. They worked much better as a team because they were working together to get home two hours earlier for the same money, and this was something they needed to achieve collectively. The company had a saving of overhead. There is also quality improvement with less wastage, etc. We must look at the incentives. Are we incentivising people through poverty wages to work very long hours? Or are we treating them as adults and saying, 'Listen, this is what we want. We want right first time; we want everything produced according to specification and we want it by 5:00 o'clock. How can we do that'? Of course, you can only have that conversation, you can only imagine that conversation is possible if you attribute agency to workers. If you think workers are capable of having that conversation, you can have that conversation. But as discussed in many of the contexts in which we were with the dehumanising of workers, it is hard to persuade management to engage with workers in that world.

Uwe Schulte

And what would your recommendation be to engage those employers? Because that then is the key, isn't it?

Rosey Hurst

It really is. We have done a lot of work on this. So again, I will flip to Bangladesh. And the reason for talking about Bangladesh is because it is a sort of concentrated case study of factories all in the same area making similar things. We did a big study with, I think, 183 factories. We worked with them on improving productivity, improving quality, hand in hand with improving human resource management and the business case was quite staggering. And in fact, we then did this work again in India and again in Myanmar the results were the same all the way through. In all cases, labour turnover reduced by about 50%, and in all cases, efficiency went up by about 33%. In all cases, workers' incomes improved, and, in all company, profits improved. On average across what was a sample by the end of about 250 factories. The business case is very strong and it is blindingly obvious, isn't it? If you treat people better and incentivise them correctly, then they will do a better job for you, and you will make more money. Interestingly the business case on its own isn't quite enough. And I think this is where you talked about social psychology earlier. This is where the psychological and cultural distance come in. And it is also where attention needs to be paid to training and sensitisation of floor managers, supervisors, the people who directly manage workers. I was in a factory once and I asked them, 'how do you choose who to promote as a supervisor'? They said the one with the loudest voice. Shouting was the key skill for a supervisor. There is a huge need to invest in better management skills in the lower ranks of management to make the business case stick and to get a real change in behaviours. In the end, it is not about standards, it is about people. It is about efficiency. And it is about marrying what works for workers with what works for business and finding that sweet spot (Fig. 4).

Uwe Schulte

I took two things out of from what you said. First, put the worker's perspective at the centre of what you do and secondly go for the root cause rather than trying to fulfil some standards. We seem to be making progress in all of this but unfortunately

Fig. 4 Textile workers Bangladesh, Photo: Impactt. Source: Impactt Limited 2013, Author: Rosey Hurst, https://impacttlimited.com/docs/2013/Report170x240v4-1.pdf

now we are being hit by COVID-19, and I guess that that makes things a lot more difficult again today. Could you outline where you see this is now?

Rosey Hurst

Yes, absolutely. What we are seeing in the global supply chain is there are kind of two types of effect at the moment, neither of which are good for workers. The first is in sectors where there is now a complete drought in terms of orders. There is a humanitarian crisis in the making in factories and workplaces where there are no orders, no wages, and no social safety net. Then there is another sort of supply chain where they are extremely busy—this might be in food supply chains; it might be in production of Personal Protective Equipment (PPE) or medical equipment. There we also see higher risk because you have workers who are already exploited being super-exploited, having to work extra hours, not necessarily getting the right payment for those extra hours, with many experiencing a curtailing of their freedom of movement. Of course, we are all of us unable to move about as usual, but I would argue it is a bit worse being locked up in a dormitory in Singapore, Malaysia, or China than it is being locked up in a nice house somewhere in Europe. These are the immediate impacts we are seeing. Looking slightly longer term though, I think there might be a correction as a result of COVID which could be helpful. This would be that those companies which are treating people as people, which are putting workers at the centre, which are not cutting corners in terms of labour cost, are more likely to be resilient and are more likely to be able to weather the storm.

But now, we already need to be thinking about what kind of labour practices will be sustainable in the new post-COVID world.

Uwe Schulte

For me a key element in all of this are two things: how much we pay our workers in the supply chain and how the access to healthcare is organised for them. How do you see that?

Rosey Hurst

Yes, absolutely. You are right. And of course, in many of the world's workplaces you have a lot of people working very, very close together, so social distancing is very hard to achieve. And you have lack of social safety nets: no unemployment benefit, no access to healthcare, and you have orders disappearing fast. Wages being cut. Companies not being able to afford to pay wages because the banks are pressing hard on them. COVID strikes at the heart of labour standards and strikes right at the heart of the global economy, particularly when we look at the supply chain. The most spectacular example of this, of course, is Bangladesh, where 84% of export earnings are from the global garment industry which is now basically at a standstill. So that turns a health crisis and an economic crisis into humanitarian crisis. We need to talk about what is the responsibility of the buyers when something like this happens.

Uwe Schulte

You raise an important point because a lot of companies are really striving to make their supply chains responsible and sustainable, and we already said that you must have certain ways of looking at your supply chain to make sure that your intention becomes reality. But there is a limit to what companies can do and where governments must step in. Or do you see this differently?

Force majeure

From Wikipedia, the free encyclopedia

In contract law, ***force majeure***[1][2][3] (French: [fɔʁs maʒœʁ]; lit. 'major force') is a common clause in contracts which essentially frees both parties from liability or obligation when an extraordinary event or circumstance beyond the control of the parties, such as a war, strike, riot, crime, epidemic, or sudden legal change prevents one or both parties from fulfilling their obligations under the contract.

Fig. 5 Force majeure. Source: Wikipedia, Creative Commons Attribution-ShareAlike License 4.0

Rosey Hurst

Well, the last crisis that affected supply chains, less deeply than this is doing, was the financial crisis back in 2007, 2008. And there, interestingly, human rights and labour rights did not have a seat at the table. Orders were cancelled, but there was no real feeling that buyers had a responsibility to see that workers were OK through that. And what I am delighted to say is that there is a far greater sense of responsibility this time round. As you know, a force majeure clause is a standard element in many contracts. It says, if something completely unforeseeable happens, we are entitled to break the contract. It is very rarely used, but I think everyone agrees that this pandemic is a force majeure[4] event. In the garment industry, a few buyers have exercised this clause to get out of their contracts with suppliers, but most have decided not to. Quite a lot of them have, publicly, said that they will continue to honour orders even if they have no way of selling that stock, and even if they don't even take delivery of the stock, they are going to continue to pay. Perhaps not full amount, perhaps not immediately, but they want to provide assurance to their suppliers that those contracts will be honoured. This is fascinating because contract law is absolutely at the centre of the global trade, and this idea of force majeure is crucial to the rationale of outsourcing production, which of course outsources responsibility. So why are these buyers going against the fundamental principles of global trade? The UN Guiding Principles on Business and Human Rights[5] are at the root of this. The UNGPs say that if a company uses the force majeure clause, its responsibility for the harm done to those workers increases because the company has just done something which has made things worse, so in other words it has contributed to the harm. Another contributing factor is the interest of investors, who are starting to look at which companies are going to come out of the pandemic in good shape? They start to look at not only which companies are in profit with decent cash reserves, but also which companies are maintaining their supply bases so that they can bounce back as demand grows. And that does mean paying attention to honouring these contracts. Obviously, there is uncertainty everywhere, but possibly this signals the end of continual subcontracting of production and responsibility with very little responsibility for human rights impacts. I think we could look back on this time and say this marks a change (Figs. 5 and 6).

Uwe Schulte

That is an interesting and, in a way, inspiring thought. It would mean that human beings only learn when there is a drastic crisis. If we take positive learnings from that, then this would be great, and I have seen some signs of that as well. When investors are speaking about more sustainable companies being more resilient, that is indicating exactly what you are saying, isn't it?

Rosey Hurst

Absolutely. This strikes at the heart of what we at Impactt do. We spend one-third of our time in global workplaces, diagnosing issues. We spend 1/3 of our time trying to sort things out on an enterprise-by-enterprise basis, getting working children

---

[4] https://en.wikipedia.org/wiki/Force_majeure
[5] https://unglobalcompact.org/library/1461

Fig. 6 Guiding Principles on Business and Human Rights (UN). Source: From "Guiding Principles on Business and Human Rights: Implementing the United Nations 'Protect, Respect and Remedy' Framework", by Office of the High Commissioner for Human Rights, © 2011 United Nations. Reprinted with the permission of the United Nations

back to school, getting people who have been in bonded labour out of bondage, etc. And we spend 1/3 of our time building policy based on our learned experience. You would have thought that, at the moment, nobody would be interested in talking to us, because everyone would be far too busy trying to keep businesses afloat. But actually, we have been completely amazed by the amount of interest in our work. Purchasing companies, but also suppliers and employers are starting to think that, if they are to survive in good shape, they need to get better at protecting workers' rights. That is not to underplay the very real crisis and the very real hardships that workers are facing. For those workers who are paid in cash, it is a particular disaster. Because if you are locked down and unable to go to the factory on payday, you do not get your pay. If you have had to go back to your home village, and you do not have a bank account, you do not get your pay. There are some very, very fundamental issues which are emerging, but trying to be positive about this, I hope that virtue will get its reward as we come out of this crisis.

Uwe Schulte
You make me think. Let us spend a few minutes on the other side of this. You know, huge demand is emerging in some other areas and that might also have an impact on human rights.

Rosey Hurst
Absolutely, yes. There are some sectors where there is huge demand, food for example, but also medical equipment, masks, rubber gloves, PPE of all sorts. We are also

seeing some quite significant human rights impacts in these sectors. Looking at PPE, these types of production systems tend to rely on migrant labour. They tend to be based in Asia, Southeast Asia in particular, and some in countries like Turkey as well. In these sectors, we see already vulnerable migrant workers being further abused because through seven-day working and extremely long hours. We have reports of people working 18-hour shifts in the packing department of a rubber glove factory, as part of a 'COVID-19 heroes' scheme, where they 'volunteer' to work on the rest day for less money than they get on a normal working day. In the meantime, they are living under lockdown in overcrowded conditions. There is no possibility of social distancing and, of course, freedom of movement is severely curtailed.[6] All our freedom of movement is curtailed at the moment, but I would argue being locked down in a dormitory with 50 people is rather different from being locked down in your house or your apartment. As is typical, health, economic, and humanitarian disasters affect the people at the bottom the most and of course social distancing is a luxury which the workers of the world cannot afford and the chances of significant hotspots with the epidemic are also extremely high.

Uwe Schulte
But there it must be in the interest of those purchasing the goods from these factories to improve the conditions because you do not want a total lockdown of your source.

Rosey Hurst
Exactly. I mean there are obviously strong commercial incentives for improving things. But lockdowns mean that it is very difficult to monitor the situation face-to-face. So suddenly the way that we are working at Impactt is, we are in regular contact with workers through my colleagues who are local to where the factories are or local to where the workers come from. Because obviously maintaining that conversation, having a sort of ongoing monitoring rather than an audit every six months, but getting news in every morning about how things are, what the dangers are, it is very helpful. We are working a lot on this kind of remote support to be able to triage issues. Workers obviously have mobile phones. So, we get a lot of footage when workers feel that social distancing is being breached or where insufficient efforts are being made. And I regret to say, in many cases, what a company says publicly about how it is a supply company and what it is saying publicly about how it is managing social distancing, is heavily undermined by the kind of footage that we get sent by workers. And I think it is very important that first, try not—particularly in the healthcare sector—to make our huge demand for some of these products, particularly the PPE products come at any cost, because we could well be finding that the cost to those who are producing it outweighs the value of the protection which those rubber gloves and other masks and things bring. If purchasers can continue to draw the line to say: 'we want to have proof of social distancing. We want you to allow helplines. We want you to allow grievance procedures. We wanted to allow remote

---

[6] https://www.washingtonpost.com/world/africa/the-kenyan-factory-that-transformed-into-a-surgical-mask-assembly-line-overnight/2020/04/08/fac04912-783e-11ea-a311-adb1344719a9_story.html

monitoring so that we can keep on checking that the best is being done'. I think that is a very important role for purchasers, and I would say that is for public sector purchasers in health systems as well as private companies.

Uwe Schulte

It's good advice and it's doable. You made me think: If I am sitting in a home office, let us say in London, and I want to secure rubber gloves from Malaysia, where I already know that the conditions under normal circumstances weren't brilliant. What do I do? You have just given some guidance because, of course, demand is high; the urgency is great, but on the other hand, those companies who provide these things at the moment have the luxury of being in high demand so they can afford also to take some precautions. And I guess those suppliers should have an interest on maintaining the health of their workers because otherwise they might not be able to participate in that demand.

Rosey Hurst

But exactly. And in fact, they cannot currently hire any new workers because of lockdowns. Trying to maximise the productivity of the workers that remain to them is very important. Particularly in these high-pressure sectors, we cannot say that the ends justify the means. And we should not be saying we must have these products at any cost. We must make social distancing, proper payment, and reduction in exploitation part of the deal in buying this type of product.

Uwe Schulte

There is a train of thought which says, if we repatriate these things, we have a bigger control over it and labour conditions will improve and so on and so forth. There are people who say, the consequences out of this are to stop global supply chains. How do you see this?

Rosey Hurst

There have been moves for some time now to bring some supply chains 'home', partly because of quality, partly because of human rights concerns, and partly because of carbon and partly for 'just in time' delivery. But what we tend to find is that when production comes home, it is not as good as it should be in human rights terms. The tendency is to keep prices artificially low by hiring the cheapest possible migrant workforces in our own rich countries, who are highly vulnerable to exploitation. We like to think that there is no such thing as modern slavery[7] in Europe or the USA, but this just isn't true. For example, British regulatory systems are not strong enough to prevent labour exploitation and modern slavery—and some systems, such as schemes for seasonal agricultural workers, actively encourage it. The impact of Covid is likely to intensify the need to bring production closer to home. But this needs to be done with far greater care and thought about human rights than has been done to date. It may be that this crisis (together with the carbon crisis) will accelerate the demise of the fast fashion model as well as prompting other environmentally positive changes. But we must remember that these changes will have

---

[7] https://www.weforum.org/agenda/2022/09/global-modern-slavery-trafficking/

significant social impacts. For example, impacts on those 5,000,000 workers in the garment industry in Bangladesh[8] and their many millions of dependents, who may lose their jobs, as well as facing direct climate impacts in their country. It is also not at all clear that green energy production is any better than oil and gas when it comes to negative human rights impacts. There is a big fat problem here for the world to solve post COVID (Figs. 7 and 8).

Uwe Schulte

I simply believe that our global supply chains will continue, they will need redesign, and they will need to be made more resilient, which is the new word and more transparent. But there is, of course, some good sense for some division of labour in

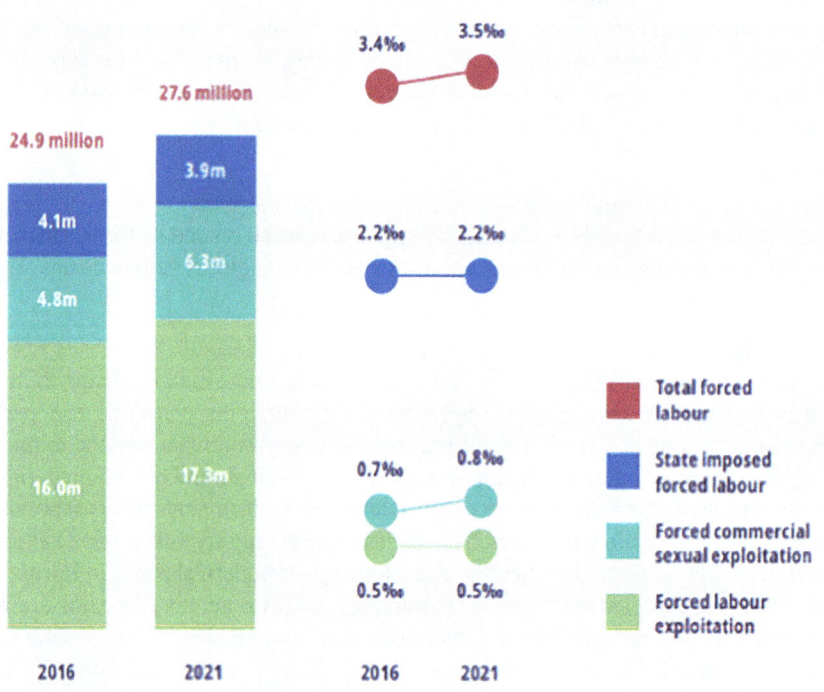

Fig. 7 Modern slavery. Source: *ILO* (International Labour Organization), 2021

---

[8] http://www.unido.or.jp/en/news/1650/

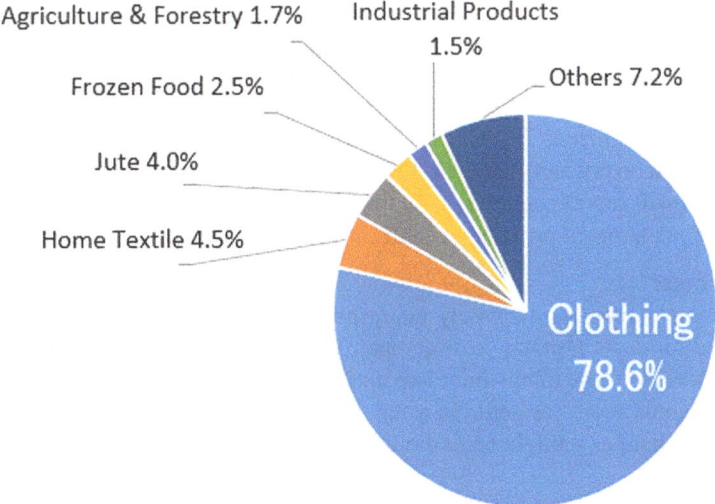

Fig. 8 Bangladesh exports by product group. Source: public domain, CC BY 4.0 DEED, Attribution 4.0 International, UNIDO - United Nations Industrial Development Organization, Investment and Technology Promotion Office Tokyo, 2015, http://www.unido.or.jp/en/news/1650/

different countries and as you said, making sure that all the aspects of sustainability are taken into account—carbon footprint being a very important one, but the social impact being another one, this must be something that when you are procuring, to be on your mind and you have to have visibility of these effects.

Rosey Hurst
And I think it goes at both ends of the supply chain, doesn't it? The decline of bricks and mortar retailing has an impact on jobs, both in terms of reductions in the number of sales staff and increases in the numbers of low-quality jobs in picking, packing, and delivery. As these changes take place, we must all, collectively, ensure that the experience of the work has a seat at the table as we start to work out what the post-COVID world looks like. We see how interdependent our world is. It is clearly in nobody's interests for there to be huge, localised, serious humanitarian impacts. And I think it is going to call for a unique collaboration between nations and between companies and governments to try and navigate way out of all of this for businesses and humans around the world.

Uwe Schulte
You are making a very important point here and we have briefly touched on access to healthcare, but we do not have to go to Bangladesh to see that access to healthcare in a situation like we are having it at the moment is something that is in the developed world also an issue, and therefore when we rethink supply chains and working conditions, and you just mentioned for example, workers that deliver or people working on the shop floor in supermarkets, we must re-evaluate their positions as well, not just those in faraway countries.

Rosey Hurst

Absolutely. I am a great believer in attempting to re-humanise people in each other's eyes and I think it is very tempting for employers and for purchasers to think about people in supply chains as being a little bit like machines. Which means the moment you think that someone is a bit like a machine, you start to treat them a bit like a machine. You do not consider your duty of care, for example as an employer. I hope that Covid will support some positive thinking on this. What is the responsibility of employers in terms of providing health care or health protection for workers?

Uwe Schulte

You outline something extremely interesting and we have to see how it emerges. The need for cross country, cross company, and a company government collaboration to develop these things in a way that our systems rather than just our supply chains become more resilient. To your point here is the possibility for a positive outcome as hard as it might be to think about this now.

Rosey Hurst

I do not know if you have noticed but when at the beginning of the outbreak everyone was in shock for at least two weeks, and there was a sort of full-on crisis mode, then companies and individuals have been thinking operationally, how we are going to manage. I think now we are in the stage of strategic thinking. We are in the stage of thinking what is it going to be like afterwards. How can we have economies on the domestic, industrial, and national levels that work, and which are human? There is something this disease has done, it brought home to all of us that we are frail human beings. And if anything comes out of this, if we can factor that into the making of the New World post COVID, I think that at least there will be some positives coming out of this disaster (Fig. 9).

Uwe Schulte

Time goes so quickly; we have unfortunately come to an end, but we have not spent any time on inequality today[9]. With the interdependence that happens everywhere, if you are sitting at home and you are getting stuff delivered to your home because you are quarantined or you rely on supermarkets working even with the risk for those people out there, we become more aware that all those people are equal and therefore we must re-evaluate our relationships.

Rosey Hurst

Those people who are doing those jobs are in fact rather more important than the rest of us. That is clear when we look at the importance of frontline workers and health workers. Hopefully that notion of equality or rebalancing will be part of the post-COVID landscape.

---

[9] https://wid.world/

Top 10% national income share

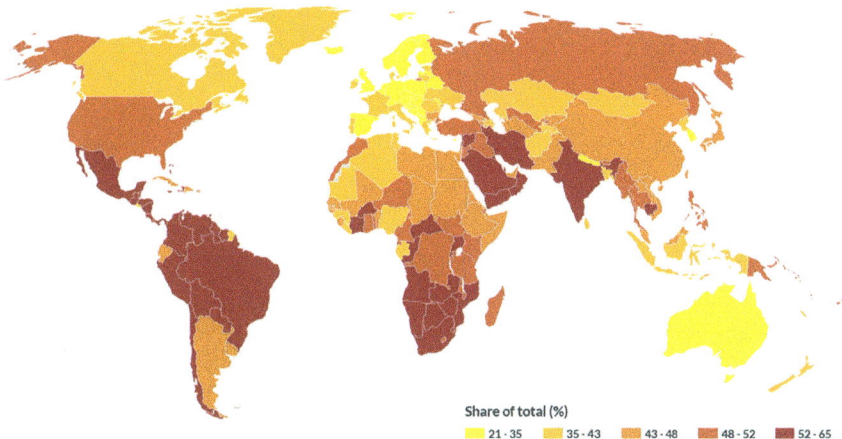

Fig. 9 Top 10% national income share, World Inequality Database. Source: World Inequality Lab, wid.world (2023), CC BY 4.0 DEED Attribution 4.0 International

Uwe Schulte
And that doesn't necessarily mean to forfeit the need for companies to thrive, it is just to re-evaluate how to thrive sustainably.

Thank you, Rosey. This was under the circumstance a really encouraging conversation. I thank you for your insights and no doubt we will continue that conversation in the future when we have better visibility of hopefully a good outcome.

Sustainable Business Transformation: A Renewable Energy Example

Recorded June 2020

Uwe Schulte

Today I will be talking to Filip Engel from Ørsted about sustainable business transformation. First, let me introduce our guest to you. Filip Engel is a vice president, sustainability, public affairs, and branding at Ørsted. Filip has a bachelor's in public administration and a master's in political science from the College of Europe. He accompanied and supported the business transformation of DONG, originally Dansk Natural Gas, to Ørsted from an oil to a 100% renewable energy company. Filip did this in several roles, like strategy advisor, stakeholder management, and VP for an area that included sustainability for the whole company. Welcome, Filip. Please tell us a little bit about yourself and your role at Ørsted.

Filip Engel

This Interview relates to the situation in 2020. Filip Engel left Ørsted in November 2023. In the meantime, Filip co-founded the Danish-based strategic sustainability and communication consultancy Koral. The views expressed here should not be seen to reflect those of Ørsted in 2024.

Hello Uwe and thank you for having me. I have been with the company for 12 years and as you said I have responsibility for our global functions within public affairs, sustainability, branding, and marketing. And when I started—at that time it was called Dong Energy—my very first task was to assist the CEO back then to write an op-ed in which we wanted to say that climate change was a problem. And that we needed to reduce carbon emissions and that we had a big responsibility to do so because we had remarkably high carbon emissions. We were one of the most coal intensive European utilities back then. That was where it started for me. And that was also where the transformation towards green energy really started for the company. And since then, it has been step by step in the green direction. Back then 12 years ago, we set a strategy where we said that we had 85% fossil fuels-based energy and 15% green, and we wanted to flip that fraction around to have 85% green and 15% fossil fuels by 2040. We reached that objective last year. So that is how fast it has gone. And me personally, I have had the privilege of supporting the business in separate roles. My first role was a strategic advisor and supporting the CEO on his presentations and speeches, and then I moved into public affairs and sustainability and then over time I was given responsibility for branding and marketing (Fig. 1).

Uwe Schulte

That sounds interesting, and we want to learn more about this. You talked about coming in and having to help writing an op-ed. The question is, what triggered this—and could you talk a little bit more about it before you answer the question about what Dong did at the time, to better understand where the decision to change came from that insight.

Filip Engel

Now that is certainly an interesting question you are raising there, Uwe. At that time, Dong Energy was a company that had coal-fired power plants in Denmark, and quite a few of them. It is interesting that today Denmark has changed a lot and has built up a strong green profile and has transformed a lot when it comes to green energy. But back then, Denmark had quite a lot of coal still. And being the biggest energy company in Denmark, Dong Energy, our story as a company is also very

Fig. 1 From DONG to Ørsted. Source: Ørsted A/S, https://orsted.dk/

much the story about Denmark's energy transition. At that point in time, we had a lot of coal-fired power plants and we also had oil and gas production, in northwestern Europe. And that was the context.

When I joined the company there had been a lot of preparations and thinking whether we should start to change as a company and what triggered that change? What triggered those thoughts? You asked me where that decision came from. And as with most strategic decisions, it is something that you prepare, that you groom, that you think about for quite some time and there was a leadership team—the CEO back then and some different people across the company—who saw a need for changing the business. And there were different drivers for that, for asking the question if we should change. And one of them was the fact that they could see that climate change as an agenda was on the rise and being a company with fossil fuels at its core, that did not seem sustainable for the long term.

We can get back to that later, but that was one reason, and the second reason was that the liberalisation of the European energy markets was kicking in, so we were looking into a reality where our legacy business was becoming less and less profitable and there were major risks on the horizon. So those are two of the main drivers. And what happened with the op-ed—if we want to circle in on that—it was very much used to set the direction for the company going forward. When we published that op-ed, we had not said that much about how we wanted to change as a company yet, so that op-ed was part of a major communication push where we announced that we wanted to change as a company. We want to go from 15% green energy to 85% green energy within a generation, which was understood as around 30 years. And that was interesting because what the communication did, the purpose it served was also to set the direction for the company. The concrete business strategy for how to do it was not really that solid at that point. There was not a clear action plan in place for how to get to that vision of having 85% green energy by transforming our energy mix. What was interesting was that the communication, not only the op-ed but the general communication that was made by the leadership back then was used to set the direction and say, 'this is where we need to go, and we need to find out how to do it'. And that was used to set the agenda externally towards our stakeholders, but also internally towards the employees and the broader leadership team back then so it is an interesting exercise in change communication, in leadership communication.

Uwe Schulte
That sounds like a big step, and I would love to hear how those two distinct types of stakeholders responded to that, so the external world and your workforce as well.

Filip Engel
If we take the external stakeholders first—so let us divide them into the political stakeholders and NGO's and then also the potential employees, people who we would be interested in interacting to work for the company and the general public. This was in a Danish context. As you know, we had activities in other countries but back then we were very much a Danish company. More than 90% of our earnings came from Denmark. So that was the context and there was a positive reaction

externally. Back then there was already a debate in Denmark about the future of energy with respect to climate change. There were a lot of political stakeholders who thought that we needed to act on that as a society. The announcement to transform the company to renewables was received positively. Of course, also from the green NGOs who had looked at the company and criticised it for how it had a very carbon intense footprint, and certainly, with that, also from the broader public, and from the people who we wanted to attract to come to work for this company. So that was overall a quite positive reaction. There was a lot of scepticism with respect to if the transformation could be done. Especially from people in the energy industry. Internally, there was also a lot of discussion about the sense in pursuing such a transformation. Now, one must keep in mind that, as I said, we were a company that had coal, natural gas, and oil. And especially with respect to coal-fired power plants, we were good at it. We were one of the leading companies globally in building highly effective coal-fired power plants and we had a strategy back then to build coal-fired power plants in different countries. We had a couple of projects in Germany and in the United Kingdom. This was very much a part of the company's DNA. It was a part of people's identity who worked here. So naturally there was a lot of questioning around whether it was the right strategy to leave something behind, we were good at in exchange for renewables which we did not have that much experience with.

Back then the offshore wind industry was extremely nascent, extremely young. You could not even talk about the existence of an offshore wind industry. You had onshore wind of course, and we had some of that also and that was becoming a more consolidated industry. But you did not really have an offshore wind industry. It was natural that many colleagues reacted with scepticism when we said that we wanted to throw away coal-fired power generation which we were good at and start doing offshore wind. I remember one episode where I met a senior colleague at the coffee machine, and we were talking about the green transformation. I remember he took a napkin and a pen and drew a chart on that napkin. What that chart explained was how our strategy would never be able to succeed because renewables were much more costly than fossil fuels. He could not see how we could ever turn renewables into a profitable business. That was very illustrative for the thinking back then.

Uwe Schulte
This is exactly what I anticipated and that of course raises the question what you think were the key success factors in turning this around? Because if you do not convince your own team about the vision the CEO obviously brought in as well as several other senior managers, then those negative prophecies might have turned out to be right rather than, as now proving to be wrong.

Filip Engel
There were a lot of distinct factors that helped the strategy along. As I said, there was a growing realisation that we needed to act in one way or another because we were starting to change due to policies such as the EU liberalisation and the European Union taking steps to put a price on carbon. The CEO managed the communication internally and externally in a strong way. To set those targets and to

communicate externally that we wanted to do this before we had the plan in place for how to do it turned out to be a clever move. The textbook approach would be to do it the other way around: build a strategy and plan and then communicate about it. But it was done the other way around. And then of course there was a third factor, which was that the organisation was changed. A reorganisation took place where talented people and capital were allocated to building the offshore wind business. Those are three drivers that helped the transformation of the strategy succeed and really took a hold in the company.

Uwe Schulte

A lot of people will listen to this with great interest because companies are facing the situation repeatedly and it is difficult to make very fundamental decisions about the business model. I hear you say: you look at what is material to you, and for your company that was the carbon footprint. And then to look at the future from a stakeholder perspective and from a market perspective, identifying new options and—and that was of course an entrepreneurial decision—to go for these options rather than defending the past. Is that a summary that would resonate with you?

Filip Engel

Yes, it most certainly does. I think a point to keep in mind is that when you talk about business transformations you often look at companies as these very rational and optimising entities that will always produce the best possible outcome. It is often how companies are also depicted in the business media. But companies are run by people. Companies try to make a profit—but how do you do that in the best way? That is where the human factor comes in. Do you transform your company, or do you stay within your legacy business? And one of the ways we humans function, is that we tend to value what we have more than what we do not have. And that is certainly one of the biases that often inhibits making the change that is needed, even though we can see some signs that we should change. We were in a situation where we did see some straightforward signs that climate change was real and that climate change would become a key factor, in the long term in how stakeholders would look at the company. Stakeholders being regulators, employees, potential employees, and investors. Back then, we were not a listed company (we were listed in 2016) but there was an ambition to be listed. We looked at that and we asked ourselves—should we change? This is very much what is important—to look at what is coming your way. Get those trends right and look at the long term. It is a difficult exercise, but this is what sustainability is about. At the end of the day, sustainability is a prism that you can look through to get an idea of how your market will shape up some years from now and then act on it to prepare for that market.

Uwe Schulte

That is a wonderful picture. I must say, I like your analogy here. And it is interesting that you talk about that human factor in this transition. But you also talk about the long-term perspective, being one of the main elements of sustainability. To get out of the short-termism, and to look at the long term which is not a widespread practice. We can see that not all players in the industry have the same vision as you did, but I think we should now look at that napkin again that said 'this is not possible'. It looks to me as if you are talking about a more successful story than your colleague at the coffee machine was anticipating.

Filip Engel

Yes, absolutely. History has shown that it did become quite a successful story. If you look at the energy markets, in general there is now consensus around green energy being the future. Most players within the energy industry are now moving in the green direction in some form, some quicker than others, but everyone is doing it. So that has certainly changed.

Uwe Schulte

What I would like to work out is the development of capacities around wind. People are now starting to challenge: 'Is there enough space to develop the capacities that are required'?

Filip Engel

Let us investigate that. Let us take a European perspective just to zoom in on a specific geography. The European offshore wind capacity was eighteen gigawatts in 2018, so eighteen gigawatts of offshore wind had been built out. Now, the European Commission published an analysis that said that technically Europe could reach 450 GW of offshore wind by 2050 in the northern seas of Europe.[1] That is a huge increase, and it is technical potential, but it still gives an idea of the potential out there. And that is a part of how the European Union sees that the continent can become carbon neutral. It will require 5 to 8 times more solar, 3.5 times more onshore wind, and twenty times more offshore wind to deliver on that ambition. So that is something about the capacity build-out that will need to take place in just the European context to reach a carbon-neutral Europe. That will allow us to halve greenhouse gas emissions by 2030 and then reach net zero by 2050 in the European Union. And that is what science says the world needs. That is of course ambitious, and it is also quite front loaded, meaning that a lot will have to take place throughout the twenties to get there. You cannot just say: 'We need to build out green energy—why do we not just do that when we get to 2040'? You cannot do that. First, because it is not possible to ramp up an industry this quickly. You cannot go from the level we are at today to a much higher level within a couple of years. You need to do that ramp-up gradually over the years. And secondly, we need to act now because we cannot wait to reduce emissions. Emissions need to come down now as well as the years after that if we want to have any chance to keep temperatures to 2 degrees, let alone 1.5 degrees. That is the situation of the build-out.

And you asked a particularly good question. How does that impact space requirements? And that is a very new discussion that we are starting to have as a European industry and are also having with stakeholders across the board. Because, if you want and need to build more, you need to take into consideration how it can coexist with other industries that are out there. For instance, transportation. If you take

---

[1] https://setis.ec.europa.eu/document/download/7d0ebed5-ddd7-4a09-920b-99b950c47146_en

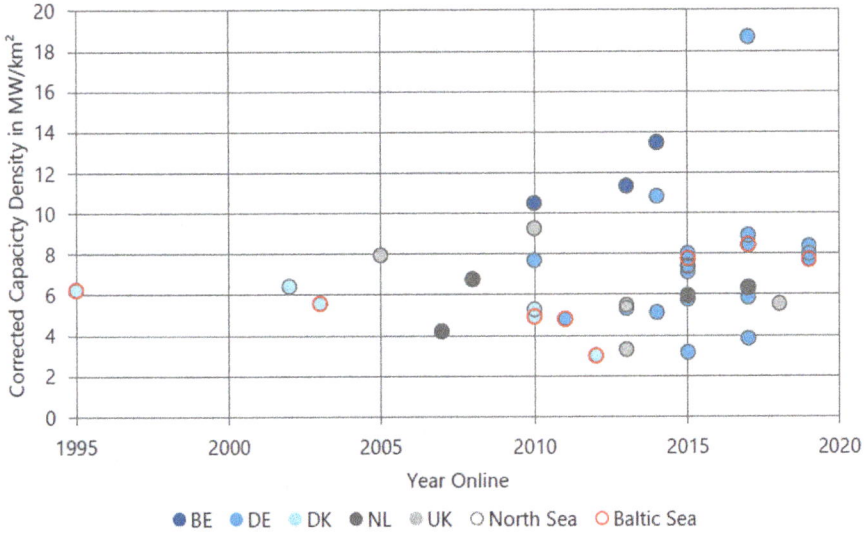

Fig. 2 Off-shore corrected wind capacity density. Source: Deutsche WindGuard GmbH, Capacity Densities of European Offshore Wind Farms, Report conducted by Deutsche WindGuard Gmbh, 2018, https://vasab.org/wp-content/uploads/2018/06/BalticLINes_CapacityDensityStudy_June2018-1.pdf

something such as defence, they also have access and use up a lot of areas at sea and the fishing industry as well. And then secondly, we need to make sure that that build-out continues to contribute to biodiversity and to protect the environment (Fig. 2).[2]

Uwe Schulte
That is of course an important question, and people have raised that around off-shore. But I understand that modern technologies come along that help you to achieve these targets.

Filip Engel
Yes, certainly. If you look at offshore wind, it is more an evolution of the technology of offshore wind. If you are thinking about how to build out offshore wind, what we are seeing is that turbines are becoming bigger and more powerful. We are still using the same technology. But we are evolving it to become more powerful and to be able to produce more. That is how it has been for the last decade. And what we see is that it will continue to evolve and refine continuously. Then of course there is an important leap technology wise that we are looking at as an industry across the board when it comes to floating turbines.[3] Floating turbines mean that you do not have to anchor the offshore wind turbine to the seabed. What you are doing today is

---

[2] Corrected wind farm capacity density considers for comparability a smaller number of turbines accounting for the reduced number of rectangles that are created by the centers of the wind turbines.

[3] https://windeurope.org/newsroom/news/floating-wind-is-making-great-strides/

Fig. 3 Floating wind turbine.
Source: Ørsted A/S, https://orsted.dk/

that you are building a foundation below waters which the turbine stands on. Now, of course, that works fine if it is more shallow waters and with shallow, I mean 30, 40 but also fifty metres. That is what we are doing today as an industry. But if you want to go deeper than that, then you would also need floating. And that is something that a lot of companies are also looking at to see how that can evolve (Fig. 3).

Uwe Schulte
I understand there already are five floating turbines off the shore of Scotland.

Filip Engel
Yes, that is one of the demonstration projects that are out there with the ambition of seeing that part of the industry taking off.

Uwe Schulte
But we are getting too much into technology now. You were already talking about a colleague who owned a napkin that told you that what you have achieved now would not be possible, and that fascinated me, so let us talk about that. The cost of renewables in comparison to other sources of energy today, can you say something about that from your perspective?

Filip Engel

Yes, I certainly can. Solar energy, onshore and offshore wind energy in most parts of the world today, it is cheaper to build that than to build a coal-fired or gas-fired power plant, and it is coal and gas you use for power production. Oil is used elsewhere, so let us just leave that aside and focus on power production. And there is a remarkable change that we have seen over the last 7–8 years. To zoom in on offshore wind: What we are seeing is that costs have fallen around two-thirds between 2012 and 2019, so we reduced costs by 66%. Regarding solar and onshore: they have taken similar paths where they have also reduced costs significantly. I think solar is the technology that has reduced costs the most. And that is of course a major game changer. And as I said, it is in most parts of the world, meaning that there are some places yet where this is not the case. And there may be several reasons for that, but it is often simply because, for instance, in the case of offshore wind, in some places you need to build up an industry to push down the price. And that industry is not there yet. Regarding solar there are of course also limits in some places of the world to how much sun there is. But solar is also even working in a country such as Denmark. The sun is shining in the summer, but I am looking out the window here, I am in Copenhagen, Denmark, and the sun is shining but it is fair to say that we are not the sunniest country in the world. But it is still cheaper here to build solar cells than to build a coal-fired power plant. That is a remarkable change and a major game changer that really kicked in around 2017. Notably for offshore wind which of course has done a lot to spur investments and in general just create faith in the green transformation and in the future profitability of these technologies (Fig. 4).

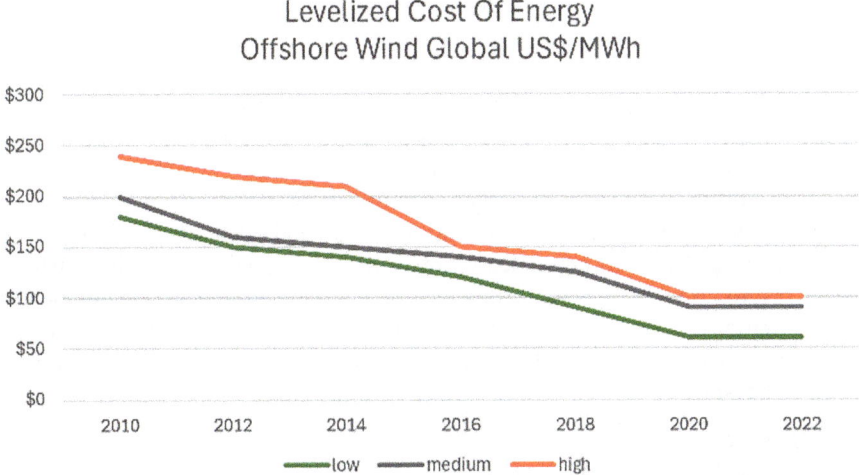

Fig. 4 Off-shore wind cost decline based on IRENA 2022. Source: Uwe G. Schulte

Uwe Schulte

I understand that in some cases under certain circumstances the full loaded cost of a wind farm can compete with the incremental cost of a written off coal-fired coal plant. Is that correct?

Filip Engel

That is correct. That is what we are starting to see now, that even if you are talking about new build, it can compete with already existing power plants, coal, for instance, which is written off. And what we are expecting is to see more cost reductions within wind and solar energy. That is really changing the game a lot.

Uwe Schulte

Do you think that when we look at places like India, where there are still quite significant plans to build coal-fired plants, that these economics might change their perspective?

Filip Engel

They are changing their perspective, but I also think that in a lot of countries there is a, let us call it a path dependency. There is a technology lock-in that is extremely hard to break out of. I am not an expert on India so allow me to talk about this in more general terms. What we can see is that if you already have an industry and that industry is strong, of course there are jobs in that. And it becomes attractive to continue to invest in that industry, even though you have other alternatives, greener alternatives that are cheaper. That is one reason you do not see an automatic translation of the fact that green energy is now cheaper than fossil fuels into that no fossil fuels power plants are being built, for instance. That is not yet what we are seeing. We are seeing it to a considerable extent in Europe and it is also happening in the USA. In Asia, we are not there yet (Fig. 5).

As I said, there are several reasons for that. You are asking a very timely and relevant question. Because you may be excused to think: 'If it is cheaper, then what is the problem? There is no problem anymore, right'? Because of rational economic access, governments will, of course, choose the cheapest alternative, right? But unfortunately, that does not always happen. A second reason is that you may need to develop different policy regimes to also build out the green energy. Because it is different. Of course, if you want to build offshore wind, then you need to look at your seabed and how to create lease areas where companies can build offshore wind. Just to take one example. Often there is not a unit within a country's public administration that knows how to do that. Capacity has to be built. There are a lot of questions about the institutional capacity to enable the transformation that we see as being increasingly important than just looking at the price.

Uwe Schulte

What you just said is encouraging, it offers businesses opportunities to make these points, engage in them, and drive the pathway for such investments. I would like to cover one more aspect: wind and solar have this issue around storage capacity and reliability of supply. Could hydrogen projects be part of the solution?

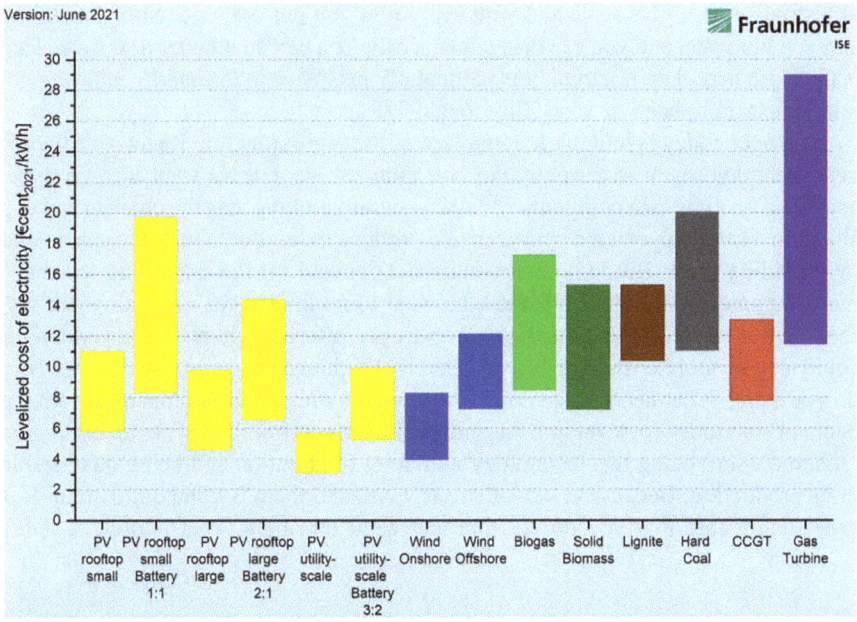

Fig. 5 Fraunhofer levelized cost of electricity 2021. Source: Fraunhofer ISE, 2021, https://www.ise.fraunhofer.de/en/press-media/press-releases/2021/levelized-cost-of-electricity-renewables-clearly-superior-to-conventional-power-plants-due-to-rising-co2-prices.html

Filip Engel

We very much think so and others think the same, we can tell. It is remarkable how the conversation around hydrogen has picked up over the last couple of years from being something that we have all looked at for many years but was a bit more marginal to something that a lot of serious players are really looking at now. And several projects are being announced to help develop hydrogen. What we are talking about here is that hydrogen is a known technology to a considerable extent. A lot of industries are already using hydrogen. For instance, in the chemical industry, it is already being used. What we are talking about is to produce hydrogen that is based on renewable energy instead of hydrogen that is, as of today, based on fossil fuels, notably natural gas. And that will, of course, contribute to reducing global carbon emissions. How can we take hydrogen and help to develop it? It is about creating a cost out journey for hydrogen. Hopefully like what happened in wind and solar energy. Allow me to go back and give a couple of words as to why that did happen. It was very much a question of providing scales to those industries. I said before that if you take offshore wind as an example—costs fell by two-thirds between 2012 and 2019. Well, this is also the time where capacity increased by six times. Each time the capacity was doubled, the cost came down a bit more than 10%. And the same happened for onshore wind and solar. That is important to keep in mind if you want to bring down costs of these capital-intensive industries. You need to give them scale. Why? Because when you give them scale, the industry learns. You industrialise, you give scale and with every unit you put out, you learn something, and you innovate, and you can bring down costs. You can do it better next time. That is the logic here. I do not think it is particularly exclusive to the energy industry, but it is important to keep in mind (Figs. 6 and 7).

Hydrogen today is looking at somewhat of the same situation. Renewable hydrogen, green hydrogen is currently not cost competitive, but we want it to go there, and it can become cost competitive[4,5]. What we are looking at is the chicken and egg situation. How can you take hydrogen and produce more of it? Well, you can do that by providing scale. But to do that you need a demand. At the same time, you have big companies on the demand side who want to go in the green direction and say, 'but there is not really that much green hydrogen offered right now, and certainly it could also be more cost competitive'. That is the chicken and egg situation—where do you start? What needs to be done is to team up with a lot of companies from the demand side to try to develop a flagship project that is going to scale up hydrogen. Offshore wind, being this technology with a lot of attention and being quite stable in its production. Because at sea—there is wind, and there is wind quite often. It is exceedingly rare that you do not find any wind out there. That is quite a stable

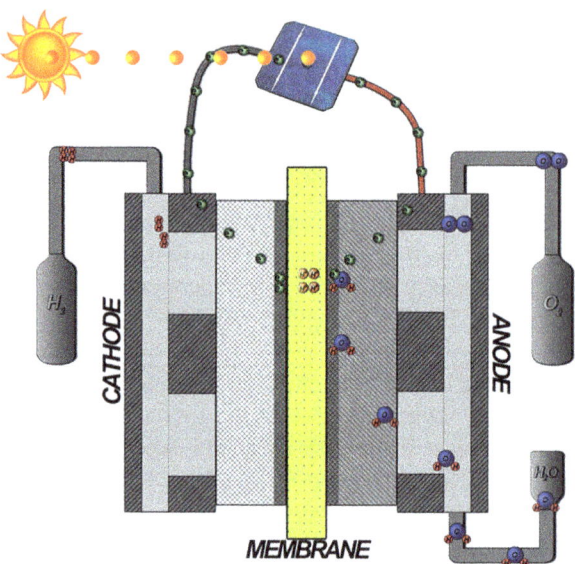

Fig. 6 Green hydrogen production. Source: Wikipedia, CC BY-SA 3.0 DEED, Attribution-ShareAlike 3.0 Unported, Author: Davidlfritz, Source: own work

---

[4] https://earthjustice.org/feature/green-hydrogen-renewable-zero-emission

[5] https://www.irena.org/-/media/Files/IRENA/Agency/Publication/2020/Nov/IRENA_Green_Hydrogen_breakthrough_2021.pdf?la=en&hash=40FA5B8AD7AB1666EECBDE30EF458C45EE5A0AA6

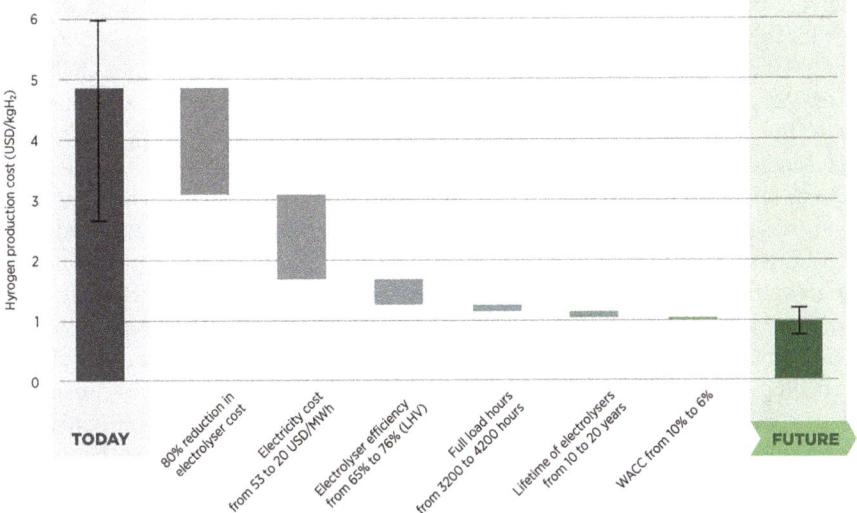

Fig. 7 IRENA cost reduction potential green hydrogen. Source: IRENA (2021), Making the breakthrough: Green hydrogen policies and technology costs, International Renewable Energy Agency Abu Dhabi

technology and one can take that energy and use it to create hydrogen. That can then be used, for instance, by big transport companies such as Maersk or Scandinavian Airlines.[6]

Uwe Schulte
That is good news and I guess what you are telling me is, because I have just decided to put in a fuel cell-based heating system into my house, that I am sort of old fashioned because even, so it is based on hydrogen, the hydrogen comes out of gas. I am backwards oriented, but that is the best I could do at the time.

Filip Engel
Well, I think what you are saying there, that probably the key insight is that we have a lot of areas where we need to transform the energy space. A lot is happening within power now and it is certainly going in the right direction. But it is still a long way to go if we want to move the world in a greener direction. Seventy-three percent of global emissions are coming from something energy related and that is really a lot, and we need to change that. We need to change that by taking our fossil fuels and having green energy instead. How do we do that? We do that by ramping up green energy, of course. If you look at a scenario with 1.5 degrees, if you want to stay there, then the share of green energy must rise to 60% by 2050, up from 11% today. The share of electricity should rise to around 50%, that is the share of electricity in the overall energy use. You need a strong electrification to be able to raise the overall energy share. Today we have the production technologies to really

---

[6] https://www.greentechmedia.com/articles/read/orsted-to-power-decarbonization-hub-for-land-sea-and-air-transport

increase power production—we have solar, and we have wind. But what we also need is to find the ways to get the power into other parts of the economy. Sorry for the small detour here, but it is important to underline that we are facing a challenge here. We are in a situation where green power is cheaper than power from fossil fuels. But we also need to take that power and get it into the other part of the economy, and that is where hydrogen can be one lever that can help to do that. That can help us build green hydrogen, which can decarbonise some of the carbon-intensive industries such as chemistry where there really are no other options today. And what you were saying regarding your example, although from your home, it is still relevant. We can only do what the technologies allow us to do, so we need to evolve those technologies. A lot of those technologies are known technologies. We have a lot of those technologies; we know what they are. Electric vehicles are a known technology by now. The components of hydrogen, as I said a couple of times, are known technology. But what we need to do is to bring down costs. We need to bring down costs, so it becomes more competitive, and it really becomes the natural choice. And that is a process that is ongoing now. But what it really requires is scale. And to have scale you need to have investment. We are already getting close to that point now regarding electric vehicles. Each year the automobile industry, the manufacturing industry, they revise their view on when electric vehicles will be cost competitive. They revise it one year down. They have done that for the last 3–4 years. That is because it is getting closer and closer. First, they said it is going to be somewhere in the late twenties. But now, if I remember correctly, they say that it is going to be in 2022. Or it is 2023, so that is close. That is the evolvement we want to see to bring these innovative technologies forward (Fig. 8).

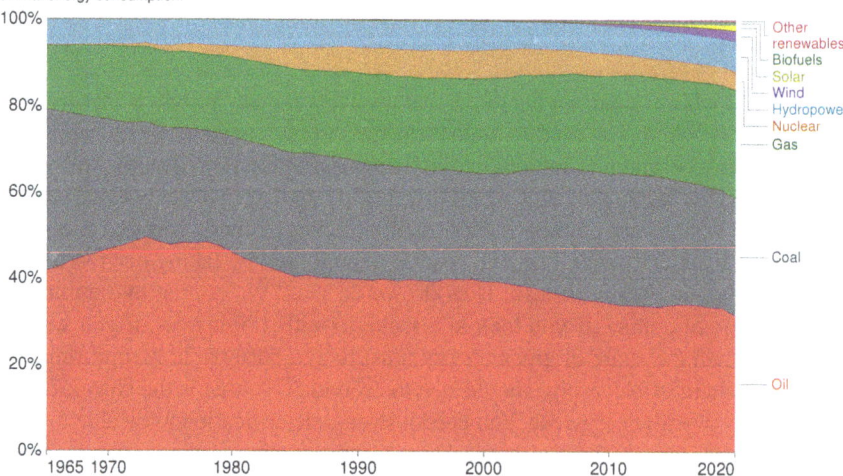

Fig. 8 Global energy consumption by source. Source: Wikipedia, CC BY-SA 3.0 DEED, Attribution-ShareAlike 3.0 Unported, Author: Our World in Data, Source: Our World in Data, https://ourworldindata.org/grapher/energy-consumption-by-source-and-region

Uwe Schulte

You have just made me feel a bit better again by having chosen an electric vehicle. So that is good news. Thank you so much, Filip you have given us a perspective of what needs doing when we start looking forward again and getting out crisis mode. Thank you so much for that outlook on renewable energy from your perspective, which was very insightful.

Filip Engel

Thank you, Uwe, and thank you again for having me.

Water the New Oil

Recorded July 2020

Uwe Schulte

Today I will be talking to Emilio Tenuta from Ecolab about 'Water, the New Oil'. First, let me introduce our guest to you. Emilio Tenuta is the Chief Sustainability Officer at Ecolab. Emilio has an MBA in general management from the Kellogg School of Management. His tenure with Ecolab includes working for its industrial water treatment business, Nalco Water. Welcome Emilio and please tell us a little bit about yourself and your role at Ecolab.

Emilio Tenuta

Sure, and thanks for having me today. A little bit about myself: I have 36 years of industry experience in water and energy. As you said, starting with Nalco Water, which is now merged with Ecolab. I guess I have got to start with my passion around sustainability. This dates to the time that I spent in southern Italy. I am first generation Italian American and I would recall times in Calabria, Southern Italy, where I worked with my grandfather on his little local farm before I knew the relevance of what water management was or soil management. He really instilled in me the importance of the role that Mother Nature has to the livelihood of society and the environment. That experience has really informed what I do today at Ecolab.

I have been leading sustainability for Ecolab for the last 10 years. My origins with the business include working from within to really drive impact through our customers. Ecolab started back in 1923 with one product called Absorbit, which was used to clean carpets within hotels without taking the actual carpet out of the room. Today we would say that product reduced energy and carbon emissions and is, therefore, a sustainable product. But back then, obviously, people did not think of it in that way.

Our business model really allows customers to work more efficiently to save money and natural resources. And since 2000, we have had ambitious goals around sustainability. And we have always met or exceeded them. In August 2020, we launched a more ambitious set of goals, and these are called our 2030 goals. We always start where we have the greatest impact, which is through our customers, in terms of helping them achieve 300 billion gallons of water savings, equivalent to the drinking water needs of a billion people. Or helping them become carbon neutral.

Obviously, water savings also deliver thermal energy savings because you must pump, treat cool and heat that water. Because of this, we have a climate impact as well as a water impact around the world. Besides accomplishing the business objectives of helping our customers achieve their goals by leveraging our solutions, my role is really driven first and foremost through the work that we do for our customers. But we also have done an incredible amount of work to drive corporate responsibility and environmental management within our own operations. We have about 100 facilities around the world, and I lead the efforts around establishing these targets and ensuring that we achieve these goals with the right stewardship practices.

Uwe Schulte
Thank you, Emilio, that is quite an impressive background. But before we get into our subject, as you are a business-to-business company, some of our listeners might not know exactly what Ecolab does today. You just touched on it a little bit, but maybe you can just very briefly summarise what you are up to.

Emilio Tenuta
People may know of Ecolab or see the brand from hand sanitisers and handwashing stations in restaurants, sports arenas, and other public venues. But we do a lot more than that. There is very little of the economy that we do not touch in terms of industries. In broad terms, our business is water, climate, hygiene, and infection prevention solutions and services. We employ about 45,000 people around the world. Our annual revenues are about $13 billion. We serve three million customer locations in more than 170 countries. Products and services range from huge cooling systems within power stations or automotive assembly plants, which require management of water, energy, and efficient business processes, to dish machines and cleaning products at your local restaurant in your neighbourhood.

As you look at our customer reach and impact in 2019, we helped save 206 billion gallons of water towards that 300-billion-gallon goal by 2030, equivalent to the annual drinking water needs of 712 million people. Along with that comes enhanced energy efficiency because water is connected to energy, and the avoided greenhouse gas emissions. At Ecolab, we refer to this as the exponential return on investment, or eROI. And this is all focused not only on saving critical resources like water, energy, carbon, and materials, but also on being more productive and, from a time perspective, reducing costs and other things. As you can tell we cast a wide net when you look at the impact we have in the world.

Uwe Schulte
I do not want to put you on the spot. I wonder how many litres these are. We will work that out separately. It is a large number and you related it to the drinking water requirements. Let us start with our subject of today. Water: The New Oil. We did choose that because fossil oil up to now has been very important and water is extremely valuable, today more than ever. Where do you see the reasons for that?

Emilio Tenuta
When most people think of oil, they think of something that is rare and expensive. When they think of water, on the other hand, they think of something that is plentiful, available, and cheap. But the reality is that water is precious and scarce, and all the water we have on this earth is already here. There is no new water. Many of us learned from our grade school studies that 70% of the world is covered in water. But most of it is saltwater, and so there is just 2 1/2% of freshwater. Just a small fraction of freshwater on this earth is available for society. I am referring to usable freshwater, mostly in rivers, lakes and, of course, we have a disappearing groundwater source as well. Today water is under-priced, and it is often cheapest in the places where it is the scarcest.

We work with organisations like Global Water Intelligence,[1] which does an excellent job. This includes tariff surveys on water, freshwater, and combined water in-and-out costs. In 2017, as an example, in a place like Amsterdam you are looking at about $6.25 per cubic metre in an area that is not considered to be water stressed. Compare that to places like Sao Paulo in Brazil or maybe Mumbai. In Sao Paulo, where you do have water stress, water is significantly cheaper; it is about $1.35 per cubic meter. In Mumbai, which is extremely water stressed, it is about $0.30 in-and-out per cubic metre. As you can see, there is an inverse relationship where the degree of water stress and what individuals and water users pay for water does not make a lot of sense. To know the real value of water, you must look at it in terms of increased water costs and the impact that has as water becomes scarcer. Operational risks, regulatory, and, of course, reputational impacts must all be factored in, as well as the societal unrest that comes from water stress conditions. To know what water is worth for your business, you really must be able to monetise those risks in terms of dollars or put it in business terms so that water users around the world can act on those risks. We have worked with several stakeholders to really think about how one could monetise those risks and created the Ecolab Smart Water Navigator. It is a

---

[1] https://www.globalwaterintel.com/

publicly available online tool[2] that can help businesses determine how water availability, quality, and current business practices impact the bottom line so that they can become smart water users and achieve business resilience (Figs. 1, 2 and 3).

Uwe Schulte

By the way, I lived through water stress in Sao Paulo when I was living there with my family. I know what it means. According to the World Resources Institute, already in 2006, a billion people lived in water-scarce regions and the estimate is that by 2025 it will be more than three billion and the water scarcity atlas was even higher. From your experience, where are the regions that are most affected by water scarcity?

Emilio Tenuta

When people think water, we think about water in developing countries—that is where the problem is. That is where people *perceive* the problem to be. They think of places like Mumbai or Saudi Arabia. That is not really accurate because water scarcity is the new normal. Not just in developing countries, but also in developed countries. If we continue on the current path, and the World Resources Institute (WRI) has done some incredible work updating the statistics around the supply–demand gap, the latest numbers are that the demand for freshwater will outstrip supply by more than 50% by 2030. Now that is less than 10 years away. As you mentioned, two billion

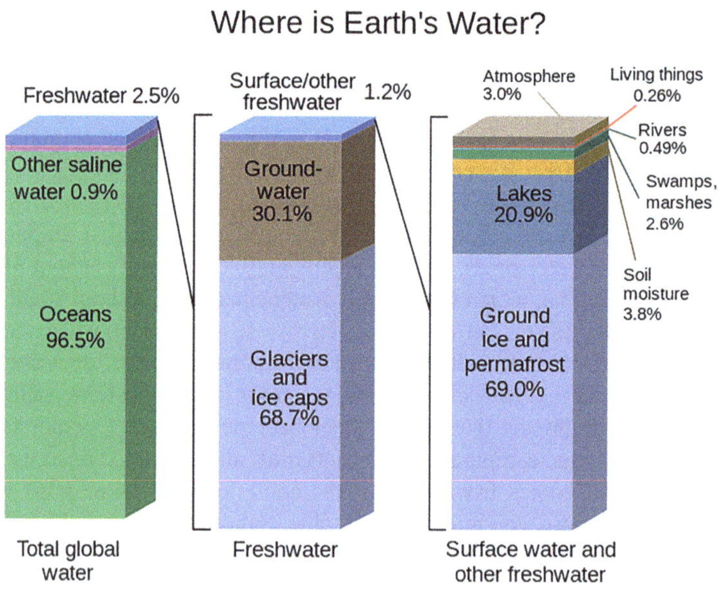

Fig. 1 Earth Water. Source: Wikipedia, public domain in the United States, Author: USGS, Source: https://water.usgs.gov/edu/gallery/watercyclekids/earth-water-distribution.html, traced and redrawn from file: Earth's water distribution.gif

---

[2] https://www.smartwaternavigator.com/

Fig. 2 Global Water Intelligence. Source: Global Water Intelligence, https://www.globalwaterintel.com/global-water-intelligence-magazine/24/2

people already live in areas that are affected by water stress and the figure is projected to increase. Today, according to the UN, one out of every nine people, almost 850 million people, have no access to basic drinking water. That is water access alone. And, of course, think about the impact that has during a pandemic, which is what we are in now, where water is critical to being able to maintain hygiene, to be able to wash your hands—to try to avoid these types of infections. This is happening everywhere, and you mentioned Sao Paulo. You will remember Day Zero back in 2015. We came within days of running dry. Or Cape Town, which was not that long ago. Chennai,[3] last year, where you had a sizeable portion of the population, nearly four million people, who had to access their water from water trucks. This is becoming an acute situation and high-income economies are not immune to this (Fig. 4).

Fig. 3 Smart Water Navigator.
Source: Ecolab, Smart Water Navigator,
https://www.smartwaternavigator.com/

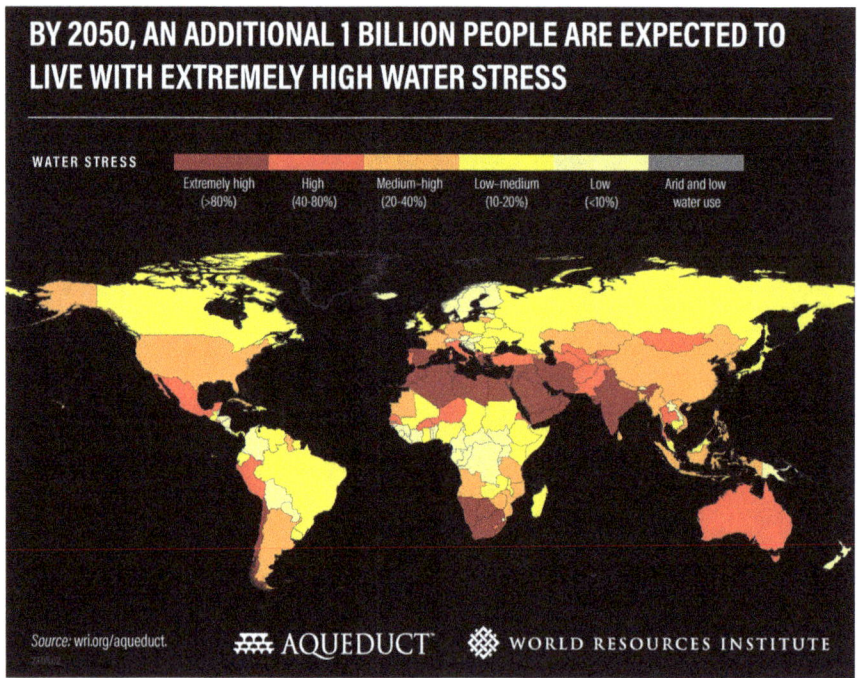

Fig. 4 Water stress map. Source: World Resources Institute/Aqueduct, https://www.wri.org/insights/highest-water-stressed-countries

---

[3] https://en.wikipedia.org/wiki/2019_Chennai_water_crisis

As you pointed out, European cities like London and Brussels have faced water issues and droughts. And wildfires in Australia, that we heard about last year, and the same for California and Texas. In other words, water is increasingly scarce and valuable, and we should not just treat it as a disposable commodity. It really needs to be viewed as a valued asset.

Uwe Schulte
I live in Germany these days and we now have 2 years where the agricultural yield was very low because of the drought. It was never heard of before to such an extent. What are the main reasons for this? What is happening?

Emilio Tenuta
Well, in quite simple terms, demand is outpacing supply. We have a growing population. In 1950, we had 2.5 billion people on this earth. Today, we have 7.2 billion. By 2050, we will have almost ten billion. That is one major factor affecting this issue. Another is economic growth. Increasingly, millions of individuals have joined the middle class, and that number will continue to grow, especially in Asia. And then of course you have the impact of climate change. There would be water scarcity even without climate change, but climate change is really worsening this issue and one of the things that we often talk about is the connection between climate and water. In many ways, the first chapter of our story on climate should be about water. Because we are largely seeing the effects of climate through the challenges around water, such as extreme weather events, droughts, floods, and other factors. We think about it, in terms of what this means to business and industry, which is something that Ecolab is on the frontlines of working with customers every day. According to UNESCO, industry uses about 20% of all freshwater.[4] We have heard that statistic, I think over the years. However, in high-income countries, notably in Europe, industry accounts for up to 59% of total water use. That is a big jump in a significant factor in terms of how we need to look at managing water within an economy (Fig. 5).

As low-income countries industrialise, their water usage trends will continue to rise just like they have in developed countries. We have done a lot of work around this with several organisations, such as the Carbon Disclosure Project (CDP),[5] and others. Water use fell by 10% since 2005, but in recent years it has increased. Since 2015, according to S&P Global Sustainability1, it has been trending up again and, according to CDP, there was an almost 50% rise in the number of companies reporting higher water withdrawals in 2018. We kind of have a good news/bad news story. The good news is that more and more companies are establishing targets and identifying risks related to water. The problem is we are not seeing that action at the local level.

---

[4] https://ourworldindata.org/water-use-stress#global-freshwater-use
[5] https://www.cdp.net
 https://www.marketplace.spglobal.com/en/datasets/trucost-environmental-(46)

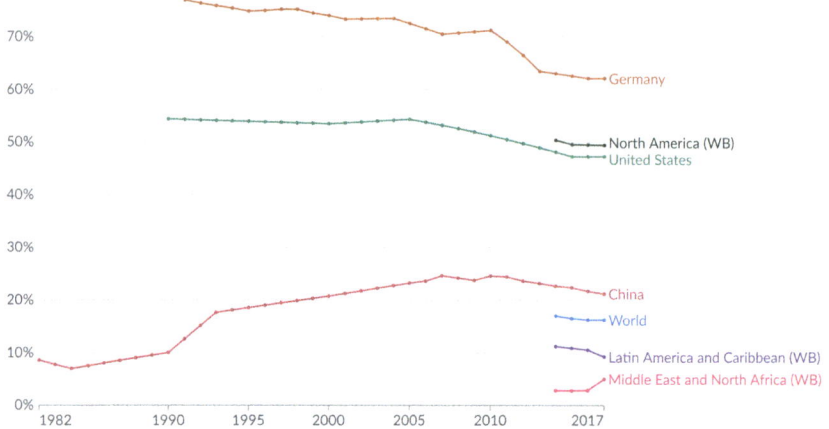

Fig. 5 Industrial water usage. Data source: Food and Agriculture Organization of the United Nations (via World Bank), OurWorldInData.org/water-use-stress, CC BY 4.0 DEED Attribution 4.0 International

Uwe Schulte

We have now talked about climate change and population growth. I see another factor, or better, other factors like pollution and unsustainable consumption. Isn't that something that we should be concerned about as well?

Emilio Tenuta

Be cautious about overemphasising consumption because it is true that we can be better and more conscientious about how we consume water and how we produce the goods and services from an efficiency and conservation perspective. I just want to make sure that we can manage water in a way that does not compromise the quality of life. If we do the right things and do them quickly, because obviously time is a factor here, we can build an economy that ensures high quality of life for all, enough clean water for all, and a thriving natural environment. Does that mean that every person can live the exact same way as, say, a typical American does today? No. We must redesign systems and rethink the way we manage water for sure.

But the idea that we must give up automobiles or refrigerators or protein sources or those things that we enjoy today, I do not think that is necessarily the case. I think we just need to really do what I call 'shore up the execution gap' around what the challenges are and what needs to be done to set the right targets and the action that needs to happen at the local level. That leads to smart water management, which is key.

Uwe Schulte

I am still struggling a little bit with the pollution issue. Is that not something that depends on where you are?

Emilio Tenuta

It is. Water quality—when you talk about physical risk, it is about quantity and quality. We spend a lot of time today talking about quantity and the UN has identified that 80% of the water in the world today is discharged untreated and that is a problem.[6] Water quality is impacting the way we manage water for organisations and society at large. The challenge is that with this gap by 2030 of over 50% between freshwater supply and demand, there are opportunities for us to take that water that is being discharged, untreated, and to begin to think about, or rethink that as an opportunity to reuse and recycle that water. Today less than 3% of all global wastewater is reclaimed and reused. And that must change to serve two purposes. One is to improve the water quality that is being discharged. But two is that we have an opportunity to take that water and repurpose it, because very little of it is being repurposed today. What instead is happening is we are using freshwater in lieu of that. And there is a connection between water, climate, and pollution. The more water we use, the more energy we use, the more energy you use, the more carbon you emit and the more that impacts the climate situation and the dilemma we are in. To me, all these factors and water quality have a role in this in terms of how we can get after the issues of discharge-quality problems. Being able to reclaim and reuse that water and make it fit-for-use back into the economy (Fig. 6).

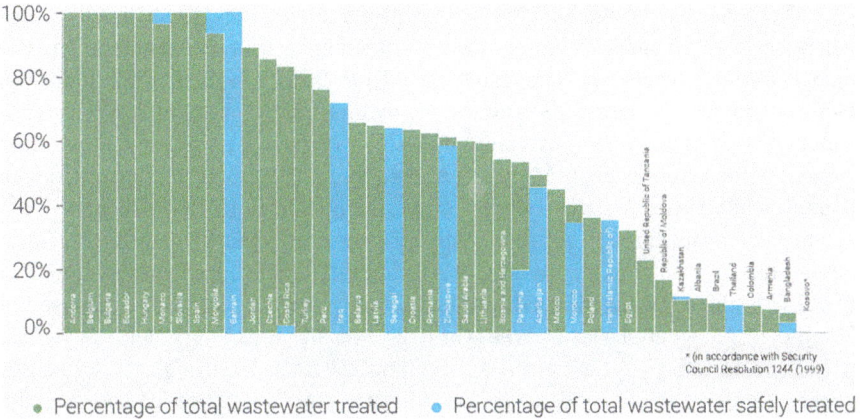

Fig. 6 Water treatment percentage in 2015, unwater.org. Source: UN Habitat and WHO (2021). Progress on Wastewater Treatment: Global status and acceleration needs for SDG indicator 6.3.1., https://www.unwater.org/publications/progress-on-wastewater-treatment-631-2021-update/

---

[6] https://www.unwater.org/sites/default/files/app/uploads/2021/09/SDG6_Indicator_Report_631_Progress-on-Wastewater-Treatment_2021_EN.pdf

Uwe Schulte

I would like to explore the climate aspect a little bit more because today I learned that there is more connection between climate and water than in my simple mind I had been envisioning before. I am glad that you have already indicated some perspective on possible solutions. Let us now talk about those. First let us dive a bit more into the connection between water scarcity and climate change.

Emilio Tenuta

Water and energy are tightly connected. Address one and you address the other. Water scarcity would exist even without climate change. But climate change really worsens the problem significantly. The effects of climate change are mostly expressed in water. We see this through droughts, sea level rise, and floods. We see extreme weather patterns. As a result, if you use less water, you are less vulnerable to climate change. But at the same time if you use less water, you also save energy because using water takes energy. You must pump it, heat it, treat it, or cool it. And because most energy generated in this world still comes from fossil fuels, if you use less water, you will also lower your carbon emissions and help mitigate the effects of climate change. But it is worth noting that oftentimes we do not think about the energy embedded in water conservation. And that really works both ways. If you help mitigate climate change, you also alleviate some of these water scarcity issues. We are on the frontlines at Ecolab, working across more than 40 different industries. And we have a unique perspective on that point in that we have recorded over 500 assessments where we worked in manufacturing facilities that use water—mostly food and beverage sector type facilities. We can say that, in those facilities, the potential water-use reductions average anywhere between 30 and 40% of that total site. The resulting potential energy savings, by reducing their water use, is somewhere between 15 and 20% in thermal energy savings. Things like natural gas and then 1-to-4% in electricity. The results vary from facility to facility, but industrial facilities can reduce their carbon emissions by up to 20% simply by lowering their water consumption. A good example of that is a very large company that we have worked with: Archer Daniels Midland (ADM). Since 2012, Ecolab has worked with them to really save and drive a water conservation strategy by improving the management of water through all their critical water circuits in their different facilities—whether it be corn wet-milling or making different products that go into a lot of our Consumer Packaged Goods products. Today, the programme is comprised of 200 projects at locations around the world. The result? Amazingly, not only did we help them become a lot more productive and efficient, requiring less water and energy, but they saved 2.3 billion gallons of water. And I would have to do the math in my head, Uwe, on the number of litres that is, but it is equivalent to the annual drinking water needs of almost eight million people. Along the way, we saved a lot of BTUs (British Thermal Units)[7] of thermal energy and CO_2 emissions by 70 million pounds. This demonstrates your point about how much water can be saved with

---

[7] https://de.wikipedia.org/wiki/British_thermal_unit

a concerted effort and the right technology. But also, how much of an impact you can have against climate just by focusing on water.

Uwe Schulte
When we talk about climate, the normal reaction is to talk about energy. But it sounds like water is the underappreciated part of this equation.

Emilio Tenuta
Absolutely. We often say that water is the forgotten chapter in the climate book. The Paris Treaty, believe it or not, does not mention the word water—not once. That is baffling and it must be corrected. It will be hard to get after climate if we do not get after water. It is part of the solution. One more example to illustrate this: we worked with a coal-fired power plant in Great Britain that had issues. It had fouling condensers, which is a problem because it obviously drives inefficiency in terms of the production of steam to run the turbine. The plant saved 22,000 tonnes of coal per year and reduced its CO_2 emissions by 53,000 tonnes. That is over a 1% reduction, equivalent to taking almost 23,000 passenger vehicles off the road. The moral of the story is that even if we decarbonise the economy, many coal-fired power plants will operate for years, even though there are fewer and fewer operating now. But just doing this one money-saving thing can reduce CO_2 emissions by 1 to 2%. There are, I think, over 6500 coal-fired plants operating in the world today. If they all did this, that would be equivalent to taking 60 to 132 of them offline overnight.

Uwe Schulte
It just baffles me when I listen to you. You already mentioned that unfortunately corporate water use is going up again instead of going down, but if it is saving water and if saving water saves energy and reduces carbon emission and more importantly cuts costs—why are not more people doing that?

Emilio Tenuta
It is a great question and I think it a very vital question to getting after the water challenges that we have with water. And the response is that water is currently under-priced, and the perception of the ROI is not high enough in the eyes of those that use it. But once a drought hits like the one you experienced, for example, in Sao Paulo and a company must deal with the dependency that they have on water, it becomes a lot clearer to them how dependent they are on water because it disrupts or interrupts their production. There are quality issues. They get skyrocketing prices and a whole bunch of other regulations. In some cases, even water rationing, as you have heard of in places like India. The real value of water must be seen in terms of that. The business risk is represented. It is not that companies are not interested in water. In fact, more and more companies have ambitious water reduction goals, and we have seen this from some of the surveys that have been done with the State of Green Business[8] each year. But they lack the expertise to achieve them. This is a challenge, according to a survey that Ecolab and GreenBiz, a large sustainability

---

[8] https://www.greenbiz.com/report/2020-state-green-business-report

Fig. 7 GreenBiz State of Green Business 2020. Source: GreenBiz Group Inc., https://www.greenbiz.com/report/2020-state-green-business-report

consultant and event coordinator, did. We found that 75% of the companies have water targets, and these are companies with a billion dollars or more of revenue. But 82% of those companies lack the tools and strategies to achieve their targets. That is a problem. Eighty-eight percent of the companies say they will take active steps to manage water use in the next 3 years. But only 44% have a plan (Fig. 7).

One big challenge is that water is not like CO_2. We emit CO_2 into the atmosphere. It has an atmospheric impact. All water is local. And that becomes a part of this challenge. Every place is different. You have climate. You have, as you mentioned, pollution. You mentioned population density. You mentioned the degree of industrialisation. What works in one place may not work in another. That is why across-the-board, corporate goals, that peanut butter spread efficiency targets across their enterprise, do not work. You must have context-based goals. Do the work at the individual facility level and empower the local teams. Act where the issues and challenges are. That is where many companies, I think, stumble. They have trouble bridging that gap between corporate-level and local-level engagement. And we refer to that as the execution gap.

Uwe Schulte
Let me share a personal experience. In another life, I was the head of a factory and one of the things I thought was silly—we were using freshwater to cool the process. We introduced heat exchangers and used the same water again for cooling, just some new freshwater now and then. The problem we got was that the local authorities said you were really flushing out all the dirt in our sewage system and your water is not coming anymore. We have a problem now. So, what do you say to that?

Emilio Tenuta
Good question, and in many ways, I go back to the risk factors that companies face. There are regulatory risk factors on top of physical risk factors, like quantity and quality, and those are things that we must really manage and measure. Some

measures are quite simple: Make sure that the team is accountable for water. You fix the leaks; you turn the water off. All those things are easy, but in situations like you mentioned, you really must have the right technology and the right measurement and monitoring to stay ahead of the challenges that you face. A good example of that for us is that we have technology from a real-time monitoring perspective that can give a process within a manufacturing setting like you describe, the intelligence that you need not only to take the necessary action, but to do it in real time. I often talk about this as an MRI system for water unit operations within a facility—being able to have the right smart sensors in place, not only to know the quantity and the quality of water and what changes in real time, but also to take the necessary steps to be able to address and remediate the problem. We often find that we continue to not have enough data. We do not really understand how water is being used. We do not know what the critical water circuits are, and we have invested a lot in building a digital capacity and capability where we have more than 40,000 digital sensors and units out across many regions that allow us to monitor water in real time. It provides us with information about everything from the condition of water and how much the quality of that water impacts the productivity and business objectives that lead to that eROI, that exponential impact, that companies are looking for, to really make the business case around water solutions.

Uwe Schulte
My learning from my experience was when you do those things, do not do them in isolation. Talk to your authorities and plan the whole thing together and then it is something beneficial for everybody. I can relate to the point you are making. At a corporate level, you set out a target. We are going to reduce on so much, but the real issue is local. But how do you close that gap?

Emilio Tenuta
Well, in many ways we often say that it starts with the ability for us to really understand the current context of water in that local area. We often talk about this in terms of four key areas. One is understanding *how* water is being accounted for, and *who* is accountable for it in terms of management of water. Two, it is the water management practices. Three, it is the right targets that are being set, not at the corporate level, like we talked about, but about the shared water challenges that you are facing in that local watershed. And like you said, that involves collective action. Being able to engage with others. And that is the fourth area, which is water stewardship. The work that you are doing within the fence line is great, but it cannot be done in isolation. Like you said, you have got to think about others outside the fence line because water is a shared resource. A great example for us is we have nearly 100 facilities globally that we, as Ecolab, have been manufacturing products that we use with our customers. We have a facility in Louisiana, down in the Gulf region. The name of the facility is Garyville. It is one of our larger water-use plants. Now, if you think of Louisiana, you do not think of water stress, but it is highly water stressed. There are challenges related to wetlands degradation. There are flood water storage issues and imbalances. There are water quality and nutrient load issues. We call it the Amazon of the United States. It is really challenged with some of the same issues. Our

facility there sources water from the Mississippi River. We extract that water. We clean it, to your point about water quality, we put it to use in our plant and then we discharge about 88% of it back. That 88% is cleaner than when we pulled it from the river. And that 12% is now consumptive use. We feel that we need to contribute a lot from a stewardship perspective to turn this into a Net Positive Water Impact facility. We wanted to replenish that water and what we did is we developed a three-pronged strategy around adopting water stewardship principles through the Alliance for Water Stewardship Standard,[9] which looks inside and outside the fence line, at the shared water challenges and builds collective action. Two, we drove a reduction in demand to the tune of almost 60 million gallons of reduced demand from the Mississippi River, but three we also upstream worked with The Nature Conservancy,[10] a large environmental NGO that does work on the ground in restoring water basins, where we worked on a project called Loch Leven to essentially replenish over 100 million gallons, equivalent to the consumptive use of that facility. Now that is a Net Positive Water Impact story and to do that, to your point about taking the corporate target and making it localised, you really must get down to that local level to understand how you need to engage with the local teams and the local authorities and stakeholders to really drive that kind of action (Fig. 8).

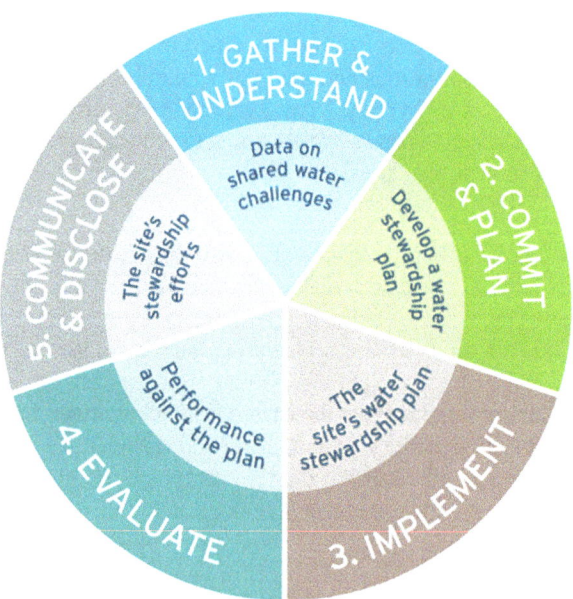

Fig. 8 The five steps of the Alliance for Water Stewardship (AWS) Standard V.2.0. Source: a4ws.org

---

[9] https://a4ws.org/the-aws-standard-2-0/

[10] https://www.nature.org/en-us/

Uwe Schulte

This resonates with my experience from the past. But at the end of the day, that is a complicated thing to do. The devil is in the details, as they say. Are you optimistic about this?

Emilio Tenuta

I am optimistic. We are on the frontline, and we have a unique perspective of the way water and other natural resources are being managed today through the multiple customers that we serve every day, and we see things. We see that there is in many ways the opportunity across these different industries and by the way, by geography. If I look at a beverage plant in Sao Paulo and I compare that to a beverage plant in Mumbai, India, there are a wide range of water-use efficiency opportunities to really improve. And I think there are opportunities for us to act to drive more water conservation. That not only saves energy, but also reduces carbon emissions. Another reason for optimism is that the incentive structure is right. It is easy to make the business case for water management because it saves money. We can make that case once you make that connection to the fact that you can save energy and that obviously saves money. It also makes you more resilient. In a world of risk, when you look at finance, and the CFOs for organisations are all about finding ways to reduce disruption to not have stranded assets. And so, we need to make sure that this is at the heart of how we look at things so that we are proactive, not reactive, when it comes to the work that we do around water. It is also important to remember that no company or industry can do this alone, and you mentioned this in your story. Collaboration and collective action are going to be required to make that happen.

Uwe Schulte

I saw that you have been instrumental in launching the Water Resilience Coalition.[11] Is that the background? Why are you doing that?

Emilio Tenuta

It is, yes, the coalition was launched on World Water Day this year. A bit of a whisper because it was on March 22nd on World Water Day. And of course, we were at the beginning of a pandemic. We felt it was important to launch this action coalition around this critical challenge that we are all facing. We launched it with 11 member companies: AmBev, Diageo, Dell, Ecolab, Gap, Microsoft, PVHCorp., Coca-Cola, Heineken, Levi Strauss, and Woolworths. The goal of the coalition is to bring scale to corporate action on water, to preserve the world's freshwater resources. First, collective action on water-stressed basins and, second, ambitious quantified commitments. We are working towards a resilient world that can adapt, which is important to the impacts of climate change with enough clean water for all. The companies have made a commitment to join and sign what we are referring to as the Water Resilience Pledge. They are expected to first make investments in their own operations, like my story about Garyville, and work towards accomplishing the pledges through overarching 2050 goals, Net Positive Water Impact, which delivers

---

[11] https://ceowatermandate.org/resilience/about/

measurable net positive impact in water-stressed basins. And that is demand and supply based. Second, our focus is on the water resilient value chain: the proliferation of suppliers in our value chains and our customers. To implement best-in-class water resilient practices across the value chain. Global leadership, raising the ambition of water resilience through public and corporate outreach, and really inspiring and recruiting more companies to join this action coalition.

Uwe Schulte
That is encouraging. But we live in times, I must ask the question, what changes due to the pandemic? Will this still be relevant?

Emilio Tenuta
The first order of business today is to stop the pandemic and get people healthy and make sure that people are healthy. But this pandemic demonstrates a key point, which is how interconnected our world is, and how globalised risks affect everyone. Water scarcity and climate change are among the global risks we face in the coming years. The lesson from the pandemic is that we must address these risks before they become a global crisis. And so, water scarcity is already a crisis in many parts of the world and is obviously impacting the effects that it has on the pandemic, namely hygiene—it is very difficult to have good hygiene practices in emerging economies when you do not have access to water. 850 million people do not have basic water access to wash their hands. Tackling water scarcity can help us not only get people healthy but also help us exit this economic downturn that we are seeing and get out of it faster. The transition to a sustainable, resilient economy will unlock the opportunities from a technology breakthrough perspective and spark new industries. This has happened every time there has been a crisis. We see this happening now. It will build the infrastructure that we need and the technology platform, which will provide hundreds of millions of people with new jobs to help us rebuild our economy. The COVID crisis also highlights, again, the importance of water in hygiene and public health, and we have got to continue to focus on these WASH initiatives and sanitation and hygiene programmes that have emerged from several different organisations. For us, with our CEOs involved, and we are seeing more and more executives really understanding the risk factors, and along with the backing of the UN organisations as part of the coalition. The Water Resilience Coalition can help make sure that we do not lapse into inaction or inactivity following this pandemic. We are going to stay the course.

Uwe Schulte
Thank you so much Emilio. This is an interesting outlook, and I must say, the number of things that really resonate, talking to others—the need to collaborate more across boundaries. The crisis highlighting issues which we knew about, but we are facing now, and they need to be addressed in a better way. They offer business opportunity if you understand the risk involved and know how to mitigate it. You have given us good guidance on that. Thank you very much for sharing that with us. We were a little bit down when we looked at all the risk problems, but you have now given us a good perspective for the future, and I learned about the link between

climate and water and that is something that I will take with me into future discussions. Thank you again and would you like to give our audience maybe a couple of guiding principles?

Emilio Tenuta

Well, I want to, first, thank you for giving us this opportunity—this platform to really share how critical and valuable water is as a resource to not only grow our businesses, but to have countries and communities thrive. I will leave you with this: We are in the middle of a pandemic right now, as we just talked about. But this pandemic will end. And we must really look ahead beyond the pandemic. By 2030, over the course of this next decade, there will be a billion more people on this earth. It is essential to rethink water so we can sustain the growth we need to lift more people out of poverty and to ensure that their lifestyles are sustainable. Thank you, Uwe.

Uwe Schulte

Thank you, Emilio.

A Global Company with a Purpose

Recorded July 2020

Uwe Schulte

Today I will be talking to João Paulo Ferreira, CEO Natura Latin America, about purpose-driven companies. Let me introduce our guest to you. João Paulo graduated in electrical engineering from the University of Sao Paulo, USP and has an Executive MBA from the University of Michigan in the United States. He worked at Unilever for 20 years. João Paulo is the CEO of Latin America for Natura and Company. Before becoming CEO of Natura, he joined the business in 2009 as VP of Operations and Logistics. Welcome João Paulo. I am so pleased to have you and please tell us a little bit about yourself and your role at Natura.

João Paulo Ferreira

Thank you very much, Uwe. For those listening to us—Uwe is an old friend. We worked together many years ago and I enjoy the fact that you are taking this course forward. Well, I think you said a lot about me. I can only add that I am married to Elizabeth. We have been married now for 27 years. I have a 16-year-old son who enjoys playing his guitar and he plays very well. I used to play with him, but I cannot catch up with him anymore, so nowadays one of my pleasures is to listen to him playing. I joined Natura ten years ago, as you said. And it is a place where I found a new way of doing business and breaking this paradox that it is impossible to reconcile economic progress with social development and environmental protection and I am very glad to share some of my experiences with you today.

Uwe Schulte
Great, thank you. As we have a global audience and there might be listeners who do not know Natura, although I doubt that, could you just briefly talk about the history of Natura and the scope of this business today?

João Paulo Ferreira
Natura is a Brazilian born cosmetics company that celebrated its 50th anniversary last year. It developed its business primarily across Latin America until 2012 when it started to bring other companies to its family. By the end of 2012, the Australian born AESOP joined our family. AESOP is a more luxury cosmetics retailer. And that is when we started to learn how to manage other businesses and other brands in the company. Then late in 2017, exactly three years ago, The Body Shop joined our group and that is when we formally became a group. Natura evolved into Natura & Co, which encompasses more than one company. At that point there were three companies: Natura, AESOP, and The Body Shop. And most recently, beginning of this year 2020, we welcomed Avon into the family. We now are four businesses with four iconic brands which turned us into one of the largest cosmetics companies in the world, one of the top five. It has been an exciting journey. When we decided we would expand by bringing other companies and brands into the family it might be worth mentioning that we had to develop a filter and that filter had to do with purpose, Uwe.

Uwe Schulte
That is very interesting, I will come back to that in a second. I find it fascinating as Natura has a special way of bringing the product to the end user, and when I look at your recent joint venture—Avon—it seems to be like closing a circle.

João Paulo Ferreira
Indeed, interesting that you noticed that. Natura was born in 1969 and in 1974 it chose direct selling as its main sales and distribution method. And that had a lot to do with the company's vision for social development. Natura was born out of two passions—cosmetics and relationships, and the belief that combined they have the power of transforming individuals and everything around them —their families, communities, society, the country and ultimately the planet. Direct selling was the logical mechanism for that to come true. This developed Natura into a more than two million consultants' network of affection, as we keep saying. Of course, we were inspired by the company that created that industry and that was Avon 136 years ago. We were so delighted that at the end of our 50-year journey, we could meet the origin of our industry—Avon—to join forces in this quest for generating a positive impact on society. Altogether we are now more than six million representatives and consultants around the world with 40,000 associates working in more than one

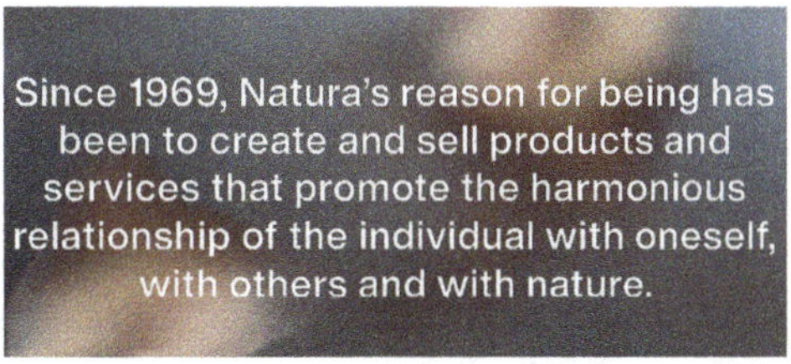

Fig. 1 Natura Reason for Being. Source: Natura & Co, https://www.naturabrasil.com/pages/about-us

> Since 1969, Natura's reason for being has been to create and sell products and services that promote the harmonious relationship of the individual with oneself, with others and with nature.

hundred countries, which shows the power of mobilising an army of people around the causes that we stand for.

Uwe Schulte

That is extremely fascinating. I am tempted to dive into it, but you already mentioned the word purpose which we hear increasingly. When you look up the word purpose, the definition is the reason something exists. In your wording you do not use the word purpose, instead you say that since 1969, Natura's 'Reason for Being'[1] has been to create and sell products and services that promote the harmonious relationship of the individual with oneself, with others and with nature. I would call that a purpose. And I would love to hear from you from your perspective what that means today (Fig. 1).

João Paulo Ferreira

Indeed, it took a few years to be able to formalise those words you just quoted. And it is a combination of the reason for being, the vision, and the beliefs. That defines the whole business model, the way people operate, the way our processes are built. One of the interesting elements of having a reason for being is that if we are not fulfilling that reason, we should not exist. I find this really fascinating and we keep checking on that. Are we doing *this*? It is not something that we are pursuing, it is something that we *must* do. If we are not doing *this*, we should not exist as a company. It took a few years to be able to formalise that idea. We believe that through cosmetics and relationships, we have that power you just mentioned of promoting self-esteem and self-awareness from which empathy is born so that each individual is able to relate to the external world, their family, society, the planet, and so on. And the beliefs, which are six, also help us bring people together. It is easy to track if you have similar beliefs or not. There are six beliefs: interdependence, continuous improvement, the search for beauty, commitment to truth, diversity, and sustainability. Either you believe in those things, or you don't. And if you don't, you should not work in this environment. Those things eventually translate into our working processes and the metrics associated to those working processes. And that is what makes this alive rather than words standing on the wall. Let me give you an example. One of our beliefs mentions commitment to truth, which is the reason we do not have an anti-ageing product in our product line. Simply because we cannot fight against ageing. We can fight against the signs of ageing but not against ageing. Time

---

[1] https://www.naturabrasil.com/pages/about-us

is the raw material of life—why should we fight against it? For those things to eventually translate into a product line or to the metrics in the distribution system, for instance, takes many years of continuous improvement. But that is what makes the purpose, or the reason for being, alive.

Uwe Schulte

Interesting; you just told me that certain trends look attractive and could create some sales volume but might not be truthful, deep down. And your purpose will help you to decide that you are not going to take that opportunity because it is not part of what you believe in. Did I hear that right?

João Paulo Ferreira

You are right, Uwe. And that has been a difficult call, many times. Sometimes it is even difficult to spot that you are facing dilemmas. But that is what we try and do. We intend to deliver socioeconomic environmental results. All our executives are awarded based on those elements. Every day we must take decisions where we must wait regarding economic development, social impacts, and environmental protection. Every day. Can we develop a new lipstick? Yes, sure. Does it have to perform nicely on your mouth? Yes. Is it reducing carbon footprint? No. Then it is not ready. We are not going to launch. Do we have to wait a little bit more? Yes, we do have to wait a little bit more. These are difficult calls, but that is what happens when you are on the edge of trying to balance different variables and optimising for the entire system every day.

Sometimes people do not even realise that that is going on. Think about some of our professionals in distribution. They may not relate back to all this 'reason for being' of the company. But embedded into their decision-making process is a variable like carbon emissions, for example. They must judge whether they are going to deliver faster, cheaper, or lower carbon emissions every day. They will have to choose whether they are going to ship by bike, by boat, or by truck. You name it. Imagine 'the reason for being' embedded in all processes of the company. There is a lot of room to improve that. There is science, social, and environmental science which continue to be developed for us to improve those things. But as it keeps evolving it gets into the routine of our teams. That is what makes this 'reason for being' alive.

Uwe Schulte

What you are telling me is that wherever you are within your organisation, one of the challenges everybody is facing is to apply the purpose in decision-making.

João Paulo Ferreira

Absolutely. That has been deployed in many sub processes of the company over the years and everyone is appraised and rewarded based on the combination of those elements.

Uwe Schulte

Let me dive a little bit deeper because I am trying to really understand you. You are saying, life is a chain of relationships, everything is interdependent, valuing relationships is the foundation of the great human revolution. How does that apply to a business like yours?

João Paulo Ferreira
Well, that is the very nature of our business. With Avon, we have six million independent representatives or consultants which are developing relationships with their customers. And it is not a one-time transaction. Trust must be built over time. Trust is not about recommending the best product for you at that particular moment. Of course, that is a critical element of our business, but it is also about understanding your emotional needs, trying to convey some of the philosophical goals of this community and trying to engage people in activities with higher purposes. Through that there is more value to be captured and distributed amongst participants, including material value, that is fair. There is material value, but there is also emotional and philosophical value. The value proposition to our network of consultants is based on three Ps. They are purpose, prosperity, and belonging which starts with the letter P in Portuguese. This is all they do. It is prosperity, both material and social. It is belonging because the network supports itself in so many ways, not only teaching each other how to act as a consultant, but also helping with family matters, emotional support, and so on and so forth. And finally, purpose—many of our consultants are social entrepreneurs. It is unbelievable, but a large number of them are community leaders and social entrepreneurs. What happens is that both, the company centrally or all the people in the network, will engage into their social projects to develop their smaller communities. That is how this chain of relationships built over time increases the value of the ecosystem as a whole.

Uwe Schulte
Let me challenge you a little bit here because it is easy to talk about purpose when everything is smooth sailing, and your company is growing. But when you hit a crisis then it becomes so much more difficult, and we are unfortunately experiencing that awful crisis of COVID-19. How have you dealt with that in the light of your reason for being?

João Paulo Ferreira
Excellent question, Uwe. I must tell you that we had no doubt about the way we would react and that was because of our reason for being. We decided we would do three things: help try to contain the spread of the disease, look after our people, and try to keep the economy active. What we did at the very beginning was to stop our factories and redirect all the available capacity to essential items—soaps and alcohol as well as concentrated alcohol which was not part of our portfolio.

Uwe Schulte
For disinfection products.

João Paulo Ferreira
Yes. We also donated everything that we could. In the first hours we asked ourselves: what can we donate? We donated a huge volume of products across Latin America to health authorities, NGOs, health professionals, etc. Interestingly enough, we had to collaborate with alcohol producers, sugar cane producers that also donated the alcohol so that we could convert those things because otherwise we would not have been able to source all these things in such a short period of time. It was a

beautiful way of having people collaborate to try and help society. That was the first thing we did. Then we sent everyone else home. We announced job security for at least 60 days because people were really scared. Then we started looking at our consultants. We extended all their payment terms so that they would not have to worry about that. Imagine the impact on the cash of the company for doing that. But we had no doubt. We were going to deal with that later. Right now, we let them rest with one problem less. We created an emergency fund for our most vulnerable consultants, unfortunately including funeral support where needed. And finally, we accelerated many of our digitalisation solutions so that many of those consultants who lost their jobs would be able to stay connected with their clients and get some minimum income to get food on their table and provide for their families. By the way, we increased their commissions on that form of commercialisation so that they will keep the same profit they used to have. Was that painful? Yes, of course. Did that impact our cash? Yes, it did. And the profitability? Yes, sure. But it was the right thing to do. Here is the interesting thing, Uwe. Guess what happened to the satisfaction KPIs (Key Performance Indicator) or loyalty KPIs that we track amongst our network of consultants? It went through the roof. Because that is the thing that they would expect us to do. Again, we are building long-term relationships. We are together for the long run. They are returning that to us. We looked after them. And in return they are looking after us. Our share of their minds, of their hearts, and of their business has increased significantly simply because they decided they would return to us what we did to them in the first hours.

Uwe Schulte
This is very encouraging because what you are saying is, that the word prosperity, for example, which you just used regarding the company purpose, was applied as a reason for decisions when you decided to do what you just described. And it sounds like it has not just been an emotional and socially correct decision, but whilst you were losing cash flow and profits in the height of the crisis, it seems to be building your business in the long run.

João Paulo Ferreira
Absolutely, Uwe. A few years ago, we had to re-examine our Natura business which was not performing well in our home country here in Brazil. It faced difficulties between 2014 and 2016. And the reason we were facing difficulties was because we were not really delivering according to our reason for being. The relationships had become more transactional rather than based on lifetime value and true willingness to develop all the potential of all the participants. And that translated in our commercial rules, in our offerings, etc. We started to lose both consumer and consultants' preference because we were similar to other companies then. And we had to go back to our reason for being and check whether our practices were in line with it. And we had derailed a little bit. We had to redesign many of our commercial practices and the offerings of some of our brands to get back to the framework that our principles define or our reason for being defines. And after we did that, we relaunched our operating model and our commercial model with extreme success. That was when the business resumed growth and resumed its health in all angles you can look

at. That is when we decided to expand again, first bringing in The Body Shop and most recently Avon. We had to go back to that essence and check, whether our practices were in line with that. Because once we lost it, the business suffered.

Uwe Schulte
That is an interesting observation, because it means that it is a constant process to re-evaluate how you develop vis-a-vis your purpose.

It is lovely that we were able to talk about this and to hear how you apply it. The company development of Natura is an impressive journey.

João Paulo Ferreira
It was a wonderful journey indeed. I keep reminding people how unusual this was and how very unlikely the successful journey was for a Brazilian born cosmetics company in this very international world of cosmetics that was born talking about nature and ingredients in 1969 when the world was fascinated by synthetics and that chose direct selling as its main sales and distribution instrument. Coming from that starting point and now reaching this magnitude of the Natura and Co business that includes Natura, The Body Shop, Avon, and AESOP in one of the largest cosmetics companies in the world, was indeed a fascinating journey.

Uwe Schulte
And it is also quite interesting for me that in your documents you do not even talk about purpose—as so many people do these days—you talk about your reason for being. That indicates that you are deeply engaged in that as we discussed already. Let us now look at another application of your purpose and that is your recently published sustainability vision 2030 which you call commitment to life. And I understand it contains three major elements. Can you talk a little bit about that commitment to life?

João Paulo Ferreira
Sure, but before I get into this, it is worth giving you some background on sustainability for Natura and how it is ingrained into our business model. At Natura, we like to transform social environmental challenges into business opportunities. That is essential, because for us sustainability is not at all to be paid afterwards. For example, you do good business and then you try and remediate the damage that you may have caused. It is actually about transforming social environmental challenges into business opportunities, so it needs to be embedded in the value proposition of the business. It is also an engine for innovation, because when you set yourself to that task of transforming those challenges into business opportunities, the only way that can be done is if it is a goal considered right at the beginning of any new endeavour, any new project, or development of any new product. It is a source of significant innovation for us, not only in products but also in the way we commercialise and regarding our business model. For that reason, we keep raising our own bar, looking at the best examples around the world. We learn from academia, we learn from other companies as much as we can. We have a continuous probe looking at what is happening around the world and we have the best available knowledge. In 2014, Natura launched its 2050 sustainability vision which was at the same time we

became the first publicly listed company ever to become a B Corp.[2] And then we set our goals to 2050. We were very ambitious and those ambitions included many things yet to be discovered. That has been pushing the Natura journey itself. As we evolved from Natura into a larger group, now called Natura and Co, including the four businesses, the four brands, we felt the need to make sure that all of the businesses, all of the brands would be aligned in those ambitions of creating positive social environmental impact for society. We look at each individual business, look at their starting point and set ourselves a goal: how can we move together, yet acknowledging that we are in various stages, transfer knowledge and get to a meaningful and most impactful position, given the size of the new group, as fast as we can? That was when we decided to launch the 2030 Natura and Co vision,[3] already including Avon. And that vision based on three key pillars was named 'commitment to life'. The first pillar is to do with fighting climate change and protecting the Amazon. How can we possibly contribute to that subject? The second one is to do with human rights and we call it 'becoming humankind'. And the third commitment is to do with circularity and regeneration. To summarise: think of a shift from scarcity to abundance and think of a shift from remediation to regeneration. This is what we are trying to capture in our 2030 vision (Figs. 2 and 3).

Fig. 2 B Corp Certification, photo: Jurre Rompa & B Lab Europe, 2019

---

[2] https://www.bcorporation.net/en-us/certification

[3] https://www.naturaeco.com/sustainability-vision-2030/

Sustainability Vision 2030
Commitment to Life

Natura & Co **Commitment to Life** sets out our commitments and actions - within a 10 year timeframe - to tackle some of the world's most pressing issues: addressing the climate crisis and protecting the Amazon, ensuring equality and inclusion, and shifting our business towards circularity and regeneration. Our approach calls for an all-encompassing business model that gives back more than it takes.

Our Commitment to Life

To address the **Climate Crisis** and protect the **Amazon**

Reduce our GHG emissions: become net zero by 2030.

Amazon: Zero deforestation.

Science Based Targets for Biodiversity; enforce the Nagoya Protocal.

To defend **Human Rights** and to be **Human-Kind**

For our associates: gender equality, inclusion of under represented groups, and living wage for all.

For our wider network:Measured increases in earnings, education and health.

Intolerance to human rights infringement in our supply chain.

To embrace **Circularity** and **Regeneration**

Full Circularity of Packaging.

95%+ Renewable or Natural ingredients.

95%+ Biodegradable formulas.

Investments and collaborative actions inRegenerative Solutions

Fig. 3 Natura Sustainability Vision 2030. Source: Natura & Co, https://www.naturabrasil.fr/en-us/

Uwe Schulte

It is a very impressive ambition and I think it merits a closer look. When I looked it up, two things really intrigued me. One was that you talk about zero deforestation of the Amazon region and secondly you talked about science-based targets for biodiversity. Can you explain that? These are quite broad targets.

João Paulo Ferreira

I would like to start with the Amazon because it is close to our business. 100% of the Natura products are formulated with at least one ingredient coming from the Amazonian biodiversity, which is transformed through science into very powerful cosmetic actives. We have had a continuous presence in the Amazon for more than 20 years, whereby we developed a close relationship with more than 30 communities, understanding their needs, understanding the richness of the ingredients, sharing benefits, paying not only for the ingredients themselves, but also for access and for associated traditional knowledge, etc. We learned that that activity helps protect the rainforest. And that in itself is a powerful insight because we are combining economic development, economic growth with environmental protection and social development at the same time. By the way, we also measure the social development of those communities. Our history proves that that is possible. It is possible to combine economic prosperity with environmental protection. We measured that in those communities and our activity helps protect almost two million hectares of forest. It is still a drop in the ocean. The only way we can approach such a systemic problem is in collaboration with governments, local state governments, federal governments, agencies, NGOs, the private sector, and the communities themselves. We are known to be a reliable actor in the Amazon that promotes dialogues and establishes bridges amongst all the agents. So, what we are proposing ourselves is the following: we will increase our own positive impact there, but moreover, we want to increase our role as a catalyst, a bridge amongst all those participants to promote systemic actions to protect the Amazon, and zero the deforestation. That is our ambition.

Uwe Schulte
Two things come to mind. One being the drop in the ocean. Because when you live outside of Brazil, for example, in Europe or the USA, you hear sad news about the Amazon. That is why it is important to understand the impact that you want to have beyond the work you have already been doing. It is important to understand why you are saying that it makes sense for you to become a catalyst and advocate and drive the whole systemic change rather than just do your bit.

João Paulo Ferreira
There are many reasons for that. One has a lot to do with our reason for being. One of our beliefs, the sixth belief of our company, is sustainability. We have to promote the maximal well-being of this generation yet increase the likelihood of an even higher well-being for the generations to come. And that is a central element. Climate change is a central element for the generations to come, so that fits into our purpose. The second one is that one of our key competitive advantages that was built over the years is our deep knowledge of the Amazon and how to translate that biodiversity and richness into unique products. Then there is the third element. We are Brazilian born, so there is no way we cannot participate in this. Those are the main reasons. Over the years that became an intangible asset of the company. We are in constant contact, we are searched by mining companies, the agricultural business, beef producers, strategist communities, NGOs. They all come to us as a group that can promote dialogues that otherwise would not happen naturally. It became a duty, not only a source of our competitive advantage, but it became a true duty for us.

Uwe Schulte
You already touched on my second question. I am very curious about science-based targets for biodiversity.

João Paulo Ferreira
Biodiversity is an area that still requires a lot of understanding. There are life cycle analysis methods developed many years ago. That keeps improving. But the biodiversity itself and its systemic impact are not totally understood. We have implemented practices, not only to honour, but to reward biodiversity even before the Nagoya Protocol (Fig. 4) on that subject. We even helped shape the Brazilian law, working with the government for more than a decade to shape the regulation around that theme. Because we have been working for so long around that team, we know that the regulation is still very poor because it fails to monetise. All the externalities

Fig. 4 Nagoya Protocol. Source: 2011 by the Secretariat of the Convention on Biological Diversity, https://www.cbd.int/abs/doc/protocol/nagoya-protocol-en.pdf

related to biodiversity fail to monetise. We have been working with other suppliers in experiments whereby protecting a certain environment you see how that whole ecosystem regenerates. What is the value of regeneration? We need to create mechanisms to value biodiversity so that we can level the playing field. A key element is to bridge between environmentalists and governments and the private sector. In the end, we need to translate all the social environmental externalities into the balance sheet of companies and governments, etc. And we reckon that biodiversity might be so complicated that it is still lagging behind in comparison to carbon footprint, for example.

Uwe Schulte
Yes. On the other hand, the COVID crisis has highlighted that biodiversity was ignored for too long, and we are putting so much stress on that system, and we are paying the price. I am very glad that we have some pioneers driving that subject and it will increase in importance. In light of the time, I wanted to, at least briefly, cover the other two commitments of yours. One is especially interesting. You want to turn human rights into humankind. What do you mean by that?

João Paulo Ferreira
What we have been witnessing through this crisis is the very negative impact of inequality. There is enough wealth generated in the world that if it could be equally spread, everyone would have a decent and dignified life. The issue that I think we are going to face in the years to come is not one of increasing the wealth that is generated, it is one of access and distribution. How will more people have access to that wealth and how will it be distributed? Otherwise, we are going to see more and more perversive effects of the inequality. This is an area where we think we can contribute a lot. Primarily because in our business model, we operate with six million independent representatives and consultants around the world, and we measure the human development index in that community. We actually stir our business model to try and increase that human development index, not only through the commercialisation of goods, but we distribute education and scholarships through that network, health benefits, etc. And we reckon we can increase that in the years to come. The primary reason we do that is that we can significantly improve the standards of living of our own huge network of consultants and reps. You multiply that number by 4 given the number of people in their households and you see the ripple effect happening there. But not only that. These people talk to 250 million people around the world in sometimes very remote areas. They can be social agents. We are not only there to transact goods or cosmetics, but there is a flow of affection and of care and of love that we have been promoting and we reckon we can do more. That is what is behind that statement.

Uwe Schulte
And at the end of the day, I guess it is good for business at the same time.

João Paulo Ferreira
Of course, it has to be. We are for profit. It is all about maximising economic, social, and environmental results at the same time. In our history, we learned that if we move all those three variables in the same direction, it is going to be good for everyone. It generates more value; it captures more value and distributes that value in a fair way.

Uwe Schulte
Understood. Let us look at the third commitment. You talk about circularity and regeneration. What are the investments and collaborative actions you look at in these regenerative solutions?

João Paulo Ferreira
That is an interesting question. Natura has been carbon neutral for many years and now we are moving from offsetting and talking about insetting, not only in terms of carbon, but solid waste and biodegradability, etc. It really requires new science. It requires research and new science and the way we do research is through open

innovation. More than 50% of our innovation comes from universities, suppliers, and research centres around the world collaborating with us. Recently, we ran a call for regenerative solutions, and we received hundreds of proposals from around the world in that area. We are also working with groups like Ellen MacArthur to help us channel some of the science that is coming to that area. And we are deploying hundreds of millions of dollars right now and in the years to come in that area and we truly think that we can become carbon positive in the near future. There still is work to be done with the companies that more recently joined Natura and Co, Avon and The Body Shop. We are looking at the carbon footprint, the solid waste footprint, and the water footprint. But we are catching up very fast and moving to circularity and regeneration.

Uwe Schulte
These are great ambitions, and these commitments actually are quite concrete, they are measurable and transparent. But there is a big question as we are going through this huge economic crisis right now—will this hold?

João Paulo Ferreira
Yes, there is no doubt. It must hold. It is what differentiates us. As I said, we are for profit. We are looking for products and proposals and offerings and ways of doing things that are ahead of other groups. We always want others to catch up in some of these areas because that is good for the planet, but we are searching for some competitive advantage here and this is the area where we chose to differentiate. So yes, that will hold.

Uwe Schulte
Thank you so much João Paulo. This is giving a lot of food for thought. A number of these things merit a deeper dive and maybe we will find another opportunity to go even deeper into the biodiversity subject, for example, which is also very close to my heart. I think it has been ignored for too long and you just gave us an example of a company purpose in action. Thank you so much for this interesting conversation.

João Paulo Ferreira
My pleasure, Uwe. We are happy to have you or any of your listeners visiting any of our operations anytime—The Body Shop, AESOP, Avon, Natura. We are glad to collaborate in any manner you can think of.

Uwe Schulte
Thank you very much.

Sustainable Tourism and Corporate Governance in Asia

Recorded September 2020

Uwe Schulte
Today I will be talking to Ho Kwon Ping, the executive chair of Banyan Tree Holding. Let me introduce our guest to you. Ho Kwon Ping graduated from the National University of Singapore in Economics and History. He started his career as a journalist in the late 1970s. Later, in the 1990s, Ho Kwon Ping joined the family business and opened his first Banyan Tree Resort in Phuket in 1994. He serves as director on several boards and was featured on the cover of Fortune Magazine. Welcome, Kwon Ping. Please tell us a little bit about yourself and your personal sustainability journey. How did you come to embrace sustainability?

Ho Kwon Ping

Thank you. Well, in fact, when I first started this journey, there were no concepts like corporate social responsibility, sustainability, or much else along those lines. And this was back in the 1970s. I suppose, the very origin of my interest is the fact that I was always a student of development economics. Economic development issues were always top of mind for me and for everything that I did, rather than business or journalism. So, when we accidentally, almost literally, fell into an abandoned tin mine in Phuket, we bought it on a whim because it was very cheap. Not having studied business, I never heard of the term due diligence and so on. I bought this tin mine because it looked like a moonscape, a very eerie, surrealistic moonscape with no trees, just sand dunes. It had an oceanside location and we bought it and I thought we would do something with it, plus my brother was an architect. I started researching, as a good journalist would do, and with the research came the discovery that the reason the land was so cheap and looked like a moonscape was because it had been completely depleted of any sustainable regenerative minerals and soils because it was a ripped-out tin mine. While trying to rehabilitate that piece of land, we began to experientially learn what you could do in terms of doing good by rehabilitating depleted areas of land. We also began to realise how you can really destroy the environment around you, very carelessly. That first encounter with the two sides of tourism made us realise very early that you could do much good but also much damage. That was 25 years ago. We never looked back (Fig. 1).

Uwe Schulte

I understand. That is quite an impressive experience. I can visualise it before my eyes what it probably looked like back then, and people can go on the Internet and see what it looks like now and that is impressive.[1] We have a global audience and there might be listeners who do not know Banyan Tree. Can you briefly talk about the history and the scope of your business today?

Fig. 1 Banyan Tree Resort, Phuket. Source: Banyan Tree Hotels & Resorts, https://www.banyantree.com/thailand/phuket/gallery

---

[1] https://www.banyantree.com/thailand/phuket

Ho Kwon Ping

Well, we never intended to develop a hotel management company. It happened partly by accident and partly by intent. The intent was to build a brand, because when I joined our family business it was not at all Banyan Tree. It was many other areas of business which my father had started, and they were all in contract manufacturing, they were in trading, there were so many different things that Southeast Asian entrepreneurs would do. But we never really owned the brand. We were generally cheaper producers of goods for other people. I had wanted to establish a brand, but I did not know what it was. This is a very long story, but partly by luck we decided to start a hotel management company. Largely because we wanted to develop the last piece of land we had at Laguna Phuket as a hotel, but no hotel management company wanted to manage it, because it did not have a beach front. Being young, ignorant, and stupid, we decided that would be the starting point of our own brand. As a result of that, 25 years later, we have about 50 other hotels, and we have six brands. We just added the last few brands 2 or 3 years ago and we are growing moderately fast. We will double the number of hotels within the next few years because of the very fast growth of Asian tourism.

Uwe Schulte

I must say, I do not have much knowledge about sustainable tourism, and I guess a few our listeners will suffer the same ignorance. Can you describe, from your perspective, what you would call sustainable tourism?

Ho Kwon Ping

Well, the interesting thing now, in fact, is that the new term is not just sustainable tourism, it is regenerative tourism.[2] And that is an area we are extremely interested in. The word sustainable tourism means that you just do no further damage to the environment, you just sustain it. But very often when you sustain it at the same level you currently have, it is not necessarily regenerative.[3] That is an interesting aspect, that we are just beginning to realise, that one can go beyond sustainability to regeneration. But let us talk about sustainable tourism. Because of mass tourism and other effects of tourism over many years, you are destroying both the physical and the human environment. It is very obvious to see for us, mainly because we are involved in a lot of developing countries from China to countries in Asia-Pacific, to Mexico, to Seychelles, to Morocco. We are in so many places where we are in very beautiful, pristine areas and generally what we see is that tourism comes in and destroys the environment. At the same time, it also destroys communities. When you look at the economic disparity between rich tourists and poor communities who service the rich tourists, you also have social contradictions that are not sustainable. Our slogan for our version of sustainability is to empower people and embrace the environment. We take a holistic view that sustainable tourism is not just about physical

---

[2] https://www.cbi.eu/market-information/tourism/regenerative-tourism#what-is-regenerative-tourism

[3] https://capitalinstitute.org/wp-content/uploads/2014/08/FINAL-Regenerative-Economies-for-a--Regenerative-Civilization-w-Case-Study_John-Fullerton.pdf

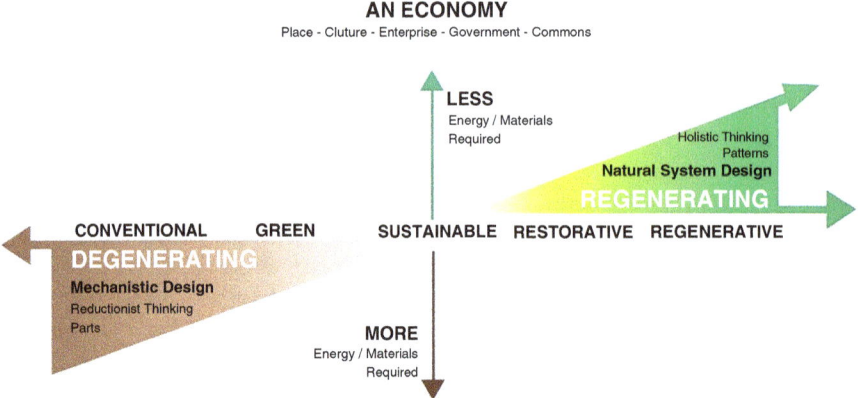

Fig. 2 Kosmos Journal Regenerative Capitalism. Source: Bill Reed, Regenesis

rehabilitation of the physical environment. It has to be a socioeconomic, social, cultural compatibility between the tourism that comes in from the outside _and_ the local community (Fig. 2).

Uwe Schulte
I understand. We will get back again to the regenerative topic. That is a key point. But you just explained environmental and social aspects going hand in hand. Can you give us an example of one of your projects to explain in more detail how you apply these principles in practice?

Ho Kwon Ping
Well, we are in so many places, whether that is Thailand, Vietnam, Indonesia, or Seychelles. In more than half of the places where we are, we usually pioneered the resort locations there. The physical part is quite simple. Usually, you come into an exceptionally beautiful pristine area. If you are not very careful about the way you design your project and the way you build it, you can destroy the natural terrain. The construction process can lead to such severe erosion, that pristine beaches and beautiful coral reefs will be destroyed. In the very physical process of building a beautiful resort you are already destroying the physical environment. That has happened so many times. It is shameful to look at the track record of tourism developers there. That is on the physical side. Therefore, when we come in, we are very careful about how we plan and design our resorts. We have our architects and stay at the site location for days on end, to make sure that we really understand the terrain. We make sure that we tie white ribbons around all the big trees, so the contractors will not just come in and raze them. From that side we have got it down pat. We make sure that in terms of infrastructure, we try to be as carbon light as we can. That is all on the physical side of it. Everything we do has to be certified by EarthCheck,[4] which is

---

[4] https://earthcheck.org/about/

one of the two largest accreditation agencies regarding the way you build and operate buildings.

The social side is a bit more complicated, because very often you find that in the local community the tourism investor generally is the only source of economic development, so they are welcomed. On the other hand, the economic disparity, the income disparity between the people who work at the resorts and the people who come and play at the resorts is so big that one day's room rate, which a European tourist would think nothing of, could equal close to a month's salary for a frontline worker. If you then do not mitigate the relationship between the tourist and the frontline worker, you may then end up with a situation where a server feels a certain servitude towards the guest who in turn feels a sense of superiority. You then develop a semi-colonial relationship, which I as an Asian and an ex-victim of colonialism would resent very much. That is why one of the bigger things we have to develop, and which is more of a challenge for us, is to create a true service culture, where that service comes from the heart and is not because the server is a poorer person of a third world country who is obliged to serve the rich European tourists.

Thankfully, because of the last 10 to 15 years, the rise in the Asian middle class has been so rapid that we are no longer seeing this great economic and quasi-racial disparity. That has been a big challenge for us at Banyan Tree, to create a real sense of pride and self-respect and a genuine sense of wanting to serve other people, and that is at the heart of sustainable tourism also.

Uwe Schulte
Your point about the social aspect of this is, you come in with such a large resort and you change the social relationships in that community as well. How do you evaluate your impact there?

Ho Kwon Ping
If you want to be accepted by the community, not only do you provide economic livelihood for the people who live around there, but you try to respect their culture. That is another aspect of what we try to do. For example, my wife started Banyan Tree Gallery. Banyan Tree Gallery is a retail arts and crafts centre within all our resorts, where we source both products that we sell to guests and products that we use in the hotel. We try to source them from the local community. We also try to feature artwork from the local community as much as possible. We try to create a sense of the locality. All of this is now becoming known as sustainable tourism, but we never knew the fancy term 'sustainable tourism'. We walked into it by simply doing. The background of my wife as a development sociologist and my own background as a development economist helped us because we had the perspective within which we could view our efforts to build a hotel management company. We were not professional hoteliers, and that is not necessarily a bad thing.

Uwe Schulte
That is a very interesting remark that fresh eyes can start things in a different way and possibly in an even better way. Let us get back to the regenerative aspect of what you were talking about. I find that extremely interesting. We are talking about

positive impact. Can you explain where you see chances to do more than just maintaining the environment and the social situation?

Ho Kwon Ping

One early aspect of regenerative tourism has been planting trees. We planted so many trees and we have a programme whereby we donate $1.00 for every dollar that is donated by our guests. And that goes into the Banyan Tree Global Foundation[5] and a programme called the Green Imperative,[6] where we then essentially try to look at areas of a society that have degenerated. It could mean reforesting areas, restoring coral reefs, or restoring lost arts and crafts. If you go into a resort area with the eyes of a development economist and development sociologist rather than a hotelier and you then ask yourself the question 'what has been depleted and degenerated from this entire community over many years'? then you basically can analyse it systematically and say what happened on the physical side. The water table has dropped, they have been practising monoculture in their agriculture, etc. You can list all these things. You also look at the social aspect of what has been happening. And then you can craft your own policies within the hotels so that you constantly try your best to restore and regenerate those lost things. For example, a lot of resort developers, including ourselves, have thousands of acres of undeveloped land which they bought because it usually is not that expensive, because it is land that is not near a beach, etc. And many people are now beginning to practise 'farm to table'[7] agriculture. We are doing that in our resorts now, where we have so much land, we teamed up with farmers, and with chefs too, to grow exotic vegetables which would have had to be imported otherwise. We save on carbon footprint, etc., by growing vegetables locally that usually are imported and quite expensive. We also grow other kinds of local crops which have been subjected to monoculture before and deplete the nitrogen in the soil. We then take all these vegetables, and we use them in our own restaurants. That is just one example. There are many areas of tourism where you can consciously practise regenerative tourism, which goes beyond simply sustainable tourism (Fig. 3).

Uwe Schulte

I understand. Now let us get to the trickier bits of this. It is great that tourism can help in the developing world to elevate people out of poverty and that cannot be underestimated at all. But at the same time this requires people from the developed world to travel there, and I suppose that would usually be by plane which has a carbon footprint. That is a dilemma. How do you see the resolution of such a dilemma?

Ho Kwon Ping

That goes to the heart of what economics is all about. Economics is all about trade-offs and trying to optimise the trade-offs. Only the very naive idealists in the world

---

[5] https://www.banyantreeglobalfoundation.com/background/
[6] https://www.hospitalitynet.org/opinion/4110588.html
[7] https://en.wikipedia.org/wiki/Farm-to-table

Fig. 3 Banyan Tree Island Farm–to–Table. Source: Banyan Tree Hotels & Resorts, https://www.banyantree.com/article/island-farm-to-table-ori9in-phuket

would think that you can do everything for good and that there is no trade-off involved. There is obviously going to be trade-offs, for example, in trade or also in travel. Radical environmentalists are now saying everyone should just stop travelling on anything that involves a carbon footprint. They should not even take trains, should not take cars, maybe if they are electric cars, it would be OK, but they should only go on holidays where they can bicycle to within a short distance of their homes. That is fine and good if you are living in a developed country. But until poor developing countries can become developed themselves that simply is going to mean that the inbound tourism from rich countries cannot be a source of economic development. That is one example of how there is no easy solution because we do know, and I think we all accept, that aircraft emissions are very negative, and the airline industry has to find its own way to reduce its carbon footprint. But if everybody just simply stops taking planes until that is done, that might ease the conscience of some people in the Western world, but it is also going to cause economic distress for many people in the developing world.

Let us talk about trade, for example. There was a recent article that said that because of COVID-19, the flower industry in the Kenyan Highlands has been destroyed. Kenya, being close to the same time zone as Europe and having a higher altitude near Nairobi, etc., has been exporting a lot of flowers to Europe. That has completely died because of COVID-19. If people take the argument that we should do everything that is necessary to simply reduce the carbon footprint in whatever we do, then that _is indeed_ going to lead to less carbon footprint, no doubt. But the dilemma there is that it will also lead to one-sided economic development. There is no easy answer and I think the whole science of economics is to really look at the different trade-offs and to very minutely, very analytically and dispassionately try to find a middle way solution for whatever we do so that the trade-offs can have the least negative impact on all parties involved.

Uwe Schulte

I understand what you are saying, and the Kenyan example is quite a strong one. I see the effects as well and we also must make sure that we do not focus on just one thing in these developments. Having several legs to stand on for each country in their development is so very important. People might say when they listen to your excellent efforts, that you are in a niche of luxury resorts and you have affluent guests which might make it easier to follow sustainable or regenerative concepts, although I do not think it is. But I guess there are learnings from what you have done which could be applied to the mass tourism segment as well. How do you see that?

Ho Kwon Ping

Well, that is an interesting point. Banyan Tree, the first and most well-known brand of our six-brand platform is inevitably associated with luxury tourism. But I have never been a great fan of luxury. We got into the luxury segment simply because it was an area that was most underserved at that time, because each so-called luxury boutique hotel would generate the least management fees. That is why big hotel management companies were less interested in managing a 50-room luxury hotel than a 500-room midscale hotel. There was a space there, we wanted to play in that space, and we got into it. But the most exciting thing from my point of view has been what I call the rise of 'rainbow tourism' in the last 20 years. Rainbow tourism is tourism, but in many different colours. Whereas in the past, tourism was always unidirectional and a single colour, which was white. Tourism going from Europe to the rest of the world. For the last 15–20 years, you have had brown, black, and pink tourism, very much so, all around the world now. Asia is rising and India is rising, China is rising, and so is the Middle East. You are getting very multi-coloured tourism and as a result of that the demand for hotels in the Asia-Pacific region is not just for luxury hotels to serve rich tourists coming in from Europe, it is to serve their own young middle classes. We are very much involved in that. The last three or four brands that we launched are growing very rapidly in China and elsewhere. They are to serve that younger, more affordable mass market. And in some ways, if you look at it even from the perspective of regenerative or sustainable tourism, it is more exciting than even luxury tourism, precisely for the same reason that you mentioned.

It is great to have a little resort charging $5000 a night in the Maldives that is practising a zero-carbon footprint kind of tourism. But does it really move the needle in any way at all? In my view, that kind of resort is largely for millionaire celebrities to come and assuage themselves of their guilt. And they feel great about what they have done, but it does not move the needle. But for mass tourism projects, if those can have regenerative aspects to them and have sustainable aspects to them, then they will have a far bigger impact than having sustainability and regeneration only in luxury resorts. To me this is a huge challenge and a huge opportunity at the same time.

Uwe Schulte

Do you already have ideas how that would work? Because you cannot simply apply what you have done in luxury resorts.

Ho Kwon Ping

No, but if you were to look at it from one perspective, mass tourism is not a bad thing. Tourism has almost become something somewhere along the line of the hierarchy of needs beyond basic needs. Most people, after a certain economic level, want to see the rest of the world around them, and it is something they desire to do. And we want to feed that basic desire for people to see the beauty of the world around them. I think we can do it with mass tourism. I will just give you one example. If the farm-to-table practice that we want to do in agriculture can be replicated for a 400-room hotel, it has a bigger impact than if you are just doing it for a 50-room hotel. If you can save water or generate your own water, if you want to have no more single-use plastic, if you want to practise using only bioplastics—whatever practices you want to implement that are going to be regenerative or sustainable, you can practise it across a much bigger platform if you are engaged in mass tourism. That is why it is very important that the people who are involved in mass tourism, like the Accor hotels or the Marriott hotels of the world, adopt these practices because they have a far bigger impact in many ways than a Banyan Tree hotel would have.

Uwe Schulte

Yes, and I think we see these tendencies and that is very encouraging. I really enjoy learning from you about sustainable tourism and, as you quite rightly put it, regenerative tourism and how your company is thriving by living these principles.

Ho Kwon Ping

It is rather ironic that you are referring to our company as thriving. Nothing could be further from the truth right now with the impact of COVID-19. But inshallah we shall be thriving eventually. The basic difference between the new concept of regenerative tourism and that of sustainable tourism, which had been the buzzword for several years, is that if you look at the word sustainability, it just means 'keeping the world as it is today'. Sustaining something that currently exists. But if what currently exists has essentially been depleted, degenerated, and degraded, then sustaining it is not enough. You must regenerate that particular situation, whether it be regenerative tourism or regenerative industries and regenerative societies. There seems to be a new mood, and part of it is now after COVID, that people are beginning to discover that sustaining something is not enough. The impact of COVID-19 has been so bad, not only on health and on economies, but also to our entire psyche that I think we are beginning to realise that out of this crisis there can be an opportunity. The Chinese word for crisis is 'weiji' which is a combination of two words, 'Wei' meaning danger and 'ji' meaning opportunity.[8] There is danger in COVID but there is also an opportunity to regenerate the world around us (Fig. 4).

Uwe Schulte

I am glad that you see it this way. I am absolutely convinced that with your very solid concept, this thriving of the past will also be a thriving of the future. I would

---

[8] The first character *wēi* (危) means 'dangerous', the second *jī* (机; 機) 'change point' https://en.wikipedia.org/wiki/Chinese_word_for_%22crisis%22#cite_note-1

Fig. 4 Chinese characters (trad. and simplified) wēijī. Source: Wikipedia, public domain, CC0 1.0 Universal Public Domain Dedication, Author: Tomchen1989, Source: own work

like to broaden the scope a little bit and get your perspective about corporate sustainability, especially in Asia. How do you see this going forward?

Ho Kwon Ping
Well, generally as an Asian businessman I have been very proud of everything that Asia has achieved in the last quarter century. However, in the field of corporate governance, Asia has generally been far behind the Western world, or perhaps I should say behind some of the European countries. I cannot say I am a great admirer of American corporate governance, which I think is laced with hypocrisies and so many platitudes about American corporate governance which is not reflected at all. I would hardly hold what is happening in America today as an example of good corporate governance. But I would say that for some European countries, some Scandinavian countries, for Germany, in my view, corporate governance seems to have been taken on more seriously, and perhaps that is because some of these countries come from a social democratic background rather than a fair capitalism background.

Uwe Schulte
You are saying that there is something to be developed in Asia in that respect?

Ho Kwon Ping
Yes, I am sorry I digressed there. I believe that Asia, in its very rapid economic development, has been successful in the rapidity of its development. Entrepreneurship is good and alive in Asia, but corporate governance has fallen very far behind. Much of that is somewhat to be expected if you are a student of economic history and you look at corporate governance even in Europe or America. Corporate governance usually comes way after a society has attained a certain level of economic development. If you are poor, you do not particularly care about corporate governance. You just try to get rich as quickly as possible, and after you have reached a certain level of affluence then you look at how to maintain it in a responsible manner. That is true for family-owned companies as well as for state-owned companies. I would say that today, there probably is a greater recognition in Asia by the stock exchanges, by regulatory authorities, by central banks, by entrepreneurs themselves, family-owned companies as well as state-owned companies; there is a greater recognition that we now must up our game. And that means we must do it in every aspect of corporate governance from gender equality to diversity and inclusivity and many other areas. We have not really been exemplary in doing what we should have been doing.

Uwe Schulte

We have only been talking about Asia overall, but of course we all know there are huge differences within Asia. How do you see these differences playing out in terms of the corporate governance agenda when you look at India, Southeast Asia, China, Japan, Australia?

Ho Kwon Ping

Well, everyone is so different. Let us just take Northeast Asia first and do a quick analysis there. If you look at corporate governance issues in Japan, in many aspects they are in fact exemplary—the security laws, the regulation of stock exchange, for example. Stock exchange and security violations are likely to be a lot less than in China, for example. But if you take a broad definition of criteria for proper governance and you take diversity and inclusivity as one aspect of corporate governance, then Japan has not done well at all.[9] Corporate governance covers many different areas. You can adopt the same template to analyse every single country in terms of ticking off what they have done, but the results are very different from one country to another. There is still quite a lot of corruption in Korea. China's corporate governance is something that is just beginning to be implemented. Then there is India and Indonesia. The large developing societies have massive corruption issues, not just poor corporate governance by companies but massive corruption. Singapore stands out, and I am not just saying that because I am a Singaporean. We stand out as a beacon of light in terms of corporate governance. But that does not mean that much because we are so small in the overall scale of things, not only in Asia, but particularly in the world. But what we do has been successful, and we are an Asian economy that came out of the developing world and economic underdevelopment just one generation ago. The other Asian countries around us are beginning to look at many practices that we have adopted in Singapore. The overall conclusion is that Asia is not a single entity. Some have done better in some areas, some have done worse in other areas, and you cannot use a broad brush and tar all of Asia uniformly. Except that overall, it is still very hard to be proud of what we have done in corporate governance. Whereas all of Asia can legitimately be proud of having lifted the bulk of our people out of poverty within 50 years, which is not an easy task when you have billions of people to deal with.

Uwe Schulte

Absolutely. When we talk about this gap that you would like to close, what do you think are the main influencing levers to drive that development?

Ho Kwon Ping

Government is particularly important for eradicating poverty, in that the political will to eradicate corruption is primary. One of the reasons why Singapore has done so well was because Singapore's first founding Prime Minister, Mr. Lee Kuan Yew

---

[9] https://www.conference-board.org/topics/sustainability-practices/sustainability-practices-2019-trends-report

(Fig. 5), would tolerate no corruption at all. Singapore's history is filled with several examples where his intolerance for corruption even reached his own friends, where he would not even let friends get away with it all, or even forgive them. We have now created a culture of intolerance regarding corruption. The first and most insidious aspect of poor corporate governance is to allow corruption within society and within politics. Because once you do that you set the tone for all companies to follow, and corruption is the most invidious source of destroying a society. The first thing you need is political rectitude. Once you have that, you also need to have an awareness within corporate leadership itself that getting rich alone is not sufficient and that we must do it in ways that we can be proud of. Education, I suppose, is another area that is very important. Our universities and business schools must produce leaders who have a true sense of leadership. Good corporate governance is not simply imposing a set of regulations by regulatory bodies, which is relatively easy to do. And I would argue that the United States is probably leading the way in terms of a massive number of regulatory bodies trying to regulate good corporate governance. I would say that it probably has failed in many cases, because the rest of society has not developed the values that really are necessary to underpin good corporate governance. Certainly, the political leadership in the United States today is setting the tone. Every company that does not want to practise good corporate governance can simply point upstairs and say 'Why should we do it? Look at the White House, they are not doing it'.[10]

Fig. 5 Lee Kuan Yew, Singapore's 1st Prime Minister. Source: Wikipedia, this image is a work of a U.S. military or Department of Defense employee, taken or made as part of that person's official duties. As a work of the U.S. federal government, the image is in the public domain in the United States.
Author: Robert D. Ward

---

[10] The comment refers to the Trump administration at the time of the recording.

Uwe Schulte

Let us focus on Asia. It is important to get a feeling on the needs for future development. You pointed out government as well as corporate leadership and education. I would argue that there is also the element of the consumer and the populace. How do you see that?

Ho Kwon Ping

I certainly think so, but if you look at economic history I would argue, and this is not an insult to consumers, that, an activist consumer movement usually comes much later in the day in terms of the economic development history of a society. Maybe that is to be expected to the extent that you have a society that is poor, any Asian society would be relatively poor, illiterate, etc. You then need enlightened elites to set the tone, because you have consumers who are not even aware of their rights. You have the electorate that is not even aware of their rights. People at the very bottom who are not aware of their rights, generally would be the last to exercise it. That is why you do need to have the tone set by the political leadership, the corporate leadership, and the educational leadership. After a generation, I think you would then have a new generation of consumers—younger, more affluent, educated consumers that begin to have more of an attitude of demanding that they use their consumer purchasing power to effect social change. Consumer power is very much evident in the Western world, but in the developing world it is just beginning to come about.

Uwe Schulte

This change process is something that a lot of corporate people are struggling with in Asia. They are asking themselves 'Is regulation, is government moving in that direction? Where are my markets moving'? What would you say to people in responsible positions in business in Asia, what they should use as guiding principles?

Ho Kwon Ping

I suppose the guiding principle must be an awareness, a genuine recognition and awareness that good corporate governance is good for the bottom line of a company. And it is also good for the so-called bottom line of a society and economy itself, to the extent that political leadership must be aware that they should be against corruption, not simply because it is unethical, unchristian, unbuddhist, unhindu, or whatever, but because it is bad for economic development to have corruption.[11] And therefore, that same awareness must be recognised by corporate leaders too, that good corporate governance is in line with good profitability, etc. There is no dichotomy between good corporate governance and good financial performance of a company. If you do not have that recognition, then corporate governance like sustainability and corporate social responsibility would just be buzzwords that c-suites and boards of directors will adopt and put out in their press releases because they think journalists like it and governments like it and shareholders like it. But they must be convinced that corporate governance is good for the company. Just as

---

[11] https://en.wikipedia.org/wiki/Corruption_Perceptions_Index

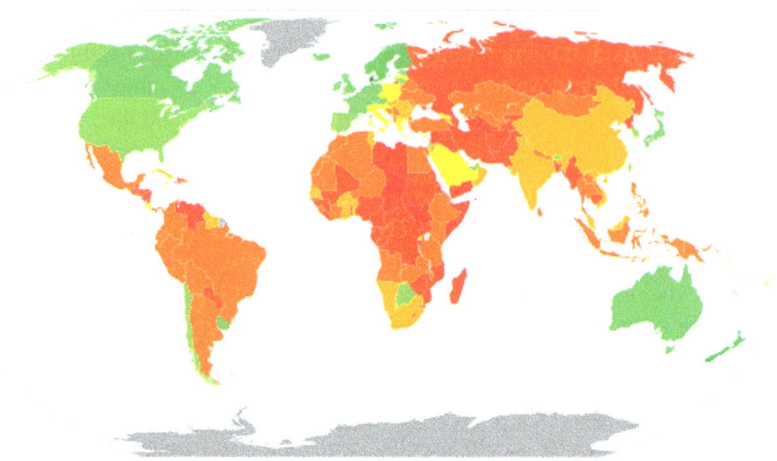

Fig. 6 Corruption Perceptions Index. Source: Wikipedia, CC BY-SA 4.0 DEED, Attribution-ShareAlike 4.0 International, Author: ConnerMiner, Source: Template used: https://commons.wikimedia.org/wiki/File:BlankMap-World.svg, Data from: https://www.transparency.org/en/cpi/2022

I have long argued that diversity and inclusivity, for us at least and for everything that I have been involved with, is not just a nice platitude, but that diversity in and of itself makes a company more resilient, more able to anticipate diverse consumer needs and ultimately it is good for the company. That recognition must sink in (Fig. 6).

Uwe Schulte
You are practising what you preach, and we started off with me talking about your good business efforts and you mentioned the situation that we are currently in. The pandemic highlights many things and puts them more into focus. Where would you see this development going? What is your perspective on corporate governance, corporate sustainability, corporate social responsibility in the next 6 to 9 months in Asia, with the pandemic still being very much alive and kicking, unfortunately?

Ho Kwon Ping
Across the world, if you take away the immediacy in terms of the public health issues of COVID-19 and how governments and companies respond to the public health aspect of it, if you take a slightly longer-term view, I think one of the most notable changes that have occurred to everyone in the world is a resetting of all our priorities in life. When the entire world is virtually locked down for months on end and we have only ourselves to spend our time with, we tend to be more reflective about the things that really matter. I know that for myself, my family, and for friends I talk to. As individual human beings we begin to realise more what really matters in life, and it is usually not luxury goods, etc., it is friendships with people you love, it is relationships that are at a personal level.

For many companies it has also been quite interesting, and it has been interesting for mine, too. On the one hand, it has been totally debilitating for my company because we are in hospitality, one of the worst hit industries. I have had to do terrible things which hardly make me feel happy and that is letting people go. Virtually almost every single company except those involved in e-commerce have had to let people go. When you have had to do that, and that probably is the most painful thing for any CEO, suddenly you are also aware that the important things are not just about profit anymore. You suddenly have become aware of all the things that used to be buzzwords—about how stakeholders should perhaps be more important than shareholders, that corporate governance should be practised in and of itself, not just for profitability, and so on and so forth. As a corporate equivalent to human beings beginning to re-evaluate their personal lives, I think many companies are beginning to realise too, that this is an opportunity for them to reset, to regenerate themselves and to re-evaluate what is important in their own company. At least I hope that is what many are doing, and I am certainly doing that. Of course, there are those who are hugely profiting from this whole pandemic, and they are just too busy making money from it that they are not contemplating the impact of this on their own company. But I think many companies are taking a more contemplative, reflective view towards how they can change themselves after this pandemic is over.

Uwe Schulte
I must say that I have seen initiatives in all parts of the world, where company leaders said that the restart after the crisis requires new rules and new principles. That is very encouraging. We now have the Corporate Leadership Council in Asia, and you are a part of that. Do you just want to say a couple of words about that initiative?

Ho Kwon Ping
Well, that initiative, like all initiatives trying to bring CEOs together, is a very good one because we live in our own little cubbyholes of our own business sectors, our own companies and the more we learn about what others are doing, not only gives us more insight as to what we can do, but also encourages us that we are not the only people doing all these things that we think are necessary to do, but that there are many other people doing them also.

Uwe Schulte
You already explained that the way to do business has to be regenerative and you mentioned the aspect of looking at the social impact of your organisation. In the USA, we have seen quite an upturn about an issue that has been there for a long time—Black Lives Matter—and more and more people are becoming aware that this is something that truly needs to be addressed at the root causes rather than window dressing. Would you say similar things are likely to emerge in Asia?

Ho Kwon Ping
Of course, I think clearly so. It is not about black lives per se, but it is the whole notion of systemic racism and unconscious bias. Not every single police officer is a bad person, not every single white person in America is a bad person, but the whole point about Black Lives Matter is that systemic racism and unconscious bias have

become such an embedded part of American life, that the recognition of the issue is the beginning of change. And in that respect, America has long had the ability to be very harsh on itself, which is good compared to some very entrenched Asian and European societies. America has that ability. What that has done for a lot of younger people in Asian societies is to question the systemic biases, systemic racism, and unconscious biases that they have in their own societies. And to question these is a good thing, and it is happening as an indirect result of Black Lives Matter in America.

Uwe Schulte
And what I am hearing from you is that corporations can play a role in fighting that systemic bias.

Ho Kwon Ping
Once you realise that about Black Lives Matter in America, and that there have been systemic biases, you know that systemic biases can exist in any organisation. If it exists in the police force, it can exist within your own company. The moral of the story is not just to point the finger at other people and say, 'see how bad they are and how great we are'?

It is in fact to look at what other people are doing and ask us what we can learn from this for our own societies and our own companies. It has made me realise that at Banyan Tree, we may well have systemic biases and unconscious biases too. Basically, systemic and unconscious biases exist everywhere where there are people. That is the basic learning point from Black Lives Matter that I think everyone should take away and apply to themselves.

Uwe Schulte
Thank you so much, Kwon Ping, for these great insights about Asia and where corporate governance and corporate sustainability will be moving. You pointed out that there is a lot to do, but I sense an optimism to take the struggles that arise from the COVID-19 pandemic as an opportunity to reflect where you are and to head towards a more advanced and balanced way of dealing with your stakeholders and thriving for positive impact from your business. Do I get that right?

Ho Kwon Ping
Yes, there is no better way to end this than the point that you just made. When I come across so many young people, I realise that this pandemic has defined an entire generation to the extent that this pandemic is the worst crisis the world has seen since World War Two. World War Two clearly defined my parents' generation globally, it was a global crisis. There has not been a global crisis like this that has affected every single individual in the world, young and old, regardless of colour or race. Virtually every single person has been affected, perhaps even more than in

World War Two. I think an entire generation of young people will define themselves by this. Young people, virtually by being young, are always going to be optimists, they are going to see that this has been an absolute disaster, but from this disaster they can create a new world. I am hugely encouraged when I talk to young people and I see their determination not to waste a good crisis, as Winston Churchill once said.

Uwe Schulte

Excellent, thank you so much. Thank you for sharing your experience and your insights. As I already said, I am sure that based on that solid ground your company will pick up and thrive again.

Business Integration of Sustainability: The Customer Perspective

Recorded March 2021

Uwe Schulte

Today I will be talking to Daniel Schmid, Chief Sustainability Officer at SAP, about integrating sustainability into the organisation's strategy and operation. First, let me introduce our guest, Daniel Schmid to you. Daniel started his career in 1992 as a consultant at Kiefer & Veittinger, a Customer Relations Management Systems Company that was acquired by SAP in 1997. In 1995, Daniel became Business Unit Manager, and, in 1999, he took on the responsibility for SAP Customer Relationship Management (CRM) Consulting. From 2004, Daniel held various senior management positions within SAP Consulting across Europe, Middle East, and Africa. In 2014, he assumed the role of Chief Sustainability Officer and is globally responsible for sustainability at SAP. He holds a degree in Industrial Engineering from the University of Kaiserslautern in Germany.

Welcome, Daniel. Please tell us a little bit about yourself and your personal sustainability journey.

Daniel Schmid

I love my family. I love sports. And community service is a passion of mine. For quite a long time, I have been a member of a service club and part of the Rotary family for more than 30 years. But in addition, I love sunny days like today when the solar panels on our roof are highly active. I also love to drive my pure electric car, which I have been doing for more than 7 years now. After 16 years in consulting, I got a call in 2008 from a board member and he said: 'Daniel, observing you from a distance, I associate your leadership style with sustainability. Am I right'? You can imagine, being on a phone call with a board member was not often the case for me at that step of my career. I asked myself what the next question would be. I was quite astonished about his observation and then he told me: 'Daniel, the board decided to establish a project around sustainability, understanding stakeholder expectations, and the task would be to define the strategic approach, the key targets and how the organisation should look like. And, Daniel, can you start tomorrow because tomorrow between 7:30 and 8:30 am you need to say yes or no'. And Uwe, already on my way home, I made the decision, and I love that job.

Uwe Schulte
Increasingly we observe that, rather than a specialist coming from environment or from communications, business unit managers and business managers move into the role of Chief Sustainability Officer. It is interesting for our audience to hear a little bit more about the rationale behind that, from your personal perspective, but also from the company perspective, how that works out.

Daniel Schmid
Let me start with the company perspective. It is obvious now that sustainability has become a core business topic. It is important that you can define and share the business case. It is a beautiful business case, but you need to explain it. You need to put it in the context of your counterparts of line of business heads, from an overarching perspective, but also from a detailed perspective, tailored to their circumstances, their current target scheme. Then you need to show your colleagues in the relevant business functions, that by including sustainability, by including this kind of holistic thinking, they will be more successful. They will more likely achieve their business targets. So far, at the beginning of that journey, I observed that people thought, you are either profitable or you are sustainable. In your role as Chief Sustainability Officer, you need to show the opposite, that by being more sustainable, you are more successful, you are coming up with the better business decisions, you will create better business outcomes and that leads to more business success, at least in the mid and long term. That is the company perspective. With regard to my role and my own perspective, I would say that it has been an experience that sends a signal. At SAP, it is well known that an SAP unit head has a profit and loss responsibility for many years and that he or she him or herself was a leader in the field in market roles, in customer facing roles with profit and loss responsibility. That suggests that having such an experience will make it easier to achieve the buy-in of your counterparts. I would say through that experience I felt well prepared to particularly manage stakeholders in an effective way. But to be honest, Uwe, I am learning something new in my role every day. And that is another reason I love my job. It is a continuous learning journey, for me personally.

Uwe Schulte

It is interesting what you say that you are more convincing because you had a profit and loss accountability yourself. I remember my days when I got into role at head office, it suddenly felt very strange. You had always been in a business unit or in a local facility and you always dreaded the visits from the central guy a bit. And suddenly you are a central guy yourself. I remember that shift was quite an important one, to not forget how it felt when these central guys came. Do you experience the same thing?

Daniel Schmid

Yes, it is important that you really put yourself in the shoes of the others, of your stakeholders, and understand their circumstances and having that experience. Uwe, in my role, when I set up the so-called EMEA (Europe, Middle East, Africa) delivery hubs, I was responsible for people in thirty different countries. You gain a lot of experience, and you understand why it is so important to bring in different perspectives, different points of view, diverse cultures, various aspects of diversity. That is why I had an accelerated learning journey in my past career, from which I can benefit in my current role. I would like to give you one concrete example. Uwe: You think that you communicate and communicate and communicate. But still you always need to check what people have experienced, what they have heard, and conduct engagement sessions with colleagues around the world. Did they really get the strategic approach to sustainability or not? You might think you communicated sufficiently, but you need to understand that from their location, they are far away from the headquarters, from the central functions. You need to repeat and repeat the sustainability messages. I started as a Customer Management (CM) consultant, so I learned to listen first, to reflect and then connect things, bringing in a strategic perspective. Change & Transformation Management was extremely key in my career.

I was employee #32. Now I am part of an organisation of more than 100,000 people. And I always had roles that gave me the opportunity to drive change and transformation. One concrete example was that I used the staircase methodology[1] to develop a vision. It is about achieving your goals step by step over the years, and that was an exceptionally valuable tool, the strategic tool that helped me to build our sustainability agenda.

Uwe Schulte

What you said very much resonates with me, that capability to listen and connect the dots and never lose sight of what you call the staircase, the top of the staircase, but being able to go step by step. That is particularly important.

Daniel Schmid

Sorry to interrupt you, Uwe, but I believe it is important for the audience to understand that, yes, you need bold, ambitious goals, but you also need to understand where you are coming from, what your maturity level is, and then break down your long-term goals to an annual base. That means what would we like to achieve this year to be best prepared for the next case, for the next decade. That is important. I would say analytical skills help, of course.

---

[1] https://www.mckinsey.com/featured-insights/employment-and-growth/staircases-to-growth

And you mentioned that I studied Industrial Engineering. Following science-based approaches is important in my role. But I have an overarching responsibility as well. Collaborating with great experts in my team and with many colleagues around the globe and other lines of business helps me a lot to learn and to understand stakeholder expectations and how to address them or how to engage with the stakeholders. And that is another beautiful element of my role which I love. In my consulting life, I had a lot of contacts with companies. Now, in addition to that contact with our customers, which I have every week, every day, I also reach out to investors, to academia, to partners, to NGOs, to governments, or internally to all the lines of business. Wow, what a wonderful role I have, I must say.

Uwe Schulte
It is truly clear that you love what you do. I have to say that I felt a bit embarrassed. I have only had a full electric car for a year now, and you have had it for 7 years, so you have really outpaced me there. One thing that was on my mind, you already almost answered. There is a balance between the business experience, but you also must know the complex area of sustainability. There are so many different elements, be it carbon footprint or be it the question of human rights, it is a complex area. And you must build that knowledge as well. Coming from the business, of course you were not completely versed in all those elements, but I hear you say, the other element which is being able to listen and relate to people is more important. What was your experience there, building that expertise, which of course everybody is looking at in your role?

Daniel Schmid
I am a huge fan of learning by doing, through conversations with experts, for example. A very tangible example is coming to my mind, when we decided back at the end of the year 2013 that all our solutions should be offered by a green cloud, meaning running all our data centres by 100% renewables. I reached out to experts from NGOs to better understand how to purchase renewables and ensure high quality of renewables. Based on these conversations, we defined around ten criteria helping us to do the right things.[2] That is one concrete example of 'learning by doing'. You need to know what you do not know and reach out to the right experts. I am surrounded by a fantastic team helping me a lot. Every day I benefit from their experience and their expertise.

Uwe Schulte
It is interesting that you reached out to an NGO giving you expertise. That is quite fascinating because I know from experience that companies often think that they know best.

Daniel Schmid
It is a journey and look, Uwe, we have defined sustainability in such a broad way, you cannot beat the experts in all these environmental, social, economic, and governance aspects. We have that broad definition at SAP—which is the right approach

---

[2] https://www.sap.com/docs/download/2022/06/1c983247-307e-0010-bca6-c68f7e60039b.pdf

Fig. 1 Carbon Disclosure Project (CDP). Source: www.cdp.net/en/

from my perspective—but you cannot have the ambition to always be the expert in all these fields. Coming back to the NGOs, those were concrete experts from CDP[3] and WWF[4], who helped us (Fig. 1).

Uwe Schulte

You said that you have such a broad definition of sustainability. SAP has expressed its purpose which is 'help the world run better and improve people's lives'. I can relate to that, it is clear, but it is also open for interpretation. Can you interpret this a little bit for me?

Daniel Schmid

We run the key critical core processes of our customers through our solutions. So, by having thousands of customers across the globe in every industry and sector, SAP customers generate 87% of total global commerce and ninety-seven of the one hundred greenest companies in the world run SAP. Now you understand that we run the business world and help the world run better and improve people's lives. Our purpose is such a great sustainability statement, and it shows you how huge the impact is that we have at SAP. We use the SDGs, the seventeen sustainable development goals as defined by the United Nations, as a compass to judge if we really help the world run better and improve people's lives or not. It becomes more concrete. And the way we bring our purpose to life is through sustainability and we have a clear definition in our business context (Fig. 2).

Let me share that definition with you. It is about creating positive economic, social, and environmental impact within the planetary boundaries or, in a nutshell, a good life for all of us within planetary boundaries. That is our definition. You can see the link from our purpose to our sustainability definition. As an IT company we need to fulfil two roles. One is—we need to have the ambition to be an exemplar, to be a role model when it comes to our own operations. Only through that we gain the credibility, and we learn to act as an enabler—the second role. Being an enabler through our solutions, helping our customers to execute on their sustainable business strategies, that is, of course, the biggest lever we have in our hands. Coming from the overall purpose, which explains the definition and the tools we need to fulfil that, it hopefully helps to better understand our purpose.

---

[3] https://www.cdp.net/en/

[4] https://wwf.panda.org/

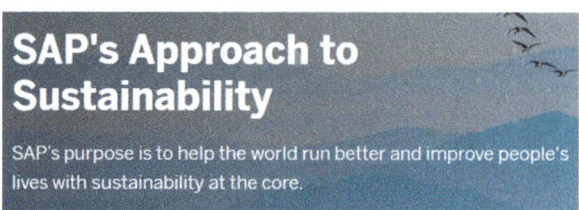

Fig. 2 SAP Purpose Statement. Source: www.sap.com

Uwe Schulte

That is clear. When you think of an IT company, of course you think about your servers and all of that and you run it on clean energy, but you have gone way beyond that. In the carbon world for example, we would call that scope three. You look at what your customers do with your IT system. We will dive into the customer element a little bit later. You also have products that help perform in that way directly and I am quite interested in your Climate 21 programme. Can you explain a little bit what you are doing there? It is fascinating because I know that several people are struggling with the fact that they want to define that scope three better. And let me explain to the audience: scope three means the carbon footprint that is along your value chain, either with your customers or with your suppliers. That is quite a challenge, I would say.

Daniel Schmid

Yes, indeed. But let me explain that a little bit more broadly. I am coming back to the two roles we need to fulfil. By being an exemplar, we learn a lot and we are extremely proud of being perceived as a thought leader and we receive great feedback. We are perceived by various ratings and rankings as the number one in the software sector, like the Dow Jones Sustainability Index,[5] or having an A rating from CDP.[6,7] But you are right, the biggest lever is through our solutions, enabling our customers to become more sustainable. Therefore, it is important that we and other companies learn to steer the business in a more holistic way. We are all well-educated and trained to focus on financial performance. But we need to add sustainability to that financial dimension. Do not get me wrong, we need to keep the dimension of financial performance, but we need to add the impact of our business activities on our planet, and on our society. So, covering the social, the economic, and the environmental dimension. And that leads to a holistic view. About the Climate 21 initiative you mentioned, imagine Uwe, when we, who's systems touch or customers' business-critical processes, embed sustainability criteria in the data model, like greenhouse gas emissions, energy consumption, water use, land use, or social indicators. That would allow our customers to have the full transparency across the entire value chain, from the suppliers downstream to the customers. Really creating that transparency across the entire value chain. With the Climate 21 initiative, we were able to

---

[5] https://www.spglobal.com/esg/csa/yearbook/2023/ranking/

[6] https://www.cdp.net/en/search

[7] https://news.sap.com/2023/06/acknowledging-sap-esg-efforts/

provide the first product mid of last year to our customers, which looks at the product footprint. Companies need carbon emissions transparency on the corporate level, but they need it as well on the plant or production level. And if they have the data on the product level, that makes an enormous difference, because then you can simulate—your value chain, your suppliers. Should I produce the product in plant A or plant B? There is a different energy mix being provided in the grid, so we could reduce emissions which could have that monetary impact and that leads to better business decisions, again, having that full holistic understanding. Let me add that I observed a lot of pledges and commitments and targets in the past year. But sometimes I struggle a little bit to understand how these companies really manage their ambitions. Because you need to know your baseline, you need to know your ambition level, you need to have the data, not half a year later, when your fiscal year is over. You need to have these on at least a quarterly basis, and really across your entire value chain. And only with that basis can you steer your business accordingly and pin down greenhouse gas emissions to fulfil your ambitious goals (Figs. 3 and 4).

The Sustainability Yearbook – 2023 Rankings

The Sustainability Yearbook 2023 considered over 7,800 companies assessed in the 2022 Corporate Sustainability Assessment (CSA). This page provides the ranking of the 712 companies selected for this year's Yearbook based on their S&P Global ESG Scores calculated from the CSA. Learn more about the Yearbook Methodology.

CATEGORY ⌄	COMPANY NAME ⌄	INDUSTRY ⌄	LOCATION ⌄
● Top 1% S&P Global ESG Score	SAP SE	Software	Germany
● Top 1% S&P Global ESG Score	Temenos AG	Software	Switzerland
◐ Industry Mover ○ Sustainability Yearbook Member	Fortinet, Inc.	Software	United States

Fig. 3 Dow Jones sustainability ranking software sector. Source: S&P Global, https://www.spglobal.com/esg/csa/yearbook/2023/ranking/

Fig. 4 CDP climate change 2022 company rating. Source: www.cdp.net/en/

Company	Score
SAP SE	A-
Publicis Groupe SA	B
Sappi	B
Sapporo Holdings Limited	B
Saputo Inc.	B
Sapphire Textile Mills Limited	D
Norsk Hydro ASA	D

Uwe Schulte

I understand, and it is important. Initially we have seen less than one hundred companies committing to zero-based emissions by different time scales from 2025 to until 2050, depending on the company and the industry sector they are in. But now almost 1500 companies are committing to those targets. Enabling measurement and certification around that will play an increasingly vital role and that is why I was raising that question with you. Of course, other people will provide services as well, but I think companies like yourselves that are in the middle and can foster collaboration across boundaries will play a vital role. Having said that, it sounds ambitious to me to be able to do this on a product level because it requires a lot of data.

Daniel Schmid

You are right. Let us look back for a moment. For decades, our customers have used our systems to be as efficient as possible. Think about ERP, Enterprise Resource Planning.[8] It is all about dealing with resources, financial resources, material resources, human resources in the best and most efficient way. But as soon as the product leaves the gate, there is no transparency anymore. But that is required for the urgent move towards circularity. And you do not only need the data coming out of your own production and logistics systems, but you also need to have transparency across the entire value chain. And that means collaborating with your business partners, with your suppliers, with your customers, and sharing these data. That is why we decided to join the World Business Council for Sustainable Development and McKinsey with the Pathfinder Project,[9] which is about sharing carbon emission data across company boundaries. We are coming from a history where companies tend to say 'These are my data. I am keeping it for myself, I do not share them'. But what we urgently need for our planet is to share these data in a systematic, standardised way, in a trusted way, where people can rely on the data to really bring down their emissions in a way you just described with having so many commitments from companies around the world (Fig. 5).

Fig. 5 Pathfinder project. Source: public domain, The Pathfinder Framework, https://www.wbcsd.org/Programs/Climate-and-Energy/Climate/SOS-1.5/Resources/Pathfinder-Framework-Version-2.0

---

[8] https://en.wikipedia.org/wiki/Enterprise_resource_planning

[9] https://www.carbon-transparency.org/pact-methodology

Uwe Schulte

You already talked about your job and your role with a lot of enthusiasm, and that you engage with so many different stakeholders. One stakeholder group I am especially interested in are the customers. As we already discussed, you must work through your customers to bring your purpose to life. That is quite a challenge, I would say. Can you share a little bit how you go about that?

Daniel Schmid

I am happy to do so. It was a journey, and it is still a journey, also internally at SAP. Sometimes when I talk to colleagues, they tell me that we need to do this or that in our canteen, or in our company car fleet. And then I tell them that they are right, but that the biggest impact we have is enabling our customers on their transformation journey with digital transformation and bringing in our SAP portfolio. That makes an enormous difference to them. But to do so, you need to understand where your customer is. And you need to understand that sustainability has clearly become a core business topic. And for us, we agreed on core sustainability priorities like climate action or circular economy or having an inclusive and skilled workforce, to ensure our investments towards enabling our customers to run their business holistically and as efficient as possible. And I am being honest, Uwe, efficiency alone will not get us there. To solve today's societal and environmental challenges, we need to bring in innovation. We need to bring in embedded sustainability criteria in our data models, in our solutions, so that our customers have the full transparency across the entire value chain. And then these sustainability criteria must relate to financial indicators. And that leads to innovation, that leads to new business models, that leads to business transformation, which is urgently needed. So again, efficiency alone will not solve today's challenges. We need innovation and digital transformation.

Uwe Schulte

I understand that but let us focus on that challenge of the customer. At the end of the day, he provides your business, and he might not share your vision of sustainability. And then the question is, how do you manage to engage with the customer to create that common goal?

Daniel Schmid

I would not fully agree with your perspective, Uwe, because I would say that, at least in the past 2 years, I have seen an accelerated movement where CEOs have understood that there is a huge risk to not finding customers or consumers anymore purchasing their goods and services, and not finding any talents in the future who would work for their company, if they do not embed sustainability in their core business strategy. And that is what I do to prepare and be best informed, before I engage with a customer. I look at their purpose and then I check the ambition level of their targets, but even more importantly, I check what they already achieved on their journey and whether sustainability really is embedded in their business strategy. Engaging with these customers and showing the connection between the so-called non-financials—we should call them pre-financials because they have a massive impact on your financial performance—has a massive impact on the value of your company and whether you are successful in the market or not, in the mid and long term. Showing that connection helps customers understand that they must change and embed sustainability in their core business strategy. Do not get me wrong, there are distinguished role models out there in different sectors and I learn a lot from them. There are different maturity levels though. There are companies looking at sustainability purely from a risk perspective, then there are the ones looking at it from an efficiency perspective, then there are the ones looking at it more from an opportunity perspective, not just bottom line but top line perspective, and the most advanced are the ones looking at it as an opportunity for innovation.

Uwe Schulte
I would like to get a grip on how you do that. Can we work through a practical example? There is a customer, you want to engage with him. Is the sales force on your side? Are they approaching you? How does it work?

Daniel Schmid
They approach me. Every day I receive e-mails from the field, from our account executives and managing partners dealing with the customer relations, reaching out to me because there are various aspects. #1 Sustainability has become a core business topic and is high on the strategic agenda of our customers across the various industries and sectors. #2 Due to that network I have in a trustful way with my peers and other companies, I can open a channel. Because of our heritage, we are well connected to the colleagues in the IT departments of our customers, with the CIO and the folks there. Having them access business decision makers in the lines of business through me is another element I can bring in as well, as an additional benefit, which is highly appreciated by our colleagues in sales functions.

Uwe Schulte
Sorry for being pedantic, but how does it work? Are you sitting together with sales in a team, discussing how to approach the customer or how does it work?

Daniel Schmid
It typically works in a way that I am asked to join the customer meeting. Before that I will have a preparation meeting with the sales team to explain what works and what does not work. And what works very well is to start with the customer and listen to their approach, listen to their targets, listen to the challenges they have on their journey to embed sustainability in their business strategy and in their business. It is challenging and there are different material topics depending on the business model and the industry the customers are in. And then I reflect on that by sharing our journey, for example. We already had a clear focus on sustainability 12 years ago, and I am immensely proud that now with our renewed business strategy sustainability is even more prominently embedded in our derived product strategy. Our board member Thomas Saueressig who is responsible for product engineering, for our product portfolio, is so committed and says that sustainability management is well anchored in our evolved vision of an intelligent enterprise, so it is part of our portfolio. Using that and sharing our learnings from our journey helps a lot in these

customer conversations. After that we can decide together where to put the focus. The carbon topic is important for every company, followed by circular economy, reporting needs and holistic steering tools, covering transactional topics as well as analytical topics. But it is important to gain the customer's trust and you can only gain their trust if you can share with them what you have achieved in your own business operations and learnings from what we call the exemplar strategy, and then use these learnings in our product strategy. One concrete example, Uwe, is that I share the sustainability dashboard we have in our hands, which is accessible for 100,000 colleagues around the clock at SAP, where they see their own numbers, not just the ones of our CEO, Christian Klein, and our CFO Dominik Asam. On earnings day quarter by quarter, they not only share financial performance, but indicators like women in management, employee retention, and carbon emissions. On the same day, the colleagues have the data in their hands, their own data. They could say that they are only one of 100,000 and cannot influence SAP's performance. They see however the carbon emissions of their team, for example, and what emissions sources lead to the performance. They have the full transparency. When I share that with customers, they tell me 'Wow, Daniel, I need that'! and then I respond that the analytical tool that lies behind the dashboard is one thing, but getting the data in is a different thing. And then we are in a business conversation about the core business processes. Many companies in the chemical or discrete manufacturing industry already run systems like SAP's environment, health, and safety solutions to proactively identify, analyse, and mitigate environmental, health, and safety risks, so they can manage their chemicals safely, or monitor industrial hygiene, or reduce their environmental impact. Many customers have already been using SAP solutions for many years. But now we have achieved the next level, having that full understanding that sustainability management is anchored in our portfolio and that we embed data, and we start with greenhouse gas emissions. But we think broadly, we think about water or social indicators, energy consumption and others, to create that full transparency that allows our customers to steer their business holistically. That is the way how we conduct these conversations. And again, Uwe, with every conversation, I learn a lot from our customers as well, often thinking 'that is a cool best practise we could apply in our own operation'.

Uwe Schulte
If I would ask your salespeople, would they say, 'it is nice to have you on board' or would they say, 'it is essential to have Daniel and his team on board to engage with customers'? It is a bit of a naughty question to ask, I know.

Daniel Schmid
It is a fair point, and I observed a change over the past years. I would say from a nice tool to a wow-effect. And as you might know, and our audience might know, the fourth quarter of the fiscal year is always the most important one. I received several e-mails from sales colleagues who told me 'Daniel, thanks again for your support, we made the deal thanks to you and your engagement and thanks to the trustful conversation you were able to conduct with the customer'. So, there definitely is a change. Today I had a call with a colleague who now has a key role in the region.

Carlos Diaz is responsible on a regional level, like the Chief Sustainability Officer, in the southern part of Europe, Middle East, Africa. Knowing that we need to better understand the challenges of our customers, what is material to them, we need to enable the colleagues in the field as well. They are not the deep experts, and they cannot be the deep experts on that, for many companies. We need to understand how we can best scale and enable them to drive the conversation with the customers in the direction where it is beneficial for both. Regarding how we develop our solutions, co-innovation is key, and it has never been so easy. That is what I learned from my colleagues in product engineering. It has never been so easy to find customers collaborating with us in the field of climate action, in the field of circular economy, in the field of holistic steering reporting. They want to be part of that journey and we need to understand their needs, their demand, what data is needed, how to ensure data consistency across the entire value chain. It is a major part of our internal methodology how we develop software in a co-innovation way with our customers. Selecting the right customers is another challenge for us, because they all tell us that they are the standard, etc. You need to select the thought leaders; you need to select the ones from each industry where you believe they are doing the right things that could help the entire industry to transform. And collaborating with them and innovating together with them is key for us (Fig. 6).

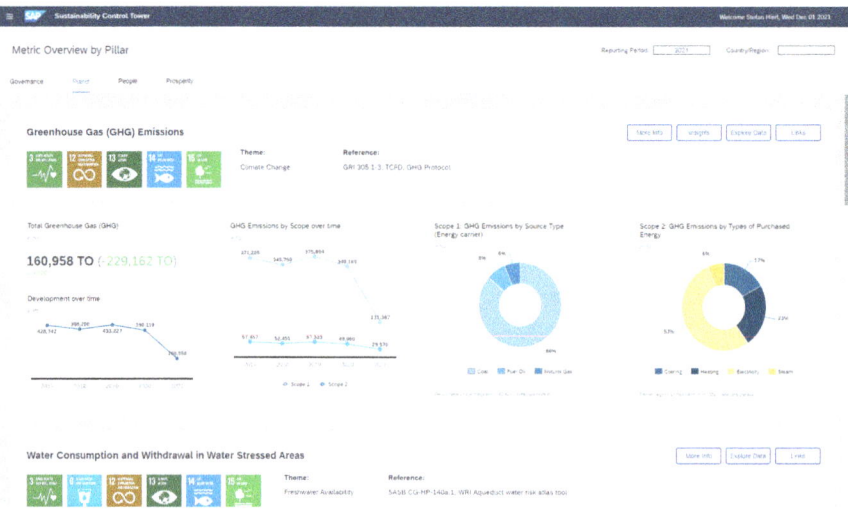

Fig. 6 SAP Sustainability Control Tower. Source: www.sap.com, https://blogs.sap.com/2021/12/14/getting-esg-reporting-and-performance-management-under-control-with-the-sap-sustainability-control-tower/

Uwe Schulte

We have not talked about reducing the carbon footprint of the SAP employees; we have talked about helping major contributors to greenhouse gas getting transparency on their data to be able to improve that. That is very encouraging because as it enables SAP to do more business. We started the conversation by saying that people said in the beginning that you either are successful at sustainability or you are successful in business, but both things do not go together. It seems to me that you just explained that things have turned.

Daniel Schmid

Yes, absolutely. It addresses these various facets of the overall business case. One is, of course, if we reduce our energy consumption in our data centres by being as efficient as possible, we save money. It has a significant impact. Regarding our own journey in the past 3 years, we were able to cumulatively avoid costs of almost €300 million in our own operations due to our focus on carbon emissions. Just to share that number with you. The other aspect is, and that leads to where I was coming from, the category of risk perspective, opportunity perspective, efficiency perspective, or strategic innovation perspective. That is why I am so proud of our renewed business strategy. You can see that sustainability now is an innovation topic, it is a strategic topic for SAP, where we helped our customers in the past to manage their top line, to manage their bottom line, and now we also manage their green line.

Knowing that sustainability is more than just green, but let us start with that, with greenhouse gas emissions and climate action that is urgently needed. S During Sapphire 2022, our customer conference, our CEO Christian Klein talked about resiliency, profitability, and sustainability. And these three terms are connected. So, it is really a strategic approach, it is a business case, it is a business approach. I am happy and I am proud that we also see that as a top-line opportunity for ourselves. But Uwe, our customers expect that from SAP too, to help them deal with the current challenges and turn these challenges into opportunities.

Uwe Schulte

I do not know whether you are able to share this, but it would be interesting to know. When you look at the recent customer conversations you had, could you share what the major requirements are that people recently are raising, challenging you/SAP?

Daniel Schmid

They are looking for data consistency, they are looking for connecting data, helping them to have that holistic view. That is quite critical, and it is important to also apply standardised methodologies which are not yet in place for all the sustainability fields we are talking about. We joined the Value Balancing Alliance [10] as a founding member to do exactly that. To cooperate with other companies, front runners and thought leaders in that field of impact valuation, and to standardise the methodology in a way that it can be implemented in a very pragmatic way. We started with the piloting phase mid of last year and the first results are remarkably interesting. Then

---

[10] https://www.value-balancing.com/

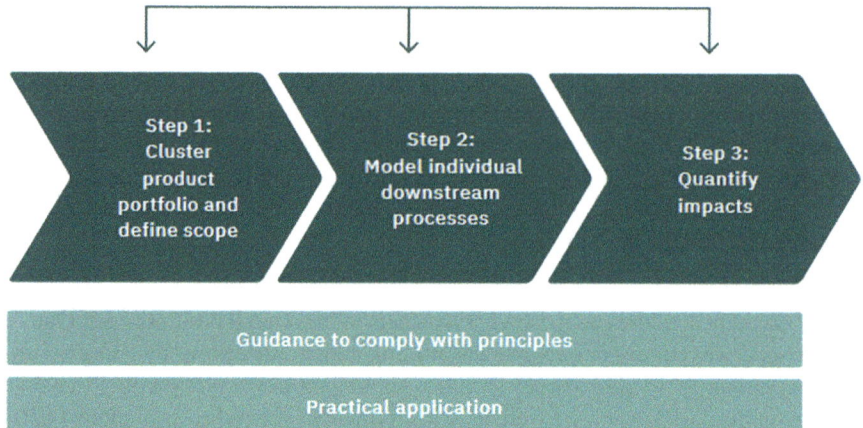

Fig. 7 Value Balancing Alliance impact approach. Source: CC BY-ND 4.0 DEED, Attribution-NoDerivs 4.0 International

we further reshaped that methodology. The basic idea is about having that valuation of impact–I am fully convinced that this is the future: Looking at what the business impact of your core business activities on the environment is, and what the impact on society is, and then putting a euro or a dollar behind that. The valuation of it is particularly important. That is what our customers are really looking for and then challenging us to help them. Look at the dynamics coming from the EU green deal,[11] the sustainable finance topic,[12] the EU taxonomy topic[13]—from 2021 on, companies need to create transparency about their so-called sustainable investment and sustainable revenue streams, Operational Expenses (OpEx), Capital Expenses (CapEx) and revenues and show that these data are used by the investors, while the investors are asked by the EU legislation to show the transparency of their investment portfolio. What investments are sustainable and what investments are not, based on their taxonomy. Dealing with that is a huge challenge for our customers and for ourselves. But do not get me wrong, it is the right direction, because the ambition of the EU is to guide the capital markets and the investments towards sustainable development, which is needed (Fig. 7).

Uwe Schulte
You raised the term addressed by the Value Balancing Alliance and that is a huge topic. Let me just point out that the Conference Board has published a report,[14] also in collaboration with you, on that approach of total impact valuation that you were

---

[11] https://commission.europa.eu/strategy-and-policy/priorities-2019-2024/european-green-deal_en

[12] https://finance.ec.europa.eu/sustainable-finance_en

[13] https://joint-research-centre.ec.europa.eu/scientific-activities-z/sustainable-finance/eu-taxonomy_en

[14] https://www.conference-board.org/topics/ESG-reporting/Total-Impact-Valuation-Overview

referring to. Monetising all impacts of a company, summarising them, balancing them out, and seeing what your overall impact is. And impact means things like the amount of training you do, the amount of water you consume, and all these elements and monetising them. And if people are interested in that, the report is available on the Conference Board website. It is interesting what you are saying is that you have now made strides in harmonising the approach, because there are lots of different approaches there, and that is, of course, what is needed to make that a more generally applicable tool, is that not right?

Daniel Schmid

Yes, absolutely. And stakeholders expect that they can compare data. But only if you can produce a standard, stakeholders can compare their performance. Reporting is one aspect, but the most interesting part of it, from my perspective, is the internal steering aspect for companies. For them to really have the full transparency across the entire value chain and the effects and knowing how they can bring in this kind of holistic thinking, Uwe. Coming from that history of financial optimisation and financial decision processes to 'Let us keep what we had and add to it, what is the impact on the environment, on our planet and what is the impact on society, on us, on human beings'. And that leads to better business decisions and better business outcomes, so that is crucial. But again, coming back to the topic where you challenged me about how we deal with customers. You mentioned the purpose of SAP about helping the world run better and improving people's lives. You see increasingly purpose-driven companies[15] out there as well. We will now pilot a methodology in sales, where we think about how we can better address that topic and drive conversations in a well-educated way with our customers about purpose, and through collaboration, because that is needed to achieve great ambitions. We currently focus on strategic accounts; we start with piloting those. I am looking forward to my first customer conversations I will have in the next days, applying that methodology, where it is about looking at these four pillars, about reaching an alignment, a collective understanding of the company purpose to mobilise, to design, and to deliver. And a concrete outcome of such a conversation is to then have an agreement to do what we call a Purpose Impact Lab. That is when we kickstart the collaboration towards a joint road map and that would include senior executives up to C-level, from both the customer and from SAP, to have these deep dive workstreams and conversations established. This is really helping our customers, but ourselves as well, to have that purpose-based conversation and driving outcomes. We have seen so many pledges, targets, and commitments, but we need to turn these pledges into real action. And Purpose Impact Lab is about real action. How to do it? How to add the baseline? What is the target? How to manage that? What innovation is required in the business model? What kind of business transformation, what kind of digital transformation is needed to support that business transformation? I am really looking forward to these conversations in the next days.

---

[15] https://www.conference-board.org/topics/sustainable-business-integration/purpose-driven-companies-lessons-learned

Uwe Schulte

That sounds very encouraging and interesting, and that merits another conversation. I am glad you mentioned two words that are close to my heart as well—outcome and impact. It is not only about ambition. Ambitions are important, but we really must manage for outcome and impact rather than just compliance and risk avoidance. Thank you so much Daniel, for sharing your work with customers. It is extremely interesting, and this is also applicable for companies beyond the IT sector. This is much appreciated, thank you so much.

Daniel Schmid

Thank you, Uwe. It was a pleasure! Thank you so much for having me.

Chemical Recycling

Recorded April 2021

Uwe Schulte

Today I will be talking to Lars Kissau, Senior Vice President, Global Strategic Business Development at BASF's Petrochemical Division.[1] We will discuss a potential answer to the plastic waste problem—chemical recycling. First, let me introduce our guest, Lars Kissau. Lars joined BASF 18 years ago as a marketing manager. He spent 7 years in Southeast Asia and China in different roles, and, returning to Europe, he served 3 years as Senior Vice President Corporate Strategy and Sustainability. Now, as SVP Strategic Business Development, he is driving the digitalisation of the Petrochemical Division that is responsible for steering relevant strategy and marketing topics globally for that division. Lars achieved his PhD in Organic Chemistry at the Max Planck Institute for Molecular Physiology. Welcome, Lars. Please tell us a little bit about yourself.

Lars Kissau

Well, thank you for the introduction, Uwe. It is a pleasure to be here. You already covered the key points of my biography. What is not on the CV, and I also did not put that on LinkedIn, is the passion behind of what is driving me, which is to leave behind a better planet for future generations. So being a chemist by training, I am very thankful that BASF has given me the opportunity to do something in that direction, in every position. That is why I am excited to be here to talk about chemical recycling. This is a great topic, and it motivates me and my team tremendously.

---

[1] Since January 2022, Dr Lars Kissau heads the newly established Net Zero Accelerator unit. In this unit, BASF bundles the extensive cross-company activities with which the company aims to achieve its ambitious climate protection goals. The unit focuses on implementing and accelerating projects on low-carbon production technologies, circular economy, and renewable energies.

© The Author(s), under exclusive license to Springer Nature Switzerland AG 2024
U. G. Schulte, *Sustainable Business*, CSR, Sustainability, Ethics & Governance,
https://doi.org/10.1007/978-3-031-58596-8_9

Uwe Schulte

Before we get started on that, we need to define what we mean by chemical recycling of plastic waste. From my perspective, it is a conversion of plastic waste through heat and pressure into the molecules that were originally the different plastics from the start. I guess you can explain this better for our audience which has a limited chemistry background.

Lars Kissau

That sums it up quite well. Usually, chemical recycling refers to technologies that break down long polymer chains[2] of the plastics into their basic building blocks. This is really the main difference to mechanical recycling in which the plastics keep their polymer structure as they are only cleaned, shredded, melted down, and reprocessed. The most used chemical recycling technology is pyrolysis, in which the plastics are converted into pyrolysis oil by treating them at temperatures of 300 to 700 degrees in the absence of oxygen. And the oil that you get can be used as a feedstock for chemical production, as a replacement for many of the fossil feedstocks commonly used today. Another method of chemical recycling is called depolymerisation.[3] In this process, you take certain plastics and you break the polymers down into the monomers. For instance, if you look at a plastic polyamide called polycaprolactone, it can be broken down into the monomer caprolactam, cleaned up and used again. This type of process only works for single-material plastics. The pyrolysis really applies for all the materials (Fig. 1).

Uwe Schulte

Lars, if you depolymerise, you break it down to the original constituent. But that only works for pure plastics, as you said. Pyrolysis goes a step further. It makes it into an oil again, but it is not fossil, it is recycled through the thermochemical processing of the plastic.[4] Is that right?

---

[2] https://en.wikipedia.org/wiki/Plastic

[3] https://en.wikipedia.org/wiki/Thermal_depolymerization

[4] https://www.pyrum.net/

Chemical Recycling

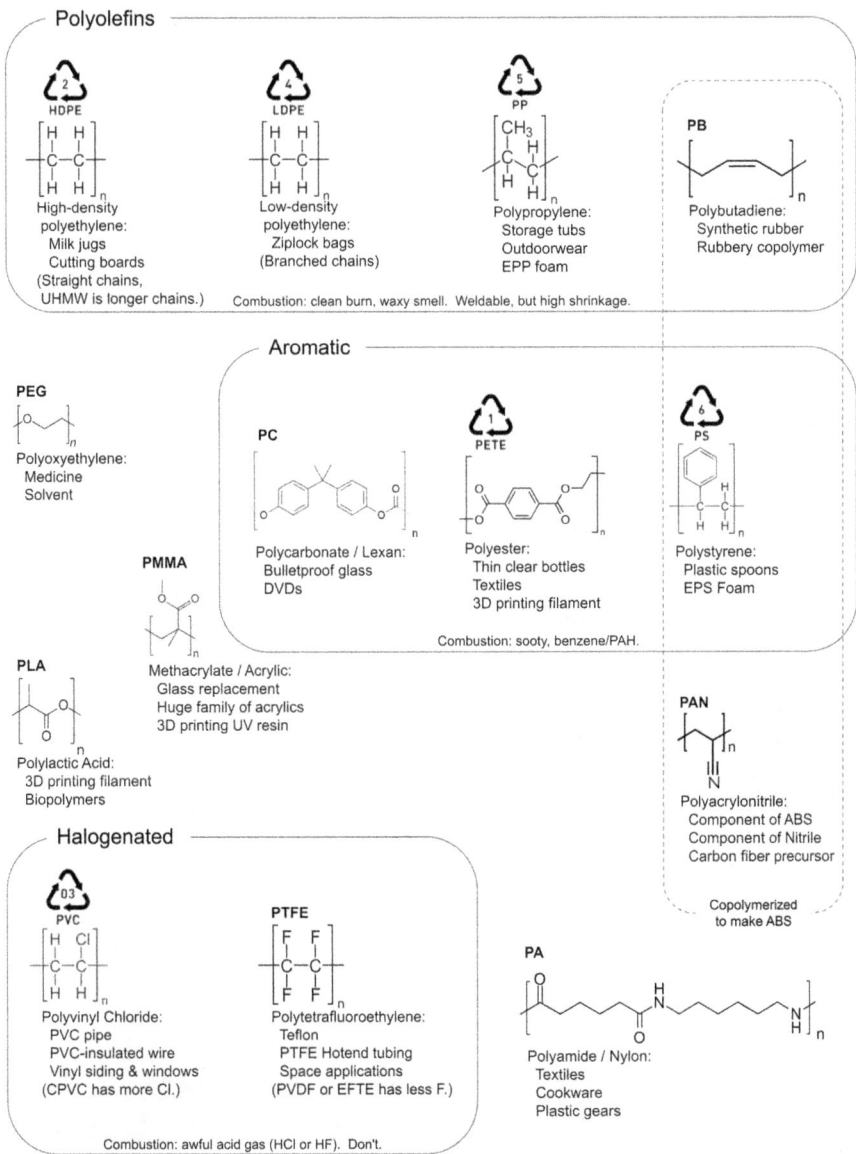

Fig. 1 Plastic polymers. Source: Wikipedia, https://upload.wikimedia.org/wikipedia/commons/5/5f/Plastics_Summary.svg, CC0 1.0 DEED, CC0 1.0 Universal, Author: Orion Lawlor, Source: own work

Lars Kissau

That is correct, yes.

Uwe Schulte

I hope that we have defined chemical recycling sufficiently. It is an emerging technology and you at BASF have launched this as ChemCycling. I wonder, how did this evolve? Where did this whole idea start in your company and how did you play a role in this?

Lars Kissau

The first idea for this project came up a couple of years ago when I was still in my role in the Corporate Strategy and Sustainability Unit. There, we had two trains of thought coming together at the beginning. On the one hand, my team and I felt that BASF should, as everybody in the plastics value chain, contribute to solving the issue with plastic waste. If you look at it globally, we have about 250 million tonnes of plastic waste produced every year and only about 20% of that being recycled. And the other two hundred million tonnes are landfilled and incinerated or, and this is the worst-case scenario, they end up in the environment. Being a large producer of mostly durable engineering plastics, but still plastics, we felt that it is important to be part of conducting business responsibly to engage in addressing the issue of plastic waste (Fig. 2).

Uwe Schulte

Lars, I am so sorry to interrupt. You just gave a definition of durable plastics. Let us explain that because there are several types of plastic here. The material I know as a consumer is when I buy something, it is usually somehow packaged in plastic. So that is single-use plastic. What you are talking about is more in my household—I have pipes in my house that are made of plastic, for example (Fig. 3). [5]

Lars Kissau

Pipes, window frames, insulation materials, structural components: these are things I would call durable, because after they have been produced, they stay in use for p20–30 years in some cases (Fig. 4).

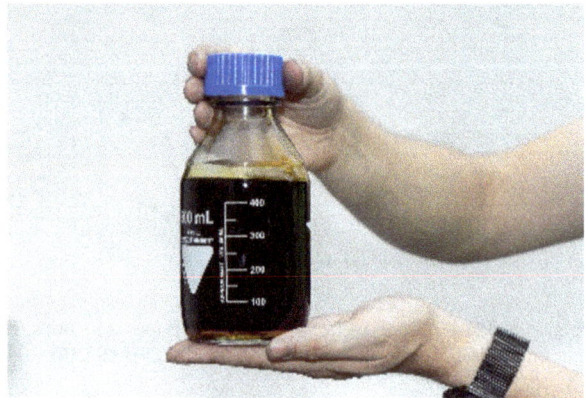

Fig. 2 Pyrolysis oil from Pyrum. Source: www.basf.com

---

[5] https://www.conference-board.org/topics/plastic/plastic-solid-waste-management

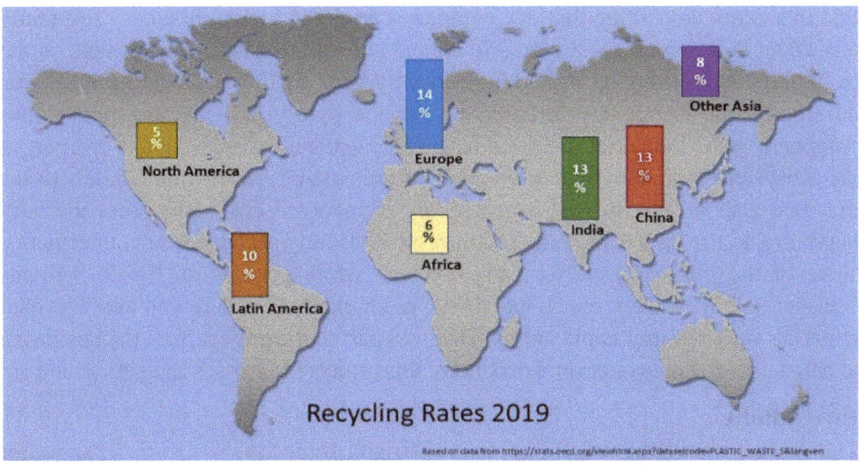

Fig. 3 Global plastic recycling rates. Source: Uwe G. Schulte

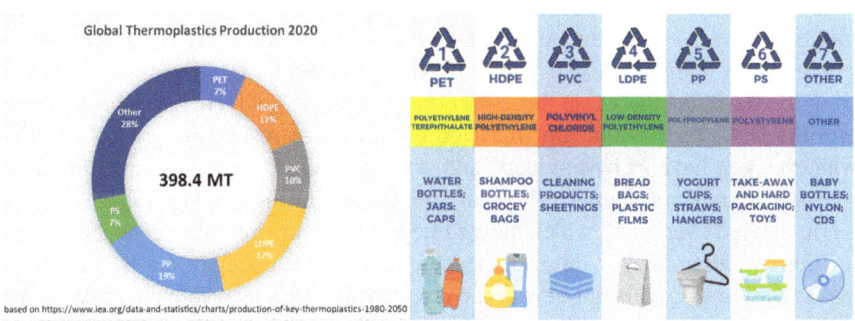

Fig. 4 Plastic types. Source: Plastics for Change, https://www.plasticsforchange.org/blog/different-types-of-plastic (right part), Uwe G. Schulte (left part)

Uwe Schulte
Sorry for interrupting, but I believe it to be important to make that distinction.

Lars Kissau
As I was saying, the second train of thought that came to that was if we want to meet the targets of the Paris Agreement and reduce CO2 emissions, we really must shift the economy towards a more circular economy. We must reduce CO2 emissions and we must replace fossil feedstocks. This was the second consideration that, aside from addressing the plastic waste issue, we saw an opportunity with ChemCycling to avoid CO2 emissions from burning plastic waste and to replace fossil fuels or fossil feedstocks for chemistry. Those were the two considerations at the starting point. The technology itself is not new. If you go back the many years that pyrolysis has been around, there have been various attempts. What we then said early on was

that this is not something that one company can do or should do alone. You really talk about building an ecosystem. We looked and collaborated with partners on the technology side, bringing it from its currently very small scale, scaling it up, and developing the technology further. Most of the pyrolysis plants are quite minor compared to the industrial scale you have in a chemical industry. That is one part of the ecosystem. And then of course collaborating with customers immediately to see that you also get the market acceptance. We involved customers from the very beginning in the project as well. You may have recently seen some announcements, some of the pilot projects we have done on white goods with Bosch Siemens Hausgeräte.[6] We have some cooperations, as an example, where you take c-cycled materials into end-user applications. That was part of the project from the beginning to help build this ecosystem and make sure this project progresses and gets scaled up.

Uwe Schulte
This project was conceived, if I got your CV right, at the time when you were Senior Vice President Strategy and Sustainability. How does that fit into the overall sustainability strategy? It is, as I can see it now, still a minor component.

Lars Kissau
Volume-wise, yes, but if you go back in history, and this is quite a telling story for me, BASF was founded in 1865 by a guy named Friedrich Engelhorn who was a goldsmith by training. And if you think about the work of a goldsmith, he learns from the start that any waste that he produces is worth gold. He really brought this into the DNA of the company, that you do not waste resources, you try to reuse whatever you have as by-products, and you try to close loops wherever possible. This sustainability thought has been in the company all along and we like to use the German word 'Verbund', which means integration. This 'Verbund' concept for production is really based on this start. The thought of conducting business sustainably and saving resources is not new to the company. What is new is the circular economy programme that we started that was announced in December 2020.[7] Trying to really move the whole industry from linear value chains to circular ones. In this programme, chemical recycling plays a key role, where we really want to scale up the technology and get to a point where we can replace significant amounts of virgin feedstock with recycled feedstock (Fig. 5).

Uwe Schulte
That makes sense for me but let us investigate this a little bit more in detail. There are several companies that have started looking into chemical recycling and you see announcements left, right, and centre. Would it not make sense that because it is such an important and crucial part of what we are trying to achieve here, to bring these different forces together and exploit the synergies?

---

[6] https://www.basf.com/global/en/media/news-releases/2021/03/p-21-161.html

[7] https://www.basf.com/global/en/who-we-are/sustainability/we-drive-sustainable-solutions/circular-economy.html

Fig. 5 BASF ChemCycling project. Source: BASF, https://www.basf.com/at/de/who-we-are/sustainability/whats-new/sustainability-news/2021/BASF-quantafuel-and-remondis-want-to-cooperate-on-chemical-recycling-of-plastic-waste.html

Lars Kissau

Absolutely. I would think it does not only make sense, but it is also a necessity that the players in the value chain and many of the companies working on similar approaches join forces. Let me give you an example if I just look at the 2018 numbers. In Europe, about 42% of the post-consumer plastic waste was recycled and the ambition, the EU target, is bringing that to 55%. In volumes that means we must recycle another 2.3 million tonnes of plastic that today cannot be recycled. Of course, mechanical recycling is well-established and there will be a certain part of the volume that can and should be recycled mechanically. But if I only assume that half of this volume of this ambition in Europe requires chemical recycling, then that is another 1.1 million tonnes of plastic. At the current scale, a normal pyrolysis plant as it is built today, is around 10,000 tonnes, slightly more. That would mean we have to build another one hundred pyrolysis plants until 2030 to at least manage this target. This is not something that one company can do; this also still requires a lot of technology development and hopefully also scale-up to build larger plants. And that is why it is necessary that companies join forces and do this together (Fig. 6).

Uwe Schulte

You just mentioned a shocking number. I think some members of our audience will be surprised to find how little is being recycled in plastic. The public has become more aware of this since we have seen plastic floating in the oceans, but it has been a problem that has been around for a long time, and I am glad that people are picking it up. Here we are dealing with is the part of plastic waste that is more difficult to recycle. If I have a single stream of plastic, as we discussed before, if I have PET, for example, and it is pure PET, that is a different thing. But in Germany, we have

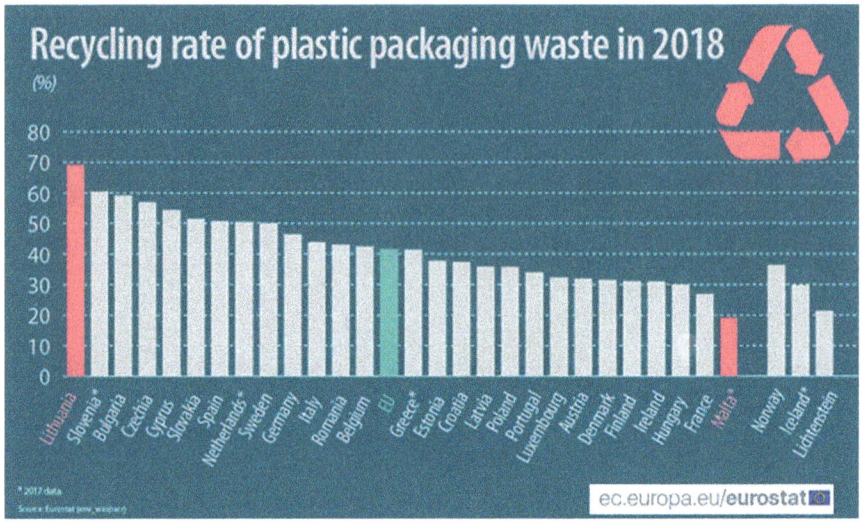

Fig. 6 Plastic packaging recycling rates 2018 Europe. Source: Eurostat, https://ec.europa.eu/eurostat/de/web/products-eurostat-news/-/ddn-20210113-1, modifications: UK data deleted as per https://ec.europa.eu/eurostat/web/main/about-us/policies/copyright

the famous 'yellow sack' and where we put soiled packaging. That is what we are talking about here, is it not?

Lars Kissau
Yes, but to be clear, a significant part of the volume of plastic waste today is mechanically recycled and I think it should be, because it is well-established, you mentioned PET. That is a stream of waste where the recycling that is set up works very well. What we are really looking at with chemical recycling are those streams, those materials that are difficult to recycle or currently not recycled. I really see it as a complementary solution, something that we can add on to what we are already doing and expand the overall volume of plastic waste that can be reused and simply avoid incineration.

Uwe Schulte
This sounds like something worth pursuing. But there are critical voices here and we should not ignore them. Let me ask you about this. People say that what you are doing, and we just talked about a lot of degrees centigrade, is not necessary. It is energy-intensive, the yield is low and, it does not save any CO_2 emissions. Why is it a route worth pursuing then?

Lars Kissau
Those are valid questions and, to be honest, at the very start of the project, this is exactly what we asked ourselves, too. Considering that you need these temperatures—does this make sense? If I look at where the process is now, again it is still early stage, the technology can be developed further, but if we look at the

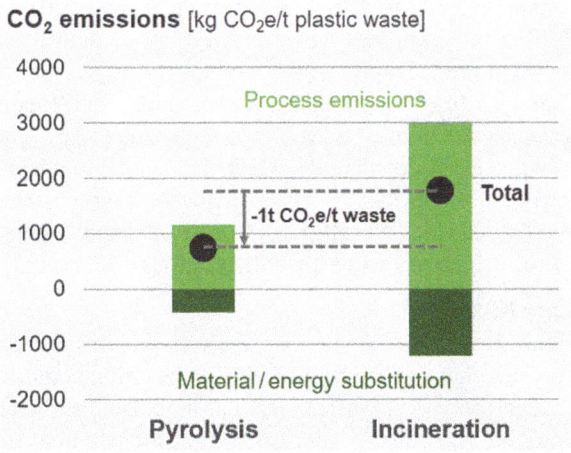

Fig. 7 Sphera life cycle assessment of chemical recycling vs incineration. Source: BASF, https://www.basf.com/global/de.html

facts—today, if you do pyrolysis of plastic waste, about 70% of the volume that you put in is recovered as pyrolysis oil. The rest is usually converted into a gas that is currently used to heat the process. In theory, you could also do further chemistry with the gas, depending on how you set it up. But there is also quite a good yield already. And again, this is on a small scale, this can and will be increased. We then also looked at the CO2 emissions, and it is important to look at the whole life cycle here. And that is where we did this project early on, a life cycle assessment. We had that conducted by a company called Sphera,[8] and we had the results that they produced vetted by external independent experts, because we wanted to make sure that it is a real rock-solid comparison. What this analysis really shows is that if you compare the chemical recycling of plastic waste to alternatives such as incineration, your CO2 footprint is about 50% less. In terms of preserving carbon for further chemical use as a structural material instead of burning it and emitting it as CO2, there is a benefit, and this is what that life cycle assessment shows. With these results, we realised that what we are doing makes sense, we are not doing nonsense.[9] This is a good project, and it has a positive contribution to both, the original aim to reduce CO2 emissions and the aim to recover carbon for further chemical use (Fig. 7).

Uwe Schulte

There is another aspect here which, in my mind, is especially important. Provided that you will work on the yield, provided that the energy balance is going to be more positive, and we are on a learning curve here—I give you that, but the other aspect for me is that you are dealing with plastic waste that otherwise has only two possible ways. Either it is going to be dumped somewhere or it is going to be burned. We

---

[8] https://sphera.com/life-cycle-assessment-lca-software/

[9] https://www.basf.com/global/documents/en/sustainability/we-drive-sustainable-solutions/circular-economy/2020-09-21_LCA_ChemCycling_Slide_deck.pdf

cannot pretend that chemical recycling is competing with pure stream recycling of PET or, for example, scraps in the plastics industry, which are pure and can be recycled immediately, which we call primary recycling. That is not what we are dealing with. We are looking at something else. What really concerns me—I have seen all these dumps and you must have seen these in Asia as well, these wild dumps of waste in the countryside, which then leak into rivers and then basically end up in the ocean. If that then becomes a valuable resource, then it is going to be interesting. But do you think we will be able to scale this to a point where in these parts of the world we can make this a viable solution?

Lars Kissau

Honestly, yes. We must. I love to travel, and this was one of the more shocking discoveries, that you can be in incredibly beautiful countries, and you turn a corner and suddenly you see a waste dump that should not be there, with lots of plastic. Or, like you said, you go swimming, or you see the pictures. This is a problem that must be solved. At the current stage of technology development, plants with 10,000 tonnes or 15,000 tonnes are small. It would be important to scale that and reduce the investment cost to bring this up. What is also important is that it makes economic sense (Fig. 8).

All the companies that are looking into this will be looking to create a viable business model out of this. That is what you mentioned. It does not make sense to chemically recycle PET or the single product streams that already have another recycling solution. There is an established business for that. That is not going to be a viable model to come in with chemical recycling. Those streams are going to be valued too high. This is where I see that chemical recycling is really an additive

Fig. 8 Plastic garbage landfill, Vietnam. Source: Böll Foundation. Photo: Lê Đình Tuyển

solution. Some streams will be perfectly suitable for mechanical recycling and other streams are the ones that we should address with chemical recycling.

Uwe Schulte

That is the recycling question but let us face another challenge here. The real work we should be doing is to completely redesign the value chains to avoid plastic and to reduce the use of plastic at least. Is that not the better way?

Lars Kissau

To a certain degree, yes. I am sure you have seen this printed in many places—the 'reduce, reuse, recycle' slogan. And I like that. Globally we are obviously using way too much of the earth's resources, so we need to reduce the use and be more resource-efficient, in any way. If we look at single-use plastics and some of the actions taken globally, it clearly makes perfect sense to reduce the use of materials in that sense. Obviously, reusing materials, designing them for a longer lifespan is important. Recycling can be part of the equation. I do believe though that plastic itself is not the problem, it is how we deal with it. There are some applications or some benefits of plastic that will be difficult to replace. It allows us to make durable lightweight wind rotor blades, build cars in a lighter way, some of the food packaging made with plastic materials preserves food and avoids wastage or spoilage of food. If we try to do that without plastic materials and some of these high-performance materials, we will incur other downsides that we do not want. Banning plastics, to be blunt, would be the wrong move because you create a whole lot of other problems. Being more careful how to design products and then closing the loops to reuse the materials is really the target state for which we should aim.

Uwe Schulte

I get that, but we should be clear—plastic forks or straws are not necessary and to avoid them is a straightforward thing. We have gone overboard because it was cheap and easy to use. Let me come back. You just mentioned the usefulness of plastic. The problem that arises, as far as I can tell, but you can correct that, is that we must put different things into the plastic material to achieve the desired performance. That then in itself raises the question how to recycle it? Because you have all these components in there which are unwanted, and in a mixed recycling they would render the recycled material, if you just remelt it, less valuable. Is that correct?

Lars Kissau

One example to consider in this respect is if you look at multi-layer packaging. We all know, if we buy packaged meat or packaged cheese at the supermarket, this is multi-layer packaging, this is not just a single little layer of foil. There are many different layers of varied materials. It is very lightweight, it protects the food from microbes, from oxygen, from moisture. There are a lot of properties that can be built into such a material. And of course, it is not a single plastic material, so when you come to the end of life there, that was your point, then the recycling is more difficult.

That is where I believe chemical recycling would be a particularly useful tool to recycle these materials. Replacing that, for example with a single plastic material, so substituting a multi-layer packaging material with a monolayer, you would have to increase the thickness significantly. You would create a lot more packaging by weight and volume, so you are making the problem of waste worse in the first step, and you might not be able to achieve the properties. This is one of the examples where we have extremely high performing materials, and we just need to make sure we close the loop. And that is where chemical recycling can be a viable solution.

Uwe Schulte
But here I must ask you, Lars, would you be able, in that process of creating that oil out of those mixed plastic materials, to get rid of all these additives and stuff that is in there, which you do not want in the process afterwards. Is that possible?

Lars Kissau
Yes, this is how the pyrolysis plants are supposed to run and deliver. The pyrolysis oil that you want to take into a chemical plant must meet a narrow specification, because chemical plants are built to a certain specified raw material. The task and the before mentioned technology development that must happen, is to further refine how the pyrolysis plants take plastics and the specification of the output. This is clearly a challenge. Depending on how mixed it is and how soiled the material is, you can have a lot of impurities in the plastic that need to be removed before you can take the resulting pyrolysis oil and put it in a chemical plant for new production. It is this purification that is already working, and this is also where we see a lot of technology development work still to be done to bring that to a further higher level and more output.

Uwe Schulte
But this is the unique positioning of this process, isn't it? Having soiled and mixed plastic materials, which nobody else can recycle easily, that would be the positioning for that residual amount. This puts it in an interesting perspective because you produce plastics and resins and therefore the question is how does that fit into your business model?

Lars Kissau
I take the example of engineering plastics that we sell today to many customers, those customers have a high interest to have products that are not based on fossil fuels or have a certain recycled content. Basically, taking plastic materials back and putting the pyrolysis oil made from recycled content into our production and producing new materials with recycled content. This is something that quite a few customers ask for and increasingly ask for, and this is also what is driving us to push the upscaling of the process.

All our integrated sites are really driven by the constant optimisation and conservation of resources. That is at the core. Whatever raw materials we use, we want to use them efficiently and preserve and not waste anything. The larger driver behind it is really this notion of moving to a circular economy. Today we have an economy where economic growth or growth of companies is very linear. The more raw materials you use, the more products you produce, the more you grow. So, it is all driven by more fossil fuels, or fossil resources being taken out of the ground and put into the value chains. And to meet the sustainability goals that we all believe should be met by 2050, according to the Paris Agreement, we will have to wean ourselves off this very linear system and move to a circular system. We cannot just continue using everything based on fossil resources. We will have to adopt and use different raw materials, and this is where the chemical recycling comes in. We want to increase the share of recycled raw materials and reduce our use of fossil resources over time.

Uwe Schulte

It is always interesting for me to understand philosophy and culture of companies. You had mentioned that from the start you were into something. And being a German, I heard the word 'Verbund.' When you go onto the Ludwigshafen site, and I used to be a customer of yours many years ago in another lifetime, 'Verbund' was the word. Please explain this a little bit more for me. It is an interesting thing.

Lars Kissau

If translated, it means nothing more than integration. But what we mean by the concept is that the chemical plants at the site are very much interconnected. The output of one plant is put into the next plant, ideally by pipeline, to convert it further for another product. But every process also creates side products. It creates waste heat or a by-product stream. And we do not just burn by-products or just release the waste heat. We try to use energy created in one process in another process so there is an energy 'Verbund', if you will. The product streams are connected so the by-product of one plant might serve as a raw material in another plant to make other products. You can think of it as a tree—you have a trunk and then it branches out and it is a little bit how the whole production setup works. Everything is very much interconnected and from very few starting raw materials you create a wealth of end products.

Uwe Schulte

That is interesting, because as you know, in the circular economy world, people are starting to say, 'we need this combination of plants to make better use of, for example, waste energy' and so new industry parks are being set up. You are saying that the Ludwigshafen site is sort of a blueprint of that sort of approach?

Lars Kissau

I do not believe you call it blueprint, but it is the same idea. The industry parks also try to do very much the same—instead of transporting materials over long distances, you put plants right next to each other, you have savings there, you have the energy integration, you have all sorts of other benefits. That is the whole notion of industry products that we not only see in Europe, but we also see that to a large degree being pushed in Asia, especially in China. The industry is moving more towards clustering in industry parks.

Uwe Schulte

That was interesting, sorry for side-tracking you here. Let us get back to the pyrolysis and something that immediately springs to mind. We are talking about a technology that is evolving, so let me ask you this—are you running another stream of feedstock into your process that is separate from the one that comes out of a fossil fuel well, or how do you do that? (Fig. 9)

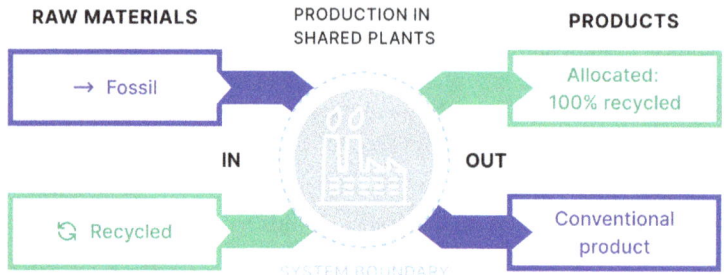

Fig. 9 Mass balance approach. Source: Circularise, https://www.circularise.com/blogs/mass-balance-approach-for-the-sustainable-chemicals-transition

Lars Kissau

No, we do not run it separately. We use the pyrolysis oil as a feedstock alongside the conventional feedstocks. For instance, we can feed it into our steam cracker and there the different raw materials are mixed, and they are then processed together. Looking at the molecules, they become indistinguishable from each other, but we are processing the volumes together. And then in terms of the end products, the recycled content is attributed in what is called a mass balance approach[10] to certain volumes of the end products. The plants are always physically connected, so they know if we feed in pyrolysis oil in one end, the products coming out at the end based on the recycled raw material are connected. We always make sure that there is a physical connection, but it is a mass balance attribution. It is best compared to what people are familiar with regarding green electricity. The electricity that you get out of the outlet in your house may not directly be produced in a local renewable energy facility, but with your purchasing decision to buy green energy, you make sure that somewhere in the grid the corresponding amount of green energy has entered the grid. This is the same approach that we use for recycled raw materials when they are mixed and attributed. The benefit of this is that if you look at the alternative of having segregated parts, as you mentioned, that you would treat it separately, you will have to build up all the plants again, you would have separate raw material streams, separate downstream units. There would be a significant investment required that would slow down the adoption of different raw materials and it might also not be economic. And as I mentioned before, it is also a scale topic. Today, the volume streams of recycled raw materials are still insignificant compared to the overall raw materials being used. This is where the mass balance approach helps to substitute fossil raw materials over time, and at the same time the customers can be sure that if they buy a chemically recycled product, the corresponding amount of recycled raw material of pyrolysis oil has been put into the system.

---

[10] https://www.circularise.com/blogs/mass-balance-approach-for-the-sustainable-chemicals-transition

Uwe Schulte

I am suspicious. You are going to charge more for the recycled material, of course. So, there is this temptation to tweak the numbers. How can I trust that mass balance? You used the green energy analogy, there are some challenges around that as well. How do you get this certified? How do you make sure that I can trust you?

Lars Kissau

We make it auditable. We also spent quite a bit of effort to make sure that we can internally trace the volumes. If you put in 10,000 tonnes in the beginning, where did the volumes get used and are we at a certain period also exactly selling that? So that is auditable. It would ruin the whole concept if you started to fool around with that. It was clear from the very beginning that this must be done properly. Both our mass balance methods as well as our products are certified according to internationally acknowledged certification schemes like REDcert2[11] and ISCC Plus.[12] Obviously, what it also requires is a certain regulatory environment that supports the use of mass balance like it does for green energy. This is also something that is a prerogative to making this technology and making this development succeed.

Uwe Schulte

It requires the pyrolysis oil to be like the fossil feedstock you are using. Does that put a limitation on the process, or can you adjust?

Lars Kissau

I would not say limitation, it puts a certain burden in terms of the purity, obviously. Look at the components that you can find in many plastics. For example, you might have chlorine, or something included and of course that would be highly corrosive in any chemical plants. These are the components that must be removed from the pyrolysis oil before we can use it. But the rest is not that difficult because chemically it is close to naphtha or comparable products.

Uwe Schulte

And naphtha is not always naphtha. It changes in composition as well, so you must have some flexibility in your process, I guess.

Lars Kissau

It is the same as a modern steam cracker has some flexibility to deal with different grades. It is not always the exact same grade of naphtha that goes into a cracker, there is a certain raw material flexibility built in (Fig. 10).

---

[11] https://www.redcert.org/en/

[12] https://www.iscc-system.org/

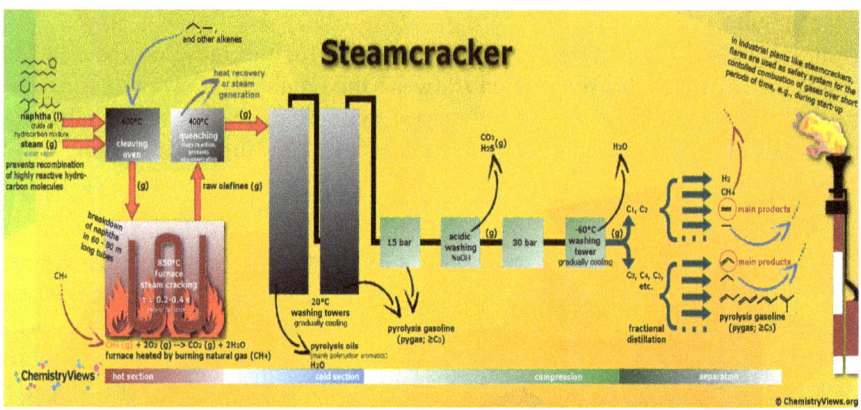

Fig. 10 Steamcracking process by ChemistryViews. Source: Wiley-VCH GmbH, a Wiley Company, V. Koester, Steamcracker, ChemistryViews 2019, https://doi.org/10.1002/chemv.201900023; reproduced with permission

Uwe Schulte

I am afraid that we might have lost the audience now. Let us just go back. The oil is the oil that can be used to be refined and a certain part of that oil could become diesel fuel for engines, but it could also be the raw material to create chemicals, be it plastics or other carbon-based chemicals.[13] To do that, you bring the oil, which is a mixture of many different chains and stuff like that, into what you call a cracker and that then segments it out. Is that what we were talking about?

Lars Kissau

Exactly.

Uwe Schulte

I am glad that I still remember that correctly, so that is great. Let us get back to the business behind that. That is what we are interested in here. I understand why you are doing it, you described that and that is part of your philosophy. Your customers, how do they react to that opportunity here? How do they respond to that?

Lars Kissau

I would say they respond with a remarkably high interest for several reasons. We are not the only company. Many other companies and many of our customers have made commitments to increase the use of recycled materials to reduce the use of virgin fossil materials. What we offer here is something that helps them meet these commitments. That is one part. And what becomes particularly interesting is that there are certain applications where, for instance if you look at food packaging, you cannot use normal mechanically recycled materials because of concerns in terms of health and purity. But chemically recycled materials, because it goes through this extensive purification and is indistinguishable from virgin material, you can use that for food packaging. Even if you are talking about a packaging material that has a

---

[13] https://www.chemistryviews.org/details/ezine/1046155/Steamcracker/

very demanding specification, we can meet that with the chemically recycled material. Or if you look at medical packaging, obviously some of those materials for medical supplies packaging can be made from chemically recycled materials without any concerns and it is fully within the regulatory requirements. This type of thing is what is really driving the interest from customers in these products.

Uwe Schulte
And I understand you already have projects where you collaborate with customers as we speak, but it must be on a relatively small scale still.

Lars Kissau
Currently yes, it is still a small scale, if you look at the scale of the overall industry. But as I said, this is a developing technology where a typical pyrolysis plant creates about 10,000 tonnes of pyrolysis oil. This is of course, in order of magnitude, smaller than one or two orders than what a chemical plant might do. This is beginning, but we are scaling this up and we see quite some interest to also take it further.

Uwe Schulte
If I am one of your customers and we agree that I now buy from the mass balance thing. I understand how it works now. I buy 10% or 1% or whatever it is. Can I then put a remark on my packaging saying that the packaging is 100% recycled? Or how does it work?

Lars Kissau
Just as an example, if we take 10% of this recycled raw material and 90% of the fossil, they are processed together and, in the end, you could of course say that of all the products 10% of the content is recycled. But you could also say that 10% of the products are made entirely of recycled materials, and that is mathematically the same. There is an interest in both. There is an interest in wanting 100% allocation or just having a certain share. Both are possible, but what we ensure through the internal tracking and tracing is that the numbers always match and there is always a physical connection. The plant that is producing, let us say a certain fibre for the textile industry, is connected to the plants that took in the pyrolysis oil.

Uwe Schulte
I understand. But let me ask a specific question because I heard challenges around that. If I take something out of the mass balance from you—if we agree I have now bought my share and the share is 100% recycled—can I make that public claim, or do I get challenged by people saying that it is not possible to do it like that?

Lars Kissau
You can claim that the product has a 100% share of attributed recycled raw material, but you are right, there is still some discussion going on in the EU on how exactly the boundaries of mass balance should be defined. There can be different ways and we try to reassure our customers by saying that we always ensure that there is a physical content. We are not adding pyrolysis oil in one plant and then allocating that to something entirely disconnected. You could also define a mass balance system completely loose. But we think that it is, like in the case of green electricity, reasonable to say that if it is connected, if we are taking a certain volume of raw

materials into our site, like in Ludwigshafen, and we continuously replace, maybe in the beginning 1% and increasing to whatever, we are achieving a certain goal which is replacing fossil raw materials and we allocate that to the corresponding end stream products.

Uwe Schulte

What you are saying is that it must have a physical connection and that makes sense to me now.

Lars Kissau

Yes, this is a view that is widely adopted. Again, you are right, there is still some discussion.[14] Obviously, there are people who believe a wider definition would be best.

There are also some requests to define it differently. Being a chemist, being a scientist, for me, the definition with a physical connection makes a lot of sense.

It is good that it is openly discussed, because in the end as an end consumer I want to have full confidence into what I am being offered. That is why I welcome this discussion. We have a clear position on the physical connection that I think is important and we would try to also convince those who are still sceptical that this is a valid approach and not window dressing.

Uwe Schulte

Let us get back to business here. So, it is small scale now, we still must do additional cleaning steps. The material is more expensive. At the end of the day, it must become competitive. What are the main cost drivers and have you got plans how to deal with that?

Lars Kissau

Yes, it is more expensive and there are a couple of reasons. Number one, the processing step for the plastic waste to the pyrolysis oil itself costs some money, the plants must be built and operated. If you look at the scale it is still quite small, and the logistics. And if you look at the fossil raw materials, in 2019, the global consumption was something like one hundred million barrels of oil a day. That is a huge amount of material as a very efficient industry. Where we are with recycling plastics and creating pyrolysis oil is quite a bit smaller. Obviously, per kg of product, it is still more expensive to transport, it is more expensive to build the plants, but we are working on really scaling this up and reducing the difference.

Uwe Schulte

Let us ask that question: 10 years ahead within the business model of BASF, where will you be with ChemCycling? 1%, 2%?

Lars Kissau

What we did not want to do is put a huge unrealistic target 10 years down the line. What we said is to put a target in 5 years' time, so in 2025, and make sure we hit that. Coming from zero, or a few tonnes, we want to go to 250,000 tonnes of

---

[14] https://www.packaginginsights.com/news/mass-balance-debate-should-the-eu-implement-fuel-exempt-calculation-standards-for-recycling.html

pyrolysis oil in 2025 that we use, process, and sell as final products. That is also quite a significant ramp-up and over that time we expect the technology to develop further and then have a steep growth curve beyond that. There is no target defined yet for 2030, but my focus right now is really making sure that by 2025 we deliver on that, make it a specific target, a concrete target and something that can also be checked whether we hit it.

Uwe Schulte

This is one for those people with the glass half full and half empty—the 250,000. I must say, this is not that far away, that is only 4 years from now and that is a substantial number in that sense. It is a small number compared to what we need to do, and you talked about the number of plants that are required. How confident are you? It is part of your bonus to achieve that target. How confident are you that you are going to make that? That would be very encouraging.[15]

Lars Kissau

I am confident and I am not just saying that because yes, my bonus is influenced by that. But seriously, I am confident. This is something that we work for, we make satisfactory progress, I am happy about the partnerships that we built to make this happen, and we have more ideas for further new partnerships to enter and to take this forward. And I believe that the significant interest from the customer side is really what is also the real driver. More customers are asking. And then also, like you said, it goes from a first pilot production with a few tonnes to a scale-up. And as our customers have success in their markets with products that are based on this recycled feedstock, we will see the demand grow. This is really what is driving us, it is not just an internal target, it is really for us meeting the customer demand (Fig. 11).

Uwe Schulte

What we are saying is that you have partnerships in place that will build the plants to create the oil, and you will buy the oil from those partners. Is that the way it is going to go or are you going to make the oil yourself?

Lars Kissau

Our approach has been that we collaborate with partners to jointly invest in various setups. We take the oil and there are many companies that are active in this field, but our interest is in taking the oil and using that. Our interest is not just in producing pyrolysis oil.

Uwe Schulte

That also makes sense because the pyrolysis oil should be produced where the waste is, rather than where your place of conversion is. But what is your role in the partnership then? I wonder, what are you providing? I am one of your partners—what are you doing for me?

---

[15] https://plasticseurope.org/sustainability/circularity/recycling/chemical-recycling/

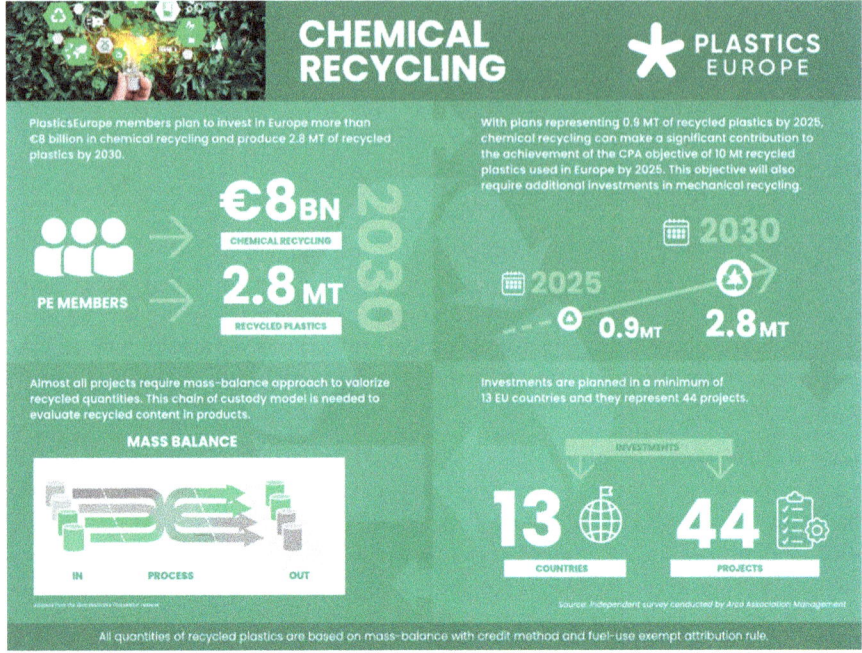

Fig. 11 Chemical recycling outlook. Source: Plastics Europe, https://plasticseurope.org/

Lars Kissau

Well, there are a couple of things. Number one is of course the offtake of pyrolysis oil. Depending on what is the raw material, whether you are using plastic waste, whether you are using end-of-life tyres, there are different outputs, and we are interested in the pyrolysis fraction. That is one contribution, and the other one is technology development. We have some experience in really scaling up new processes and we collaborate with our partners on taking the technologies and scaling them up. Also, further developing, especially the purification step, to take out the impurities from the pyrolysis oil and create a pyrolysis oil that can be used in a steam cracker alongside the traditional raw materials. That is on the technology side. It is of course also a financial investment that we do and then the offtake of the pyrolysis oil.

Uwe Schulte

Lars, I am extremely glad that you made this point because in The Conference Board, we just recently published a new report on the future role of business in society. And one of the important things that we mentioned there is to achieve the goals of the United Nations Sustainable Development for 2030.[16] Companies cannot be on their own, they must collaborate with others. We must break down the barriers

---

[16] https://www.conference-board.org/topics/sustainable-business-integration/role-of-business-in-society

of the limits of one factory, or one site, or one company. And you just made that point. What is happening here is that some people really focus on creating that pyrolysis oil, you provide financial resources, you provide development resources and most importantly you guarantee the offtake, so that we can be confident about your commitment to develop this further with partners. That is something that applies here, but it applies in many other industries as well. If you think about achieving sustainability targets, think about collaboration. Thank you so much for that, Lars. Anything else you would like to emphasise in this context from your side still?

Lars Kissau

No, I think I can just thank you for the opportunity to talk about ChemCycling. Of course, there are many other things that we are doing in terms of moving to a circular economy, but that would fill another podcast. But seriously, thanks a lot. It is important to have discussions and talk about the pros and cons and the difficulties. These developments moving to a circular economy, like you said, do require companies and investors and different people to collaborate in new ways and to have an open discussion to also have this societal acceptance for what we do. And I really appreciate the opportunity that we could talk about this, and I hope we can do this again. Circular economy is a fantastic topic with many more subtopics to consider.

Uwe Schulte

Excellent. Thank you so much for sharing these insights. A company that is so well-established like yourselves is looking into innovative technologies to create these solutions to existing problems. It is much appreciated, thank you very much, also for being open-minded in terms of the critical aspects here that still must be sorted out. Thank you so much.

Sustainability and Science: For Impact and Value Chain Resilience

Recorded May 2021

Uwe Schulte
Today I will be talking to Gayle Schueller, Senior Vice President, and Chief Sustainability Officer at 3M. Gayle is responsible for the 3M sustainability strategy across the global 3M enterprise. These efforts span from healthcare and safety advances to vehicle electrifications and intelligent transportation. Gayle started at 3M's corporate laboratory and has over 20 years of technical and business leadership experience. Gayle's previous assignments include Directora General and VP for 3M Mexico and VP R&D and Design for 3M's consumer business. Gayle has a PhD from the University of Virginia in Material Science and a bachelor's in physics from the New York State University.

Welcome, Gayle. Please tell us a bit about yourself and your experiences in the world of science.

Gayle Schueller
Thank you, Uwe. It is a pleasure to join you and the Sustainability Centre. I have been involved with science since before I was born. My father was a high school chemistry teacher. He instilled that idea of science since I was a very small child. My mother taught special education, which gets to some of that drive for impact that we in the sustainability space have. Every summer we would go camping and visit places like national parks, so the whole science and sustainability bug hit me very early on in my life. I have gone on, as you mentioned. I was inspired by science during my classes as a school student and then chose to major in physics and then came on to Graduate School and Material Science as a PhD. Since then, I joined 3M. It is a very exciting science-based company and as you mentioned, the diversity of the portfolio and the types of businesses that you can work with at 3M, while applying science in so many ways, has been something that has really been exciting for me in the way that we can have an impact broadly around the world.

Uwe Schulte

Yes, I can hear that you are quite passionate about science and education. People might think that science in a corporation like 3M is mainly playing a role in R&D and that it is something for specialists. But with the pandemic and the climate crisis, we experience important input from science on many fronts. How do you see the role of science in business?

Gayle Schueller

That is a great question. And while you are correct that there is an important and critical role for specialists and R&D scientists to be advancing specific scientific areas of expertise, whether it is from developing the right tape backing to addressing a global pandemic, the last year or so has been unprecedented. I know the word is overused at this point, but it is because it is an excellent word for this purpose. We are just seeing the importance of science being at levels that we have never seen before, and at personal levels, whether it is with the global pandemic or the way that you address safety associated with the pandemic or global issues like climate change. 3M publishes an annual state of science index,[1] looking at locations all around the world and getting feedback about people's perceptions about science. And I am pleased to say that the perceptions of science around the world are increasing, recognising the value, recognising the importance to daily life, whether it is from being healthy and safe on a day-to-day basis or addressing the fundamental natural concerns we have related to sustainability. I think we are waking up to it more (Fig. 1).

Uwe Schulte

That is very encouraging. Are you doing this survey with your people or your consumers and customers? How do you do that?

Gayle Schueller

We have 13,000 people participating across 13 countries around the world. It would only be by chance that a 3Mer would be involved in this survey. It is general population, and we are looking for insights. We have a scripted set of questions that we have been asking over the last 4 years, so that we can calibrate and see improvements or

---

[1] https://www.3m.com/3M/en_US/state-of-science-index-survey/

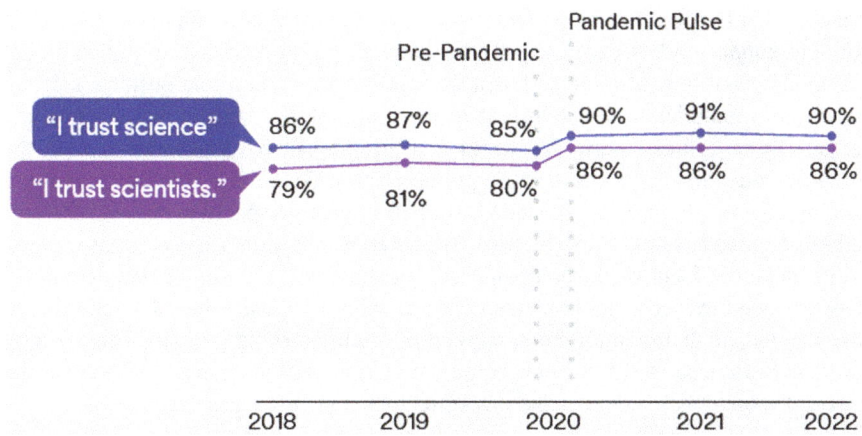

Fig. 1 3M State of Science survey. Source: 3M State of Science Index, 2022, https://www.3m.com/

negative effects, changes over time. There also are specific questions that we ask more about, based on what a specific environment it is. In fact, in 2020, we conducted the survey twice, because we started conducting it pre-pandemic and then needed to go back, because we realised that some of the views that people had around science might be affected by that, and that is indeed what we found.

Uwe Schulte
Did you see any major differences between the different regions of the world?

Gayle Schueller
There are many things that we have seen. There are some countries that have a much higher confidence in science, others have less. It is very interesting to look at on a country-by-country basis. In fact, this could be an exciting separate podcast to go into specific details. There is a lot in there.

Uwe Schulte
The pandemic obviously focused minds. But there are other things that must concern a company, like the climate crisis or biodiversity loss. And that will influence business development. How do you see this from a corporate perspective?

Gayle Schueller
In fact, tying back to that state of science index, we found that after the pandemic and health related effects, the number 2 factor, even in the year of 2020, was that people were concerned about climate and biodiversity. We know that companies and other organisations around the world have both, a responsibility, and an opportunity, to do more in this space. We believe that collaborating is really the way we make this happen. Because companies can offer that ability to scale, they can support resources for innovation, and it creates business models as well. While there are challenges that are presented in these spaces, I believe very strongly that science is the way to help address these challenges. Having a commercial mindset to how

making that happen is an important piece of it. You mentioned some of the electric vehicle enhancements early on—those things come in response to major global challenges, but they also create business opportunities. The same goes for shifting from more materials-based solutions to more digital. We believe that science is a great way to address those challenges and bringing forward, whether it is in the broader educational system or in corporate efforts. We believe that this is really a way to advance both, what is needed from an impact perspective, but also the creation of great business opportunities. And we are not alone. Investors are seeing more and more focus on the companies, they call it ESG, Environmental, Social and Governance Practices, and how that connects with both, what the track record is of a company and their commitments, and current actions going forward. There is a lot more to be done, and 3M in fact is committed to invest more than $1 billion over the next 20 years to help advance the investments that we have as a corporation.

Uwe Schulte
That sounds impressive. I am wondering how you make sure that, within 3M, you stay on top of science, because science is not something static, it develops itself. We had warnings about climate change many years ago. Not many people took it very seriously in the early stages, but then more and more evidence emerged through the scientific method: forming a hypothesis, testing it with experiments, falsifying or verifying a hypothesis and in the latter case turning it into a theory. How do you make sure, you stay on top of that advancement of science?

Gayle Schueller
You have two questions there and I would love to answer them both. The first one I heard was about this science culture and staying current. The second one I am hearing woven in, is about addressing climate change. Answering the first question—we have a long-standing culture around science that we have talked about. In fact, our technical forum is celebrating close to its 70th birthday right now.[2] That means that for 70 years, we have had a group of technical employees who have engaged to discuss science. And it is very organic. We have approximately 10,000 members around the world, as well as about 1000 events per year. Some of them are big, like our annual event which was virtual this year, or some of them can be small where maybe there are 10 specific subject matter experts meeting on a topic of interest, which might be next generation solar energy or advancing types of abrasives or something related to electric vehicle charging technologies. That group helps guide where we are going from a scientific perspective and create this organic approach with our 15%-culture,[3] where you can spend up to 15% of your time working on things that you are passionate about. We have 51 different technology platforms that are mixed and matched to create different solutions for the enterprise. I could go on and on talking about some of those. Who knew that traffic signage solutions from the 1950s could lay the pathway for dental amalgams that help teeth look and feel

---

[2] https://hbr.org/2013/08/the-innovation-mindset-in-acti-3
[3] https://www.3m.co.uk/3M/en_GB/careers/culture/15-percent-culture/

like natural teeth. The idea is, the scientific community coming together, staying aware of what is going on in megatrends, bringing together different technology platforms, and evolving those technology platforms. It is a key place in how we stay advancing. We also have governance and management systems ranging from our technical council to our corporate technical operating committee that help guide these things. We have a very robust system on how we continue to advance on the technology. Within that, I mentioned this technical forum. One example of ways that we stay current, is that we have a technical form chapter that we have had for a few years now. That is our climate chapter which is very much focused on all things related to climate. They publish 101, 201 and maybe even 301 classes for people around the company of all backgrounds, that they can take to stay abreast of what is happening in science. Also, this year, in January of 2021, we established a science for circular chapter, so really advancing what is happening in terms of that global circular economy and how we can make materials stay in play for the longest amount of time. When it comes to goals and staying advanced on those goals, we take a 'math with a path' type of approach. As a scientific body, it is very important for us to make sure that we understand when we set an ambitious goal, what exactly our math is to get there, what the key programmes are, what the key investments are, and what impact they have. Earlier this year, we announced our set of new environmental goals, designed to achieve carbon neutrality by 2050, while reducing our footprint 50% in the next 10 years, reducing our water use 25% in our facilities over the next 10 years and returning higher quality water to the environment after the use of manufacturing. Just last week, we announced our commitment to reduce the use of virgin fossil-based plastics by 125 million pounds (lb) within 5 years. All of those are developed with this 'math with a path' type of approach (Fig. 2).

Fig. 2 3M technical forum session in the early 1950s. Source: 3M, https://multimedia.3m.com/mws/media/1712400/3m-century-of-innovation-book.pdf

Uwe Schulte

First of all, I was very tempted to go off on another tangent when you talked about caring for teeth, based on signature for traffic.

Gayle Schueller

I would be happy to go there, but maybe that is off path for today.

Uwe Schulte

Let us stay with your targets for a second because it is very interesting that they are mathematically founded. And after that, I would like to come back to circular again, because I always get very excited about that. But let us stay on climate. Climate neutrality by 2050 is a very ambitious target, as we have seen that countries are struggling to agree on it. Even so, we have a new boost of initiatives now, which is of course very exciting as well. How do you see that? Have you defined steps how to get there over time?

Gayle Schueller

Absolutely. That has been the core. And that is the reason it took us longer than perhaps some of us would have liked, to come out with a carbon neutrality goal. We have mapped all our facilities on a global basis to understand what the impacts are for any given facility. We have also gone across our key value chains in the enterprise. For 3M, maybe tape manufacturing would be one of those areas, or adhesive coatings. Things like that would be examples of value streams. They might cross many businesses or many different locations. When they go facility by facility, we map out where our footprint is, whether it is from greenhouse gas emissions or energy usage or even things like water or waste. And then we understand where we can make the biggest impact the fastest. We also overlay that with where the existing technologies, the known technologies are, as well as the ones that are emerging quickly that we believe we have high confidence in. And we only use those that are primarily based on existing technologies, plus a reasonable estimate of those that are emerging that we think have high confidence. We go through project by project, going after specific facilities and specific processes. Mapping that 'math with a path' to carbon neutrality was a major effort, and one for which I am proud of the team and how they pulled it together. We have done that layout, looking at what projects need to be done in 2020, what projects will be done in 2021, 2022, and so on, to get to that neutrality by 2050. But perhaps, even more inspiring is to get to a 50% reduction in our carbon emissions by 2030. And in doing so, we have specific project, specific capital investments that must be done and we look at what the cost is, what the technology confidence is, the number of resources applied, and when it needs to happen to meet that goal. As a global manufacturing company, we are largely based on that manufacturing footprint. Where we see our own operational footprint being highest, is in our manufacturing sites. Many times, that equipment is something that you purchase and lasts a long time, decades even. That is why it is critical that we get ahead of this from early on and that we take those most important equipment steps at the right times. When equipment is either being revamped for maintenance reasons or as new products are coming on and we are adding new capabilities or new equipment, that is the time to make those key changes. And then in parallel with that, we are doing things with that value chain mapping as well. How can we go about making our adhesives the lowest footprint possible, how can we go about choosing the right backings for tapes, for films, that have the best carbon footprints? And that is an important part of what we are doing.

Uwe Schulte
Let us get back to the circular one, because that is something that is extremely important. We just published a report on the challenges of solid plastic waste recycling and how far behind we are against the ambition to really recycle everything. But recycling is not everything, because circular really means that we continue to use the same resource repeatedly and you call it science for circular. Can you explain this, maybe in an example where and how you apply that concept?

Gayle Schueller
We have a strategic sustainability framework that we work under and referenced it. It is all based on our ambition to apply science to improve lives. It gets to our vision statement; it is core to who we are. We know we are science-based, and we know our global breadth, and the areas we touch give us the opportunity to have that global reach and touch people and improve lives all around the world. That strategic sustainability framework has three pillars: Science for circular, science for climate, and science for community.[4] We have talked a bit about science for climate. Let us talk a little bit more about science for circular. Our overall ambition around science for circular is to design solutions that do more with less material, advancing a global circular economy. This is something that neither 3M nor any other company does on their own. This must be done in collaboration, perhaps more than anything else that we do. We have put in place a sustainability value commitment that helps bring this to life. This is a requirement, that every new product we develop must advance a global good. In the case of circularity, this might be for example Scotch-Brite sponges. They are made from recycled plastics content. There are other examples where we take adhesives that are made from plant-based materials. We always make sure to do a life cycle analysis in those cases, to make sure that the carbon footprint makes sense. But we can use plant-based materials, we can use recycled content, and we can always design to do more with less material, what we call de-contenting. Those are all very important pieces of both the circular economy and the work that we do to have our new reduction of plastics goal, so those come together. The commitment around reducing the dependence on virgin fossil-based plastics by 125 million pounds (lb) or 63,000 tons within 5 years is leveraging all those pieces, recycled content, plant-based materials and using less materials. It is across our products, with the Scotch-Brite example I have provided, as well as across our packaging. You might be interested to know that 125 million pounds (lb) is roughly equivalent to 5 1/2 Eiffel Towers by weight (Fig. 3).

---

[4] https://multimedia.3m.com/mws/media/2292786O/3m-2023-global-impact-report.pdf

Our commitment

We use a science-based approach to reimagine what's possible as we rise to the challenges that are most material to 3M and critical to our planet and its people. Our goals and environmental, social, and governance (ESG) metrics reflect a heightened commitment to thinking holistically about how our people, products, and operations can all contribute to a better and brighter future.

Fig. 3 3M sustainability commitment. Source: 3M, https://multimedia.3m.com/mws/media/2292786O/3m-2023-global-impact-report.pdf

Uwe Schulte

To be very honest with you, I have not been in Paris for a while, and I do not know how much the Eiffel Tower weighs. Anyway, you just whetted my appetite again with something you introduced and that was science for social. I have not seen that on your website, I am ignorant about that, I am sorry.

Gayle Schueller

We developed our strategic sustainability framework about 2 1/2 years ago, bringing together a dream team of leaders across the company, representing every function, every business, every geography. And we knew that science needed to be at the root, but what we were trying to determine was what the right pillars were to have within our strategic framework. Climate was the one that jumped out first because that was very clear. Then we knew that we needed to have a materials piece, so that got to the science for circular. We really liked that we had two Cs, so our third pillar is around science for community. And the community portion is yes, how our products help people's lives, reducing healthcare acquired infections, helping people be safe in the event of a global pandemic or other types of safety issues, etc. But it is also about how we engage in our communities, how we promote and advance science, technology, engineering, and mathematics (STEM) education,[5] how we help ensure equity for people with all types of underrepresented backgrounds, whether it is in our own workforce or in the communities where we work and play, helping make sure that there is a world where we all want to be living. We think that these three pillars of our strategic sustainability framework really align well with the UN SDGs and other major global approaches to sustainability and ESG.

---

[5] https://en.wikipedia.org/wiki/Science,_technology,_engineering,_and_mathematics

Uwe Schulte

There are the community effects that you have with your products, but there are also the effects that you have on communities by operating there. Does that extend to that as well?

Gayle Schueller

Absolutely. This gets to programmes that we have, like 3M Impact,[6] which is skills-based volunteerism all over the world, where 3Mers are spending time in the communities to partner with different NGOs on critical issues and bring the expertise in addition to a pair of hands. They bring the expertise either as a scientist or a designer or a business leader, where they can really help an NGO advance. We have some wonderful examples of that. Additionally, it gets to some of our sustainability goals around things like engaging, where we have facilities in water-stressed and water scarce areas. We have a very small fraction of our facilities in those locations. And where we do, we make sure that we have special engagement with those communities to make sure that we are doing the right thing from a water stewardship perspective and partnering with them on their greatest needs. We make a point when we are hiring to have that balanced diversity. We have diversity goals around enhancing the diversity of our global workforce, as well as goals in the United States around improving their racial diversity specifically, and really bringing through school programmes, STEM programmes in the schools all around the world. We have active programmes like our Visiting Wizards Programme, where scientists visit schools. We are looking forward to getting that started in a face-to-face section once we get past the global pandemic. But we have also done a Science at Home Programme[7] which is accessible online to people all over the world, where you can see individual science experiments practised by individual scientists and it is designed to help students expand their scientific curiosity or classrooms work in new ways around the world. There is a lot going on.

Uwe Schulte

That is something very much needed. We talked a lot about science, and science education is so important. It benefits you with your recruits, and you also make sure that you give that back as well.

Gayle Schueller

Absolutely, and even in the bigger sense. If we are going to successfully address these global challenges, whether they are health related or environmentally related, science is going to be at the core of that. The more great minds are inspired to work on scientific challenges, the better it will be for all of us.

---

[6] https://www.3m.com/3M/en_US/company-us/about-3m/3m-impact/

[7] https://news.3m.com/2021-08-11-3M-Science-at-Home-Learning-Resource-Delivers-Free-On-Demand-STEM-Education-Anywhere,-Anytimeucation/science-at-home/

Uwe Schulte

This is a very important learning. We started by saying that the pandemic has highlighted when people start applying science, then we were able to fight the pandemic in quite an impressive speed. I would like to come back to your point about collaboration very briefly, because this is such an important point, that companies applying science and driving sustainability, cannot do this on their own, as you mentioned. How do you go about that? How do you approach others to join into the effort?

Gayle Schueller

That is a great question because absolutely no single company, no single NGO, no single government at any level around the world can address these challenges completely by themselves. It just is impossible. When it is within our products, we work closely with both our customers to design in solutions that really help address footprint and address impact for society, but also with our suppliers. We have a supplier responsibility policy, and we have our supplier sustainability solutions library that we use to reinvent products. Those are ways that we do within our product portfolio. Other ways where collaboration is critical is working with governments on what the key regulations are, that need to come into place. How do we ensure that they are truly science-based and not just a political artefact? Another question is—how do you bring everyone along? One of the things that we have done in the last year, that I am really excited about, is a partnership with the United Nations Global Compact on the SDG ambition. That is the Sustainable Development Goals Ambition Programme[8] aimed at helping companies, big, small, medium enterprises. Help them make sure that sustainability principles are brought into their core business values and strategies for their business. It is one thing for companies like 3M and our large suppliers and our large customers to be doing things but getting it across the whole portfolio of the business world and aligned with what society and governments are wanting, is really where we need to get to. We are eager to take an important role in that at individual and collective levels.

Uwe Schulte

Let us look at the aspect of sustainability and supply. When I talk to senior managers, they often complain about the complexity of their portfolio. They might have 10 product lines with 100 different items in each of them. I guess, for this conversation we need to calibrate this a little bit. In how many different industry sectors, does 3M operate and how many different products are you selling?

Gayle Schueller

Those are more difficult questions than you might have thought. Our passion for science and innovation spans our entire enterprise, but the way we organise is around global business groups to help best serve our customers: safety and industrial, transportation and electronics, healthcare, and consumer. These groups beneath them have 23 business units which use 51 technology platforms from across 3M to innovate thousands and thousands of products and solutions. Our products and

---

[8] https://unglobalcompact.org/take-action/sdg-ambition

solutions are brought to market through approximately 70 different countries with manufacturing footprints and being sold around the world in many more.

Uwe Schulte

That sounds quite complex to me, it is very impressive. One of the things I took from our conversation about science and business was the passion you conveyed around science and the clear integration of science into 3M. Maybe I have a suspicion that explains, why you can be so innovative. Many people recognise that in 3M. In recent times, I have used two major products of yours. One is the self-adhesive tape and the other one is the face mask that I am wearing. Looking at such complexity and knowing that people in less complex organisations are already struggling to create visibility across their value chains. How on earth are you managing?

Gayle Schueller

Well, it is always a challenge, because as you can imagine, with that much diversity in products, and you just mentioned 2 examples of the thousands and thousands, there are many different pieces to the supply chain. Overall, we have a sourcing policy and practices that we engage for all products and all suppliers. It is called our supplier responsibility code. We send out annual communications each year, we engage in our meetings with those suppliers about all the key expectations that we have for the supplier responsibility code. Then we prioritise across the portfolio of raw materials that we purchase. There are the ones, where it is important for us to do specific deep dives across sourcing classes. One that comes to mind is the work that we have done in the pulp and paper area, where we have gone deep, working not only with our first-tier suppliers but with tiers beyond that. We start with each of our first-tier suppliers across the board, with what I described regarding the supplier responsibility codes, annual communications, touching base on key responsibilities. But then we choose to go deeper, much like we do when we were talking about our carbon footprint. Choosing where the biggest impact can be made and where there maybe needs to be some help across different suppliers.

Uwe Schulte

That is something very close to my heart. When I was still in a fast-moving consumer goods company, I remember travelling all the way to Indonesia and seeing how these plantations were destroying the natural habitat. Therefore, going beyond tier 1 is very important, but I also realised there and then how difficult it was. How do you do that?

Gayle Schueller

Well, it is certainly a complex challenge. We believe that there are a couple of key places that we start up. We have looked at, as you described, getting back to where the actual harvesting location is, and that is very challenging in our supply chains. The first step is to map our supply chain from pulp and paper mills down to the source of harvest. We started doing that back in 2015 when we first established the public pulp and paper sourcing policy. The first step was to include this traceability as a requirement in our policy for all our suppliers. Then we began developing tools

Fig. 4 Earthworm Foundation. Source: Earthworm Foundation (EF)

and resources as well as training our suppliers across the world on it. One of their early challenges was about getting our suppliers to be comfortable sharing this level of information. It was not a common request at that time, and I am still not sure if it is now. But it is an expectation for us, and we have been working for the last several years to help make that happen. We have seen significant progress as they have learned how we work with them, they have seen the value of it, they have been willing to share more and collaborate more. It has become, I hesitate to say easier, but at least more manageable. We have a global cross-functional team that works to implement the policy across all regions of the world. Additionally, we partner with a global non-profit called Earthworm Foundation.[9] This Foundation provides expertise in implementing responsible sourcing policies and improving forest management practices across the entire global supply chain. They have a deeper understanding of forest policies, forest practices, whether it is in Indonesia or Canada or anywhere in the world. We implement these practices both through our own operations, our policies with our suppliers, and in collaboration with Earthworm Foundation (Fig. 4).

Uwe Schulte
That is a good example of what we already discussed—you cannot achieve sustainability on your own, you must collaborate. Can you explain a little bit more how you cooperate with that foundation?

---

[9] https://www.earthworm.org/about-us

Gayle Schueller
They help us review the information that we receive from our supplier surveys and then they overlap that with geography and industry specific knowledge, so that we can work together to conduct a desktop risk assessment of our overall supply chain. We then use these assessments to help prioritise our future work with our suppliers, tier 1, tier 2 and beyond, and to learn more about our suppliers' responsible sourcing and sustainable forestry practices, so that we can share some best practices. To date we have engaged over 90% of our global pulp and paper spend on a global basis, and we have over 75% of our spend traceable to the forest area that has been reviewed for our risk assessment process. We continue to further the supply chain engagement by conducting web conferences where we help with training, or we help sharing best practices across suppliers. We also engage in virtual or in-person meetings, including field assessments, which are an important part, as you mentioned previously, to directly see what is happening and discuss important issues. As part of these risk assessments and in combination with other tools, we evaluate our suppliers' level of conformance to our policy. When there is a situation where we have some concerns that the supplier is performing to the level we would expect, our first approach is to work with them on action plans. That has been an important piece of what has built confidence with our suppliers, that they have learned that if they are falling short in one area, we are there to help them improve. I am proud of our team that has done that. They have really built a lot of credibility and they have helped raise the bar overall. Because we know these issues cannot be solved overnight. And if we stop sourcing from somebody, maybe somebody else would just pick it up. So, if we can help raise the performance and help raise the awareness of how you can do this in a responsible and financially viable way, that is a great way for us to help advance continuous improvement in the pulp and paper supply chain.

Uwe Schulte
Gayle, that sounds very interesting and important, because a lot of our audience will have the problem to go beyond tier 1. I also hear this from TCB members. And of course, you have such a complex value chain, so many different products. You have chosen the path of focusing where you dive deep, and I think that is an important learning. But you mentioned that suppliers see the value in this deep dive. Can you explain a little bit more where the benefit is from a supplier perspective?

Gayle Schueller
There were maybe some questions about that, but as we have developed over the last several years, we have now mapped a significant part of our global supply chain, particularly in the pulp and paper space. And it is now becoming rare for us to find any new pulp or paper mill around the world that has not been identified some place in our supply chain. When we engage those higher tier suppliers, we always start with a direct supplier and in many instances, we have multiple suppliers coming from that mill. But then bringing more parties along in our journey helps us communicate the expectations and drive overall improvement. For example, we are starting to connect different suppliers who are sourcing fibre from the same area. For example, last November, we co-hosted a webinar for our suppliers sourcing

material from British Columbia. It is important to bring multiple companies together to discuss the overall landscape, the collective challenges that they face, our expectations and to talk about how we can work together to transform the overall supply chain and lift the performance of the overall industry. We are seeing areas where these efforts are being put into policy implementation across overall supply chains. Suppliers who did not previously have responsible sourcing processes or policies, are developing them. We have also seen suppliers enhance their existing policies and build due diligence systems and management systems into developing their own traceability systems. They are really advancing their own practices. We have even had suppliers invite us to visit sourcing areas that have complicated challenges, so we can join them in discussions about how to improve overall. There is more and more that can be done together, sharing those best practices, learning from each other, and raising the performance of the businesses and the industry overall.

Uwe Schulte
Pulp and paper are a good example, and it is interesting how you approach it. I am wondering whether you can apply these learnings to other value chains in your business.

Gayle Schueller
Absolutely, and we are. As we mentioned, it is about prioritising whether it is about a specific part of our manufacturing processes or specific target supply chains of materials that we source. We talked about pulp and paper. Another example is conflict minerals. We do apply these overall principles to all our suppliers, but we particularly identify areas where there may be some risks or impact that we can help advance. When we talk about conflict minerals, we are looking at specifically sourcing suppliers where we have content associated with tin, tantalum, tungsten, gold, and other materials of concern.[10]

Uwe Schulte
Other people would, for example, have cobalt on that list, but you do not.

Gayle Schueller
Yes. In these cases, we are working with our tier 1 suppliers to identify smelters or refiners associated with the minerals being sourced and then determine their country of origin, whether they have received and passed a third-party environmental or social compliance audit. If there are concerns or risks in the process, we work again, like we talked about before, with the suppliers and the smelters and refiners to help make sure that they are meeting our expectations of what a responsible supplier should be. And us working with them is part of what we do across the portfolio, whether it is with pulp and paper or conflict minerals. We have the supplier responsibility code, we also have a responsible minerals policy for our programme, and we do annual outreach, we have global contract templates that we use around the world

---

[10] https://www.responsiblemineralsinitiative.org/about/faq/general-questions/what-are-conflict-minerals/

and make sure that we have terms, conditions, and supplier engagement approaches that comply with all applicable laws, policies, and our responsible minerals approach.

Uwe Schulte

What you have done is where it matters most for you, you have created more visibility across your whole value chain, not just tier 1, but the whole value chain. And I am wondering—the new thing that everybody is talking about is supply chain resilience. Is that work you do to improve your sustainability performance, be it environmental or social? Does that also help your business to have a more resilient value chain?

Gayle Schueller

It is interesting. There is a lot of discussion now about enterprise resilience and supply chain resilience. Fundamentally, I think that this is a natural evolution of good business practices. We have long had the philosophy, the approach of producing and sourcing where the product is being used. Regional self-sufficiency is a term that we used at some point. The idea is that we can be sourcing locally, and we can be manufacturing locally and supplying locally. The pandemic has brought this to light in a whole different set of ways. We produce N 95 respirators—you mentioned your face mask. We produce different types of personal protective equipment all around the world. And when the pandemic first hit in China, we had a significant manufacturing capability in China that was fully loaded and fully ramped up to produce in China, similarly in the United States and Europe, and growing more and more with operations and efforts in other countries around the world. And it has been a very important piece of sourcing, to know that we have second sourcing, to know that we have local sourcing across our portfolio. It always has been, but I think increasingly now whether there are challenges of a global pandemic, challenges of risks in supply chain of all varieties or even climate challenges, which could wipe out one supplier. It is very important that we have resilience in our plans for being able to produce if one supplier were to go down or if one region of the world has a particular impacting event. That global resilience is a very important piece of our business strategy.

Uwe Schulte

Having that visibility and making sure that you have sound production and engagement practices, you improve the resilience as well. Is that what you are saying?

Gayle Schueller

Like many things, there is a whole spectrum regarding resilience. There are times when there are parts that are most challenging, there are parts that are least challenging. And that gets to that prioritisation that we have been talking about. If we have a situation where we have a single source of a critical material, we put a lot of attention there. Where in the supply we think that there might be some risk from a social or an environmental perspective, we put a lot of attention there. Those are really important factors for us when we think about both the immediate viability of our business, but also the long term.

Uwe Schulte

And what we have seen in the pandemic is that people start to realise, addressing social issues is not just to be a good citizen, but it also makes good business sense because people in very difficult, precarious working conditions, under the conditions of a pandemic, will not be able to work and then supply chains break down. These things are very interconnected, and I think we are starting to understand that better.

Gayle Schueller

I totally agree. Environmental, social pieces come together very strongly in the sustainability space. And for us to go along those ambitions of the Brundtland Commission, we need to live in ways today that can allow future generations to live well also. I think we need to be looking at all those different components. Yes, locally, but also globally, environmentally, and socially.

Uwe Schulte

Yes. Thank you so much. It was great of you to share these insights with us and explain how the collaboration with suppliers works for you. And it is inspiring to see that you can make it work beyond tier 1, and that is something that we will take out of this conversation.

Gayle Schueller

Thank you very much. It is a continual journey and we do not do it alone. I look forward to the continued collaboration and gleaning new insights that we can apply as well. Thank you for having us, thank you for having me.

Business Success with Purpose

Recorded June 2021

Uwe Schulte
Today I will be talking to Geraldine Matchett, Co-CEO and CFO at Royal DSM. First, let me introduce our guest, Geraldine Matchett. She joined DSM's managing board in August 2014 and became Co-CEO in February 2020. Geraldine holds a bachelor's degree in physical and human geography, from Reading University in the UK and a master's degree in sustainable development from Cambridge University; Geraldine is Co-chair of the Prince of Wales Accounting Sustainability CFO Leadership Network. The network brings together leading CFOs to help embed the management of environmental and social issues into business processes particularly of course through the finance function. Welcome, Geraldine. Please tell us a bit about yourself and how as a finance person, you got involved with sustainability.

Geraldine Matchett
Yes, hello and thank you very much for having me. And who am I? Well, as you said in your introduction, I am a geographer at heart, physical and human geography, but in my life, at some point you also need to earn an income. That is what took me into finance. And as a result, I have done most of my career in finance as a CFO, and indeed I am currently now also a Co-CEO, which is nice, but I have been known as a little bit of a Maverick CFO because of my background. And I have to say that one of the things I have always had on my wall is a map of the world and looking at the flows of goods going from one continent to the other and the flow of people. And

---

Editorial Note
DSM and Firmenich have merged in May 2023, establishing a new company that brings together two large communities in nutrition, health, and beauty. With a 30,000 strong team dsm-firmenich will drive reinvention, manufacturing, and combination of nutrients, flavours, and fragrances.

one of my favourite inventions is Google Earth. That is fantastic. You can zoom in, zoom out and if you have been brought up in geography, the fact that societies thrive partly through their interaction and their way that they behave with their physical environment is common sense. That is my mindset and has always been for a long time. Looking more carefully at that interrelationship between societies thriving, which means companies thriving and the physical environment. Looking at books like Collapse, which looked at the civilisations that collapsed not because they were unsuccessful but because they were too successful, and they consumed themselves out of resources. It is this book by Jared Diamond, which I like very much and that sets your mind into: Hang on a second—how can we as societies choose to succeed by taking care of our physical environment as much as our own needs. And yes, that is who I am. And that is why embedding sustainability, embedding, environmental consideration and social consideration in how to drive a company, is what makes me extremely excited to be where I am right now.

Uwe Schulte
Sounds great, but we must make a disclaimer here because for all those aspiring students of geography: you can make a living out of geography as well. It might be a bit more difficult, but it can be done. I hope you confirm that.

Geraldine Matchett
I fully agree.

And to be honest, at the time I was a student in geography, when climate change was still a big debate, my master's at Cambridge was all about whether this climate change really exists and what are the facts, et cetera. Now this is not a debate. The question is, what are we going to do about it? And to be fair, that was the faculty of geography, and it is now today's hottest topic and there is space for everyone. I would happily have stayed in the geography science part as well, but at the time there were more careers to be had. Trying to link the two with business as well.

Uwe Schulte
We are glad that you have done what you have done, but our listeners are not necessarily familiar with what Royal DSM is doing as a company. I understand it

originally stood for *D*utch *S*tate *M*ines, but you have gone through several metamorphoses. Can you tell us a bit about that?

Geraldine Matchett

Indeed, DSM is not necessarily a household name because we are a business-to-business (B2B) company. If I start the story with 'Once Upon a Time', DSM was indeed the Dutch State Mines, the coal mining company of the Netherlands.[1] And overtime, of course, the future of that activity became very dubious. The company said, well, let us see how we transform into something else, which led to transforming into petrochemical refining. For a period. But that as well, based in the Netherlands, is not something extremely easy when you are not backward integrated into oil fields. That got divested and bit by bit we transformed ourselves into whom we are today, which is effectively an 85% nutrition, health, and bioscience company. We are the world's biggest producer of what makes food nutritious: micronutrients. Vitamins, Omega3,[2] Probiotics,[3] Prebiotics,[4] and that is for humans and for animals. We are the leading company in the world in that and there is a lot of chemistry in that, but there is also a lot of biotech in that. And then we have 15%, which is in specialty materials that go into mobile phones, cars really focused on recyclability, circularity, bio-based type materials. So fine chemistry and biotech, that is who we are today. And to give you an idea of size, we are about a ten billion turnover company with about twenty-four thousand colleagues around the world. We are a Dutch listed corporation in terms of our headquarters and our origin. From Dutch State Mines, we like to think of ourselves today as DSM standing for *d*oing *s*omething *m*eaningful (Fig. 1).

Uwe Schulte

Wow, that is a positive change of acronym. I had not heard that one before, but it is a huge transformation, and I would love to hear a little bit how sustainability played a role in that. I understand that you were looking at your capabilities and at scenarios of what is ahead of you, is my understanding correct there?

Geraldine Matchett

Yes. Sustainability is at the core of our transformation beyond the transformation of the portfolio changes which have taken place over decades. But if I look particularly at the last 25 years of our history, our transformation is very much anchored in the Dutch corporate law and what I mean by that is in the Netherlands as a managing board, we are accountable to all stakeholders. It is not shareholder capitalism; it is

---

[1] https://www.tudelft.nl/en/ceg/about-faculty/departments/geoscience-engineering/sections/resource-engineering/links/coal-mining-in-the-netherlands/former-mining-companies/state-mines

[2] Omega−3 fatty acids are polyunsaturated fatty acids characterised by the presence of a double bond, three atoms away from the terminal methyl group in their chemical structure.

[3] World Health Organization (WHO) defines probiotics as 'live microorganisms which when administered in adequate amounts confer a health benefit on the host'.

[4] International Scientific Association for Probiotics and Prebiotics (ISAPP) produced the following definition of prebiotics: a substrate that is selectively used by a host microorganism to produce a health benefit.

Fig. 1 First Dutch State Mine Wilhelmina 1906. Source: dsm-firmenich, https://www.dsm-firmenich.com/corporate/home.html

stakeholder capitalism, and it is embedded in our articles of association. In effect, we are virtually a B-Corp[5] by definition and that is why you see a lot of Dutch corporations being leading in sustainability and business because we have been thinking about it for a long, long time. We have been what we call a triple bottom line company for 20 years plus[6] people, planet, profit and that gives us an exceptionally long heritage as an environmental and socially conscious company. And it is interesting that when we introduced incentives that mirrored that objective, 50% of our short-term and long-term incentives are anchored on financial performance. But 50% are on people and on planet and this at that time made the first page of the Financial Times. It was like, oh my God, what is this listed company 100% free flow? Getting distracted about all these things around people and safety and engagement and greenhouse gases, and that was we are talking here. More than 12 years ago, so it was a bit scary at the time, but it was also very much what has been driving our transformation. Because we have an important saying in our company, which is "you cannot call yourself successful in a world that fails". No matter how great your share price, no matter how great your financial performance, if it is at the detriment of the people around you, both upstream and downstream, then are you successful? When you take that mindset, you start caring about your impact on the society around you, about your impact on your direct physical environment, so your own

---

[5] https://www.bcorporation.net/en-us/
[6] S. Chapter 1 for more background on triple bottom line

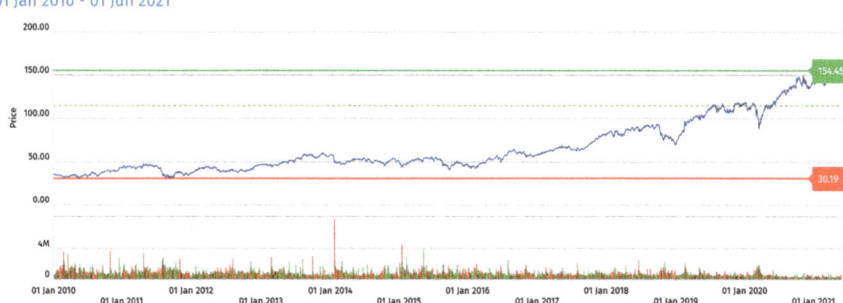

Fig. 2 DSM share development 2010–2021. Source: dsm-firmenich, https://www.dsm.com/corporate/investors/shares/share-performance.html

water consumption, greenhouse gases, et cetera, but also what you are doing to the whole chain. What are your behaviours driving in terms of changes for your suppliers and are you supporting your customers because we are a B2B, we are in the middle of the food systems. We are not in agriculture, and we are not in a consumer brand. But we are at the link of the two and that is really what has been underlying our transformation. Building over a long heritage of triple P to become a leading ESG stock and very much a purpose-driven organisation from the inside.

Uwe Schulte
I do remember it. It is longer than 12 years, I am certain. But I remember that, and I have ever since had a sort of internal watching brief on DSM. When I look at your share price development, those people were extremely worried at the time. They were very wrong. You are doing all right, I would say, but let us focus a little bit on that because repeatedly when I talk to CFOs for example, they say "this is all fine, but show me the money". You as a finance person. Is it a compromise? Do you have to forego your financial performance or how do you see it? (Fig. 2)

Geraldine Matchett
This is a long-standing debate. Can you do well financially if you also invest in the longer term now? The world has changed a lot. I will not deny that when we started on this journey, when we were one of the few companies who were doing this, we were doing it a little bit in secret. We did not make a lot of noise about it when we were on investor roadshows, we would focus on financial performance, and we would keep that a little bit to ourselves to the point that it would even surprise some investors because about 35% of our investor base is in the USA. Unless particularly asked, we would not put it forward. Now the world has changed massively and if I look today, I am talking for listed companies and where often the dilemma is the most striking because you must perform on a quarterly or 6-monthly cycle. You are challenged to defend your financial performance. Yet it is true that some of these considerations require forward thinking and consistency. But if I look today at what is happening in the markets, we have between 40 and 50% of our shareholders subscribing to principles of responsible investing. A big, substantial chunk and we are

realising that of course a lot of money is invested through passive index funds. That is a substantial number and the pure ESG funds are now coming to over 10% of our shareholders. But more importantly, it is part of everybody's conversation when you are a listed company, what are you doing about these things? So today it is virtually becoming a qualifier.

I think the world has moved a lot and interestingly it got even further accelerated by the pandemic, which was not an obvious outcome of last year's challenges. But if I zoom out to those, who are not in a listed company: why does it make sense? And it makes sense as the finance director in many ways, we tend to use the structure when it comes to sustainability in three buckets: reduce, enable, and advocate. When we talk about 'reduce', we are talking about our own footprint. It can be reduced or improved, it depends, but it is all about de-risking your own future. If you do not improve the way you operate at some point it is going to catch up with you. You have technologies which are outdated, and you start getting hit by new regulations which are becoming increasingly stringent in all industries. And therefore, by making sure that you are staying ahead of the curve, although there is a bit of an investment at first, you are setting yourself up to be at the right place at the right time. If you wait until the regulations force you to change, you will be a laggard in your own space. Other competitors will have done it and you have not. There is a huge element of de-risking. The easy one is of course reducing the cost of inputs, the cost of divesting waste streams, et cetera. But that is the very minimal part. The bigger part is how do you stay ahead of the fact that society is evolving on all the criteria, particularly when it comes to environmental impact, energy mix are these kinds of things, but also to be fair on social aspects. And that is the next big hurdle for a lot of companies to anticipate what is sustainable livelihoods going to do and how do we look at these things. This whole bucket of reduce is quite easy to see the business case: the de-risking factor.

The second bucket is 'enable'. And what we mean by that is what you are doing as a company to enable both your suppliers and your customers to reach their ambitions. We are in the food space in the food system - what we worry about is customers for instance, wanting to ensure that they can provide products which are healthy for humans, but also healthy for the planet. There is an increasing pool of innovations. We have had customers who said: "listen, we have an ambitious Scope 3[7] road map. We need you to be on top of your greenhouse gases". Quite easy for us because we have been doing it for a long time because we did the reduce part. But this is a competitive advantage. Or if they are looking at regenerative agriculture[8] or switching diets towards more plant based, how can we support? This is all linked to their ambition. We have introduced a methodology; we call it Brighter Living Solutions[9] and we measure all our sales against it. Either it is market leading from an eco plus point of view, so ecologically or it is market leading socially on the social impact.

---

[7] Scope 3: up- and downstream Green House Gas footprint
[8] https://regenerationinternational.org/why-regenerative-agriculture/
[9] https://www.dsm.com/corporate/sustainability/brighter-living-solutions.html

And our target is - and we are there now- that 65% of our sales are market leading in either ecological or social criteria. And when you do that, and you set yourself that target, the advantage is that you are embedding it in the daily activities of your whole organisation. That can be done in any sector. Finally, the reason it makes sense also financially is if you go and 'advocate'. I will give a quite simple example, which is hardcore hotwired in our financials. We have been advocating for meaningful price on carbon for many, many years. We introduced an internal price on carbon 6 years ago with €50 per tonne, we are increasing it to €100 per tonne. It is driving our capital expenditure innovation decisions; it is also driving the way that we drive performance. And we have also been very much structuring our equity and our debt financing linked to performance on these targets. We have a revolving credit facility for a billion linked to our greenhouse gas reductions for example. The advocate is also linked to the environment in which you operate, so all of that the long and short is as a CFO, not only does it make sense, but it is also necessary.

Uwe Schulte
It sounds to me like a CFO is well advised to get to know the environment a little bit better they are operating in, otherwise they might be outperformed by competition before they know it. You opened a Pandora's box by saying what your carbon price is. Carbon is a huge discussion and a particularly important one. With the EU Green Deal and the idea of cross-border adjustments, we will see a very volatile field there for a while. It is interesting that you have taken again a precocious position to say we base what we do on something that is a very sensible price rather than what is currently being discussed.

Geraldine Matchett
Absolutely. And I do want to point out here that we are a sector which has a carbon footprint. It is not as if it is a paper tiger and some companies make big claims, but to be honest, their footprint is nothing other than taking the plane. We have real production facilities. We have 1.5 million tonnes of CO_2 emissions. Broadly, we are bringing it down, we have an absolute reduction road map at least 30% by 2030. Of course, aiming for zero and we are an engineering and very much a science-based organisation so when we put these things out there, we have a real road map behind it. But it is important and that is the role of the finance to embed this in decision-making at the meaningful price because some people may say: why do you not take the current market price? Well, since I started, it used to be below €10 in Europe and now it will be at €50 in no time. And that is why we are shifting now to one hundred because we believe that that is on the horizon within a very normal business period, so not 30 years out, but within the next 5 years and that impacts our decision.

Uwe Schulte
I would love to go on about the carbon price because a lot of people are interested in that as well. We have another conversation about that another time. But the

Conference Board has recently published a report on corporate purpose,[10] and you mentioned that already. And you featured prominently in that report with DSM. But there are several companies, ill advised, having just rebranded their vision statement, and they are calling it a purpose. You at DSM are doing it very differently and it would be interesting to hear what your view is on what a company purpose really is.

Geraldine Matchett

I hope that having spoken a bit about the history and our roots highlights the fact that a purpose comes from your deep inside. It is not something which is a one-time exercise of the corporate branding and communication team that can suddenly change your purpose. And it is important to try and have something that truly resonates with the people inside the company. That is the most important. This is not a PR position, and so ours has evolved from being a triple P (people, planet, profit) company to being a strong ESG embedded company to this statement of doing something meaningful. And it matured into being increasingly explicit about what our purpose is: our focus on our nutrition business, which is health through nutrition, health of people, health for the planet. Health for the people is the essence of what we do because we are all about micronutrients, about immunity, about the right health, about the health of animals. People, thanks to the quality of nutrition that they are getting, but health for the planet is very core to all that we have done on sustainability, and we have tried to capture that in creating 'brighter lives for all', which sounds very generic-but the *for all* is important. Because it is this concept of you cannot be successful in a world that fails. It really is 'brighter lives' in the impact and in our behaviour resonating with the people we work with and to the societies and communities that we work within. We do find that it is helpful to attach a purpose to Sustainable Development Goal themes and if you are able to say: this is what we can bring to the world. Why is it that the world is a better place if we are successful, that is the best question to ask yourself and therefore that should be our purpose. Why is it better that you are successful and not another company? Well, that is maybe because you have strict rules on your environmental footprint and how you manage the social and environmental impact of clothing, which is a big challenge. Any company should truly ask themselves: why is the world a better place if we are successful? In answering that question, you will get to your true sense of purpose, and then it is about having the courage to speak it out because some people say, that sounds a little bit airy, fluffy, but it is amazing how it resonates. It resonates internally. It resonates then for talent. When your people now say: "I want to work for this because what you say makes sense". They can feel it immediately. This is real. This goes deep. So that is really where purpose should be coming from.

---

[10] https://www.conference-board.org/topics/sustainable-business-integration/purpose-driven-companies-lessons-learned

Business Success with Purpose

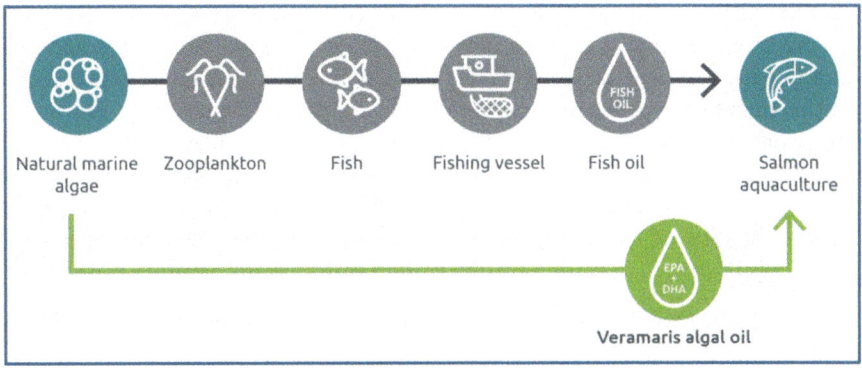

Fig. 3 Salmon farming with algae feed. Source: dsm-firmenich, https://www.dsm.com/corporate/markets/animal-feed/replacing-fish-with-algae-with-veramaris.html

Uwe Schulte
But Geraldine, there is another aspect here which I think is important because, you can have a fluffy statement, but you can also have a nice one like yours. But you might still not be living it. One of the things that I have seen that people have been—sorry to be saying that—blasting out a purpose statement, but then living another life. And the pandemic has shown this on some occasions that people were not living their purpose.

Geraldine Matchett
That is even worse. One mistake is, you may be doing the right things, but you try to define a purpose which is disconnected from what you do. It is not that you are doing dreadful things, but that the two are not coordinated. The other one, of course, is that if you make statements that are unsubstantiated that is a challenge. For instance, in our case, it has been instrumental to embed our ambitions internally through our innovation pipeline. We do ideation around climate ideation for innovation and that is how we got to some rather weird outcomes like working on how much methane cows burp. You do not get there if you are not really working your purpose of saying how does our science and technology and knowledge of nutrition impact climate change? And this is one of them. If we looked at, for example, the nutrition of aquaculture, salmon is full of Omega 3s, which is good for the health of people, but unfortunately, we are fishing out the oceans to feed the salmon, the oil that makes them rich in Omega 3. We looked at our biotech capabilities and realised that we can produce that oil from the algae itself, so we can feed the salmon directly from the algae,[11] which avoids fishing out the sardines out of the ocean to get the oil. These are examples (Fig. 3).

And in fact, to really be credible and to build the trust that your purpose means something, you must have it embedded in who you are and your targets. What are

---

[11] https://www.dsm.com/corporate/markets/animal-feed/replacing-fish-with-algae-with-veramaris.html

you committing to externally? But also, of course, in how you do business and what you are bringing to your offering. For example, if you make equipment and you want to have a climate claim, you have to show that you have done something to your product to be you leading the world in the right direction on energy consumption or on circularity on whatever the levers that you have at hand. But it is indeed important, and we find that it focuses the mind on the organisation if you commit publicly to ambitions, because then it sends a strong signal. There is not just talk. It is something that we are willing to hold ourselves accountable to going forward.

Uwe Schulte
I have just learned a new thing: you are putting salmon on a veggie diet. That is interesting.

Geraldine Matchett
Well, interestingly, the salmon is like a big, big fish, but the small fish eat the same thing, and indeed they can go straight on an algae-based diet.

Uwe Schulte
You mentioned that recruitment and retention of people is an important part of purpose as well. But again, if you are not living your purpose, it will eventually backfire rather than the over simplified relationship of having a purpose statement and your retention rate goes up. It is not like that at all. Could you please give our listeners your view of how purpose and financial success go together?

Geraldine Matchett
Particularly to finance colleagues: make it part of the core of your strategy of your business mission and of what you feel your function should be bringing to the whole company. This is not something for another department or embedded somewhere else. Of course, it is everywhere, but effectively we have seen the finance profession evolve over the decades based on the needs of society, from local business to globalisation. You needed IFRS standards,[12] etc. The world needs the finance function to embrace sustainability as its core, and it is happening as we speak. Go and embrace it and encourage. Particularly the tone comes from the top. Encourage all your colleagues to live it daily and it pays off. I can confirm it is not a trade-off. It is an essential building block for short-, medium-, and long-term success.

Uwe Schulte
You are a purpose led organisation and we had an interesting discussion about what that means and how it is incorporated. What is the reason you have related your purpose now to the United Nations Sustainable Development Goals (UN SDGs)?

Geraldine Matchett
What is key here is that for a long time and you are right, we discussed a little bit our origins and how far back DSM has been a triple P people, planet, profit company and SDG stock, but for a long time, it was very niche. So ESG was investing.

---
[12] https://www.ifrs.org/

People had their own ideas and their own themes, et cetera. And now what the UN has done very well is effectively create, in my view, a language around which we can anchor certain themes and certain ambitions, and those are the Sustainable Development Goals. What we have done when we defined our strategy as Royal DSM, the world's leading company when it comes to making food for humans and animals nutritious with all the micronutrients, the vitamins, the omegas, probiotics all of that. What is it that we can really have an influence on? To be specific, we have anchored for our nutrition part of our business around 4 SDG's. SDG-2 Zero Hunger,[13] because we are in the food space and hunger is not only about calories, but also about malnutrition, which, unfortunately in today's world, we still have seven hundred million people suffering from hunger and two billion from malnutrition. There is a long way to go in that zero-hunger ambition. And then there's SDG 3,[14] which is about good health and well-being, and that is in economies where it is not about people dying of starvation. But to be fair, the health outcomes are not good, and we saw that last year in the pandemic that poor nutrition leads to chronic diseases, non-communicable. The most obvious are obesity, diabetes, cardiovascular issues, respiratory issues, and how does better nutrition lead to better outcomes. So that's SDG 3 and our contribution there. And then we have 12 and 13. 12[15] is a bit broader. It is about responsible consumption and production. And this is really about the production of food. The most impacting human activity on the physical environment is agriculture, is production of food and that has been the case for many, many civilisations, and therefore responsible production of food, which is not the case today as we waste one-third of the food. That is not a responsible way of neither producing nor consuming, so there are a lot of things to be done on SDG 12 around the food systems. And finally, SDG 13[16] is climate action, so there are multiple aspects of the food systems being linked to climate change. On the one hand, agriculture is the second biggest activity in terms of greenhouse gas footprints, and the food production. It is the second biggest guilty party and at the same time it is the biggest victim straight away right now through big climate events like drought and floods. It is estimated that the desertification[17] is currently forcing forty million people a year to relocate off their land because they cannot grow anymore. There are huge interrelationships between the food systems and climate. What we have done is, and it does not mean that the other snags do not matter; of course, we have SDGs around inclusion and diversity around all the aspects of water. We try to really bring down from a strategic shaping, where are the areas where we can have the most impact and those the ones that we have identified and then we really work on those in terms of our innovation pipeline, the work that we do with our suppliers, upstream, the work that we do with our customers downstream. We always say you

---

[13] https://sdgs.un.org/goals/goal2

[14] https://sdgs.un.org/goals/goal3

[15] https://sdgs.un.org/goals/goal12

[16] https://sdgs.un.org/goals/goal13

[17] https://en.wikipedia.org/wiki/Desertification

Fig. 4 UN Sustainable Development Goal 2. Source: https://www.un.org/sustainabledevelopment/. The content of this publication has not been approved by the United Nations and does not reflect the views of the United Nations or its officials or Member States

Fig. 5 UN Sustainable Development Goal 3. Source: https://www.un.org/sustainabledevelopment/. The content of this publication has not been approved by the United Nations and does not reflect the views of the United Nations or its officials or Member States

cannot be successful in the world that fails and that means you cannot do it on your own either. We chose the UN SDG's that we can work on with the people, with the companies in our value chain to make a meaningful impact (Figs. 4, 5, 6, and 7).

Uwe Schulte
Geraldine, from my perspective you just said an important sentence: we have chosen the SDGs where we can make really an impact. And that is a key point. Sometimes people get a bit critical. There are too many SDG"s. But what people must realise is we have a common language; we have scoped out what needs doing to develop the world and it is important that different people focus on different things where they can do something. And I am always getting worried when I see company web pages where all SDGs are mentioned. And then I am asking: where are you going to focus your attention, where are you going to make a difference?

Geraldine Matchett
Yes. And here, it is especially important for anyone listening to understand there are two sides to it. On the one hand, you must have a health check. You cannot cherry

Fig. 6 UN Sustainable Development Goal 12. Source: https://www.un.org/sustainabledevelopment/. The content of this publication has not been approved by the United Nations and does not reflect the views of the United Nations or its officials or Member States

Fig. 7 UN Sustainable Development Goal 13. Source: https://www.un.org/sustainabledevelopment/. The content of this publication has not been approved by the United Nations and does not reflect the views of the United Nations or its officials or Member States

pick and say we are great here, but we are making really a negative impact elsewhere on the whole suite of SDG's. You must commit to a minimum standard of at the least, do no harm. That is where, for instance, ESG rankings are important because they look at all the SDGs and all the aspects, and they try to say: OK, you don't only get positive points for what you do well, but we will also look at whether you are doing harm elsewhere because that is not great either. It is important to realise everything is interconnected. But when it comes to having a positive impact and linking it to your purpose, you must be clear where it is that you can lead to market transformation to system change and that can only be in your areas of strength, so that is how it is not either or. Indeed, the world is a little complicated. It does take quite a few SDGs to cover all the important themes and we see that as well in the investing world. Shareholders, on the one hand, will do a scan to make sure that there is nothing offensive in what the company is doing. That is your qualifier with regard to impact on SDGs. And then there is your ability to be extremely successful in the context of changing markets and that is the opportunity side. There is the downside and the upside and SDGs are helpful in both.

Uwe Schulte

Thank you for pointing that out. It is important to be clear that we are not compensating one with the other. We must be at least neutral, but what we are aiming at is positive impact of course. Let us get a bit more concrete. You mentioned zero hunger and you talked about malnutrition. Something that is close to my heart is there are so many children still affected by malnutrition and that will jeopardise their whole life.[18] You can share with us a couple of examples what you are doing in this field.

Geraldine Matchett

You are right that malnutrition in the first thousand days of life, which includes within the mother and after birth determines the neural development, particularly of children, for their life. If you do not have the right nutrition in those first thousand days of life, you cannot recover later as a result. We are the leading company in the world when it comes to the knowledge and the science behind micronutrients. We have been for many, many years working with development agencies and saying be careful when you say zero hunger people think calories, they think people dying of lack of energy. But in fact, that is only half the problem. Of course, it is the first one, because if you die, you die. But malnutrition and stunting are chronic in still a lot of countries for a lot of children, and stunting is the outcome of a deficiency in micronutrients. What brings a lot of hope is the realisation that it is about malnutrition has really got embedded in the strategies of World Food Programme, of UNICEF, of World Vision, of the Big NGO's, and UN organisations trying to help these populations that are in this critical survival mode. We have been working with micronutrient supplementation of, for instance, the World Food Programme. The main thing they will deliver on site is something called super cereal plus, which is a porridge, which has of course a lot of calories, but also now is rich in micronutrients. We have been working with UNICEF for now many, many years on sachets of micronutrients that people can sprinkle on whatever it is that they are eating. Is it rice? Is it whatever it is that they can have. If they add this, they will get the minimum requirements of micronutrients. It is really focused on pregnant mothers, young mothers, and children. But there is a nicer example which goes beyond that because that is still relying on aid agencies, which currently are doing a fantastic job. Last year was a terrible year. There has been an improvement in the number of people suffering from hunger and extreme poverty every single year for 10 years, and last year we reversed, and we are 10 years back, so it is not a good picture. In the context of a conversation at the World Economic Forum many years ago, there was an observation of saying, is it not a bit frustrating that these agencies import the food into Africa to help the starving populations of Africa and its grain coming from Europe, from the USA? Is there not a way of producing food in Africa for Africa and they talked to us, and they said: Hey, DSM, would you be interested and able to see if we can do that differently. So we created Africa Improved Foods (AIF),[19] which is a

---

[18] https://www.unicef.org/reports/state-of-worlds-children-2019

[19] https://africaimprovedfoods.com/who-we-are/

Business Success with Purpose 195

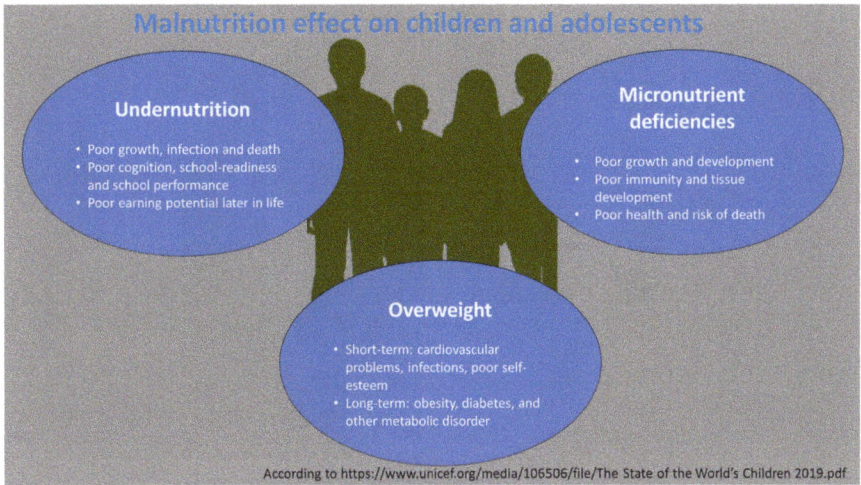

Fig. 8 Effects of malnutrition on children. Source: Uwe G. Schulte, Source: Unicef

very successful public private partnership structure where we invested in a production plant for this super cereal plus in Rwanda in Kigali and it is a joint effort of the Development Bank, of the Netherlands FMO,[20] of the UK CDC,[21] of the World Bank through IFC[22] and ourselves and we decided why do not we make super cereal plus in Africa for Africa? And if we fast forward now 6 years, we have a big world class standard production facility in Kigali that firstly employs three hundred plus qualified people. It really created an environment to up the skills and replicable skills in the country. We source grain from 130,000 smallholder farmers in East Africa, in Rwanda, Uganda. That was critical for livelihoods, and we are reaching 1.6 million people with nutritious food. The impact of this project so far has been creating $1 billion of added value for East Africa because it is effectively ticking two boxes at the same time: development and aid and of course, fighting malnutrition. These are the kind of things that we need as a world to be better at doing. It is really building the trust between the various stakeholders, including the local governments, including the farming association and cooperatives, so that you have an impact across the whole chain so that it is sustainable. This is something that will keep going. It does not need subsidies. At one point it stands on its own legs. You have transformed the system as opposed to philanthropy or aid, which unfortunately as we know, is like a tap, it is on, or it is off and then it is over when the tap gets closed (Figs. 8 and 9).

Uwe Schulte
Is that something that you will be able to replicate in other parts of Africa?

---

[20] https://www.fmo.nl/about-fmo

[21] Now: British International Investment: https://www.bii.co.uk/en/

[22] https://www.ifc.org/en/home

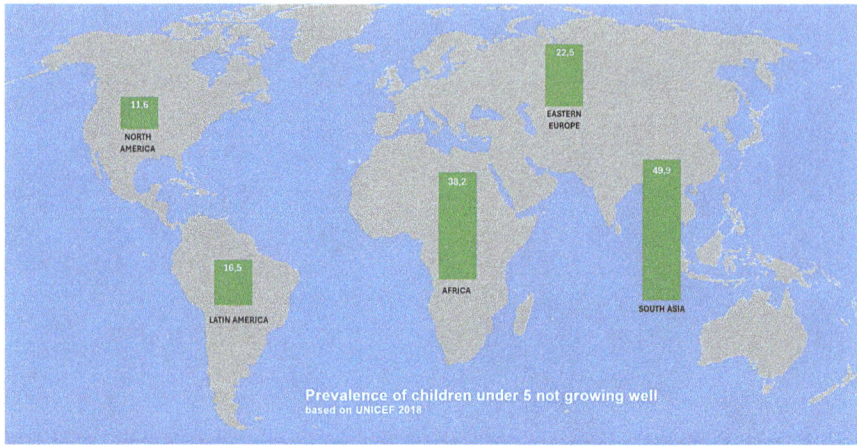

Fig. 9 Prevalence of children under five who are not growing well (stunted, wasted, or overweight), 2018. Source: Uwe G. Schulte, Source: Unicef

Geraldine Matchett

Rwanda is the one that is the most mature. We are now looking to replicate in different countries. Ethiopia, Kenya, and we are looking at Nigeria, so the continent. In that mindset, we also do egg hubs. We are looking at how do you facilitate the emergence of small farmers who can produce eggs in an effective way, because eggs are from a micronutrient content, an especially important source of micronutrients, particularly for school programmes and for children. So why are eggs extremely expensive in most emerging countries? It is a luxury, and yet it is a rich source of micronutrients. So how do you create egg hubs and facilitate an entrepreneurial sort of ecosystem emerging around that? We are looking at collaborating with the millers of grain to fortify stable foods to a much bigger degree than has been the case so far. I gave you one example out of many, but this is all anchored. This is not philanthropy. This is what we are strong at in all geographies of the world. And we are challenging ourselves to make sure that we are really reaching mouths around the world and not just in more mature and wealthier economies and it is scaling. It is nice to see but it took a lot of perseverance, because the trust, unfortunately, is often not there, that the private sector genuinely means to do the right thing. And there is still a bit of distrust when it comes to getting these things going of what is in it for you, and why are you wanting to do this? And our answer is: we believe that this mix, that anything that makes a lot of sense will be sustainable and is worth doing over time. But to get started you need different stakeholders to get together and have that common mission (Fig. 10).

Uwe Schulte

Now that is clear. I mean you already mentioned, which fascinated me, that you are turning salmon fish into vegetarians. So that is another part of zero hunger?

Fig. 10 Africa Improved Foods (AIF). Source: Africa Improved Foods, https://africaimprovedfoods.com/

Geraldine Matchett

Yes. if you think about the situation on this planet and this is the geographer speaking, the world population has tripled in the lifetime of my mother, so in 1950 there were 2.5 billion people on this planet. Now there are 7.8 billion depending on which estimate you want to take in one lifetime, and the reason I am mentioning this is that during exactly the same period, the number of people in extreme poverty has shrunk from 70% of world population, 70% of that 2.5 billion to below 10% of a much bigger number, so strong in percentage terms and in absolute terms, but there is a big but to this. It was achieved through the industrialisation of food systems. It is the only way we were able to feed three times more people and it has its consequences, which is the environmental impact of intensive agriculture, and we are seeing that come up all over the place. What we are looking at as a company, is saying how can we anticipate and help transition the food systems to something more sustainable that can still feed the existing population. There is the estimate that we are going towards ten billion. Let us see whether that happens. But nonetheless, even sustaining eight billion people on this planet is a challenge. We look at where are the environmental impacts of the food systems and what can we do in the case of fish. Aquaculture is seen as a useful source of protein and of Omega 3s, and therefore salmon is healthy to eat. On the other hand, aquaculture uses fish oil from the oceans, so to grow one salmon you must fish out between 10 and 20 fish from the ocean. Squeeze them, get the oil because that is what makes the salmon rich in Omega 3. The fish in the ocean get the Omega 3 content from algae and we have the technology to produce directly from the algae. This rich oil is used in infant formula for many years. It is a very trusted source of Omega 3, but we found a way to do it at scale. So currently we are indeed supplying the aquaculture industry with omega-3 oil directly from the algae which has a fisheries benefit, which addresses what was a resource ceiling that the industry was hitting. But it also means that salmon can have more of it because they were getting less and less, and therefore salmon was becoming less nutritious. It has a health impact and so it is good for people, and it is good for planet, and it is indeed leveraging some of the science and innovation that exists in the world. But you need to scale.

Uwe Schulte

Now let us get to another SDG and let us talk about climate action. But we can, bring it back to agriculture because there are the, let me use the word farting, cows. It is burping that creates the methane. Whilst methane is not as persistent in the atmosphere as carbon dioxide, it is on a like-for-like basis contributing many times more to global warming. I understand you have addressed that but let me put a little nudge here: some people are saying we will go to another way of creating that sort of protein in the future. So not solving the cow problem itself but creating meat protein in an unusual way is the solution.[23] How do you see that?

Geraldine Matchett

Yes. these are all the exciting things we like to think about. Indeed, a couple of things on agriculture being the second biggest contributor to greenhouse gas. And within that, there is of course the use of soil and taking vegetation away and all these issues of deforestation, but livestock is indeed a big contributor. Methane is twenty times more potent than CO2 in the atmosphere. And it is something that can be addressed with a lot less infrastructure requirements than a lot of other solutions. So how did we investigate this? We did a climate related ideation exercise and that goes back more than 10 years and thinking what we in our space of nutrition do about climate change. We identified methane burped by particularly cows, but all ruminants. And through adding a quarter of a teaspoon of certain feed ingredients, we can reduce the methane burped by cows by at least 30% and in some cases up to 50 to 60% and it is just tweaking a little bit that digestive system so that it does not create as much methane. This is going through all sorts of testing on 10,000 cows, all sorts of herds. And at first when we started doing that, we were told, why are you doing this? Who cares about methane burp by cows. Now all the dairy companies have a big challenge. The spotlight is on them, on the environmental footprint of the dairy herds. There are various aspects to the footprint because it impacts watersheds, etc. But the climate impact is part of the footprint of the country and in big dairy countries like the Netherlands, where we are based but also in New Zealand, there is a good example. This is meaningful and New Zealand is the first country in the world that has set a target to reduce methane from livestock as a national target. And we have dairy companies who are out there with explicit targets of carbon neutral milk and a low methane supply chain. It is part of their Scope 3, so that is where we are today. But to your challenge. And, it is going through the final hoops of registration, regulation, etc.[24]. This will go commercial very shortly in countries like New Zealand and in the whole of the EU with the EU Green Deal and the farm to fork strategies.[25] That is all part of where we fit. But to your challenge is the world going to be getting meat from a different source. There are two topics. One is, should we go away from animal-based proteins, dairy or meat and go to plant based? This is more the flexitarian type of diet, so a transition to less animal based, more plant based. We are working on all of that because we are in human nutrition very strongly and so we also look at what makes human nutrition nutritious. And we are helping companies who are developing these alternative offerings to make sure that the nutrition is there and the environmental footprint. When it comes to more lab-grown meats, whether a cell is grown as part of a sheep, cow, or pig or whether it is

---

[23] https://en.wikipedia.org/wiki/Cultured_meat

[24] https://www.dsm.com/content/dam/dsm/corporate/en_US/documents/media-backgrounder-introduction-bovaer_update-march-2023.pdf

[25] https://food.ec.europa.eu/system/files/2020-05/f2f_action_plan_2020_strategy-info_en.pdf

in a lab, it needs nutrients and therefore we are scanning all the technologies around the 'Impossible Foods' type companies. There are a lot of technologies out there that are trying. But the cell still needs the same building blocks and so we are looking at the nutrition within the liquid in which these cells are grown. Because in effect it is the same science, it just comes in a different shape. So it could be that if you project yourself in 10/20 years that there are some technologies that are scalable, affordable and that will provide some degree of, I do not know if you can still call it animal-based protein, that is produced in a different way. But we need to also be very mindful about these topics, there are different geographies on this planet and for some the challenge is still malnutrition and access to enough protein at a very affordable price. And this setting is a long way from being very affordable.

Uwe Schulte

There is also the question of the energy bill that is attached to it. But it is something worthwhile watching. And I see that you are having an eye on it. That is reassuring. It is impressive how you have had a long-term perspective on your R&D programme. For some people certain trends come as a surprise. You solve problems that some people did not even see coming. Unfortunately, we must end. It is so lovely speaking to you and listening to all the projects that are happening in your company. But could you help people wanting to transform their business as you have done successfully? What are the key things to watch to become a more sustainable business?

Geraldine Matchett

Indeed, we could keep talking for hours. These are all exciting things. And at the core of what we do, but maybe if we zoom out and take a broader picture for people who are in different areas, I think that the three things I would advise are as follows. One is it is important to redefine success. What does success look like and define that in the context of market transformation. Why will the world be a better place if you as a company are successful and when you answer that question you often find that you must work with your upstream, your downstream, your suppliers, your customers, your stakeholders. Broaden the conversation in the company of what the success really looks like and then you will start identifying not only your purpose but also what are the important things on the three horizons. Horizon 1 is today, Horizon 2 is in the near future and then there is Horizon 3 what is out there on the horizon, what should we be aiming for? So that is one. The other one is about visibly embedding those ambitions. We call them triple P so people, planet, profits internally wherever you can, whether it be through your system, your system of incentives, not because people are driven by money per say, but it is a strong signal of what the company feels really matters. But also, through external commitments, so have the courage to go out there and put some bold ambitions of how you want to have an impact as an organisation. The third one we touched upon already is focus on the areas where you truly matter to the world. It is important to do a health check that on your SDGs you do not do any harm, that at least you are neutral. Preferably you are positive on all, but at least do no harm, but really do the exercise of identifying which ones can you have a meaningful contribution and then really focus on those. Internally and with the stakeholders, not only private sector, but also public sector and NGOs and say how do we work together to move that. I would say be courageous. And what you will be rewarded by is, you will become a talent magnet. People love to not only have successful careers, but if they can add to having a positive impact. Everybody loves that. I have not come across one person who says I do not care. It is worth it. And sometimes you will fail. Sometimes you will trip over. Not everything will work. Innovation is always a risky thing to do because you must try things out. Then it is all about the usual number of experiments you can take in terms of capital allocation. But I think if you anchor it around the finding success, visibly showing what you are aiming for and being focused in those areas, you will be on a good track.

Uwe Schulte

Absolutely. Thank you so much. It was a very enjoyable listening to you and your experiences and giving that advice. Thank you, Geraldine.

Social Innovation

Recorded June 2021

Uwe Schulte

Today I will be talking to Kim Dabbs, Global Director of Social Innovation at Steelcase. First, let me briefly introduce our guest. Kim Dabbs is a social entrepreneur, advocate, and innovator who is leading social innovation for Steelcase. Prior to joining Steelcase, she served as Executive Director of the West Michigan Centre for Arts and Technology. She holds a Master of Public Administration from the University of Michigan and a Bachelor of Science in Art History from Kendall College of Art and Design. A warm welcome to you, Kim, and please tell us a little bit about yourself and how you got involved with social innovation.

Kim Dabbs

Thank you so much for the invitation and thank you for having me as a guest on your programme today. When I think about the history of how we all land in the jobs that we have, it always, for me, has rooted back in purpose and passion. I have always had this incredible desire to make a difference in the world, and I have had the great privilege of doing that with many different non-profit organisations, non-government organisations, both in the USA and now here where I currently live in Munich, Germany. My time has been very varied between education, between public policy, and now leading social innovation for the company I work for—Steelcase.

Uwe Schulte

Kim, it is encouraging to hear that passion. But before we get started with your subject—not all our listeners will know what exactly Steelcase does. Could you please talk a little bit about Steelcase and its commitments.

Kim Dabbs

Steelcase is the global leader in creating amazing work environments for so many different people throughout the world. We do that in corporate environments as well as healthcare and education. My relationship with Steelcase started as a non-profit organisation, as a beneficiary of Steelcase's partnerships, when I led the West Michigan Centre for Arts and Technology, before I became a part of their family. At Steelcase, we have a long history and a long commitment to sustainability and to our core values around the environment and social impact around doing business that is good for society. My draw to Steelcase, which is now a little over 5 years ago, was when you understand the impact that a company has in the environments and in the experiences, people have in their everyday life, whether that be in the corporate sector, and for the kids that I was working with directly, it was in those education environments. It really drew me to understand what I can do and how we can leverage Steelcase as a business to be that force for good and continue that commitment throughout the world. We have made a lot of, I would say, bold goals that are not new for us. We are over one hundred years old, and we operate in many different countries throughout the world. We have always had a lens towards people. We have always had a lens towards human centricity and the way that we design and the products that we deliver, but also in the commitments that we keep as a company.

Uwe Schulte

I guess, quite a few of our listeners will use some of your equipment, be it a desk or something else.

Kim Dabbs

That is right. So many of the partners at The Conference Board are Steelcase partners and clients as well. And we always welcome that opportunity.

Uwe Schulte

Let us get started. We want to talk about social innovation and its potential for business. Before we dive deeper, I think we should try to give a definition of what we understand social innovation to be.

Kim Dabbs

I think, quite simply, all innovation is social. When we think about the world and the lens that we take to design both experiences and products, I look at social innovation as making sure that we are taking a holistic look at the impact that we have in the world for all of our stakeholders, whether that be clients or employees, our dealer partners who are throughout the world, our suppliers and everyone else.

Uwe Schulte

But what would your criteria be to say that the impact is positive? Because that is what you are saying—there will always be a social impact. But it could be on either side, of course.

Kim Dabbs

That is right. I think designing through that lens of social innovation is such a critical and key differentiator to how businesses do business. For us, I always look at leveraging our business as a force for good, which is language that you are starting to hear increasingly throughout the world through a social innovation lens. I would say our key stakeholders on the social innovation side are people, the communities where we live and work, our employees, how they engage. We always look at that as social innovation impacting communities and building places where people can thrive, where people have a sense of belonging. At Steelcase, what we say is we unlock human promise. I love that because it is so true. When we think about every aspect of that work experience, what can we do to ensure that employees are thriving in their work, that employees feel a connection to the work they have? Also, like you said, taking a holistic look at that understanding and the implications of the choices that they make to be a positive force for impact in these unusual times. When I think of social innovation, I really laser focus in on that vision for the future where we have equity in our communities, where quality education is accessible for more children and more communities, and most importantly, where we are living in an environment that is sustainable. Those are the things that will guide our choices.

Uwe Schulte

What we want is that well-being is something for everybody, equally. Is that what we are saying?

Kim Dabbs

That is right. For everyone to have that sense of well-being and understand what those dimensions are, everyone must have equitable access to those opportunities.

Uwe Schulte

One crucial element of course, is access to education and education itself. Could you give us an example or two how Steelcase is operating in that field?

Kim Dabbs
One of our social innovation projects that we just launched is called a social innovation lab.[1] This is a pilot that we tested, and we were trying to figure out how we start to leverage our global scale, our knowledge, our networks of experts to come together to move the needle on positive social impact for students throughout the world. One of the things that we believe very strongly in, when it comes to social innovation, is that you must design with the community, not for the community. It is in that act of co-creation where true and lasting change can happen. It is where you start using methods and frameworks like design thinking[2] in their truest form to empower and engage communities, where the change is going to impact them the most.

We started our journey with a social innovation lab. This was during these past 18 months when entire communities across the globe were going through Covid, when we were having this uprising of voices around racial equity. And it was this opportunity for us to bring together all our community partners and say: 'What is it? How can we use this time and leverage this time of global disruption to close the gap between equity and education, well-being, and those educational environments'? We posed a global challenge in multiple communities throughout the world, and we had hundreds of people participate in what we consider an open innovation approach for social innovation. Everyone came together, we learned together, we tried to tease apart aspects of the questions that we were asking, understanding those insights that we needed to learn about why there existed a gap in access to education, why some students were thriving in environments, and some students were just being left behind. And through this process, we had hundreds of people, over thirty different countries come together and explore. We selected fifteen of the topmost promising ideas, where people were able to pilot and evaluate that approach or that intervention within their local community. And we provided them seed funding and some of the experts from the world's leading organisations when it came to innovation methods and mindsets, whether that be The Massachusetts Institute of Technology (MIT)[3] or IDEO[4] or different organisations. And what came out of that were small, focused experiments that are going to start to tip how programmes happen, how access to equitable education happens within their local communities. What we then do at Steelcase is make sure that when they are delivering that in their community we serve as a springboard or a catalyst to make sure those stories are shared with multiple communities throughout the world. And we really try to leverage our scale to share those insights because we know change does not happen the same way in every community. Those beautiful nuggets that translate across borders and across communities need to be shared and connected, that is how change happens.

---

[1] https://www.steelcase.com/socialinnovationlab/

[2] https://en.wikipedia.org/wiki/Design_thinking

[3] https://www.mit.edu/innovation/

[4] https://www.ideo.com/about

Uwe Schulte

That sounds like a very encouraging initiative. On the other hand, a big challenge to do this right throughout the pandemic. That must have been quite cumbersome to get this going. Is there a possibility to share a concrete example of a solution that inspired you?

Kim Dabbs

When you talk about disruption and so many community partners,—we have hundreds throughout the world—like you said, it is a complex process to build and launch during a global pandemic across borders, across languages. But we also needed to find latest ideas and we needed to accelerate and seed the existing ideas and communities that already had some momentum behind them. One of the other programmes that were closing the gap on equity and education was a programme that is called Camp Ignite and it is in rural Romania.[5] The students there did not have equitable access to education, nor did they have access to devices, nor did they have access to the Wi-Fi, or any Internet connection. All these barriers existed when we think about how we start to design these interventions. We collaborated with our local teams to see how we might close that gap between equity and education during this pandemic. They created an opportunity being considered a girls empowerment camp. What they saw was that one of the barriers to equitable access to education was just gendered outcomes. Girls did not have equitable access to the same education or the same rights as their male counterparts. Our team includes Romania. They decided they wanted to do something about that. They created what they call Camp Ignite and they pulled together over one hundred girls from throughout rural Romania to go through a weeklong camp that was designed to teach resilience, autonomy, and authentic voice. All these things that were going to be so important to their experience. And as they were doing this, we had to make sure that to deliver this during a pandemic we needed to leverage our partnership, so making sure that the girls had devices (Fig. 1).

Also, one of the insights that they learned is that we can tutor girls and give them access to opportunity in their educational settings to make those gains and to have the confidence within their school systems. But they also needed to teach boys, what that relationship looked like and how the dynamics of power and privilege were at play. They ended up having a camp for boys and a camp for girls, and then they finally all came together, and it was this beautiful moment of sharing, and really seeing an understanding 'this is the difference'. Not only were they more engaged in school and having access to the technology and tools to be able to finish their education, but they also made commitments to how they were going to strengthen their local community. I think these holistic approaches, when we think linearly about how you close that gap between equity and education, it is not always through those formal channels. A lot of it has to do with the culture and then married with

---

[5] https://www.steelcase.com/eu-en/research/articles/topics/social-impact/camp-ignite-sparks-equitable-opportunities/

Fig. 1 Steelcase Camp Ignite 2019. Source: Steelcase Inc., https://www.steelcase.com/eu-en/research/articles/topics/social-impact/camp-ignite-sparks-equitable-opportunities/

the process, tools, and space, to make sure that everyone has those equitable opportunities in communities.

Uwe Schulte
That is an interesting example and I think one could spend more time to really learn how you approach that. But let me ask you a more generic question. With these initiatives, it is important, but often difficult to measure impact and avoid unintended consequences. How do you make sure that you keep that under control?

Kim Dabbs
We take a design thinking approach, a very human-centred approach. Instead of jumping into situations and engagements where you have built something based on a lot of assumptions, we try to do a lot of small, focused experiments. And to get away from those unintended consequences, we design with the community, because the community is going to understand the ecosystem much better and much faster than anyone else does. When we think about who is going to see the blind spots that anyone has, coming in with a global lens, we are going to have the access to scale, and we are going to have the access to resources in new and diverse ways. But at the local level, the community has such beautiful access to knowledge resources, making sure that they understand what formal and informal systems are at play within their community, to know exactly how to design for those unintended consequences that many people do not see. Those small, focused experiments are super important to get instantaneous or quick feedback to it, and not design something so huge that by the time that you land it, the situation has changed. If we would have designed a global programme 2 years ago, imagine what the past 18 months would have done to all those plans. Having an agile approach, leveraging things like design thinking

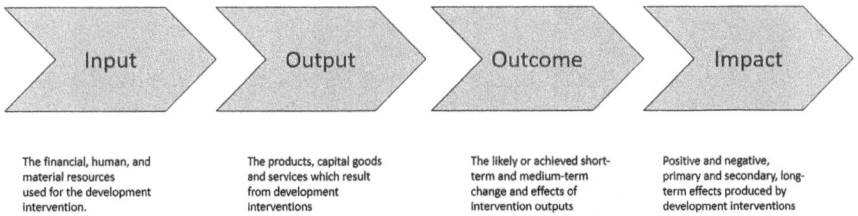

Fig. 2 From input to impact. Source: Uwe G. Schulte, Source: https://www.oecd.org/dac/results-development/what-are-results.htm

is key and critical to that agility. And then making sure that the people that are impacted by the outcomes are the ones that are designing and informing what that looks like, is foundational. That is the way that you start to mitigate a lot of that risk and those unintended consequences, because you become incredibly intentional about how you design. And then finally, we align all our impact measurements to the Sustainable Development Goals at a remarkably important level, much like many of your partner companies and organisations. But we do that through a theory of change framework. Instead of just looking at inputs or activities and stopping at outputs, which are like those metrics 'number of kids served' or 'number of classes taught', we try to take that next level jump to say that we really want to get to outcomes and impact (Fig. 2).

How many students are going through higher education or how many students are reducing that gap on quality education? We try to make sure that we have systems and processes in place that measure progress instead of just activities.

Uwe Schulte
What you are saying is such an important thing, and that is true whether you do social innovation or any other impact that a company might have. It is so important that when you are setting yourself goals, it cannot be about just changing processes. It must be about measuring real impact. That is important and thank you for highlighting that. You already mentioned the United Nations Sustainable Development Goals. I guess, that is part of how you decide where you want to engage. I have seen that many times people spread themselves thinly by doing too many things at the same time. How do you set priorities?

Kim Dabbs
For us, it was important that when we align to our core business, where can we make a difference? Where do we have it within our scope, tools, geography to be able to move the needle towards positive impact? And what is going to create the conditions for the future of work, which is what our core business is? How do we design those environments? How do we make sure that that future is for everyone? Reducing inequalities was critical. We know that that is just foundational to who we are as a society and making sure everyone has access to opportunity. For us, education was critical because we know that to have equitable access to opportunities, we need everyone to have access to education. And then finally, sustainability has been core

Fig. 3 Steelcase SDG priority goals 4,10, and 11. Source: https://www.un.org/sustainabledevelopment/. The content of this publication has not been approved by the United Nations and does not reflect the views of the United Nations or its officials or Member States

to who we are and what we do for over a century. And we know for people to have equitable access to opportunities and education they need healthy environments to live and thrive in. We said that in the social innovation space, these are the three areas that we really want to focus all our investments and all our impact, measure all our progress in the communities where we live and work through that lens (Fig. 3).

Uwe Schulte
That is the priority setting around the subjects you want to tackle, but there is also the element of 'your role is global', so there is also the question—where do you engage, in which parts of the world?

Kim Dabbs
We decided that we are going to engage in all those communities where we live and work. Our employees, our teams are incredibly important, and they are critical to our success in delivering holistic impact in the community. My goal is—as we have taken a look around the world and taken a look at those three impact areas of equity, education, and the environment—I am one person, our executive team is only so many people—in order to do this, we needed to build a movement to engage all of our employees throughout the globe. And by doing so, we have targeted specific locations where we have a presence, where we have a critical mass of employees, where we can make a lasting difference in that community. We created a programme which we call our Change Corp. And the only prerequisite to form a Change Corp in the location is that you have at least two people, a duo, that is critically passionate about equity education, or the environment and we work with them to identify different community partners in different ways that meaningful change can happen. For us, to build that global movement, we have prioritised those locations where we have employees and where we know we can dedicate resources, because it is more than just money. We can donate money to a lot of different communities throughout the globe, but we want sustainable, lasting change. We want the knowledge of our employees to enhance the impact within a community. We want to make sure that we do not parachute in and then leave the next day. We are a part of that fabric of the community and to have holistic change, we need to be a holistic part of the solution.

Uwe Schulte

Yes, I understand that, and it sounds ambitious, I must say, to do this everywhere you are. And let me challenge that a little bit. I mean, there is Kim sitting in Munich and Steelcase is in how many countries, 130?

Kim Dabbs

Not that many. But yes, we have a lot of countries and a lot of locations throughout the world. We started this approach, and it is ambitious. I remember speaking to some of our senior executives as we were proposing this new strategy and rolling it out. And they were saying: 'This is Steelcase. Your issue is not going to be trying to recruit people, it is making sure that you have opportunities for everyone that wants to get engaged'. Because as soon as we opened this Change Core Programme[6] so many people came running through the door to say, 'I want to do this in my community'., whether that be an operations engineer in Pune, India, or whether that be one of our salespeople in an office in San Francisco.

The projects and partnerships that they are creating are inspiring. We live in an incredibly volatile world. Social innovation at its core, we see some of the darkest parts of struggle in the human condition. And the other side of that is seeing so many people join hands throughout the world to try to make a difference in those areas. It fuels me to keep going every single day to see how committed our employees are, to see how committed our community partners are to making a difference in the world and making sure that we are embedding those policies, those practises in everything we do.

Uwe Schulte

I still admire the fact that you have set remarkably ambitious standards, and you have certain principles like bringing design thinking in, involving people from the onset, and to do things with people jointly. To maintain that standard throughout the world must be a challenge.

Kim Dabbs

It is always a challenge. I think that gap between aspiration and reality, whether that be in social innovation or anything else, that gap is always going to exist. I always worry, that because that gap is always going to exist, people will not try. For me, I would rather set some bold goals and race towards them because this is forever work. I cannot think in my career or in my lifetime that equity, education, and the environment are suddenly going to be solved in my tenure, in my role. But what I can make sure is that we have calibrated the systems for people to be audacious, to run towards progress, and to make sure that they care and are part of their community.

Uwe Schulte

Kim, excellent. You just made an especially important plea for 'just do it', get on with things when you see something needs doing, involve everybody, have the goal in mind, but do not be hesitant and have all those constraints in your head. We very

---

[6] https://www.steelcase.com/discover/steelcase/esg-overview/social/#highlights

often had the conversation in this podcast around 'show me the money', and in the last podcast I had with Geraldine Matchett from DSM, it became noticeably clear that forward-looking CFOs do not ask that question anymore, they do not talk about why, but how. And that is what I would like to ask you. What is it that drives Steelcase to engage in social innovation?

Kim Dabbs
At Steelcase, we have been doing this an exceedingly long time. We have always had a commitment to the communities where we live and work, throughout the world. For us, social innovation is just a natural extension of who we are and what we do. I think, how social innovation has been delivered has changed throughout the years, and it has changed through different lenses of employee expectation, community expectation as well as wanting to really be a leader and an example for how to use business as a force for good.

Uwe Schulte
Let us just spend a couple of minutes on each of those elements—equity, education, and environment, and how that relates to your business. I can see the point that you provide equipment for educational institutions. That, I can see. I also know that you have been looking into the environmental impact of your products and your production for a long time. But equity, driving against inequality—how does that relate to business of yours?

Kim Dabbs
Well, I think it does not just relate to the business of ours, it relates to all businesses. To me, equity, education, and the environment underpin who we are as a society, who we are as a company and doing so through a lens of humility. We do not have all the answers and we are not going to have all the answers, and this has been a journey of learning, understanding, and making sure that these stay priorities within our company and the companies of those that we partner with.

Uwe Schulte
I understand but let us become a bit more concrete. Let us say, I am your Chief Operating Officer and I have certain objectives. Then Kim comes along and says that we should really take some time off our people here and they should collaborate with the community on how to make sure that girls get education, as we discussed. What is in it for him?

Kim Dabbs
I think companies can take two different approaches to impact. This is where a paradox exists, but many want short-term immediate impacts. And we know that social change is long-term impact, and it is through that horizon of understanding the difference between the two. Do we want everything right now, which we do? We live in a company and a country in a world where there need to be immediate deliverables. That is just a part of life. But we also understand that the complexity of systems has become increasingly known in the management space and the strategy space and more as a globally integrated world that we live in. And the pandemic

absolutely exacerbated and highlighted how interconnected everything is. When you say equity, or equitable access to opportunity, or quality education, or the environment, they do not exist in silos. They cut across every single decision that everyone makes in the world. When we think about that and the choices that we are making for that operations person on the floor, we know that long term, if we have a thriving community, if we have an educated workforce, if we have the conditions for everyone to be able to have that equitable access to opportunity, that ecosystem is only going to get stronger in the long run, even though it may take more investment in the short.

Uwe Schulte

Let me look at that. In my past life, I was a works manager at some point in time, and I can relate to what you are saying. When I engage in the community I am in, then I will make sure that people will want to work for us and people who have a good education are more valuable partners in business than if they are poorly educated. I see that relationship, but it takes some doing to convince people who like this short-term cause and effect thinking, to think about systems and the longer term. How do you achieve that inside Steelcase that people have a different approach?

Kim Dabbs

I feel like I have had a fantastic opportunity to be able to design and deliver that strategy because we have such an amazing executive team that roots everyone in our core values.[7] When we talk about talent pipelines, which we absolutely invest in, when we talk about the ecosystems—important, they are all integrated. We know that is going to create long-term impact for the company. And truly, as I go into my strategy discussions, as I talk to different members of our leadership teams, consistently someone will come back and say: 'But is it the right thing to do'? They are not asking me for complex algorithms. What they are saying is: 'Does this adhere to our core values'? If it does not, if this choice that we are making is not aligned to the core values, it is off the table. And for me, working in a function like social innovation, that is crosscutting across all those functions, whether that be talent management, or the environment, or sustainability teams, or legal, or anyone. Throughout the world, consistently people will root themselves in our core values. I know that we are living in a time—I say this with all humility—I know we are living in a time where you are hearing this from a lot of companies. But truly, when those decisions are being made, it is asking first—is it the right thing to do? Is it the people centre thing to do? (Fig. 4)

And second, how does this impact our business? How does this impact the culture, the ecosystem? Are we driving decision-making down? Are we making sure that people have equitable access to opportunities? What are those policies that we can strengthen to make sure that it happens? Understanding that fundamentally, it is rooted in who we are as a company. Then secondarily, yes, we want everyone to

---

[7] https://www.steelcase.com/eu-en/people-planet/

Our Values

Using our core values to guide commitments and fuel action, we're shaping a future that continues to protect the environment, fosters transformational social impact and sustains a culture where all people feel empowered.

- Act with integrity
- Tell the truth
- Keep commitments
- Treat people with dignity + respect
- Promote positive relationships
- Protect the environment
- Excel

Fig. 4 Steelcase core values. Source: Steelcase Inc., https://www.steelcase.com/

have access to opportunity and we want to have that rich, diverse, unique point of view that only comes when there is diversity within teams, within companies.

Uwe Schulte
You made several points that I would love to dive into. But let us get started on the challenge you gave me which is that we hear this a lot from other companies. To be honest with you—we do not. Luckily, in the podcast series, we have now had it on several occasions, and I am immensely proud that we found these companies that not only say it but mean it. It is so important. Purpose is the new resilience. There are some buzzwords around and purpose is one of them. Sometimes people do not discriminate well enough between what their values are, and what their purpose is. One is how you apply yourself towards your purpose, of course. For you it seems living your purpose, your values, is ingrained in all the people you have in your organisation that they will challenge each other whether the decisions they make are aligned with the purpose or not. That is in stark contrast to companies employing a communication agency to change their vision statement into a purpose statement. That approach will backfire because people in the organisation will see that reality and what you aspire to on paper is not aligned.

What I gather from what you are describing is that there is a lot of energy coming out of that alignment that you are having. And now my question—long winded one—does that spark distinct types of innovation? We are talking social innovation here, of course, but product innovation—does that condition that we just described help that process?

Kim Dabbs
Absolutely. I think about what I consider holistic value. We are starting to understand that this design process needs to have and hold so many different voices, and that innovation happens when you have diverse teams, when you have different perspectives both inside and outside the company. We are partnering with an organisation right now, G3ict,[8] and designing and developing a global blueprint for

---
[8] https://g3ict.org/

Fig. 5 Global Initiative for Inclusive Information and Communication Technology. Source: G3ict, https://g3ict.org/

inclusive workplaces of the future. This was a wonderful opportunity to say that our values of treating people with dignity and respect, promoting positive relationships, all these things that we want to do, also need to be embedded in the processes that we have, or be it design, engineering, whatever that is. Are we making sure that we are partnering and getting those voices to the table that will help us broaden and deepen how we work, what insights we have, what perspectives we are hearing and listening to? And then using across the entire company processes like design thinking which have this collaborative moment at the onset that is rooted in empathy. Not just one person's voice, but truly rooted in empathy to understand what users are experiencing, what people in different communities are experiencing. How do we collectively design for that? (Fig. 5)

And I think when culture is partnered with the process and the right tools, that inclusion happens, not just in a person-to-person interaction, but holistically in the entire process. And those are the types of experience that we are trying to create, and we are on a journey, just like everyone else. I say these things, not saying that we have all the answers to diversity, equity, and inclusion. We do not have all the answers to the environment or the equity. But I can tell you that I am committed to partnering, to learn. I am committed to sharing what works and what does not work. I am committed to making sure that this is across functional, between functions within Steelcase, and across sectors, across geographies, and across industries.

Because all these things need to come together, not only aspirational, but we need to take what we are learning and embed the same things within different systems throughout the world. Because of the complexity of those systems, when something works, I always go to my counterparts. The Conference Board is a fitting example. I always reach out and say: 'Hey, who else is struggling with this? Because we have learned about this on this side. But who is doing well on this part'? And it has always been a beautiful collaboration in this moment for industries to come together and start to share, because not one of us has the answer.

Uwe Schulte
As you are mentioning The Conference Board, which is much appreciated. We just did a working group on the future of business and society[9], and you already mentioned some elements. Having a long-term view is one, embedding sustainability in all the decisions you make, we also pointed out transparency, being transparent to the outside world, we have not discussed that yet, being an advocate of the things,

---

[9] https://www.conference-board.org/topics/sustainable-business-integration/role-of-business-in-society

you believe in, taking a public stance, you already pointed out that as well. And the last point I think is an especially important one. People must rethink, how they work, you mentioned partnership. At Steelcase you have developed a culture over many years, but when you reach out to other partners, you do not necessarily share the same values. How do you make sure that you drive these partnerships in the right direction, with empathy of course.

Kim Dabbs
Every company culture is going to be different. And just like with environmental sustainability, the maturity of an organisation on that journey is different for everyone. I see that, and I understand that as we go into different partnerships. What stays the same though is, I always like to enter in those conversations asking what the change is that you want to see in the world, what is it towards which you are really driving? And then when we can find a connection, is it around education? Is it around equity? What piece of it? Do you really have a unique point of view where you can move the needle? Then it is easy to find collaborative and complementary opportunities to really move the needle faster. I think coming to it through a learning posture, if you can build that learning culture within the partnerships that you have, as well as laying the foundation towards a shared purpose versus how our company culture is the same. If you have the shared purpose, you can start to build in and design in the rest.

Uwe Schulte
Do you experience more difficulties in some parts of the world than in other parts of the world to the openness of such a collaborative approach across company boundaries?

Kim Dabbs
Absolutely. I always find that in more embedded or mature markets—when I say mature, it is just where they have had a longer history of us doing business in that location—it is almost harder to get momentum, because those systems are so deeply embedded and you get a lot of 'things have been done that way', so there is a lot of reasons why it cannot happen. I find in those resilient or emerging markets there is so much that happens with so little. They always find a way to get it done. And by nature of being scrappy, people just partner, and they partner happily because they know 'this is what we do here, and this is what we do to get it done'. And I always love jumping into those design sessions because we can run far and fast together, because there is such an open mindset and a learning mindset to be able to get things done collectively.

Uwe Schulte
You are working on a good basis of company culture and values. But I still hear from several companies that remote working has some benefits of course, but it also has the difficulty to create that sense of being together. You are in the business of also looking at home offices and similar work environments. How do you manage to maintain that momentum, that good momentum that you have talked about, under these conditions of so many people working remotely?

Kim Dabbs

I believe it is with intention that those organisations and those companies that make the work experience top of mind and critical to the success of their organisation, are the same ones that are going to come out of this hybrid work or whatever choices organisations are making globally, to have that hyper focus on whether it is remote collaboration, whether it is in person, whether it is across geography, across boundaries. Those that care about the experience of those that are collaborating with them day-to-day have made intentional rituals, intentional activities, intentional guidance to help their employees navigate this really challenging time. And to me, from a social innovation perspective, working from home is such a privilege for many. Working from home or distributed work—this is all through such a lens of privilege. And this is a huge equity issue that we are going to have in our lifetime. There are so many people coming out of this pandemic that are going to be left behind, that have been left behind, because they did not have the same equitable access to opportunity. And the workplace starts to unify that, it starts to mitigate some of those inequitable outcomes that are happening. The faster we can recognise and understand the inequality that exists by saying 'you cannot come into the office, or you do not have this, you need to work x number of days from home', not really understanding the human side of what that means through an equity lens.

Uwe Schulte

The ability to work from home, as you said, is a privilege. Those people with two small kids, or three small kids running around the kitchen, the families with both partners working, sitting at the kitchen table trying to work from home, would not consider that a privilege. But it is still a privilege, compared to those who have no access to Internet or equipment. Absolutely, I am with you on that one. What I would like you to do is to get yourself into the shoes of our listeners who have been inspired by the approach and would like to get started on this. What do I need to change to engage with my company in social innovation?

Kim Dabbs

It is the same. What is the change that you want to see and what is the change that you can make in your core business? You talked a little bit about how The Conference Board is having these types of conversations, and the role of business in society. And when I think about that on a corporate level there are some things that you would need to take into consideration. What are those culture levers? Do you have a culture where it is more focused on individual contributions or is it a top-down hierarchical approach? Because for any ESG movement to begin, for social innovation to begin a movement forward, you are going to need to drive some of that decision-making down, and you are going to need to embrace the fact that you are building a movement of lots of different employees and lots of different locations, and they need to be empowered to be able to do that. Is your culture calibrated for that individual? The transparency is critical. You talked about transparency. When do you think about the spectrum—are you only doing it to be responsive or are you looking for that long-term impact? How does your collective action reflect those commitments and your progress towards those commitments? Are you using your business and only talking about monetary impact or are you using it on the other end of the spectrum as a force for good? And where do you want to be on that spectrum? Make some goals there when it comes to leadership. As you are doing that too, make sure that it is aligned to your core business. If you are trying to be a purpose-driven company, or if you are trying to do that within a company as a social entrepreneur, the most progress you are going to make is when you align that purpose to actual impact that you can control. And then embed and institutionalise within your own company to give it that long-term momentum. The last thing is that authenticity. Understand that this is a learning culture. To have trust, you need to be willing to go forward, not knowing all the answers. Go forward with the understanding that it is going to take collective action, that you are not going to be able to do this on your own. There are going to be mistakes that are made. With the strong community partnerships, with strong relationships with employees, you are going to learn and get better. Have those tough conversations, and then keep moving forward. Because that forward progress is critical. I think, those four areas of leadership, transparency, trust, and collective action are the recipe for how you can start to build that internal culture. And once you understand where you sit on those spectrums, you will be able to understand what progress you are going to be able to make.

Uwe Schulte

One of the points you just said, and all of them were extremely important, but one resonated extremely with me. You said it in different words, but making sure that what you want to achieve and the capabilities of what your company can do, must be aligned. You must see where you can make an impact. To see, where is the material impact you have on all your stakeholders. That is an extremely key point and you have found those with equity, environment, and education—I got the sequence wrong again. Very impressive, thank you so much. Unfortunately, we are running out of time. But thank you for sharing these insights. And again, listening to you and your passion has been inspiring. We wish you all the success to continue. Thank you, Kim, and goodbye.

Energy Transition Scenarios

Recorded September 2021

Uwe Schulte
Today I will be talking to David Hone, Chief Climate Change Advisor at Shell. First, let me introduce our guest. David joined Shell in 1980 after graduating as a Chemical Engineer from the University of Adelaide in Australia. He has worked in refinery technology, oil trading and shipping for Shell. David is a Board Member of the Centre for Climate and Energy Solutions in Washington,[1] USA and the Global Carbon Capture and Storage Institute[2] in Melbourne, Australia. He was also a long serving Board Member of the International Emissions Trading Association[3] until the end of 2022 and was its chairperson from 2011 until 2013. David posts regularly on his Shell Climate Change Blog and has also authored a 2016 book on climate change, 'Putting the Genie Back, Solving the Climate and Energy Dilemma'. It is an immense pleasure to welcome you, David. As a start, could you tell us a little bit about yourself and how you got involved with scenario planning?

David Hone
Thank you for inviting me to the podcast today. Scenario planning really came out of my involvement in Shell with the climate issue. I had been in Shell for the first half of my career, doing all the things that you talked about, and then an opportunity came up in what was then the corporate centre around the climate change issue. It obviously had a link, although this was 20 years ago, not entirely clear then how it would link to Shell's long-term strategy, but nevertheless it was clear that this was a topical issue.

---

[1] https://www.c2es.org/about/
[2] https://www.globalccsinstitute.com/
[3] https://www.ieta.org/About-IETA

I applied for and started this role in the climate change space in Shell. At the time, sitting with the scenario planners, although it was not in the scenario team. There was an immediate constructive interaction because, and this was 2001, the scenarios were already talking about the climate change issue and how it was growing in scale and what it would mean for the energy system in the decades ahead. We had worked together very closely over many years. Then the opportunity came up for my job to be in the scenarios team about 4 years ago now. That happened. But of course, the job itself has changed enormously over the years. In 2001, I was Shell's climate change person. There was one person. Today, if you look at the full scope of energy transition and carbon management technologies and all the other things, there are hundreds of people involved in, not in climate change, but in the reality of the issue and how it faces Shell. That is how I got into the scenario team. This is a natural fit when you look at the climate issue and how the world responds to this challenge. It is bread and butter for scenario planning, it is what scenario planning is all about (Fig. 1).

Uwe Schulte

This leads to my next question to you. A lot of people talk scenarios all the time, and a lot of people talk about scenario planning. But it is worth our while to step back a little bit and say, 'What is it, what is the objective'? How do you approach this in principle?

David Hone

For some people, it is a bit of a dark art, and we still get talk around that in Shell that we all go off and hide in the corner somewhere and produce scenarios and no one is quite sure what happens. But that is not the case. There are many ways of looking at the future and thinking about the future. One way is to do forecasts. You look at where you are today. You are producing widgets, and the global widget demand is growing by 1% per annum. You calculate a forecast, and you say, 'By 2030, the global widget demand will be x and our market share will be this'. All that assumes, of course, that the status quo of widget demand, the use of widgets, the continued growth of that market just continues as it has in the past. Forecasts can be especially useful, particularly for shorter term things. We use forecasts a lot in the oil industry to look at short-term demand changes and things like that. Scenario planning really tackles this from a distinct perspective. It looks at what happens if the demand

Fig. 1 Putting the Genie Back, book by D. Hone. Source: Shell International Ltd., https://blogs.shell.com/category/sea-level/

pattern changes completely. What happens if a better widget emerges, and somebody invents a different process or a different approach to the service that you are providing? Or the political stability that you relied on in the country where you manufacture or produce your widgets suddenly changes and you cannot access your facilities anymore. Scenario planning is there to stretch the thinking of forecasters into places that they may not be comfortable thinking about. It applies a methodology to what might otherwise be a random collection of thoughts about, 'What if the future changes'? Well, the future will change, and here is a structured approach to thinking about that and producing two or three or however many you feel is appropriate different views of the future, but based on real trends and real developments that you can see today. But extend it out so that they become the dominant theme of the day. That is what is behind scenario planning. It is to stretch the mindset and stretch the thinking of planners, of strategists so that they can really get their heads around completely different outcomes, but nevertheless very plausible outcomes from where we are today. We have seen a lot of that in the last few years with big political changes in certain countries and the ramifications of that going forward.

Uwe Schulte
I believe one of the key points about scenario planning, as I see it, is not just necessarily to be able to predict what the future is really going to be like, but to have a

mindset that prepares you for potential significant disruptive changes and what the implications are, so that you are much better prepared when these changes occur.

David Hone
Well, exactly. And in fact, it is not about predicting the future at all, because nobody can do that, or at least nobody that I have ever met.

Uwe Schulte
There are some channels on TV that claim that.

David Hone
Well, there are people that have some good guesses, and they are right, but if you have enough people guessing, then eventually somebody will be right. The way you described it has brilliantly encapsulated it. It is about preparing you for the future and letting you see some of the alternatives that might emerge.

Uwe Schulte
We cannot feature the details of the structured approach here, but it is a very structured approach, of course, and that helps you to focus the mind and have a methodology. But what we should do is encourage people to have a look at that methodology and apply it to their business, because it is so helpful and there are possibilities to create certain signposts to say, 'Along the line, when you have developed some scenarios, which are the more likely ones, in which direction will it go'?

David Hone
We do not assign probabilities to our scenarios. What we do is that we produce a set of plausible scenarios. All of these could happen. But then to start to say, 'This is more likely than that'. you start to get back into forecasting.

Uwe Schulte
That is not what I meant. But once you have these weigh-out scenarios you can say that along the line, the next years you will see in which direction the things are going and then fine-tune.

David Hone
That is true. One of the post-scenario steps is to establish a framework to look at signals and signposts and start to get a feeling for how things are changing, and they are evolving in a particular direction. That is another step that is part of the scenario planning process, yes.

Uwe Schulte
You have done a massive exercise of applying your scenario planning methodology on various levels of potential global warming. Can you describe the scope and the approach of that exercise?

David Hone

In February this year, we released what we call the 'Energy Transformation Scenarios'[4] and these are three scenarios that look at separate ways in which the energy system might develop. They have their roots in a piece of work that we did last year call 'Rethinking the 2020s'[5] which was a piece of work that looked at how the 2020s might radically change because of the pandemic. The pandemic was seen as a big enough disruption to the global normal status or status quo, to mean that the 2020s and potentially beyond would be different. We identified in that piece of work three real tensions that are playing out. There is a tension around what we call 'Wealth' which was the desire to rebuild quickly and get back to normal. You see that with a lot of the stimulus bills going forward and the desire of economies to just get everything back together again. There was a second tension which we called 'Security' which is about countries becoming more inward looking and thinking about their own circumstances in the pandemic. But that starts to shut down the global economy to a certain extent, because it starts to upset the good cooperation that you need for the global economy to work properly. It dampens trade a bit. And you see some examples of this. My own country, Australia, is wrestling with this, 'Do we shut ourselves off or how do we open up again'? It is a challenge. And then the third tension was the recognition that coming out of the pandemic the health and well-being of society is more important than anything else. And this is not just the health of people relating to Covid. It is the broader aspect of health and well-being. These three tensions which we can see pieces of today have led to these three scenarios. These are the roots of scenario planning, 'What are the big tensions that you see around you'? A scenario called 'Waves' where there is a push to rebuild, that climate change does not get addressed as early as it needs to be, but there is a recognition of that as we go into the 2030s and then you get a wave of change in terms of moving away from fossil fuels. There is this island scenario that came out of the security drive where it just all goes a bit slowly and even by the end of the century, we are not at net zero emissions. Emissions are slowly coming down but not at anything like the pace necessary for meeting the goals of the Paris Agreement. And then the third scenario which we called 'Sky 1.5' is really encapsulating this drive for health and well-being and it leads to big change, it leads to environmental change, it leads to changes in people's mindset around how they consume, what they do, how they behave, and that delivers on the goals of the Paris Agreement. These are the three scenarios. These three scenarios are plausible. The Sky one is particularly stretching because it requires a lot of change. But you can see some of those elements today emerging out of the pandemic, not completely but nevertheless, all these three scenarios are still in play (Fig. 2).

---

[4] https://www.shell.com/energy-and-innovation/the-energy-future/scenarios/what-are-the-previous-shell-scenarios/the-energy-transformation-scenarios.html

[5] https://www.shell.com/energy-and-innovation/the-energy-future/scenarios/what-are-the-previous-shell-scenarios/rethinking-the-2020s.html

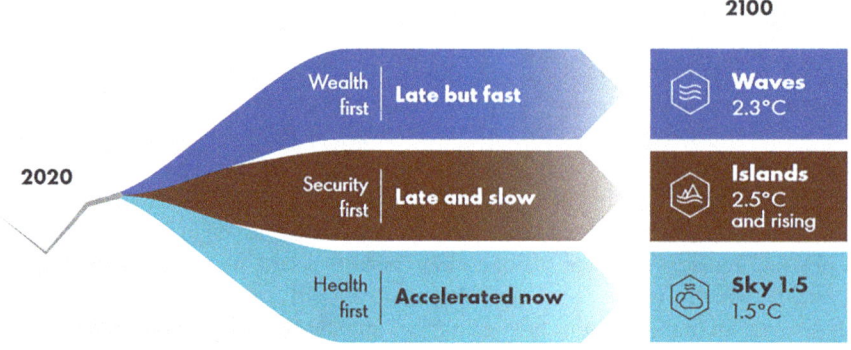

Fig. 2 Shell global warming scenarios. Source: Shell International Ltd., https://blogs.shell.com/2021/02/10/exploring-the-energy-future/

Uwe Schulte

Before we get into the details of these scenarios, and it is extremely interesting and challenging to the mind, can you talk a little bit about what the inputs were? Because it looked to me that you made a lot of quantitative analysis before you produced these then qualitative scenarios.

David Hone

Well, it is a combination of the two. The work around identifying the key tensions in society is a qualitative discussion. We do that independently of quantitative analysis initially, although the quantitative part starts to feed in very quickly. And we set up workshops last year where we invited a broad range of external stakeholders who are experts in different fields, in social trends. We had an epidemiologist come in. You can think of several different people in the room or in the virtual room as it was. They helped us through the process because the scenario process does involve looking widely outside as well. It is quite difficult to just do it yourself. You must take external input to stretch your own thinking as scenario planners. We went through that process. But within the scenario team, we have a strong modelling capability and we run a system called the World Energy Model[6] which takes inputs from the likes of the International Energy Agency, all sorts of data sources that we get about energy demand and energy use. It takes in econometric data on GDP and GDP growth and population data from the UN. We use that to model the energy system going forward, but we drive it with some of these qualitative pieces. Obviously, it is numerical, but you turn these qualitative thoughts into numerical drivers in terms of growth rates or in terms of the desire of policymakers to put in a carbon price, for instance, or whatever emerges from your storylines, and then you model the energy system going forward. Then there is a bit of an iterative loop between the qualitative

---

[6] https://www.shell.com/energy-and-innovation/the-energy-future/scenarios/what-are-scenarios/shell-scenarios-energy-models/world-energy-model.html

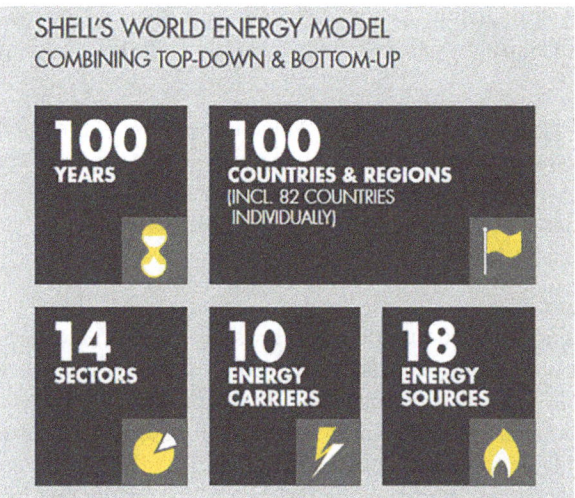

Fig. 3 Shell's world energy model. Source: Shell International Ltd., https://www.shell.com/news-and-insights/scenarios/what-scenario-planning-models-does-shell-use/worldenergy-model/_jcr_content/root/main/section/simple/call_to_action/links/item0.stream/1651505502658/2ee82a9c68cd84e572c9db09cc43d7ec3e3fafe7/shell-worldenergy-model.pdf

and the quantitative to arrive eventually at a story that is both substantial in its thinking but also backed up by a set of numbers that are physically possible to happen (Fig. 3).

Uwe Schulte

Let me see whether I understood this correctly. You have an energy model that has relationships between population growth, GDP development. And you then tweak certain knobs in that model based on your qualitative assumptions and say, 'What if this were to happen? Then this would have these knock-on effects and therefore these are then likely outcomes'.

David Hone

Yes, that is broadly it. That is a good description. But of course, the knobs are in their hundreds, there are not just a couple of dials on the front. There are hundreds of inputs to this, but that is what is going on. And then the model itself is quite a complex model because it considers the costs of technologies, the availability of materials, the availability of resources. If you want to go off into a world where more natural gas is burned, for instance, you cannot just do that because you think it is a clever idea or you think that there are pushes in that direction. You may run into resource constraints that do not allow that to happen. And that is similarly true for things like metals where there is a big drive for metals because these are key components in the renewable energy system, cobalt in batteries, nickel in batteries. There are limits on the resource availability of these, either the capacity to mine them or the physical quantity available globally. In a scenario you must start to build in those types of constraints as well, so that you cannot produce an implausible story.

Uwe Schulte

I understand that this is a lot of knobs, which is clear. We will no doubt get to each of those scenarios and the implication. I just want to ask you a question now which is almost impossible to answer, but I will ask you anyway. What do you think, based on what you have seen from the scenarios, will we be able to get to the Paris Agreement goals of 1.5?

David Hone

Well, that is quite a loaded question, is it not? Our 'Sky 1.5' scenario is called 1.5 for a reason. It is a scenario that meets the goals of the Paris Agreement in a particular fashion. And I say that because what happens in the Sky scenario is that we overshoot 1.5 around the middle of the century. But there is a mechanism within it which is using large-scale air capture and large-scale reforestation to rebalance the atmospheric carbon and start to bring it down a little bit, so that by 2100 you are back to 1.5. It is not a huge excursion, it gets to about 1.7, 1.8°C. To limit warming to 1.5 and not go above it looks extraordinarily difficult from today's perspective.

As we saw in the recent IPCC (Intergovernmental Panel on Climate Change) report[7] we are at 1.2 degrees now of warming, relative to preindustrial level. The carbon budget that is associated with additional warming to 1.5 is now so limited that it is consumed in under 10 years. Unless you had extremely rapid emission reductions in the space of a decade it looks like we are headed for an overshoot. But it is still a plausible story that we can recover from that and leave this century with limited warming.

Uwe Schulte

That is depressing and getting only a small light at the end of the tunnel for us. We must dive deeper into that. Now, I was intrigued by your mentioning that you really started about this rethinking the 2020s in the light of the pandemic. How do you see the connection between that and the energy system panning out? I know that you said depending on the tensions, how they develop, but how do you see the development in the light of today?

David Hone

Well, the pandemic has challenged the global status quo, there is no doubt about that. It is just a question of how it has challenged it. As I said, there is this desire to rebuild, but it has also left many people thinking about their longer-term well-being. We think that those sentiments are not short-lived sentiments, that this has been a big enough disruption to change things. And there are also physical changes. For example, nobody is talking about us all going back to work in the same way as we were working in 2019. At Shell Centre in London, they have leased out half the building to somebody else, simply because there is a new ethic around the way in

---

[7] https://www.ipcc.ch/ar6-syr/

which people work, the flexibility that the company wants to give everybody, the time which people want to spend in the office versus working at home. We have already started to establish changes.

For instance, will business travel ever return to exactly where it was in 2019? It will not stay at the extremely low level that it is now. But a year and a half, and by the time we are done it could be more than 2 years of zoom meetings and travelling to conferences virtually and presenting at conferences virtually, that leaves people with a new way of doing things. Of course, the technology has moved to help us do this better than we were doing it in 2018 and 2019. We have imagined in the scenarios, particularly in the 'Sky 1.5', that these changes embed themselves in society and lead us off into a different energy future, just simply for those reasons, let alone the sentiment and the feeling around it and the political forces behind it as well.

Uwe Schulte

I understand the mobility one, that is clear, and that is at least 20% of the carbon as far as I get it. But would the pandemic have an influence on the choice of whether you insulate your home, or whether companies are moving to hydrogen, for example?

David Hone

Well, not immediately. It might have an impact on people insulating their home simply because they are spending more time there and they realise that their house is not quite as comfortable as they thought it was, so they start to make changes and they make their home environment more suitable for a higher level of occupancy. But no, it does not immediately lead companies to require moving to hydrogen. That obviously comes out of a political process. But we saw this in the speech given by the Chinese President a few months ago where he declared that China would be at net zero emissions by 2060.[8] And he linked that back to the pandemic. It was a speech and speeches are written by speechwriters, and we can take it for what it is. But nevertheless, he made the point that the situation we find ourselves in has made us stop and think about where we are heading as a society and the pressures that we are bringing to bear. The pandemic emerged out of environment, out of environmental stress in the areas around Wuhan. We do not know exactly, is it because of overuse of that land. But nevertheless, he made that linkage and he said that we must look more broadly at how we are living in this world. And one of the aspects of that is ensuring that we are not changing the surface temperature conditions, and therefore we are going to be at net zero emissions. Those linkages are there, they are tenuous. This is what the scenario planning has brought to light, that it is changing people's mindsets. And mindsets eventually lead to substantial change.

Uwe Schulte

Absolutely. And I think for business the conclusion of what I just heard you say is, 'Have an open mind on the possible developments and do not just extrapolate from

---

[8] https://www.cnbc.com/2020/09/23/china-claims-it-will-be-carbon-neutral-by-the-year-2060.html

the past'. That is a crucial point. What we also see now is that some people are talking about reshoring, shortening supply chains and all of that. That might increase energy usage because that is less efficient than the global division of labour, of course. So, there is also the contrary going on.

David Hone

Well, there is, and that is built more into the island scenario. And that is a scenario where you do not meet the goals of the Paris Agreement. That is why you do scenario planning, is that you try to stretch your thinking around these different parameters and look at how they might emerge and how they might change the system with which you are dealing.

Uwe Schulte

What I would suggest is that we briefly look at each of the three scenarios and say what the basic assumption are and what the likely outcome would be in terms of climate.

David Hone

Yes, we can do that, and the climate outcome is something that is related to each scenario, it is something that we have worked on with MIT. Whilst Shell has a big energy modelling capacity in-house, we do not have a climate modelling capacity. We work with the Massachusetts Institute of Technology,[9] their joint programme. They remodel our scenarios to look at the climate impacts of our energy stories and in particular, of course, temperature rise but also some of the other impacts related to that.

Uwe Schulte

Let us take one by one. We start with the one that left me with a small light at the end of the tunnel, 'Sky 1.5'.

David Hone

'Sky 1.5' is a scenario that emerges from a rethinking by society that their health and well-being is particularly important. As we come out of a pandemic, this becomes the dominant thread through society. But also, it is supported by the fact that the pandemic is a global problem, and it is only ultimately going to be solved by global cooperation. In this scenario, there is an increase in global cooperation because of the pandemic that puts in place the necessary linkages and coordination and cooperation necessary between countries to also resolve other problems, particularly the climate issue. The pandemic lays the foundations for what I think in 2018/2019 was wishful thinking. We will suddenly all get together, and we will solve this problem. But in fact, the pandemic has forced us to get together, and in this scenario forced us to get together in a positive way. We come out of it with a new mindset around solving global problems but driven by the fact that we have just had to solve a major global problem. We are not there yet in terms of international cooperation but think a couple of years down the track and you are coming out of

[9] https://globalchange.mit.edu/sites/default/files/MITJPSPGC_Rpt348.pdf

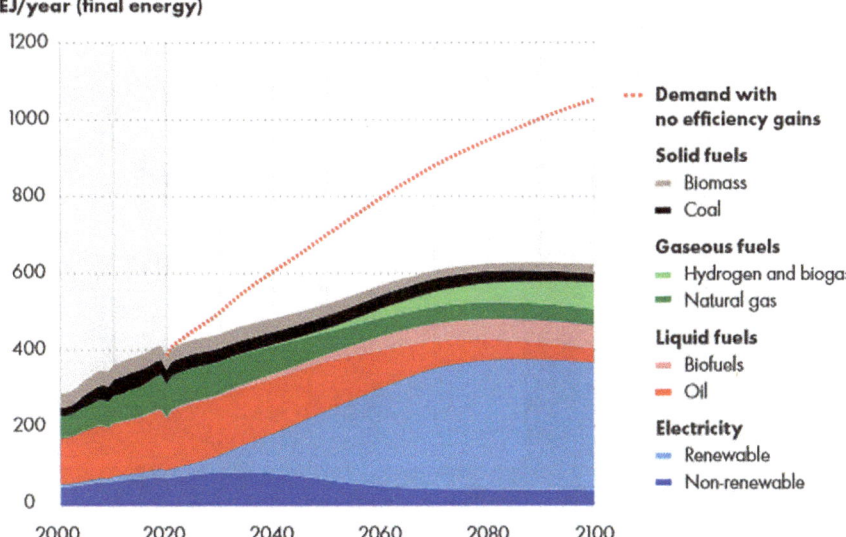

Fig. 4 Shell 1.5 degree Sky scenario. Source: Shell International Ltd., https://aperc.or.jp/file/2021/5/21/S2-1+Powell.pdf

this with a new sense of purpose globally. Then that leads to a much faster resolution of changes required in the energy system to head towards the goals of the Paris Agreement. For instance, now we have a carbon price in Europe that is around €60.00 in the emissions trading system.[10] Very few other places in the world have that. You can imagine that overtime that might cause more tension because industries in Europe are saying, 'Well look, we are exposed to something that others are not exposed to'. But in the 'Sky 1.5' scenario, you do not see those tensions emerging. You see other countries quickly looking at what the EU is doing and putting in place similar systems. Everybody goes forward together. That is the important thing. What you see is that the energy system starts to change and starts to change quite quickly, emissions start to fall quite rapidly in the 2030s. By 2070, the energy system has reached net zero emissions, but in fact globally we reach net zero emissions before that, because part of this international cooperation leads to an end of deforestation and in fact, large-scale reforestation to help adjust the carbon balance in the atmosphere. We are globally at net zero emissions in the late 2050s, and this delivers by 2100 an outcome of around 1.5°C (Fig. 4).

Uwe Schulte
I see, and the opposite scenario is the one where everybody looks after themselves?

---

[10] https://climate.ec.europa.eu/eu-action/eu-emissions-trading-system-eu-ets/development-eu-ets-2005-2020_en#phase-3-2013-2020

Total primary energy by source

	EJ / year														
	1980	1990	2000	2010	2019	2020	2025	2030	2040	2050	2060	2070	2080	2090	2100
Oil	131	136	154	174	192	172	194	198	199	192	179	161	142	121	98
Natural gas	51	70	87	115	140	136	144	152	161	160	148	134	120	105	91
Coal	76	94	97	153	159	151	159	160	154	144	129	108	88	69	54
Nuclear	8	22	28	30	30	28	31	31	25	21	31	43	55	82	120
Hydroelectricity	6	8	9	12	15	15	16	16	18	19	19	18	20	21	23
Biofuels	0	0	0	3	4	3	5	6	12	21	35	49	58	62	55
Biomass and waste	10	12	14	19	26	26	29	32	39	49	59	68	78	90	99
Biomass - traditional	21	26	29	29	27	26	25	26	27	27	24	19	15	13	11
Geothermal	0	1	2	2	4	3	4	5	8	12	17	23	28	32	39
Solar	0	0	0	1	4	4	6	10	23	40	63	95	124	153	189
Wind	0	0	0	1	5	5	7	10	13	16	18	21	24	30	42
Other renewables	0	0	0	0	0	0	0	0	0	0	0	2	2	3	3
Total	303	369	421	540	607	568	622	647	678	704	723	740	755	781	823

Fig. 5 Shell 2.5 degrees Islands scenario. Source: Shell International Ltd., https://www.shell.com/news-and-insights/scenarios/what-are-the-previous-shellscenarios/_jcr_content/root/main/section_1789847828/promo_copy_142460259/links/item0.stream/1652119830834/fba2959d9759c5ae806a03acfb187f1c33409a91/energytransformation-scenarios.pdf

David Hone

Yes, that is the island scenario. I find this to be a slightly dystopian scenario. Some of my colleagues do not like that word, but it becomes quite an inwardly looking scenario. Nationalism is on the rise globally, put in part by the pandemic because one way of addressing the pandemic is to hunker down locally, lock yourself in, not work with others to solve the problem and address your nation state. You can see elements of that in play today as well. Countries do this for what they think are good reasons, but it does not necessarily lead to the best outcomes. In this scenario, you see that become the more dominant theme. It leads to a slowing down of the global economy, it does not grow as fast, it leads to poor outcomes in trade. It does not mean that nothing happens on the energy front because individual countries or regions still pursue their own agendas. They may shift rapidly in some parts of the world to new energy sources. But it does not happen as a global effort. In that scenario, by the end of the century, we are at around 2.5°C of warming, and we are not done yet. Although emissions are falling and you do in fact reach net zero emissions in the first half of the next century, you plateau around 2.6 or 2.7 degrees at the end of the day. And that is well above the goals of the Paris Agreement and brings with it, of course, implications of significant adaptation in the future (Fig. 5).

Uwe Schulte

Sea levels rising and more heat waves and other severe challenges, absolutely. I guess, the third scenario then is the middle ground?

David Hone

Yes, it is middle ground in terms of temperature, but it is not middle ground in terms of the energy system. The scenario is called 'Waves' and it starts off with us coming zooming out of a pandemic. Zoom is the wrong word to use today. We come rushing out of the pandemic with this great desire to rebuild. We have put the pandemic behind us. It is because of the vaccination programme or because of a combination of vaccination with recognition of how to track and trace, and all these things come together. But we put the fear of Covid behind us. It is all about rapid rebuilding and reestablishing economies. You get a surge in emissions in the early years and a surge in energy demand. You get a surge in GDP. But the problems of issues like climate change and social issues like inequality, they are still there. And they re-emerge quite quickly, so by the late 2020s you are starting to get a pushback. Society's going, 'Well, hang on. This is all incredibly good. We have recovered from the pandemic, but we have not addressed any of these problems and they have become worse'. And that leads to quite an automatic reaction and a very rapid push away from fossil fuels. Whereas 'Sky 1.5' is a concerted effort to reduce emissions, and you can reduce emissions without necessarily moving away from fossil fuels completely, by using carbon capture and storage. In the 'Waves' scenario it is just like, 'Right, we are going somewhere else. We are going to do this differently'. It heads off into a specific direction of ending fossil fuel use. Technologies like hydrogen emerge very rapidly in the 'Waves' scenario, even faster than in the 'Sky 1.5' scenario. Because these are the technologies that can take you away from fossil fuels. Now, it does not meet the goals of the Paris Agreement because you have this early surge in emissions and an early and continued temperature rise. But by the end of the century, you are at net zero emissions, the temperature rise has plateaued at 2.3°C, which is certainly above the goals of the Paris Agreement. But nevertheless, the climate issue has been resolved at a level. It is not the most desirable level and that will still require significant adaptation going into the twenty-second century. But the fossil fuel era has ended by 2100 (Fig. 6).

Uwe Schulte

When I listen to your three scenarios there are two conclusions, I draw from that. One is, regardless of whether we are going to be first more inward looking, or whether we are going to globally collaborate, or whether there is a first urge to drive GDP and then recognition of what is going on—regardless of the three, climate emergency will catch up with us and require action. So regardless which direction we take, eventually it will get to us. And that is the second conclusion I draw from that, because they are linked to time scales when we start to act decisively, and that determines how much extreme weather events and other catastrophic consequences humanity will have to suffer.

David Hone

Yes, and the IPCC laid this out very clearly. There is more to come from the sixth assessment report,[11] but we saw the first part of the report in August. And we certainly saw it in the 2018 report that this is where they made the case for 1.5, limiting

---

[11] https://www.ipcc.ch/ar6-syr/

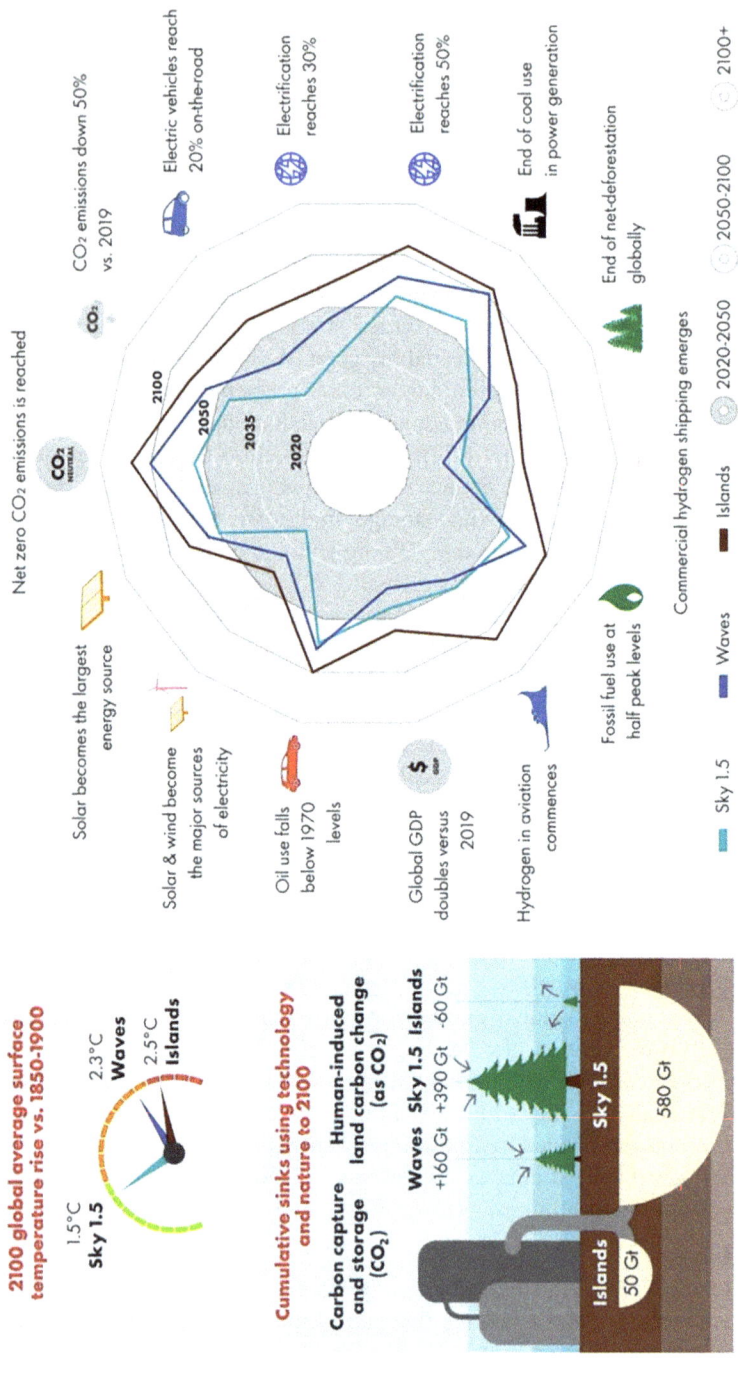

Fig. 6 Overview Shell Sky, Waves, Islands. Source: Shell International Ltd., https://blogs.shell.com/2021/02/10/exploring-the-energy-future/

warming to 1.5. No amount of warming is a good thing but limiting to 1.5 was at least manageable. As you get to two and above, you start to have consequences that potentially mean notable change for society. In this report that came out in August they talked, for instance, about sea level rise beyond 2100. Whilst that will not impact the people who are alive today, it is a legacy that will be left. They talked about sea level rise of potentially many metres and only small shifts in temperature. They do not deliver centimetres of change; they deliver metres of change. Over a period of five hundred years or something, that is a legacy that others will have to deal with. That was the first time that the IPCC had really got into the details of that long-term legacy. We talk about the climate emergency because it is imperative that emissions start to fall soon, or immediately actually. But in fact, the consequences of not doing this play out over the millennium and they continue to play out.

Uwe Schulte

I am talking to someone who works at Shell, so I must ask you—when you look at these conclusions, what does that mean for the oil and gas industry?

David Hone

It means that the oil and gas industry must change, or the energy industry must change, I should say. The way it changes and the speed with which it changes is something that companies like Shell are thinking long and hard about. In all the scenarios, even in 2100 and into the twenty-second century, there is still some use of fossil fuels. In the 'Waves' scenario it is modest. It is in the petrochemical sector. Our society today is physically built with carbon. Many of the goods and many of the products that we use start with carbon chemistry, hydrocarbons, and all the plastics we use, or many of the materials we use, many of the constructions, materials, insulation. All of this comes out of carbon chemistry and the obvious source of carbon is oil and gas. We are not going to have a society that is not using carbon. It is a question of where they get it from. That society could get the carbon from the biosphere, either directly from the atmosphere absorbing CO_2, or from plants, making bioplastics and things. But that is requiring carbon for 8 to 10 billion people. That is a very large-scale impact on the biosphere. No matter how we go forward, there are going to be impacts that we must deal with, or changes that we must deal with on a global scale. Anyway, the oil and gas industry will have to change. There is no doubt about that. Shell is very cognizant of that. We have talked about that on our strategy day a few months back. But we are also here providing energy as one of many companies for the eight billion people that need it today.

Uwe Schulte

Fair enough. But for example, people say we do not need to base mobility on carbon.

David Hone

No, it is certainly shifting to electricity. For a large chunk of the mobility services, it looks like electricity will be the mechanism. But you must generate that electricity. Okay, we can generate that from renewables, from wind and from solar. But then equally, you must build, if you look at the scenario, something like a million large wind turbines globally. Well, they are made of steel, and they sit on cement foundations. All of those are manufactured with coal and natural gas, with limestone that when you turn it into cement releases CO2. It is not just a question of generating the electricity. Our whole society has been built over the last two hundred years on making use of fossil fuels to deliver the energy that we need and provide the carbon for the materials that we use in society. And that is not going to change all at once. It will change and if you and I could be here in one hundred years' time, I think it would be quite different. But it is of those types of time scales that are necessary to completely turn over this system.

Uwe Schulte

Let us come back to a point you just made—the steel industry and the cement industry. Obviously, both those industries are looking into alternatives as well. Have you considered that in this scenario?

David Hone

They are. Yes, for instance, just last week or two weeks ago, a consortium of European companies announced that they had made the first small production runs of green steel.[12] This was steel that was manufactured through a hydrogen smelting process rather than a metallurgical coal process. The chemistry behind that has been understood for a long time but turning it into an industrial process is yet another step. They have done the first production run from a small plant.[13] The technology is very promising and let us assume that the technology is adopted globally. Let us just make that assumption. And in fact, in the 'Sky 1.5' scenario and in the 'Waves' scenario that is what happens. You then must rebuild or retool hundreds of blast furnaces around the world. And we are still building blast furnaces using metallurgical coal as the proposed feedstock. That takes time. They are not all going to change overnight. Because what must happen in the real world is that first we run the pilot plant, and we establish that the process is a viable process. And that has now happened. And it happened quite quickly actually. But then one of these companies is going to have to make their first bold step and build a large-scale production facility that runs 24/7, that does not have any problems with hydrogen supply, all the things associated with that. They are going to place a big commercial bet on that. And let us assume that is successful. But are you going to have fifty companies around the world all simultaneously placing that same commercial bet? Many of them will say, 'We will just watch and see what XYZ steel company is doing and if it is as successful as everybody thinks, we are in there'. But they may wait, and you can understand why they may wait, because there is still uncertainty and, they do not yet have secure long-term supplies of hydrogen, because the green hydrogen production chain, whilst it is getting going, it is not mainstream yet. It is producing hydrogen around the world in tiny quantities still. It is growing quickly (Figs. 7, 8, and 9).

Shell has just put in what soon will not be the world's largest electrolyser[14], but was a few months ago, in a refinery in Germany to produce hydrogen. I have already

---

[12] https://climate.ec.europa.eu/news-your-voice/news/hybrit-story-unlocking-secret-green-steel-production-2023-06-20_en

[13] https://www.h2greensteel.com/

[14] https://www.hydrogeninsight.com/electrolysers/chinese-companies-take-top-three-slots-in-bnefs-list-of-worlds-20-largest-hydrogen-electrolyser-makers/2-1-1355610

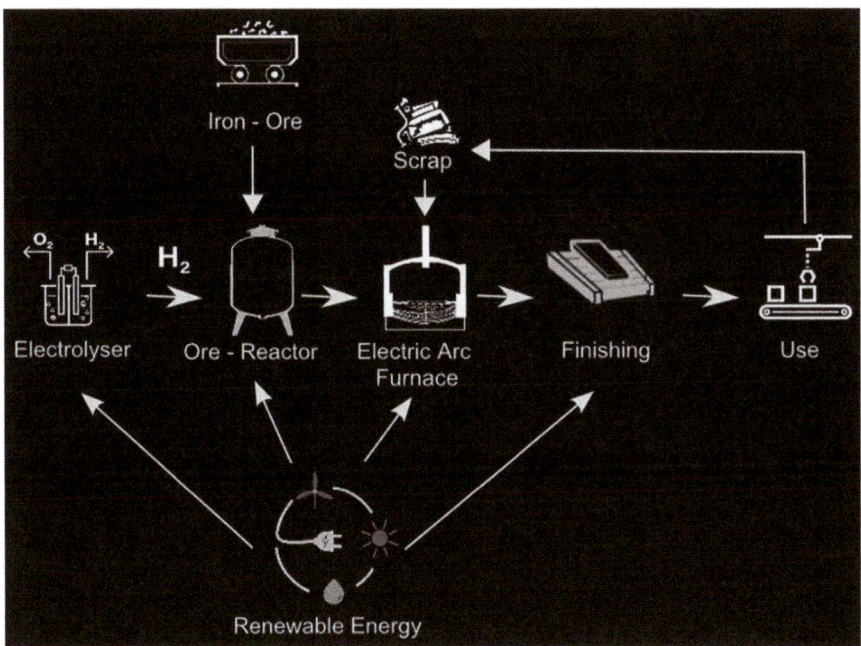

Fig. 7 Green hydrogen steel process. Source: Uwe G. Schulte

Hydrogen costs from hybrid solar PV and onshore wind systems in the long term

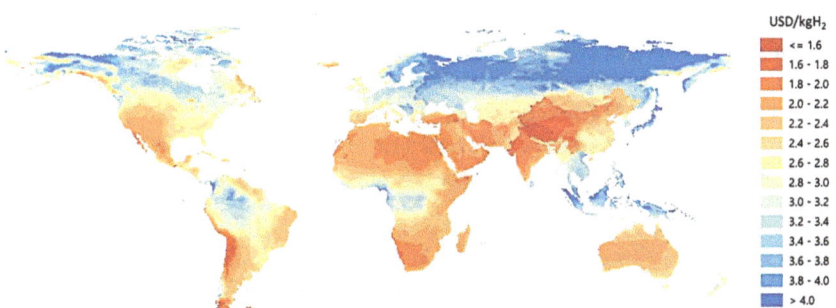

Fig. 8 IEA: green hydrogen cost. Source: IEA - International Energy Agency, https://www.iea.org/reports/the-future-of-hydrogen, Creative Commons Attribution 4.0 licence (CC BY 4.0)

read that there is a company in China building a larger electrolyser, which is good because it means that the technology is progressing rapidly. But that takes time and in our world energy model we try and factor all that in. I know there are lots of people who just feel we should change from fossil fuels now to solve the climate issue. And everybody would like that to happen. But there is a real world out there that is ticking along.

2022	Manufacturer	Annual Capacity	Country	Electrolyser type (ALK=Alkaline)
1=	Longi	1.5GW	China	ALK
1=	Peric	1.5GW	China	ALK/PEM
3	Sungrow	1.1GW	China	ALK/PEM
4=	John Cockerill	1GW	Belgium	ALK
4=	Thyssenkrupp	1GW	Germany	ALK
4=	Auyan	1GW	China	ALK
4=	ITM Power	1GW	UK	PEM
4=	Plug Power	1GW	US	PEM
4=	Ohmium	1GW	US	PEM
10=	Cummins	0.6GW	US	PEM
10=	Nel	0.6GW	Norway	ALK/PEM

Fig. 9 Bloomberg top 10 global electrolysers. Source: BloombergNEF

Uwe Schulte

That is correct. And what your scenarios do, they install a sense of urgency. Because what we see is that time is of the essence. And I completely accept that there are these scale-up problems, but on the other hand, I have just recently seen an article.

David Hone

Well, I would not call them problems. It is the commercial reality of taking new processes, getting them, and mainstreaming them.

Uwe Schulte

That is fair and I accept that. But you see, I have just seen an article[15] talking about the ten biggest polluters in terms of carbon dioxide for electricity production. And it is only ten plants that produce a lion share of carbon dioxide by having the wrong type of coal, for example. They are all coal-fired plants. Sometimes we might be able to address that. My home country Germany has one of them, Poland has the biggest carbon dioxide producer, all based on coal. If we just address those ten, we could already have a significant impact. Sometimes it is good to be bold in your ambitions as well.

David Hone

Yes, I agree and there are several examples of that around the world in various places. It is the case that the five or ten biggest blast furnaces in the world, and I do not know what scale they operate on, are half the emissions or something. It is nice to say, 'If only we could just change those'. But for all we know, two of those blast furnaces might be brand new, just started up. And they have had significant investment in them. Are the owners going to want to tear them down again? Well, that comes back to this commercial reality. I just use that as an example. I do not know the details of the blast furnace industry, but it would not surprise me.

---

[15] https://iopscience.iop.org/article/10.1088/1748-9326/ac13f1/pdf

Uwe Schulte

Collaboration is the essence here and we must see how these ambitions can be addressed. What you just said has implications not only for the oil and gas industry. How would you see that panning out for everybody else? How should they look at this and how should they approach the insights from your scenarios, if you are in any other industry?

David Hone

There is no industry that I can think of that is not dependent on oil, coal, and gas. There are lots of companies that say, 'We are only using renewable electricity'. But that is for their immediate operations. The fact is that they still have factories, and those factories are built with steel and cement and that they are dependent on trucks to move their goods in and out of the factories. And the trucks are running on diesel, and they run on roads and bridges that are made of cement and bitumen hitch, so they are not carbon neutral. They are operationally carbon neutral, but again, they are embedded in the carbon society as much as anybody else. This impacts everybody in an equal way. We are all in this together. Every business is going to have to start to think about what is in their supply chain and how do they change that, and how do they work with other parts of the supply chain in a sectoral type of approach to change things? It is nice to say, 'Well, I just buy renewable electricity, therefore I am out. I have done my bit'. But in fact, you have not. You have done one small piece of your bit. And there are many other parts that you must put your mind towards.

Uwe Schulte

That is the famous Scope 3 discussion, of course, with all the implications of what you do as a business up and down your supply chain.

David Hone

Correct, yes.

Uwe Schulte

I am glad to say that more companies are recognising this now. I guess what you are saying is to be aware of these impacts and do something about it. You are doing something about it as well?

David Hone

Well, we are. Shell is collaborating with its customers, with its customer base, with the supply chains to find ways of moving away from the fuels that they conventionally use. The aviation industry in our scenarios shift to hydrogen, so you run aeroplanes on hydrogen. It is not just about Shell producing hydrogen and turning up at Heathrow or Schiphol and saying, 'Well, there is hydrogen available, guys, use that', because there is no aeroplane that currently burns it. It must be some sort of cooperation with Boeing, or with Airbus. But then they do not actually make the engines. Pratt & Whitney and Rolls-Royce make them. And then, of course, the airports themselves must be ready. There is no point of an Airbus hydrogen plane turning up and Shell has not, or anybody else has not actually produced any hydrogen for it, nor does the airport have any facilities to hold hydrogen and refuel it. Sectoral cooperation is going to be especially important to get all this to work, and then that takes time. You must build up those coalitions and get them to effectively make some big bets and go forward.

Uwe Schulte

You have just made a key point in the sense that we can see all of this as a big threat to business, but we can also see it as huge opportunities to build new business models, new coalitions, new collaborations and develop innovative solutions together. I do not think anybody is going to go back to your island scenario in this anymore.

David Hone

I agree. There is huge opportunity, and you only must look at what has happened in the digital world in the last 20 years to look at the opportunities. Companies like Blockbuster and Kodak come to mind, and everyone thinks, 'Oh well, they did not see it'. But in fact, the number of companies that have emerged—who would have imagined Netflix and all the other companies replacing Blockbuster? And the fact that every year we take, it is some astounding number that every few months we take more photographs than have ever been taken in history. That imaging industry has transformed itself and is enormous today compared to the days of silver pallid photography, which of course was Kodak. Opportunity abounds, and for Shell it is finding that opportunity and making the most of it.

Uwe Schulte

Absolutely. And, to our audience, all the details of the three scenarios can be found on the Shell website if you want to dive a bit deeper into where we could only scratch the surface. David, I would like to thank you so much for enlightening us about scenario planning and the implications on climate change. Unfortunately, we were not able to really dive deep into any of those subjects, but for the audience, if you are interested you will find more information on the TCB website and on the Shell website. Thank you, David.

David Hone

Thank you very much for inviting me today.

Ocean Plastics

Recorded October 2021

Uwe Schulte
Today I will be talking to Chever Voltmer, Plastics Initiative Director at Ocean Conservancy. First, I would like to introduce our guest. Chever worked at the Office of Ocean and Polar Affairs at the US Department of State, where she was the lead for international marine debris issues, overseeing US engagement on this issue in the United Nations. And she was an active member of the US Foreign Service in Poland, Guyana, Russia, Ecuador, Bosnia, Herzegovina, Ukraine, and Estonia. She spent a year as the Director for Central America and the Caribbean at the office of the US Trade Representative. Chever holds an Undergraduate Degree of Economics and Russian Studies and holds a Master from the National War College where she was a distinguished graduate. Welcome, Chever. Please tell us a bit about yourself and how looking after the ocean has become such an important part of your life.

Chever Voltmer[1]
Good morning, and first, thank you so much for having me. It is a real honour to be here. Like most people, my connection to the ocean is, primarily, a personal one. I grew up near the ocean both in the United States and abroad, and my earliest memories are of the beach. In fact, my earliest memory that I can think of is of the screen door which kept me away from the water with its childproof lock, and I think I must have spent a lot of time staring at it when I was a child. When I was eight years old, my family moved to Saudi Arabia, and I learned to snorkel on the Red Sea outside of Jeddah. I have spent much of my life on, in, or near the water. I am a swimmer. I

---

[1] Since September 2022, Chever is the Senior Policy Advisor at The Circulate Initiative.

Chever Voltmer joined Ocean Conservancy in September 2018 in the role of Plastics Initiative Director. She left the organisation in April 2022. The views expressed here are hers and may not reflect those of Ocean Conservancy at this time. The transcript has been lightly edited for clarity and length. Notably, Ocean Conservancy's Trash Free Seas Alliance®—referenced occasionally throughout the interview—sunset and ceased operations in 2022.

was a competitive swimmer in college. I am a kayaker. I am an avid scuba diver. And so, I was always trying in the Foreign Service to find a way to connect with the ocean and with water-related issues. For example, when I served in Guyana, I was part of a team that inspected the shrimp fleet there for turtle excluder devices, which are devices and nets which allow turtles to escape fishing nets. And when I was in Ecuador, I tried to keep illegal fishing out of the Galapagos marine reserve. When I came back to Washington, my last job at the State Department was as the lead for marine debris, working in lots of different organisations, you mentioned some of them—the UN, G7, G20, and APEC. So, when I was ready to leave government, this was a very natural transition for me.

Uwe Schulte
Before we get going, I think we should clarify a definition. When we speak about ocean this encompasses the world ocean, which is all intercontinental connected saltwater covering the majority of the earth's surface. And when we speak about Atlantic, Pacific, Indian, these are just geographical divisions of that one big ocean. Having gotten that definition out of the way, please tell us a bit about what Ocean Conservancy is doing.

Chever Voltmer
Sure, thank you. Our tagline is that Ocean Conservancy is collaborating with you to protect the ocean from today's greatest global challenges and that we create science-based solutions for a healthy ocean and the wildlife and communities that depend on it. What does that really mean in practice? It means that we work on an entire range of ocean issues. Some of our programmes include efforts to combat climate change and ocean acidification, which is related to climate change in the ocean, smart ocean planning to use the ocean resources as efficiently and safely as possible, sustainable fisheries, and then we have some placed-based work in the Arctic and Florida, and then of course the part of the work that I do, which is the Trash Free Seas Alliance, which is dedicated to keeping trash out of the ocean.

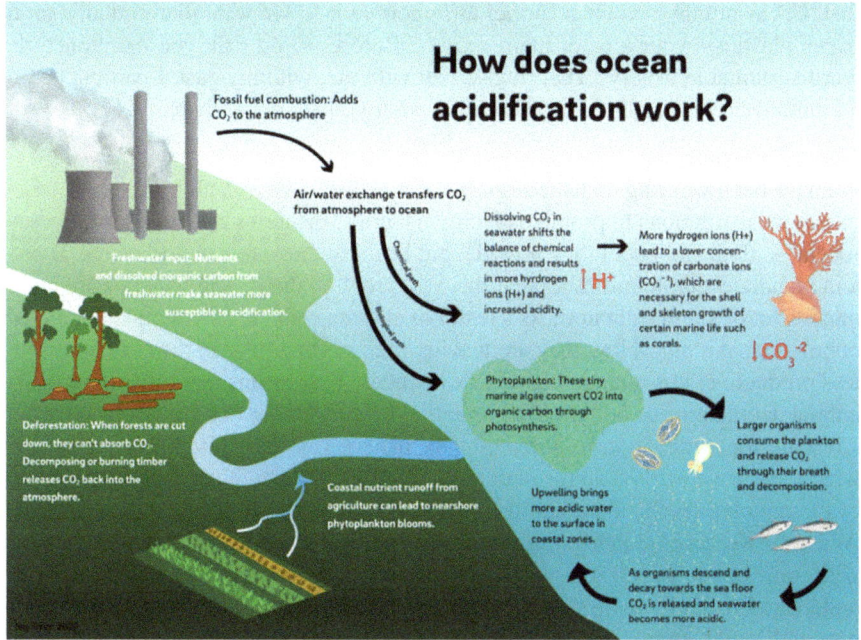

Fig. 1 Ocean acidification, Scripps Institution of Oceanography. Source: Sky Smith, California Sea Grant

Uwe Schulte

Some of our audience might not be familiar with the term ocean acidification. In my understanding we are warming up the earth, more CO2 gets into the atmosphere, when CO2 gets into the water, it forms carbonic acid, and that makes the ocean more acidic and that is bad, for example for coral reefs and other marine life.[2] Is that correct?

Chever Voltmer

That is perfectly correct. Coming from Maryland, it is bad for crustaceans and animals with shells, so shellfish. I live in a place where we are famous for our blue crab, and more acidic water dissolves the shells of those animals. It is having a massive impact on fisheries, and in fact we are doing some work to understand better how those rising ocean acidity levels are affecting shellfish, particularly in the Pacific Northwest, but hopefully they will get to Maryland, where my beloved blue crabs are (Fig. 1).

Uwe Schulte

Acidification is also bad for climate change because the absorption of CO2 in the ocean will reduce, something that really needs avoiding. We should be aware of

---

[2] https://scripps.ucsd.edu/research/climate-change-resources/faq-ocean-acidification

that. Let us not dive into that further as important it is, we want to eventually get to ocean plastics—your area of main activity. Before we do that, you mentioned the word sustainable fishery.[3] That rings a bell with me, with my past. I participated in an initiative there. Tell us a little bit more what you are doing there.

Chever Voltmer
We have been working on fisheries issues for about 25 years and it is really focused on practical solutions to problems facing fisheries. Fisheries are important, not just for the ecological benefit they provide, but because they are a major source of protein and many communities around the world rely on them. And fisheries are really under a lot of stress right now. As a result of climate change, for example, many fish populations are migrating, they are leaving their normal ranges, they are becoming less productive, less abundant, and less resilient. That means that other threats like habitat degradation or pollution are affecting fisheries more. We are working hard to advocate for a transition to climate-ready fisheries in the United States and elsewhere. We have worked on the national level in the United States, but also on some of the regional levels, including the Pacific fisheries, the Gulf of Mexico fisheries. And then we have an interesting, innovative project that is science-based, to work with some of the world's top scientists using advanced computer modelling to better understand fisheries ecosystems, including the human impact to help identify simpler and better approaches to fisheries management. It is a computer modelling system that figures out how individuals interact with fisheries. It collaborates with local communities and fishers to assess the model across all kinds of different fishery systems, but particularly in Indonesia, and helps to identify simple ways to change fishery management to make it more efficient and more ecologically friendly (Fig. 2). [4]

Uwe Schulte
I see three tensions here. There is the nationality, nations wanting their fair share, whatever that fair share might be. Then there is the livelihood of the fishing community. And of course, the sustainable living of the creatures in the sea. How do you approach that? How is that balanced?

Chever Voltmer
I think you have gotten to the heart of the problem with fisheries, because fisheries agreements can take years to hash out. And so, it takes years to hash out whose quota is how much. But the reality is that the fish are moving. Now you have places that have a quota for fish, but no fish. And you have places that have more fish, or the fish are just simply disappearing altogether. Modelling to understand what is sustainable and how you can manage the fisheries populations for optimising it for everyone, is some of the work that we are doing. I do not pretend to be an expert in the computer modelling piece. There are some very smart scientists at the University

---

[3] https://en.wikipedia.org/wiki/Sustainable_fishery
[4] By Hannah Ritchie and Max Roser—https://ourworldindata.org/fish-and-overfishing, CC BY-SA 4.0, https://commons.wikimedia.org/w/index.php?curid=120854565

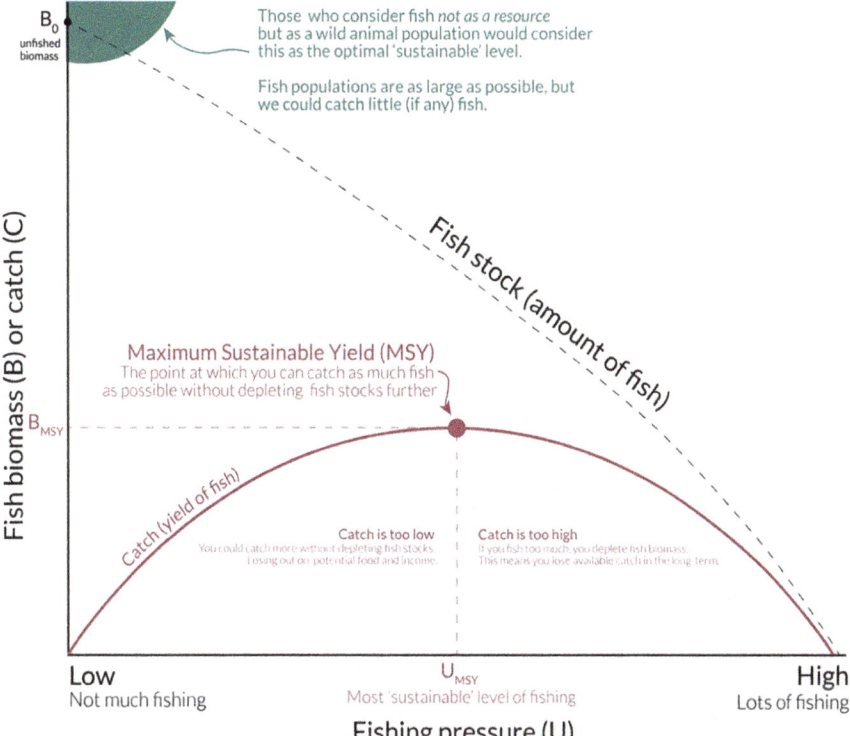

Fig. 2 Sustainable fishery. Source: Wikipedia, CC BY-SA 4.0 DEED, Attribution-ShareAlike 4.0 International, Author: Hannah Ritchie and Max Roser, Source: https://ourworldindata.org/fish-and-overfishing

of Oxford who are helping us with that.[5] But it is really a challenge to balance all these things. The reality is that a well-managed fishery provides enormous ecosystem services, but also services to people, and it is a sustainable resource if managed properly, and that is the trick (Fig. 3).

Uwe Schulte

This could be a theme for a whole podcast on its own. But still, before we get to the plastics issue, which of course is the biggest concern now, I was fascinated by how Ocean Conservancy started and what you are doing every year. That beach cleanup, can you talk a little bit about that?

---

[5] https://ora.ox.ac.uk/objects/uuid:76b28509-7fd5-419f-82a0-b312334152a2

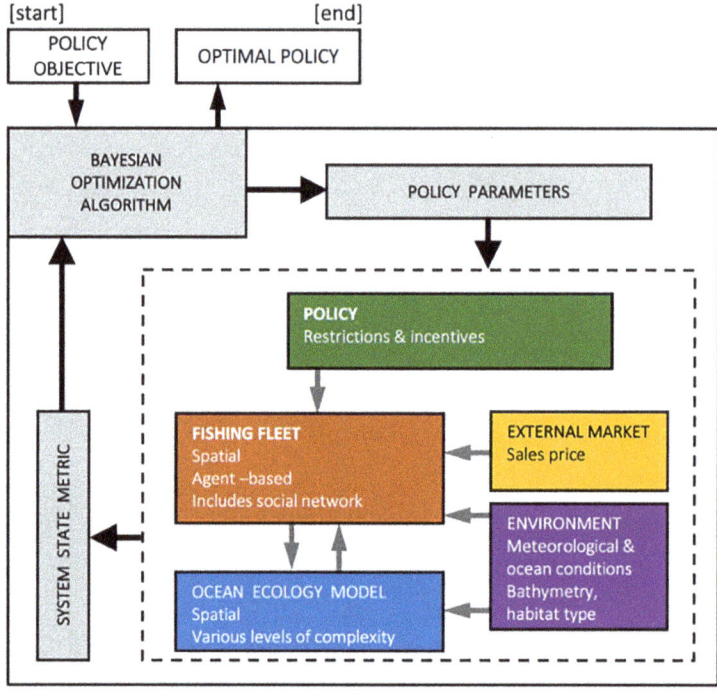

Fig. 3 The POSEIDON model of ocean fisheries. Source: Springer Nature

Chever Voltmer

Sure, I can. The International Coastal Cleanup [6] was a little over a week ago. Not this past Saturday, but the Saturday before, I spent the day on Kingman Island in the Anacostia River of DC, volunteering with the team that organised one of our flagship cleanups. For 35 years, Ocean Conservancy has organised the International Coastal Cleanup. It is the world's largest volunteer beach cleanup. I think in 2019, we hit a million volunteers globally, so it is not a small thing. One of the things that is interesting about our cleanups is that from the very beginning, for 35 years, we have been collecting data on what we are finding in the ocean. We started with paper data cards where volunteers could check 'I found a bottle', 'I found a bag', 'I found a straw', those. But in the past few years, we have introduced an app, so now you can download it on your phone. It is called Clean Swell[7] and, as you collect trash, you just tick off what you are finding, and we use that data to understand what is happening in the ocean. We have the world's largest database on marine debris. It is called TIDES,[8] it is open source, freely available, and it is used by all kinds of people for all kinds of research. We use it, we publish a report every year, The

---

[6] https://oceanconservancy.org/trash-free-seas/international-coastal-cleanup/

[7] https://oceanconservancy.org/blog/2022/05/16/building-clean-swell/

[8] https://www.coastalcleanupdata.org

International Coastal Cleanup Report. We just released our 2020 report a couple of weeks ago where we publish everything that we found. We published the top ten items that our volunteers found on beaches and riverways around the world. What is interesting about the International Coastal Cleanup is that we have been doing this for a long time, but it is still evolving. One way that we are evolving is the following. Through the pandemic, what we have seen is this huge increase in the use of personal protective equipment (Fig. 4).

According to some researchers, the planet is using, and this is a number that is almost inconceivable to me, 129 billion face masks every month and sixty-five billion gloves. This stuff is making its way into the environment. To understand that impact, we started tracking a new category last year, which was personal protective equipment. We added that to our data cards and to our app, and this data in turn informed a report we just put out in March. Let me quote a couple of headlines from

Fig. 4 Data from Ocean Conservancy's 2019 International Coastal Cleanup®. Source: Ocean Conservancy, https://oceanconservancy.org/wp-content/uploads/2020/10/FINAL_2020ICC_Report.pdf

this report: 94% of volunteers that we surveyed found personal protective equipment on the beaches during the cleanup last year and just between July and December of 2020, of last year, our volunteers picked up 107,219 items of personal protective equipment. And this is even though our cleanups were drastically curtailed because of the pandemic. We really do get to see what is happening, the changes in the environment in real time.

Uwe Schulte
This is something of some concern that I had not thought about, protecting humans could be detrimental for other species. It is a very astute reminder of whatever we do, we should always have the environment on our mind as well. Thank you for alerting about that. And it is interesting that this database TIDES can help people and companies to look at what of their products and packaging is ending up in these ocean cleanups. Thank you so much for doing that and sharing that data with everybody. That is excellent. What was the oddest thing you picked up last week?

Chever Voltmer
I know what the oddest thing is that we picked up last week. We pulled up an entire electric scooter out of the Anacostia River. It looked like its electronics had been stolen, but it was one of those rental scooters we have. I do not know if they are as popular in Europe as they are in Washington DC, but you can rent bicycles, scooters, little motorcycles. It is a little motorcycle we pulled up out of the river. That got our poundage up because it was so heavy. That was the oddest. We had an unopened bottle of olive oil; we had all kinds of things. It is amazing what you find when you start digging around.

Just one thing for you. If you do not live near an ocean, but you live near a river, you can also make a substantial difference because most of what leaks into rivers makes its way to the ocean. And we are also doing some research on tagging trash. And I was talking to one of these leading scientists a week ago and she said that already in June she had put some tagged trash into the river and some of it is already turning up 800 or 900 miles away within three months. It is amazing.

Uwe Schulte
Within three months, my goodness. Let us get to that challenge. Can you share with us from your perspective how big the issue is?

Chever Voltmer
As I mentioned, we have been doing this cleanup for a long time and we have been logging what we find, and what we found is that over the years gradually, even though we were mobilising more volunteers and picking up more trash, we could not keep up. And finally, I think in 2017, all top ten items that appeared on our top ten lists were plastic. We started to understand that we were never going to clean our way out of this problem, that we needed a more holistic solution. We convened a research group to try to understand how much trash might be leaking into the ocean. And they published the first foundational research about the quantity and the sources and the fate of plastic pollution. That paper was published in the journal Science in

2015.⁹ And it estimated, it was the first estimate, that eight million metric tonnes of trash are leaking into the ocean every year, and that was 2015.

Just at the end of last year, we published an update to that research of that first baseline, and that latest information indicates that eleven million metric tonnes of trash are leaking into the ocean every year. They have been found everywhere; plastics are everywhere. They are finding them on the summit of Everest, they are finding them in the Mariana Trench, which is the deepest trench in the ocean, they are finding it in small air particles, we are breathing it. To me, the saddest of all is that they are finding it in beer. Because microplastics have made their way into water, and when you use it for making anything else, you are finding it in beer, in table salt, in everything. We have research that shows 1600 species have ingested plastic and 1300 of those are in the ocean. It is everywhere at this point.

Uwe Schulte
Yes, but eleven million, that is a fair share of the whole production. That is a really worrying thought. Going to the source where these things get into the ocean is so important. Can you talk a little bit about how you approach that?

Chever Voltmer
Sure. 100% of plastic comes from humans, so this is a human problem, we have made the problem. How do we get at trying to fix it? Our strategy at Ocean Conservancy is three-pronged. One is that we need to prevent trash from getting into the ocean in the first place, and that involves reduction, really rethinking our relationship with plastic. What do we need? What do we have to have? What can we get rid of? And the second piece really involves managing that plastic that we do need, trying to improve waste management. What we found is that 80% of the trash in the ocean is coming from land. And of that, most of it was never managed properly in the first place. It was never collected. It was never cleaned up.

Uwe Schulte
Before you go on, sorry for interrupting, you just said that 80% comes from land. In my simple mind, I thought it was much more, so where are the other 20% coming from?

Chever Voltmer
From boats. A lot of it is fishing nets, abandoned, lost, and discarded fishing nets which, if you think about it, can be a lot of plastic by weight, because they tend to be heavier than things like plastic packaging, which makes up the other 80%. By weight 20% comes from seagoing vessels, which is both trash chucked overboard but also mostly abandoned, lost, and discarded fishing gear.

Uwe Schulte
That is a significant thing, so that brings us back the full loop to sustainable fishery again. Are there ideas how to reduce those? Of course, I understand that sometimes

---

⁹ https://www.science.org/doi/10.1126/science.1260352

Fig. 5 Abandoned fishing gear. Source: Joel Baziuk, Global Ghost Gear Initiative

a net gets broken, and it disappears into the sea and the fisher cannot do anything about it. But you also mentioned discarded nets. What can we do there?

Chever Voltmer
I have a colleague at Ocean Conservancy, a counterpart that is running the Global Ghost Gear Initiative,[10] which is an initiative that helps governments, fishers, and NGOs work together to tackle this question of abandoned, lost, and discarded fishing gear. They have best practices framework for fishers to help them avoid this unintentional loss. They have programmes that help with the return of fishing gear. Trying to find places to receive the gear and then also work on gear marking so that gear can be attached to specific fisheries and then gear recycling. An entire range of issues through the Global Ghost Gear Initiative, which I think now has over 106 members, including 20 something countries and the USA joined last year. I was happy that the USA finally stepped up to do its bit there (Fig. 5).

Uwe Schulte
Excellent. I happen to know that a U.S. company that makes carpets is collecting used fishing nets. That shows that companies can have a positive effect. I understand, if it costs something to get rid of and you are on sea anyway, you could just cut the line and then it is certainly ghost gear. I have just learned that expression. That is interesting.

---

[10] https://www.ghostgear.org/

Chever Voltmer

Just one word about ghost gear and the reason we care so much about it. It is the most destructive form of marine debris because fishing gear is designed to capture and kill marine life. And if it is abandoned, lost, or discarded, it still does that. Many of these nets will drift around, they will fill with fish, they will sink, the fish will get eaten, they will rise again and fish again. And this can go on for a long time. That is why tackling ghost gear is also an important part of the solution.

Uwe Schulte

Coming back to what you talked about regarding the size of the problem and that we find plastic everywhere now including, and I think that might frighten quite a lot of people, in beer. There is a very selfish reason we should be doing something about this because we are not only doing harm to the ocean, but we are doing harm to ourselves. Doing harm to the ocean is already doing harm to ourselves, because our life would not be possible if the ocean would not be functioning.

Chever Voltmer

Correct, yes. And then there is this function of—do you really want to eat plastic? I do not. The research on whether it causes harm to human health is inconclusive now. But even so, I do not think there is anyone out there who thinks that eating plastic is good for you, at least at a minimum, right? We need to find a way to get it out of our food chain. If it is in salt and water, beer, and air, that is not good for any of us. I would just say that the fact that it impacts marine life, this impacts the ability to fish and fishing yields, it impacts even your ability to enjoy a wonderful day at the beach, which is something that every human should be able to do.

Uwe Schulte

Even so, if you live in a landlocked place because there are certain governments that do not let you out. But you are right, everybody should be able to enjoy a lovely day at the beach, that is for sure. Let us get back to the point where I interrupted you. Rivers are a huge source of getting the unwanted material into the ocean. What can we do to work on the source? The cleanup is necessary, I understand that, but going for the source might be a better way.

Chever Voltmer

Yes. We call that last chance capture. If you can get it at the river before it gets to the ocean, that is your last chance to effectively collect trash, because once it gets into the open ocean, it becomes very expensive and physically difficult to collect. We have a project in Vietnam called Splash,[11] that stands for Strategic Plastic Litter Abatement, in the Song Hong. The Song Hong, or Red River, has a biosphere reserve at its delta, so it is an important ecologically sensitive area in Vietnam. We partnered there with a group called the Centre for Marine Life Conservation, which is an International Coastal Cleanup partner. We have given them support to build and install five trash traps in the Red River. And what is interesting about this proj-

---

[11] https://oceanconservancy.org/blog/2021/01/06/cleaning-arteries-vietnam/

Fig. 6 Trash trapper, Centre for Marinelife Conservation and Community Development. Source: Ocean Conservancy, https://oceanconservancy.org/blog/2021/01/06/cleaning-arteries-vietnam/

ect is that our trash traps are locally designed and built. They are the opposite of some of these very high-profile trash traps that you see in the news. We call them cheap and cheerful. They are inexpensive and they are easy to build, easy to design, easy to install. Our first one is already in the river. We are collecting trash; we empty it every week and we do data analysis on what we are finding. We are using that analysis to inform our outreach to local communities. One interesting early data point, we still have not confirmed it yet, is that we expected a lot of fluctuation in the trap due to seasonal weather variations. You have a rainy season and non-rainy season. We thought we would find a lot more in the rainy season, but we are also finding that culture plays a key role in the flow of trash. For example, we saw a huge uptick in trash in the river around Lunar New Year, which is when Vietnamese people traditionally clean house and get ready for the holidays. We will need more data to confirm this, but it is already giving us ideas for how to design effective behaviour change campaigns. Because you must understand what the problem is before you can figure out how to solve it (Fig. 6).

Uwe Schulte
Now, that is interesting. Can I ask an indiscreet question? I have just learned a new thing—trash trap. I wish some of these hate speeches would get a trash trap. How much is it? How much does one of those cost? I know you are in prototyping and everything, just order of magnitude.

Chever Voltmer

Well, we got a grant from the Benioff Ocean Foundation and the Coca-Cola Foundation for this project.[12] It is $1,000,000 for our five traps, but that is not just the traps. That is also all the baseline research we are doing around how much trash was flowing into the river before the traps were installed, the building and installation of the traps, and then the monitoring and community outreach around the traps, as well as all the things to get the site permits and do the research for how and where to put the trash traps in. It is cheap if you think about some of the trash traps we have seen that cost about 50 million a pop. It is cheap.

Uwe Schulte

I agree. And it is about scale. What I learned is, in the beginning we thought that some of the major rivers are the main source of plastic, but we now learned through recent studies that more like one thousand rivers are causing 80% of ocean plastic pollution that comes from rivers. That means we must really do cleanups in one thousand rivers. That requires a solution that is affordable for the regional community. So, if you produce something like that, that sounds promising. When we talk about the ocean plastics problem, as far as I understood what you said, we have two tasks ahead of us: one is that we should make efforts to avoid plastics leaking into our environment, which means that we must do much better at recycling. But we also must avoid plastics where we can. And still, and that is the second thing, even if we achieve all that, we have already made quite a mess of it. So, we must do a big cleanup job anyway. Chever, let us talk about how we can avoid plastics.

Chever Voltmer

If you think about how to keep trash out of the ocean, the simplest thing to do is to not use that item in the first place. There are places that are already working on this, and I will give a shout-out here to the European Union. The European Union has banned, as of this year, certain single-use plastic items, things like plastic cutlery, plates, straws, stirring sticks. And I raise this because if you look at the top ten list of items we find on beaches and waterways around the world, all those items are on that list. If you think about something like a straw, it has a short life span. There are some people who need a straw for medical reasons, but most people do not and can live without a straw, and yet it causes so much harm to marine life. Getting rid of those single-use plastics that are at considerable risk of leaking into the ocean, really is a smart strategy because it gets rid of them, but at the same time, it improves the quality of what is left in the waste stream. That is a smart strategy that Europe is pursuing. And in the United States, we are a little bit behind on that, but we are starting to think about how to reduce our use of packaging because packaging is the other thing that ends up in the ocean very frequently.

---

[12] https://www.coca-colacompany.com/media-center/benioff-ocean-initiative-and-the-coca-cola-foundation-announcement

Uwe Schulte

It is interesting we say straw and we do not think about why it is called straw because in the old days what we would do is take straw, cut it, and have a straw. That was completely sustainable. And now we make it out of plastic. Avoidance is one thing. The other one I believe, is that our recycling systems are, I cannot even say broken because they have not even been properly established in the first place. At The Conference Board, we authored a report about a plastic solid waste recycling, and it was a revelation to me.[13] Do you see it the same way?

Chever Voltmer

Yes, thinking about recycling has really changed the way I look at the world and thinking about how you can build a circular economy. And this looks vastly different in separate places. In the United States and in Europe, for example, we do a reasonable job of collecting our trash, but we still have a long way to go on recycling. In our part of the world, we collect it, but then a lot of it gets landfilled or incinerated or exported to developing countries. In the developing world, the problem is a little bit different. They have trouble collecting it, but in some places where they do collect, the recycling rates are as good or better than ours.

What we need though, regardless of where we are starting from, is to build strong recycling systems because they are the prerequisite for a more circular economy. You must collect the stuff to reprocess it and turn it into something new. And this is an important challenge, and it is broader than just plastic pollution because it gets at climate change and other existential issues, trying to figure out how to live within our planetary boundaries.

Uwe Schulte

You are right and a lot of people got frustrated when they experienced that even though they separate trash, it then is not properly recycled. There is a big job to do and I am glad to say that the issue seems to have been recognised now, and that an increasing number of responsible companies are starting to really engage and say: 'This is not just something for somebody else, but we have to make sure that we introduce that sort of infrastructure'. And I guess that will help you with your job, will it not?

Chever Voltmer

Yes. And thank you for bringing the issue of companies into it, because the reality is that companies are the ones who make the products that we buy and use. So, they need to think about what they are making and what happens to it at its end of life. And while this is their obligation, the reality is that they cannot solve this problem on their own either. They are beholden to whatever recycling systems their products are going into, which varies around the world. Thinking about how to tackle this problem at state level, at a company level, and at an individual level, think about the complexity of that and how to do that. There is work for everyone here.

---

[13] https://www.conference-board.org/topics/plastic/plastic-solid-waste-management

Uwe Schulte

I must say, I am not a great fan of burning plastic waste, but I would rather burn it than put it into the ocean. Let us make sure that anything we can get our grip on, does not get leaked into the environment again. I know what you mean when you said that in some parts of the world trash collection and separation is not established, and we have these wild sites that heavily leak into the environment. That gets us back to something that we discussed already, but I think we should spend a bit more time on it. Avoiding that the stuff gets into the river or when it is in the river to get it out of the river. Let us talk a little bit more about it. I understand you have that startup project in Vietnam you talked about. What I like about that approach is that it is financially scalable because this problem is big, but there is also the issue of having to be careful how you do this because you could do a lot of harm in the cleaning up exercise. Can you talk about that?

Chever Voltmer

Sure. The process in Vietnam to get the permits to issue the trash traps, and this may be the case everywhere, but my experience is really in Vietnam, was an exceedingly long, months long permit process. We had to engage with every single stakeholder that uses the river. It is used for navigation, it is used for washing and cleaning, it is used for drinking water, it is used for all kinds of purposes for recreation. Dealing with all the stakeholders, the local government, the national government to understand that where we were putting the traps was both, sustainable for the community and for wildlife. We have been very encouraged; we have not found any wildlife in our trap yet. We think it is well-designed to allow for wildlife to pass through it without problems. I feel good about that piece, but it is a crucial element to make sure that you are thinking about doing no harm as a first principle.

Uwe Schulte

Now, when you get the plastic out of the water, what do you do with it?

Chever Voltmer

That is an excellent question and a lot of it depends. It depends on what is available in the local community. This is the same for the trash that we pick up in our cleanups. One of the things that we are working on is trying to build and create more sustainable recycling value chains with all this trash that we collect. It is harder said than done because the answer looks different in every place. But trying to figure out how to give this trash a second life is something that we are thinking about a lot. For example, our global ghost gear team has a new project they are launching called the North American Net Collection Initiative, they call it NANCI.[14]

---

[14] https://marinedebris.noaa.gov/removal/collaborating-across-borders-north-american-net-collection-initiative

Uwe Schulte

Let us just be clear. Someone might not have listened when you explained this wonderful expression ghost gear. Please elaborate again what ghost gear is, before we go on.

Chever Voltmer

Ghost gear is abandoned, lost, and discarded fishing gear. Our team that works with fishing gear has a new project. When they collect these nets in North America, around Mexico on the U.S.-Mexican border, they are going to be recycling them. They have partnered with a company that works with recycled fishing nets and turns them into other things like skateboards, sunglasses, and other consumer products. Each solution may look a little bit different, depending on what is available and where you are, but we are starting to try to work on not just picking up the trash, but building circular value chains for it.

Uwe Schulte

Let me challenge you a little bit. That might not be circular, but at least it takes it out of the equation, so that is good and excellent. We already talked about what companies should be doing in the first place to avoid plastic or to build recycling systems and using recycled plastic. We know of the challenges of course—if you are in the foods industry you must avoid contamination. Let us not talk about this now, but these are challenges that the companies are facing. But companies are living up to this now. What can they do to help you with your cleaning efforts.

Chever Voltmer

I think you have touched on it, and you are right about the circularity piece. The dream is to turn a bottle into a bottle, right? And we are not there yet. But you are right, that should be the gold standard. In terms of what companies can do, beyond thinking about their own operations and their own usage of plastic, is starting to think about collective action. I say that in the sense that as I mentioned previously, nobody can solve this problem on their own. It is going to need acting by everyone. Whether they are working through their trade organisations or engaging in policy or in partnerships with organisations like Ocean Conservancy, they can help. They need robust recycling infrastructure to meet their own goals. But they need to work with others to get there. I will give you a couple of examples of how we are doing that. I mentioned previously that many countries struggle with collecting their trash because it tends to be expensive. At the same time, to the extent that any of the trash is being picked up, it is being picked up by informal sector waste collectors. And these people typically live in exceedingly difficult and unhealthy, if not dangerous conditions. They live on the margins of their own societies, and they are viewed as an obstacle to progress. And in some cases, they do not even officially exist. But from our perspective, from an ocean conservation perspective, they are frontline heroes because they keep trash out of the ocean when no one else does.

We at Ocean Conservancy started to wonder, what if we viewed these fifteen million informal sector waste collectors around the world, not as part of the problem, but as part of the solution? Could we find a way to empower these informal sector waste collectors? Could we find a way to help to incentivise them to keep low-value plastic, which is the stuff that gets into the ocean, from leaking into the waterways? And if we could get them to pick it up, could we find end markets for it? Our goal was to do this in a way that would create, what we like to call, a triple bottom line—an environmental, a social, and an economic benefit. That is where our project which is called ASPPIRe, which stands for Advancing Solutions to Plastic Pollution through Inclusive Recycling, was born. The ASPPIRe Project[15] is supported by Ocean Conservancy's Trash Free Seas Alliance and that is a group of companies, conservation organisations and scientists who are all working together to keep trash out of the ocean. They are supporting the programme.

And we built a partnership with several organisations that are real experts in working with the informal sector, we are operational in Colombia and Vietnam. Our goal is to improve the working conditions and capacity of informal sector workers to devise incentives for helping them to collect more of this low-value trash and then to connect them with the markets for the materials and governments for support. As part of that project, we are holding conversations with each of our steering committee members, each of the companies, and asking them very explicitly what they can do to help us find a home for this material if we can get it collected. And I am very pleased to say that all of them are taking this very seriously and they have really done a great job of reaching out beyond their sustainability teams to bring in their procurement teams, their design teams, their engineering teams to help us see if we cannot find a way to make some progress on this. That is exciting.

Uwe Schulte
It is interesting, you say these are fifteen million and that is obviously an estimate, an underestimation. But also, I like the idea to say that these people can help us if we can help them. It is great that you found companies and I understand why companies are necessary here and that they must play an active role because they must find a market for the material that is collected. We must improve the living conditions of these people. I guess it would be useful to work with local NGOs there as well.

Chever Voltmer
Yes, we are collaborating with local partners in both Vietnam and Colombia. These are organisations whose mission is to work with these groups. They were excited, and they have been really interested in this connection to the ocean. Because for them it is a way to raise the status of informal sector collectors and to get recognition for the environmental services they are providing. One of our partners was so enthusiastic, they organised a beach cleanup and they invited local politicians, and they paired politicians with informal sector collectors. I was proud to see that each of the collectors had a big button they had made that said, 'my job protects the ocean'.

---

[15] https://cecr.vn/en/workshop-on-sharing-experiences-and-lesson-learned-in-implementing-the-project-advancing-solutions-to-plastic-pollution-through-inclusive-recycling/

Uwe Schulte

Nice. That should get the juices flowing in the local politicians, I guess. That is good news. Are you planning to extend that beyond those locations?

Chever Voltmer

We are in discussions now on a second year of the programme, so we are really thinking through what the next step is. We are also collaborating with other partners, for example, the Platform for Accelerating the Circular Economy, PACE,[16] about how they might help us scale it even bigger. Because at the end of the day, we are an ocean conservation organisation. Our dream is to really make the case, prove the case, and then find partners who can help us scale it. We have used that successfully for some of the other work we have done, particularly on finance. We are hoping to do the same trick for this project.

Uwe Schulte

I understand. What you just mentioned is something that we see everywhere—sustainability initiatives cannot be done by one party in isolation. These are always collaboration efforts. Obviously, you are a keen collaboration partner. I think if this podcast encourages one or two companies to contact you and start supporting you, it will be beneficial for them as well, because as we have just seen, new business models can spring from that and that can also be helpful for improving your brand image, for example. Now, are there other things that companies can do to support the efforts that you are doing?

Chever Voltmer

Sure, let us talk about another initiative. You mentioned for example that there are a thousand rivers that trash flows through to the ocean. What all these bodies of water have in common is that usually there is a city somewhere on them. And that is where the trash is coming from. So, another project that we are doing that is supported by several our corporate partners is called Urban Ocean[17]. The idea behind that is that cities have responsibility for waste management but have not really been part of the conversation around marine debris. And if you talk to mayors, which I have done, they may not list marine debris as their top priority, but our interests really align because they do care about things like greenhouse gas emissions, jobs, public health, tourism. And our idea was: could we embed marine debris solutions into broader city strategies so that it delivers co-benefits both for their priorities and ours? Right now, we are working in eleven cities, including six learning cities around the world. We brought them through this programme, we brought in world-class scientists, and they did studies in each of the cities to think about their circularity opportunities and challenges. And we convened stakeholders around that scientific research, and now they are creating, identifying, and prioritising what they want to do, what their solution set is. Each city looks a little bit different. Then the capstone event will happen next year where they will pitch their proposed solutions to potential funders and

---

[16] https://pacecircular.org/

[17] https://resilientcitiesnetwork.org/urban-ocean/

partners. We are really encouraged by this work, and we are actively recruiting and looking for people who want to partner with cities. In some cases, for example, you may find that a company is headquartered in one of these cities or has big operations in these cities or wants to get engaged for other reasons. They may have a manufacturing facility or whatever. But we are really encouraged by the uptake of this. We have had cities banging down the door begging to join the programme around the world. We think that we have hit on something. When I went to the Resilient Cities Summit, they all wanted to talk about this problem. It says to me that there is a real need to think about the issue at the municipal level. That is where a lot of companies can get engaged because that is where they are. They are in cities, they are operating in cities, they are working in cities, and that is where their employees are.

Uwe Schulte
Yes, that makes sense and that is interesting. I guess, all they must do is to contact you, so that is great. I just had another thought. You mentioned that wonderful database. Wonderful in the sense of that you provide the data, not so wonderful by the fact that you have so much data about trash, because that means there is a lot of trash. In your cleanup exercises, you collect the coastal trash and you put it into a database. If I remember correctly, it is called TIDES. I would have thought this could be a useful source of information for companies to better understand where their packaging, etc., is ending up. Have you ever had conversations around that already?

Chever Voltmer
Yes, we have had a few companies come to us and look at the data. Part of why they come to us to collaborate with us is because they see that they have a problem. As I said, we have a lot of big consumer companies who collaborate with us trying to understand what the problems are. They all have different strategies for how to solve the problems. Some are really focused on reduction, some are really focused on recycling, some are focused on substitution, substituting plastic for something else. But they do keenly watch the data and pay close attention to it. I would also say that other groups, not Ocean Conservancy, look at this data and try to extrapolate what the impact of a specific company could be. If you make a product in bottles, what percentage of that share might be yours and then using that to pressure companies.

Uwe Schulte
But it is fine because at the end of the day, we must stand for what we do and deal with it. And what I learned again from our conversation today, is tackling the issue at the source. It is better than having to send out ships onto the ocean and try to collect stuff there. And I understand that once it is in the ocean, getting it out of the ocean is the most difficult part because you can do a lot of harm to the environment at the same time.

Chever Voltmer
And it is also expensive. It is much cheaper to stop things at the source than it is to try to clean it up once it is in the environment. And that is true for most pollution issues. Tackling is a critical issue, and I will say this: we have lots of, what I would

call, frank and open discussions with our corporate partners and I am always pushing them to do more as they know. But they usually thank me at the end because they know on some level that they need to do this and that having these kinds of conversations is helpful for them and it is better than having regulations or other things imposed on them, although you need those too. But figuring out solutions collectively is good for them, and it is good for us.

Uwe Schulte
What was it, twelve million metric tonnes? That is a lot of stuff.

Chever Voltmer
Eleven million metric tonnes, yes.

Uwe Schulte
That is a problem that we should attack collectively and, Chever, it is kind that you shared what you are doing. You are doing your bit and companies must do their bit. And today we might have been able to describe a little bit how this could be done. It is very encouraging to see that you are tackling it, for example, with your project in Vietnam, trying to find means of cleaning up rivers in a sustainable way. Thank you for sharing all of that and we wish you a lot of success in your efforts.

Chever Voltmer
Thank you so much. I really want to emphasise that companies do have a key role to play in this, and they are part of the problem, but they also can be part of the solution.

Uwe Schulte
Absolutely. And thank you for making that point.

Sustainable Packaging

Recorded May 2022

Uwe Schulte

Today I will be talking to Ken Bowles, Chief Financial Officer at Smurfit Kappa Group. Please let me introduce our guest for today. Ken joined Jefferson Smurfit Group as a Treasury Accountant in 1994 and has held several positions in the finance functions of the group as it has gone through various changes. In 2016, he became Chief Financial Officer. Ken holds an MBA from the University College of Dublin. Welcome, Ken. Please tell us a little bit about yourself and how sustainability has entered your personal and professional life.

Ken Bowles

Good morning, Uwe. And thank you for taking the time to talk to me about sustainability. It is a topic that here at Smurfit Kappa we are passionate about. It is interesting, we have been talking about it since 1934 and it seems like the world has woken up in the last 5 years to our way of thinking. I suppose a little bit about me. I just turned 51 a couple of weeks ago in isolation as had COVID, so not the best birthday I have ever celebrated, but never mind. I am married to my wife Elaine. We have been married for 16 years, together over 20, we have two wonderful sons—Jack and Adam, 15 and 14. And they are everything teenage boys should be. Wonderful most of the time and an absolute pain some of the time. That is their job. I have been with what was the Jefferson Smurfit Group and is now Smurfit Kappa for 28 years. A considerable proportion of my life has been spent in the group rather than outside of it. That is where sustainability interacts with the personal though, because I am a consumer, like you are a consumer, like we are all consumers. At a very personal level, every time we go into a supermarket, we make a choice. And every time we do something in our lives, it is a choice around how we do that. Drive, walk, run, cycle, take that plane to a meeting that is short. Buy that plastic bottle rather than refillable. And they are all simple choices that the consumers make. I suppose, what I try and do is ask myself whether I can connect that back to the bigger, broader picture about where we see it as an organisation in that kind of conversation. Which is—it is our products that are sitting on shelves, it is our products that are designed to make the world a better place from a recyclability perspective and hopefully from a climate perspective, because of the intensity of how we produce those. But you cannot be in Smurfit Kappa, and you would not be here this long if sustainability were not something you were (a) passionate about and (b) drove your everyday decision-making. Irrespective of the roles I have had over the years, they have always been impacted by sustainability. I remember back in 1995 drafting a paper at that point for the management team on sustainability accounting, which had become something that was going to be here quite soon. That was 1995 and I am certain it was not the best piece of work I ever did, as a 24-year-old at the time, but it just shows you how long the conversation has been. We have been trying to have the conversation, but it has never really kicked off. And like I say, it is over the last 5–10 years where people have been really engaged. I have been lucky enough in this group to travel the globe with us, and when I go to places like Colombia, where you see biodiversity and biodiversity management in action and the interactions between nature and how you can actually have sustainable businesses, yet support the flora, the fauna, the Andean bear, the people, I think that connects right back through to the person. It is with a wonderful sense of pride that I work in Smurfit Kappa, and everybody here does. But when we wake up every day it is about: how do we make this business more sustainable? How do we help our customers be more sustainable? And that is the drive. Everybody talks about economic profits, and they are important, because the simple reality is if you do not make a profit, you cannot invest in everything else and you will not have shareholders because there will be no returns. While we might like the idea of profit, sometimes it is a necessity to ensure that you can drive for everything you want in business. Fundamentally, it comes down to—like you, I am a consumer. And my choice is at the supermarket shelf, what drives me from a personal sustainability perspective, and then I try and link that back to what my customers might need on a broader scale from a business perspective.

Uwe Schulte
I get that. This is already quite a passionate plea for sustainability. Of course, I like to hear that. But Ken, while Smurfit Kappa is a €10 billion Revenue company with

almost 50,000 employees worldwide, I am afraid not all our audience will be familiar with what your company is doing. Could you please enlighten us a little bit?

Ken Bowles

I will try. You are right, we are one of the world's biggest companies that nobody has ever heard of, and we are broadly #50 in the FTSE 100, so we are a large organisation from a market capitalisation perspective. We operate in 36 countries and, like you said, almost 50,000 employees. Some people mistake us. Smurfit Kappa sometimes gets broken down into—we are not the little blue fellas who live in history, and we are not the sportswear manufacturer either, or some kind of combination of the two. We are Smurfit Kappa, and do you know why nobody would really hear about us? We are predominantly a business-to-business (B2B) company. But I can guarantee to you, if you are in a supermarket and you are picking your product off the shelf, or you are in a shop and you are looking at a display unit, or if you receive something to your house in a corrugated packaging, or you have bought a television or refrigerator or car parts, there is a fair chance that that box is a Smurfit Kappa box. We are the largest producer of corrugated packaging in Europe, we are the only pan-regional producer of corrugated packaging in Latin America, and we have been around since 1934, so we have been one of the longest in the game. We started off as a small box maker here in Rathmines, which is about four kilometres from where I sit now, to be built into, quite simply, a very impressive, large Irish success story. Among with many other companies, we are good at this. But you will not have heard of us and that is okay, we are okay with that. We like flying under the radar, but as a business model, Uwe, it is quite interesting, because when I joined back in the mid-90s corrugated packaging was seen as something that was used to get something valuable to somebody else. It was never seen as the product.

The evolution through my time here is that we have broken a lot of that B2B as a philosophical thing to be more business to consumer (B2C). It is the consumer that will consume our product on-shelf, shelf-ready packaging,[1] or the other container being the only box. I have seen this shift from transport medium, secondary packaging to packaging being the merchandising medium and the market medium, and that is wonderful because that leads you into a whole place of innovation. And indeed, it makes your ability to impact from a sustainability perspective much more real because you are directly connecting with the consumer. Yes, world's best kept secret in terms of our impact on sustainability, but we are okay with that (Fig. 1).

Uwe Schulte

I get that. Let us dive a little bit deeper into the products that you provide and let me understand a little bit about where they are coming from, how you produce them, and what the sustainability aspect is.

Ken Bowles

I suppose, the sustainable aspect is quite simple. It is a circular business, or we aim for it to be as circular as possible. In a quite straightforward way, we take seven

---

[1] https://en.wikipedia.org/wiki/Shelf-ready_packaging

Fig. 1 Example shelf-ready packaging. Source: Smurfit Kappa, https://www.smurfitkappa.com/de/products-and-services/packaging/shelf-ready-packaging

million tonnes of post-consumer waste, and we make beautiful boxes from it, and we will see that box anywhere between 7 and 10 times in its life cycle. And because of the biodegradable nature of the product, we are certain that when that product goes back to nature, it goes back to nature leaving no impact. You will not find our products on beaches; you will not find our products in seas. And if you do, they will have returned to nature very quickly, because the product is biodegradable. What do we do? Like I say, we collect seven million tonnes of post-consumer waste, so our product is broadly recycled. We do use some Kraft-paper[2] in our products, but we use those for certain products where you need strength, and they are travelling long distances through supply chains. We are Europe's largest producer of Kraft liner, which is the grade that, to keep it simple, comes directly from trees versus recycled boxes. But the reality is, even a recycled box has some Kraft liner in it because it needs strength. And as you recycle boxes, fibres get shorter, so they lose some of that strength. Our business model at its heart is to take waste and create product. And we run what we call the integrated model. We make all the paper that we need for the boxes we supply. Why is that important? It is particularly important from a security supply perspective, and particularly in the last few years where supply chains were stretched, and demand was so high. Getting product to shelf became the challenge for a lot of our customers, and our ability to ensure that our product got to them, and they got their products to their customers was very much business positive in that sense. We collect the waste, we make the paper, and then that paper goes to a network of corrugated plants all around the group, making a multitude of products. Anything from the very large boxes that you would find in the automotive industry, for example, or the chemical industry to—we have a beautiful bag and box

---

[2] https://en.wikipedia.org/wiki/Kraft_paper

operation where you will find wine for example, which is always the traditional product, but you get much more products like water in those now. We make a lot of on-shelf packaging, so when you walk to a shelf and you take a product directly out of the box, which is shelf-ready packaging. That removes the need for transport packaging and the decanted model of old. The product becomes the marketing medium. We make point-to-display, those pop-up things you see in supermarkets and around campaign time, Christmas, Easter, those. That is us. We do a lot of e-commerce. A lot of boxes that you will find coming to your front door, particularly in the last few years, would have been Smurfit Kappa boxes. Not necessarily the biggest and well-known brand, but we tend to partner with a lot of brands who work through that platform. And we like the idea of the higher end of that business in terms of helping brand owners who may not have e-commerce model to build that out in a way that supports their brand identity and their brand reputation. And then we have a huge agricultural business, so agricultural trades, in-field filling machines, things like that. Our business, to break it down, I would say it is about 75% Fast-Moving Consumer Goods (FMCG), and then the other 25% is broadly split between industrial volumes of 5–6%, agricultural volumes 10–15%, and then you have e-commerce discretely in there for the rest. But e-commerce pervades everything now. Everybody has an e-commerce model. We have an internal debate sometimes with what e-commerce is. Are DHL an e-commerce company now or a delivery company, UPS, and others. E-commerce is everywhere; It is in all our volumes. It is fair to say that if you pick up a product on a shelf and you turn it upside down, you will see our beautiful logo on the bottom of it. And all we ask is that when you use this, you give it back to us and we can make more boxes with it (Fig. 2).

Fig. 2 Roermond Circular Paper Mill. Source: Smurfit Kappa, https://www.smurfitkappa.com/de/sustainability/approach/our-circular-business/roermond-case-study

Uwe Schulte

Now, you have raised several points here, but first—I am coming from what you call FMCG. These are the Fast-Moving Consumer Goods companies. Some of our audience might not be familiar with some of the abbreviations. The other ones are B2C and B2B. You are dealing with business partners rather than consumers, but you are more engaged with consumers now, because you already do shelf-ready packaging, which you mentioned. Shelf-ready packaging means that the original packaging is used on the shelf and there is no extra transport packaging. You already explained that. And then the famous Kraft liner, and I want to dive a little bit deeper there. Fundamentally, you get boxes back, and we will talk about how you get boxes back in a second, but you get boxes back and you recycle them. You said you can do this even 6–7 times and that is impressive. But yes, for the strength you need some of the original material, and that means forests. Do you own forests? Is that where you get the original material? And of course, as you know, and that is my second question, managing forests in a sustainable way is also a challenge. Can you say something on both things please?

Ken Bowles

The only place we own forests right now is in Colombia, and we did own forestry in Venezuela before. We left that country, or our assets were taken from that country, is more appropriate to say. We do have forestry in Colombia which we manage, and then in Europe where we need trees, we have arrangements with local land or government agencies, as it would be in Sweden, to supply those trees. But you are right though. If you are going to be sustainable and if your model is supposed to be sustainable, then it has got to be sustainable irrespective of where you touch that circularity piece. When we talk about the trees that we take packaging consumes less trees than agriculture or indeed furniture making or house building.[3] We tend to take some of the products that are not used for something else, and then we take those off to make paper with them. Parts of the branches, some of the trunk, but the body of a tree goes towards furniture, house building construction and equally sustainable ways of making those products. It does come back to you how you manage those forests. And indeed, older trees consume less CO_2 than younger trees, so there is always a need to make sure that the forest is pruned and kept alive in that sense, by creating space for newer, younger trees to grow, taking out some of the older trees that maybe are not as efficient as they might be,[4] and using those for paper making and construction and everything else. But all our products we aim to have either Forest Stewardship Council (FSC)[5] certified, or Programme for the Endorsement of

---

[3] https://knowledge4policy.ec.europa.eu/sites/default/files/Sankey_diagrams.pdf
[4] https://www.ncasi.org/wp-content/uploads/2021/01/NCASI22_Forest_Carbon_YoungVsOld_print.pdf
[5] https://fsc.org/en

Forest Certification (PEFC).[6] We work with the WWF in Colombia,[7] for example, where we do have forest and they have certified our forests as FSC. Where we do consume products like that, we always drive to make sure that the certifications are there to make sure we are doing it in a sustainable way. And that is especially important for our customers too. Our customers want to make sure that the product they are getting from us is delivered in the most sustainable way possible. And we can only do that by certifying forestry as being sustainable, and we can only do that by doing the same on the recycle side, in terms where it comes through. But we always do, and it is a very delicate debate. I can understand people, when they see images of forestry being deforested that they naturally assume that this is the terrible thing, and it is when it is done incorrectly. But if you have been as long around as we have, and indeed some of our peer groups who are equally big consumers of forestry, it is important to get past the visual imagery. Europe would have planted more trees over the last number of years than they would have consumed, and largely because it is a carbon sink industry. We do need those trees to help the overall climate pattern. But also, we do need those to grow and take the place of older trees that are not needed anymore. And in Latin America, those growth patterns happen quickly. From a small seedling to a tree happens much quicker than in Europe. You get better turns on a forest there using pine and eucalyptus and those kinds of brands. But I think it is fair to say, and I probably speak for my peer group here, that when we look at how we approach forestry, and we would not be the biggest consumer in that sense or the biggest owner of forests, I think we all have the same mindset which is: as organisations we are at our hearts, foresters, paper makers, box makers, sustainable and sustainable practises run through us. I think it is, like all these things, about us educating the population and what actually happens in forests, and not sometimes to believe some of the worst aspects of deforestation, where we see forest being taken out to create room for agriculture, for example, where maybe that could be done slightly differently. While we might take trees out, we always replace them. That is the fundamental point. Whereas that does not necessarily happen in other industries, which is where I think the bulk of that problem might lie (Figs. 3 and 4).

Uwe Schulte
From my own experience, having been purchasing boxes, I am afraid to say not with you but also with other suppliers—it can be dreadful. One of my biggest challenges was Indonesia at the time where certain companies did not have a sustainable way of running forestry. And I saw two issues there. One was biodiversity because there were really devastating effects, and the other one was also the effect on the Indigenous population there, taking away their livelihood. Do you have any views on that?

---

[6] https://www.pefc.org/

[7] https://www.smurfitkappa.com/newsroom/2020/smurfit-kappa-announces-new-partnership-with-wwf

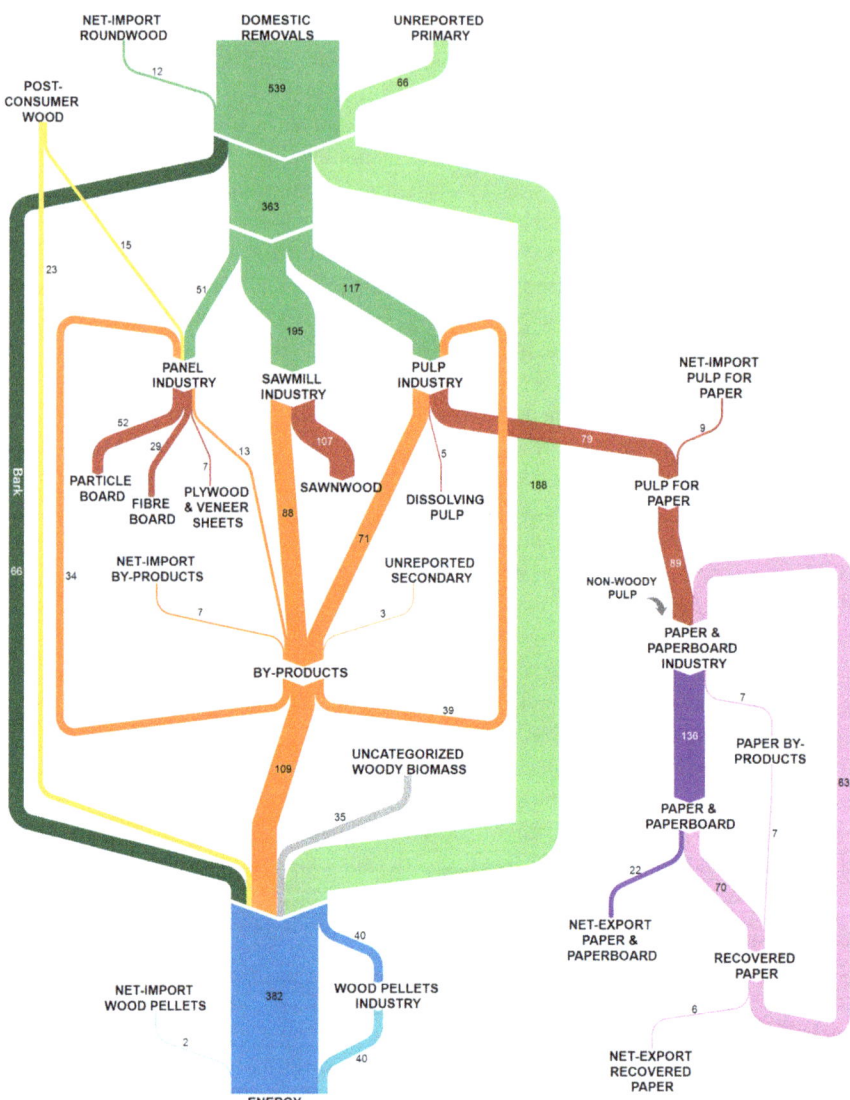

Fig. 3 Sankey diagram wood biomass EU 2017. Source: European Union, 2022, Sankey diagrams of woody biomass flows in the EU, Release 2021, Years 2009–2017, https://knowledge4policy.ec.europa.eu/sites/default/files/Sankey_diagrams.pdf

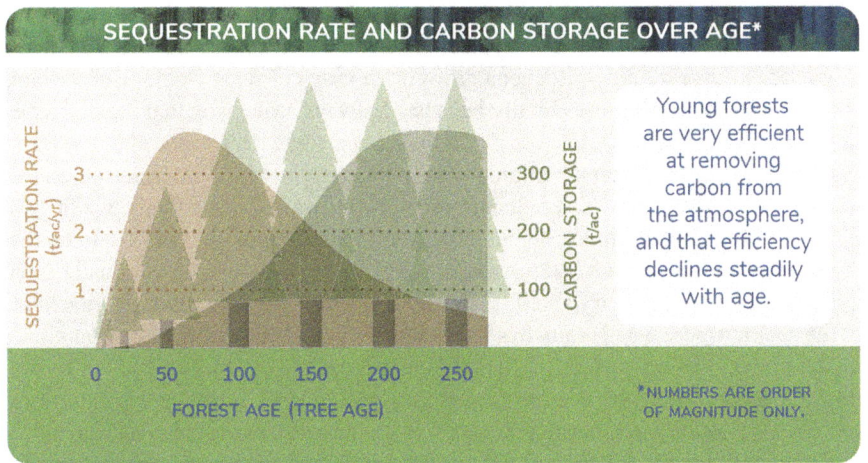

Fig. 4 Carbon storage by tree age. Source: NCASI 2021, https://www.ncasi.org/wp-content/uploads/2021/01/NCASI22_Forest_Carbon_YoungVsOld_print.pdf

Ken Bowles

Not specifically on Indonesia because we never operated out there, but I think where we do operate, we tend to collaborate with the local communities. Particularly in Colombia, where we would have a lot of farms, we tend to collaborate with those communities to make sure that we are respectful of their traditions. A lot would collaborate with us. And we do not tend to get into displaced lands or displaced people, that is not our place to be. Issues do arise from time to time, but we deal with those in a very upfront way. It again goes back to the heart of Smurfit Kappa. When you think about how the paper making industry has grown up over the last century/century and a half, most papermills started in the middle of a town, and then the town grew around it. You see that a lot through the Benelux, particularly in the Netherlands and through Germany, where you get that. In Latin America, similarly, you have a different economic environment there, where somebody like us coming in and creating businesses, creates many opportunities for people to have employment through generations. We see a lot of generational people coming into our company in the sense that the father, the son, the mother, the daughter, the sister will all work with us. That is a responsibility too. We take our place in the community very seriously. And Tony Smurfit[8] our CEO particularly would have a maxim that says that when you get to the end of your career in Smurfit Kappa, you need to be able to look back and say: 'I did some good'. And the reality is that I do not think any of us would feel good about ourselves in Smurfit Kappa if we look back and said that it was fine, but that community was just a pain for the last 50 years. And that is not what we do. I know our guys in Colombia and there are a lot of Indigenous people, which is where we really see it. We spend a lot of time with the leaders of those communities,

---

[8] https://en.wikipedia.org/wiki/Tony_Smurfit

making sure that everything is okay and making sure that we are respectful. We would give over lands to what they need, and we would take lands what we need. We work extremely hard with cocoa growers, in terms of what we do. But we have a keen sense of biodiversity equally because it always strikes me that the conversations on climate always get driven down the carbon route. But we need to start having a serious conversation about biodiversity loss. Because it is as important to me. The simple reality is, you can reduce carbon all you want, but suddenly, we find we have no water. That is a much bigger issue. But to your point—we worked hard, that does not mean we have not had problems over the years, and we have not had to deal with those. But what we try and do is ensure that we respect the rights and the lands of the people where we operate. It is fair to say, we would be seen as a good employer in about every country we are in, in all the countries we are in. But that is down to the hard work of the local teams and ensuring that their connections with the communities are strong and that that concept of giving back as an organisation and, if you like, building the village around us, because that is as important as making the product in it.

Uwe Schulte

I agree with you. We cannot have a real reduction of carbon without thinking about biodiversity and vice versa. This is important. We started off by you explaining how circular you are, and that is very impressive. What we did not touch on so far is where you get all these boxes from to have that high percentage of recycled material.

Ken Bowles

Based on what has been coming through my door at home for the last two years, the most of it comes from my house from what my sons have bought. I suppose we get it from everywhere, is the broadest answer. But to break that down—we collect at the back of large supermarkets, take someone like Walmart in Mexico, which has about 2800 stores. We collect at the back of that. Same in North America where we operate. We have arrangements with city councils in the UK, or in Germany, or companies like Veolia, where we arrange to take the waste, they sort the waste, and we take it from them. We have our own collection facilities, so we have several of our own recycling plants or reclamation facilities where we bring product in and sort it. And we have people who in some other countries bring stuff directly to the gate, where we take it. And that equally for domestic waste and post-consumer waste. The local authorities sort and collect it through those recycling bins, and we would get something back there. Also, about 25% of our material comes from ourselves. When you make a car, you get a box and you run it across the machine, and it cuts out the little clippings to make the box. All those clippings come back to us too. Equally in those plants, we would have a recycling system where any of that product comes back. It comes from everywhere. The issue we have is that big supermarkets are a very efficient system for collection, domestic environments are not. It comes back to almost full circle, back to what we talked about at the start which is—what can we do as individuals to help that problem? And what I would say is, the more you can recycle properly and get back to us, the better chance we have of making that circular model even stronger. In Ireland, we have a green bin for

Sustainable Packaging

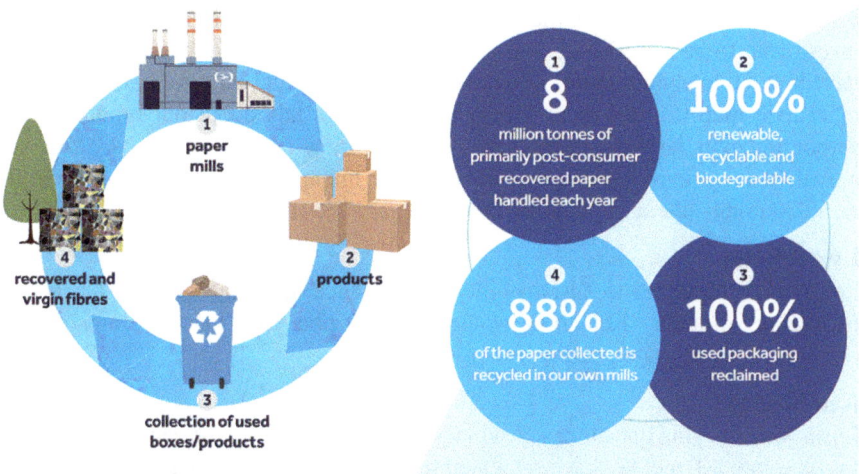

Fig. 5 Smurfit Kappa recycling process. Source: Smurfit Kappa, https://www.smurfitkappa.com/-/m/files/publications%2D%2D-global/sustainability-reports/smurfit_kappa_sustainable_development_report_2022.pdf?rev=e2161db1df74451ca8dfc031214638d4

recycled materials. It is making sure that it is clean material, it is not contaminated with other things you put on top of it or commingled. The cleaner we get it back, the better. We have multiple sources depending on the region and the place we are in. The biggest issue though in the last few years is around that pure drive towards e-commerce and particularly during 2020, 2021, and COVID-19. Our ability to get that domestic consumption of e-commerce material back has been a challenge, it is fair to say (Fig. 5).

Uwe Schulte

I understand. You will be pleased to hear that I have an extra bin just for paper, and that is collected separately and probably ends up in one of your plants. Just a quick question on that one. That is of course an energy-intensive process to make that into nice new corrugated. How do you deal with that element of your sustainability?

Ken Bowles

When we think about our footprint in terms of CO_2, an intensity sits in the paper mills. The box band machines by themselves are a lower intensity from a CO_2 perspective. They would consume electricity and they are clearly fossil based, but a big, intense production are the paper mills. How do we do it? It is investment, it is investment in cleaner tech, it is investment in newer boilers, it is the removal of fossil towards biomass and those. A couple of years ago we put a new boiler into our kraft liner mill in Nettingsdorf (Austria), the boiler slightly bigger than the one you get in your house, about 134 million Euro, and that has taken 40,000 tonnes of CO_2 out of our system. We are going to do a similar project in our Cali paper mill (Colombia), about $100 million worth, and that will take about 140,000 tonnes of CO_2 out of our system. Our paper mill in Zülpich (Germany) has a couple of investments where it will be the first carbon-neutral mill in our group. It is constant investment, to be honest with you, Uwe. It is linked to some conversation we may have in a while about targets, and how we set targets, and then we have an investment road map to meet them. But really, when we talk about our products, that carbon intensity happens in the paper mills and how do we reduce that? You can only do that by investing in newer, cleaner tech, and more efficient and bigger boilers to do things like burn biomass or multi-fuel rather than fossil.

Uwe Schulte
Let us now move on to sustainability performance and examples of sustainable packaging solutions. Ken, how would you describe your material impact with respect to energy, water, carbon footprint, and waste?

Ken Bowles
It is a wide-ranging question, so I will try and fill as much in as I can, and please, if I miss some, ask me. We have set a goal for 2050 to be carbon neutral. That clearly is something that will move over time because carbon neutrality will become all GHGs in time, all greenhouse gases. Neutrality will be really the standard when we get to 2050. I think it could either be new standards coming in around biodiversity loss and things of that, but now we have a target or an aim to be at least net zero by 2050. Within that we like to set more firm targets. We have a target to be 55% less CO_2 by 2030, and we are very much on track for that target. We just issued our Sustainable Development Report for 2021 and we are about 42% as we stand now, so very much on track for that one. That target is firm because we have set out a series of projects from a capital perspective that will achieve that. That has always been our philosophy. We tend not to set targets that we do not believe we can meet. There is always a difference between ambition and target, and both are valuable. But you must be able to manage both in the context of how you are dealing with your stakeholders and the reality situation. Net zero by 2050, 55% by 2030. And 80% of all our footprint comes from what we do in paper, where we get the biggest impacts is in our paper system. If we focus there on reducing energy use, so using less energy to make the same type of products. Clearly the move to more renewable types of energy—biomass, green electricity. And for context, if we split our scope 1, 2, and 3, about 50% of our emissions are scope1, which tends to be mostly gas at the mill sites. About 15% tends to be Scope2, that is really electricity throughout our corrugated system. And then the balance is really Scope3, we will call it 35%. And that is going to be our focus in the more near term. We are well set on Scope1 and 2, and a bit more work to do on Scope3. But we have been validated by the Science Based Targets Initiative (SBTI) at being below 2%, which is the best in our industry. That has really been a great achievement by Garett Quinn, who is head of sustainability, to get there because it is not an easy project. It is a lot of engagement and to achieve that result is fantastic. And that means that we know we have external assurance for our 55% which is always valuable for stakeholders. It is like everything, people say: 'Well, how are you going to get to net zero by 2050'? The honest answer is that we do not know yet. The reality is that you go past 2030, modern technology will take their part, will hydrogen play a big part, will reuse, and recycle get better

in terms of carbon intensity and less so? But it is important to have the ambition out there, and it is important to drive the organisation towards that goal, and within that set targets that are achievable. If you like broad strokes, that is where we sit on carbon. We could have lots of targets around waste to landfill reduction, which will absolutely hit before 2030, we want to bring that to zero. The chain of custody target of over 98%, meaning that our customers have full certainty over the greenness of the supply chain. And the last bit then is about water intake. It is a funny target for us because we do not consume water as an industry, we process water. What we do is put water back into the environment in a much cleaner way than it came to us in the first place. Because to make the kind of paper we make and as beautiful as it is, you do need clean water and that is what we aim to do. And clearly, they have benefits for local communities too, in terms of the overall water supply. We do not impact the water table in that way. It goes back to the part of the conversation we had earlier, which is when we think about our business model being circular, that must start with limiting the impact on the environment and the resources you take from it in the first place. You cannot just focus on the end of life. You must go right back to the start together, and make sure that you leave as little or no footprint as you can. And that is really what the targets are designed to do.

Uwe Schulte
I must say, Ken, I would be extremely glad if a few people who made net zero commitments and are now saying 'Oh dear, we had not realised what Scope3 is all about' will listen to what you just said. I would rather have very realistic targets than just putting something ambitious out there and having no plan how to achieve it. That I think is extremely valid. We should just clarify an expression you used—chain of custody.[9] Could you just explain that? Not everybody understands the forestry implications.

Ken Bowles
The world has got ever more concerned about not only the product they are consuming, but how that product is consumed and made in the first instance and where, in our case, the fibres for that product come from. Our customers are really interested to make sure that forestry does not come from any conflict wood. For example, the current conflict in Russia and Ukraine—the wood now coming out of Russia is designated as conflict wood, and so would fail Forest Stewardship Council (FSC) certification.[10] We could not and we do not use anyway, but we could not use that wood in our products for our customers, because we could not guarantee them chain of custody of their product. We built a system that says that if you get a box of Smurfit Kappa, as would any of our major customers, you can look back through the production of that product right back to the source of fibre and we can tell you the source of fibre and the certification around it. For example, our forestry we own in Colombia has been certified by FSC for a long number of years now. And equally

---

[9] https://en.wikipedia.org/wiki/Chain_of_custody
[10] https://fsc.org/en/fsc-standards

the fibres we secure from third parties and the paper we buy from third parties are equally chain of custody certified. We are not unique in that, but I think it is valuable for our customer to be able to say to their customer, the end consumer, that your product does not impeach any laws around conflict wood, or the modern slavery act,[11] or in certain industries you have issues around child labour, for example. That is an important statement. And then, people will see that on boxes, if hopefully at the end of this people will begin to go into supermarkets and turn boxes upside down like I do to see what is on the end. And if they do, they will see little things like FSC, and then they will know that this box is sustainably made and comes from sources that have been certified to be non-conflict. That is quite valuable for the consumer, I think, and getting more valuable in a world that is becoming more aware of those kinds of topics.

Uwe Schulte
I just realised that I asked you about an expression you used, and we both used the expression Scope3. Let us just make sure that our audience is also aware. I think 90% are but let us just make sure. Scope1 and 2 are under your control, it is your production and the energy you directly buy. Scope3 is whatever happens upstream in your supply chain and in the use and the final disposal of your product. That is scope3, right?

Ken Bowles
Yes. I suppose, our Scope3 is where we can have the greatest impact for our customers. When our customers set targets for 2030 and beyond, where they are impacting mostly probably is around Scope3, and that is where they look to producers like us and their packaging suppliers to help them. Our own Scope3 is a number, but our greatest opportunity is enabling the reduction of Scope3 emissions for all our customers. It is a terrific opportunity.

Uwe Schulte
That leads us directly to my next point, Ken. At The Conference Board, we always say that companies must be aware working for a positive impact in sustainability implies collaborating with others. You talked about your customers. Can you give us an example of how you collaborate with customers to do something about that?

Ken Bowles
I was going to say hot off the press, but in the case of this product cold off the press is more appropriate. It is a product called ThermoBox, for example. Traditionally, you would have things like fish being shipped long distances in EPS or expanded polystyrene containers. We have a view I think, which would be shared, that EPS is not the most sustainable product in the longer term, in terms of its production, or indeed its recyclability, or the end-of-life solution. In our case, we look for alternatives for customers that are looking for a more sustainable way of that.

---

[11] https://en.wikipedia.org/wiki/Modern_Slavery_Act_2015

Uwe Schulte

EPS is that white, fluffy material—polystyrene.

Ken Bowles

No matter how hard you try to not make it go all over your floor and carpet, it always does every single time. As a five-year-old child it is a wonderful toy, as an adult trying to get rid of it, it is just a nightmare. It just appears everywhere. But it is exactly that, and it is mostly air, but the 1% is the bit we worry about. We invented the ThermoBox, or the guys in the business did, and it is 100% recyclable, and that is the first thing. And you can keep food at even lower temperatures than you might be able to do with EPS. It clearly gives a benefit from the end consumer around: 'I know my packaging is now sustainable. And I know that my products from a food safety perspective are better because the temperatures are lower'. But the real benefits then come through the supply chain. If you think about EPS, it is pre-made, comes in the shape you need it. Corrugated by its nature can come flat. We find this equally with agricultural trades. You can store them flat, so your ability to store much more of your raw material or your packaging product is much greater with ThermoBox. You store flat and when you need it, you just erect it and then off you go. That can be handy, especially in busy times. How we solved the problem with a different customer was that they found that when they were busy, they ran out of the reusable plastic crates that you see in supermarkets. They ran out of those when they were busy. So, we replaced all those with corrugated board, which meant that they never ran out. But also, they could print on them for campaigns, so they became much more of a marketing product than a transport product. But back to the ThermoBox. The ThermoBox is a similar thing—you can print on it, you can make it campaign-based, you can do whatever you want in terms of colours. But logistically you store flat, your supply chain is always full in terms of packaging supplies. You can see how it can have a wonderful application, not only in the retail sector, but clearly through e-commerce also. Because e-commerce boxes are becoming the norm in terms of how we might deliver things. And the ThermoBox fits the e-commerce environment just as much as it fits the retail environment. It is ways like that where we collaborate with the customer. We have a concept here of trying to understand the customer's pain. Sometimes it is not really that they are looking for a different type of box. Sometimes it is that they are looking but have not figured it out yet. But the questions are: Where are they on that sustainable journey? Where are they on the brand promise and what the consumer wants from that? And that is where something like the ThermoBox fits in perfectly (Fig. 6).

Uwe Schulte

I used to be one of those procurement guys, but it is so long ago that I have forgotten about it. But one of the mantras was always that you should not try to invent everything yourself, but you should really collaborate with your suppliers because they might have ideas of solutions which you have not even dreamt of being possible. And this sounds a little bit like it. I am almost dared to say why we have not had this earlier.

Fig. 6 Thermo box. Source: Smurfit Kappa, https://www.smurfitkappa.com/de/products-and-services/packaging/thermobox

Ken Bowles

I suppose that in some ways the technology has not been there in terms of things like food contact and being able to ensure those, being able to work with a box that can go through the supply chain like that. And some is quite simply because as an industry and particularly Smurfit Kappa, we did not think like that before. If you came to us in your former life, you would have said: 'Ken, my box costs too much. I need to reduce the cost of my box'. Which I am sure you did. And we would have said: 'Well, okay Uwe, we will re-engineer the box slightly, and there you go'. Whereas now we do things with customers the way that we say: 'Okay, well, let us think about the problem in a different kind of way'. It is not that you get the savings from changing the box fundamentally or making it a different box from a cost perspective. We re-engineer the box that says that you get twice as many pallets on a truck and therefore you take half the trucks off the road. And you do not only reduce the logistics cost, but also, take out the CO_2.

What if in our relationship we re-engineer the box, but you get sustainability savings? It is that which changed conversation, particularly Smurfit Kappa. We really are in a unique place on this. The customer can get any box they want, but is it the box they need? And is it the right box? And these are the richer conversations we were able to have, and our teams have with our customers. We see that around us in everything we do. But those are the more discreet bits. The ability to impact things beyond the re-engineered box, particularly from a sustainability perspective is ever more valuable. In that case, I gave you we took 1000 trucks off a year, and we saved them 500 tonnes of CO_2. You could argue that it is free for them. They get the benefit, but clearly, we get the relationship, so it works both ways.

Uwe Schulte

I understand that this is a mutual beneficial point, and this is a crucial point beyond just your specific case. People are starting to realise that. In the good old days people said 'let us avoid risks' when they talked about environment and social impact.

Nowadays, people start to understand that this is a new frame of thinking and therefore new innovations come about. And your ThermoBox is an excellent example. Let us dwell a little bit longer on your transport savings, because this is an especially important one. Because again, we are looking at a system rather than just a specific product or something like this. Can you extend that a little bit more so that our audience understands how this is done?

Ken Bowles
We start off with a fundamental problem, that when you are shipping corrugated, you are shipping air, and so distribution and logistics become ever more important. Paper is great because big reels of paper can go anywhere. And they can go by rail or boat, so they tend to be less impactful from a CO_2 perspective in terms of from where they get there. But Trucks on roads—we know that corrugated does not travel more than 250 km. But that can be a lot of trips. And for our customers then, they clearly must get their product to wherever it is going. And 75–80% of our customers are FMCG, so food, beverage, those kinds of sectors. Their products are going to supermarkets and retail environments across a much bigger network than ours. So clearly for them the carbon footprint can be greater. The more we can do to impact that—and again, it goes back to Scope3 because this is part of their Scope3 emissions—it is helpful. We did something for a windscreen manufacturer for the automotive industry. They came to us looking for a box that would be more mono material and so we engineered a box that is mono material, such as corrugated, but fits twice as many screens on a truck as before. That makes people think: 'Okay, I have to think about this differently now, because I was not expecting that'. And that generates a much greater conversation than in other products. We had somebody come to us who was not a customer. But what was happening was that their box was being crushed in transport. When it got to their customer, it was being rejected because the box just was not working. Go back ten years, we would have just said: 'Okay, we will make a stronger box and that is great, isn't it'? But we said: 'Well, do you realise that you have got three products here (it was wine for a retail environment), and they are different price points, but I cannot tell the difference between the price points. Can we take it away and not only look at the problem around the crush of the box on the truck, but can we look fundamentally at what your box is doing'? We took it away, re-engineered the box, and re-engineered the design. And they ended it up with 17% increase in sales. That was verified by a third party because of the changed design. That is where innovation plays a part. That customer did not want anything but: 'Can you please stop my box being crushed in transport'? And so, they became a customer, not only a customer, but then a customer that felt: 'Wow, this goes beyond just the box manufacturer. This crowd can help us increase sales'. There are many things like that around the group. We have a customer in North America, and they would be sustainable by nature. They make a product for the household environment that helps reduce the energy footprint of homes. But the product problem was when the customer opened their box, it had polystyrene inside as a protective coating. You get this disconnect between what you tell me, that you are sustainable, and your product is sustainable, yet I am dealing with unsustainable

Fig. 7 Honeycomb packaging. Source: Smurfit Kappa, https://www.smurfitkappa.com/products-and-services/packaging/hexacomb-packaging

products. We have a product called Hexacomb which is, to keep it simple, like honeycomb in terms of shape. It is corrugated board trans-versed which gives it great strength. We replaced all the polystyrene in that case with Hexacomb, which means then when the customer opens the box, they are met with one mono material, fully recyclable packaging. One bin to put in, not having to worry about the environmental impact because it is all going back to be recycled. The customer then clearly has a situation where his brand promise is meeting his brand packaging. There are just some examples, Uwe, of where those things fit (Fig. 7).

Uwe Schulte
When I am listening to all these innovations and they are impressive, I must say, I have come to the point where I ask myself—do we still need plastic in packaging?

Ken Bowles
Yes, we do.

Uwe Schulte
Oh dear, I thought I asked the wrong guy.

Ken Bowles
Sometimes the conversation can be misunderstood. What we are interested in is reducing waste, we are about waste reduction. A box that is engineered wrong and is too big for the product, or has air inside it, or is too heavy, that is all equally waste. A box that takes too much CO_2 to produce is waste. When we think about plastic we think about waste. I think what we say is that if there is a more sustainable alternative to the plastic product, and we can do it, then that is the space in which we play. You think about something in that space like, for example, recently we launched a thing called the Toplock box. In supermarkets you have those rigid plastic containers for detergent tablets, and they have a click top box that is secure for children. For a long number of years, we could not crack the security aspects of that. But we have now, and we have a child lock, child secure version of that and corrugated, and that

Fig. 8 Detergent box with child safety closure. Source: Smurfit Kappa, https://www.smurfitkappa.com/products-and-services/packaging/toplock-detergent-box

is on supermarket shelves now. There is no reason that plastic container cannot be replaced by a corrugated alternative, because it fundamentally is more sustainable. But then there are lots of ways that plastic plays a part in avoiding food waste. Sometimes you get products wrapped in cling film that preserves the food life length. We are not interested in creating a different kind of waste problem by moving to corrugated, but we are interested in removing waste where we can. But plastic clearly has a part to play. We have not invented the see-through water bottle yet, but when we do, we will go after that. But for the moment, there are certain products where plastic clearly has an advantage. It goes back to the waste conversation, and within that very much around the end of life. We know that our product will return to nature in a brief period. That is the key differentiator between our product and other products, which is that you do not see our product on the beach, you do not see it becoming an island in the Pacific, people do not have a problem in terms of what they might do. It really is about end of life (Fig. 8).

Uwe Schulte
I am glad you say that. At The Conference Board, we have also spent some time looking at the consequences of plastic waste and what can be done about it. And I think building a good infrastructure for creating a much better recycling will be one of the big challenges.[12] This idealistic view that we can get rid of all the plastic is not the way to do this, but to make it circular as you have already done now. Thank you for making that point. We talked a lot about environment, but you are running many plants. You are working in the recycling business, you are managing forests, there are also social aspects like paying living wages, making sure that communities

---

[12] https://www.conference-board.org/topics/plastic/plastic-solid-waste-management

you operate in thrive. Can you tell us a little bit about that aspect as well? Because sometimes that is put to one side.

Ken Bowles

We operate in 36 countries, 48,000 people. We have a very keen sense of our social responsibility to all those people. The first of which is to make sure that they go home safely every single day. That is the primary concern. We benchmark ourselves against the living wage[13] and we pay above the living wage for over 95–96% of our employees, and where we do not, there are either legal local reasons or we will catch up. And some goes back to history, because if you think about paper mills, they started in small towns and towns grew around them, so you always have a deep connection back to the community in which you operate. Where we see some of the richer aspects of our Chief Sustainability Officers activities is through Latin America where clearly communities do not necessarily always have the advantage that some of our more developed European communities do. We always try and impact those communities a little bit more, through either community centres in Mexico City, in El Salvador, we have schools in Colombia, we do something similar in Argentina. You will not see us screaming and shouting about it, you will not see us making a big play of it. But if people go on to our website, they will find a thing called our open community brochure,[14] and they can see a list across the world of an example of some of the small projects we have done in the local communities. But we see ourselves deeply connected to the environment in which we operate from a people perspective, but also from a planet perspective. We operate forestry in Colombia. We do that in conjunction with the local communities there. And we created employment for the local communities there. We built most of the infrastructure to a point where we have generations now working in our factories and farms. I was at an awards ceremony here in Ireland. When you get to 25 years in Smurfit Kappa, we have a small lunch for everybody who is at that. I sat at the table with somebody from a plant of ours in the West of Ireland and him, his two brothers, his father, and his grandfather have all worked for Smurfit Kappa. Collectively, they had something like over 88 years of experience. That speaks a lot for who we are. And that is not atypical. I have been around the group, and I know many fathers and sons who work in the organisation, mothers and daughters, brothers, and sisters. We had a conversation earlier on about my nephew, who works in the business, who disowns me at every opportunity and has a different surname, so nobody knows who he is. It is a very familial place and Tony our CEO is superb at fostering that idea. It comes back to you, you can do the E and the G, you can do those, but if you do not do the S and if you do not really do the S, you will be found out. We do not live in a world, where you can avoid the S anymore. We have had conversations before, and the S is capitalised now. In a post Covid world where people are going: 'If I deal with the economic part, then I will get the governance right, I will make sure people are OK'.

---

[13] https://www.globallivingwage.org/about/what-is-a-living-wage

[14] https://www.smurfitkappa.com/-/m/files/publications%2D%2D-global/sustainability-reports/our-open-community-2021.pdf?rev=3ebc3d758d444c3ba5258e7d7781dbee

Fig. 9 Graduates of Smurfit Kappa's Back to School Programme. Source: Smurfit Kappa, https://www.smurfitkappa.com/-/m/files/publications%2D%2D-global/sustainability-reports/our-open-community-2021.pdf?rev=3ebc3d758d444c3ba5258e7d7781dbee

The next few years we will really see how people were dealt with by the organisations during Covid. There is going to be an interesting conversation around retention, around attraction and talent, and about the types of organisations that people want to work for. And I suppose that is really where it comes to us. We want to be an organisation that people want to work for, and you can only do that through your values, and our values are loyalty, integrity, and respect. We try and live by every single day at Smurfit Kappa. And that applies to the local community, and it applies to all our plant managers, and it applies to everybody here in Dublin at the head office and to everyone we meet. Some people when they get to know us, they are slightly blown away by the culture at Smurfit Kappa. I realise I say this as somebody who has been in the organisation for 28 years and I am clearly institutionalised, but there is a reason I have stayed for 28 years too. And it is the people, and it will always be the people because that is what makes you get up every day, come in, sit down, go through everything you have to go through, because we make the products we make, with the people we make in the communities in which we make them (Fig. 9).

Uwe Schulte
Thank you so much, Ken. I must say that I must remind our audience that we have been speaking to the Chief Financial Officer, and Smurfit Kappa is a growing, very profitable business. People might have not believed that when they just heard you the last two minutes. It is just a symbol that only companies where the leadership from the innovation to the supply chain to sales and to finance have fully integrated sustainability. You can be successful in the long term, and you have just exemplified that. I really appreciate that. And thank you for giving us hope that circularity in the packaging industry is not just a pipe dream.

Ken Bowles

Oh no, it is a reality and Smurfit Kappa is living it daily.

Uwe Schulte

Thank you so much and goodbye.

Sustainable Procurement

Recorded June 2022

Uwe Schulte

Today I will be talking to Thomas Udesen, Chief Procurement Officer at Bayer. Please let me introduce our guest for today. Thomas, after several years in timber trading from Africa and Asia, had a procurement career at Johnson & Johnson (J&J) which led him to become the CPO EMEA in 2010. Thomas has now been the CPO at Bayer for almost 10 years. He is also a Steering Committee Member of the Chemicals Industry Initiative 'Together for Sustainability' and the co-founder of the 'Sustainable Procurement Pledge'. Thomas holds an MBA from the Cranfield School of Management. Welcome, Thomas. Please tell us a bit about yourself and how sustainability has entered your professional life.

Thomas Udesen

Uwe, first, thank you very much for inviting me and I am very thrilled to talk to you and, of course, to all the listeners. Yes, sustainability is a big part of my life. I guess through my career as you described it, I have been living very closely with the topic of sustainable growth and how modern industry can have a positive or not positive impact on societies across the world. And you mentioned timber trading. Those were really my formative years back in the 90s. I was working in Ghana and Indonesia and through that had access, and visibility, to the things that were done in the right way, but also, I did see when things were not really working in the right way. That of course, gave me a lot of opinions around how business should be conducted as it moves forward. Then I had the pleasure of joining J&J. I was sitting with the EMEA team and that was really at a time where topics like palm oil, some may remember the KitKat campaign, were featuring. I had the pleasure of becoming part of the work that Unilever was setting up in terms of the Palm Oil Alliance and later the RSPO (Roundtable on Sustainable Palm Oil). That whole wave got me very much involved. Then of course, with Bayer being a large multinational, also with a lot of legacy in more heavy industry and chemicals it has just been a natural progression for me as well. That is how I ended up here. I do have a total firm belief that we as industry, as business, as society need to protect what is here to protect us. The whole notion of sustainability, people, and planet, combining it also with profit is really something that I am a strong advocate for.

Uwe Schulte
That is an impressive past, especially the timber trading intrigues me. But let us look at the present. Most of our audience, of course, will have heard about Bayer, but could you highlight a little bit what the company is doing today?

Thomas Udesen
Through a series of organisational changes over the last decades, we are a Life Sciences company that is organised in three divisions. We have the pharmaceuticals business; we have our crop science division and then we have our consumer health division. It is a company of 100,000 plus employees. It is based in Germany. We have a strong history, it has been around for almost 160 years by now, so it is one of the foundational pillars of German industry, but also one of the leading dimensions when it comes to Life Sciences. The mission of our company is 'health for all, hunger for none'. Again, we are in human health and working to ensure that we have sufficient nourishment and food available.

Uwe Schulte
We all know that you have gone through major demergers and have completed a widely discussed acquisition. Can you describe that journey very briefly?

Thomas Udesen
If you go 10+ years back in time, Bayer was a company that also had activities in commodities like rubber, products like plastics, there was pharmaceuticals, etc. A very conscious choice was made in 2016 to really focus on Life Sciences. We separated from the plastics business, polyurethane, polycarbonate which is Covestro today. We disengaged ourselves with the animal health business, which is in Elanco. And we had the big acquisition that you mentioned, the Monsanto Company, also a couple of years back, as well as the over-the-counter consumer health business for Merck. It has been 5/6/7 years of constant change, which is now where we have

landed. We are in human health again and in crop science, making sure we have food and that is really where we feel we also should be.

Uwe Schulte

You already stated that vision 'health for all and hunger for none'. That is generic. It is a nice one to go for, of course. But can you give us a bit more detail what that means?

Thomas Udesen

Well, as a society, and I am sure all the audience will agree with that, we are having growing populations. It looks as if we will move towards ten billion and that puts a lot of stress on our society. How do we keep people healthy and have a long, healthy life at an affordable cost? So, a lot around recent technologies. We have just gone through Covid, which again shows the vulnerability that we have as society. We have the firm belief that solutions for our healthcare need to be found through science, of which there is a lot going on and some promising prospects that we saw with the speed of the Covid vaccination. That is the health part. But at the same time, if we want to make sure that people have enough to eat, we also need to become much better at using the land we have. We must increase the food production and increasing the yield. None of us would like to see that we continue to take over more forestry land or, in a way, make sure that the growth of the population has a detrimental impact on nature around us. And we believe, that can only happen through separate ways of looking at industrial agriculture and making sure that there are modern technologies possible to increase yield at preferably even reduced space. Climate change has already had quite an impact where we see that the landmass anyhow is being reduced year on year, and that drought continues to be a challenge. Our focus again is health and food. We are really at the centre of the human challenge in the next decades and that is what drives all of us. That is what makes it a very purposeful place to work as well, and sustainability in our operations and in our supply chains, which is where I and the team of Procurement come in. That is where we have a huge role to play (Figs. 1 and 2).

Uwe Schulte

It is very tempting to dive deeper into that whole area of regenerative agriculture. Let us not do that now because our focus is Procurement, of course, for the discussion when we have the privilege to talk to a Chief Procurement Officer. That transition we just talked about, that is a huge thing. You get rid of certain parts of your business; you focus the business around a very clearly structured profile. How was that incorporated or conducted through Procurement? What influence did that have on Procurement and how did Procurement have an influence on the process?

Thomas Udesen

For any portfolio changes, whether it is an acquisition, a licencing deal or divestiture, Procurement is in from the very beginning, at the ideation point, because there is a whole degree of due diligence that needs to be taking place in which we are involved. But when it comes to our divestitures, these are people that we know, these are our colleagues, these are great businesses that we believe would be better

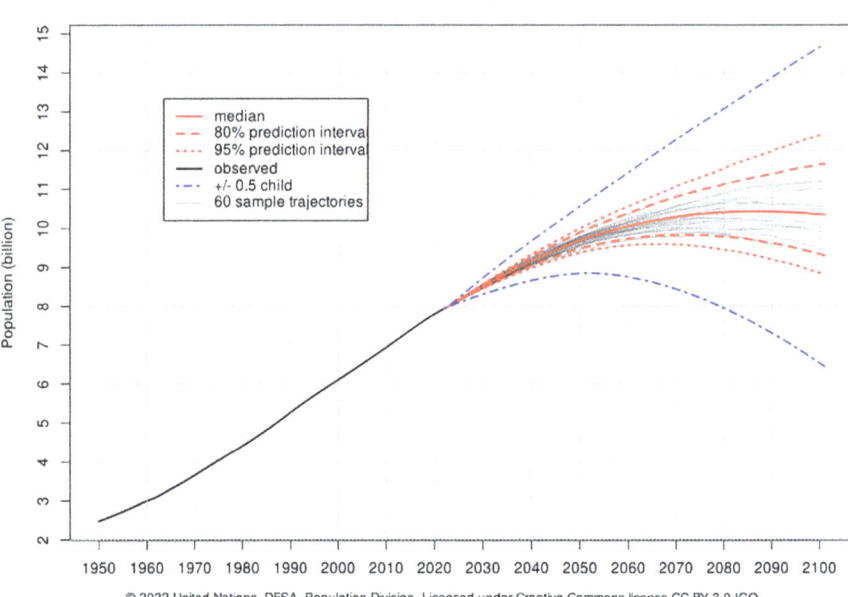

Fig. 1 World population projections. Source: Wikipedia, CC BY 3.0 IGO DEED, Attribution 3.0 Intergovernmental Organization, Author: United Nations, DESA, Population Division, Source: https://population.un.org/wpp/Graphs/Probabilistic/POP/TOT/900

served under a different ownership. A lot of our focus goes to how we make sure that these businesses continue to be successful and that we can make sure that our colleagues find a new home, either as a stand-alone as we saw with Covestro where they can create their own identity, or as part of another company, as we saw with the animal health with Elanco. It is making sure that all these transactional aspects, specifically for Procurement are being considered. This is along with contracting, with transparency, how do we make sure that the practices of the past are being put into place, that systems are recreated, that purchase orders are transferred? These are exceptionally large and complex processes. We have a dedicated team that is making sure that all these portfolio changes are made in a way that the future home of our colleagues is also one that is likely to make them successful.

Uwe Schulte
You now talked about this important part when you say goodbye to people that you know and portfolios you know, that have given you scale in some aspect. But also, the acquisition is, of course, a big challenge because as far as I recall from my past, the first thing is that everybody turns around to Procurement and says, 'Where are the savings'?

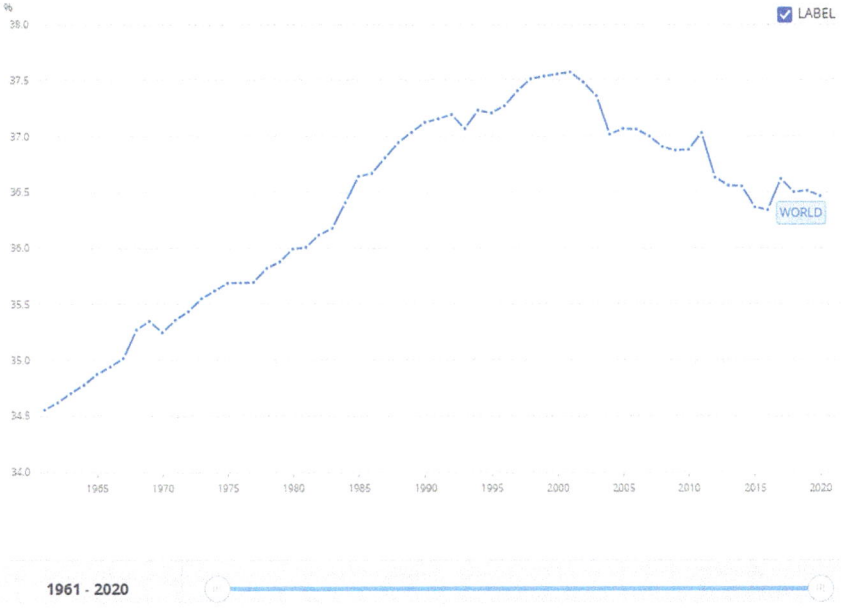

Fig. 2 Global agricultural land (% of land areas), World Bank Data. Source: CC BY 4.0 DEED, Attribution 4.0 International, The World Bank, https://data.worldbank.org/indicator/AG.LND.AGRI.K2?end=2021&start=1961

Thomas Udesen

The topic of synergies is, of course, a big topic in any acquisition and here there are diverse ways that you assess that during the due diligence. And then after the deal has been made, and that is the same with us, we typically create clean room teams where dedicated people are being put into the clean room and you make sure that they are able to assess what it is that you can do, as and when the deals are approved by the relevant authorities. That is what we did with all these things. People are being dedicated, knowing that of course, if the deal does not go through, they cannot go back to their Procurement jobs of the past. Making sure that that is done in the right way, which is step one. But then when people have all the data, we can see where we have overlap and where we can do things better. We have category strategies that will define what we should be doing, with whom. And you can do a bit of a gap analysis and try to put more concrete ideas behind the opportunities that you assumed in the very beginning. And that is what we did with Merck OTC, but also with the Monsanto acquisition. Get those teams, so that when day one happens and the curtain is lifted that we have teams ready to take those work packages and start to pick up the phone, making sure that the synergies can be delivered. And then the heavy work of integrating systems, integrating contracts, working on the cultural dimensions that will always follow when two cultures are coming together. That is what we have been working on, also in our team.

Uwe Schulte

When you talk about cultures coming together, I think in every merger that is the biggest challenge. Our theme is sustainability here, so obviously two sustainability cultures were coming together in the case of Monsanto. What was the role of Procurement in finding the common ground on sustainability?

Thomas Udesen

Every organisation, every team has something that they are amazingly good at and that has been the primary focus of their existence and that is what we also recognise. Our approach was really to sit down and compare practices early, in fact, when the legal boundaries also allowed for that to happen. What we found out was that particularly in Monsanto, they had a very advanced approach when it comes to topics like supplier diversity, inclusion on small, medium-sized enterprises, where they had a lot of active programmes in the USA but certainly also in Latin America. That was an area where there was a lot of advancement. Same with seeds, how do you engage with growers to make sure that they are educated and that there is capacity building so that children go to school rather than going into the field? Those were aspects that we took along from the Monsanto Procurement practices. Bayer, through our strong legacy of chemistry have very mature practices when it came to topics like energy conservation, process optimisation, supplier engagement around 'Together for Sustainability', industry collaboration. And that is what we then brought in here, and it was really in the mixture of those two practices that we then also defined what our path forward is. We have done a lot in the last couple of years. We updated our supplier code of conduct; we made very bold commitments when it comes to sustainability in general, including size, space, target initiatives, commitments on CO_2 reduction, and human rights. That is what we agreed that we want to focus on the period towards 2030. And now it is rolling up the sleeves and getting on with it and deliver on those commitments that we have made to society.

Uwe Schulte

We discussed that aspect now. We will not dive into the controversy of legal things around the Monsanto acquisition. That is for experts to discuss. We are talking about sustainability here. I understand that you developed three lines of engagement for sustainability, and I am interested how that relates to Procurement people at Bayer now.

Thomas Udesen

What is it that we want to focus on as Procurement internally in our organisation and how do we engage with our suppliers? A lot of it has been around the first line of defense which is our code of conduct where you will see that all our expectations have been very clearly outlined, much of which is built on the United Nations Global Compact Principles.[1] It is, of course, having all the dimensions around CO_2 reduction. It has the human rights. It has responsible care around water and energy consumption. Those are the minimum expectations and we have been clear to our

---

[1] https://unglobalcompact.org/take-action/

suppliers, that if you are not able to commit to this, we will start a more detailed dialogue where potentially we will have to walk away because that is really the minimum. But one thing is—how do you make sure that this is happening? And that is where we have assessment programmes, we have audit programmes, we have these principles reflected in all our contracting, we make sure that it is part of our tenders[2] as a sizeable portion of the decision-making. That is the first line, if you will. How do we make sure that Bayer and all our practices are hardwired and executed against? The second level here is around industry collaboration, because the topic of sustainability is so enormous and complex that any company in a way assuming that they can do this on their own is on the wrong path. We already figured that out a decade ago. In 2011, Bayer co-created two industry initiatives: 'Together for Sustainability' (TfS)[3] that you talked about, the chemical industry, as well as the PSCI, the 'Pharmaceutical Supply Chain Initiative'.[4] And the idea behind both of those is that we should not duplicate things like assessments and audits, because these suppliers who often serve multiple players, multiple customers will end up filling in questionnaires which all have a little bit of variability rather than fixing the problems that they have. We standardised, we agreed on templates, there is a mutual recognition that one audit for one is an audit for all. And with that, we have been able to dramatically reduce the documentation requirement for our suppliers and start focusing on implementation. That initiative, TfS specifically, started with six companies 10 years ago. We are now 37 members. The most recent, Lenzing, joined from Austria. We have the first Japanese company Mitsui & Co., we have Chinese. We represent more than 500 billion of sales. We have 17,500 assessments conducted in this forum. We believe strongly that partnership, doing things together in a pre-competitive domain, making sure obviously that all the antitrust requirements are respected, is the way forward. We would advocate for anybody who is not yet in an industry group around sustainability that they should find some friends quickly and find ways of moving forward together. There is this African proverb, I think you have heard it. But again, 'If you want to go fast, you go alone. If you want to go far, you go together'. That is the whole philosophy around how we change our supply chains. The third dimension is around individual engagement, and that is where people are encouraged to do community activities and educate themselves when it comes to Sustainable Procurement. You mentioned the 'Sustainable Procurement Pledge'. This is one domain where people have a chance to educate themselves, become part of communities that care, and who also want to make sure that the knowledge of how I actually do things differently is then also distributed from peer-to-peer, role models are seen, and that is what it is. We do three lines: it is the company; it is the industry, and it is the individual in our organisation (Fig. 3).

---

[2] https://en.wikipedia.org/wiki/Invitation_to_tender

[3] https://www.tfs-initiative.com/

[4] https://pscinitiative.org/principles

Fig. 3 TfS member companies. Source: Together For Sustainability, TfS Membership – status June 2022, www.tfs-initiative.com

Uwe Schulte

We should dive a little bit deeper into the vision that Bayer has and how Procurement is contributing. You talked about how you work together with others and in my experience, many of these collaborations are excellent, giving suppliers clear procedures and expectations. But when we are looking at the impact, for example progress versus paying living wages, not a lot of progress has been made so far. How do you see that?

Thomas Udesen

Every organisation has their different levers as far as what is relevant in terms of impact. I think one of the most basic items/actions that the organisations should have, is to establish where it can have a positive impact on our society around us. Certainly, the supply base is of significant scale for most of the organisations. We have, just by the nature of our business, different areas where we have a significant impact. Being in the agricultural business, it is obvious that we have big impacts when it comes to topics like child labour, making efficient use of water, minimising the deforestation that we also see across the world. Behind each of those topics we have programmes, we have had programmes for decades in many of these cases, and we make sure we engage with local NGOs to have the positive impact that we think we should have in those topics. Looking at the supply chain though, there are other dimensions that become relevant. Many of us are looking at the environmental dimension. Bayer has signed up for the 'Science-Based Target Initiative', so our own decarbonisation topic is an exceptionally large thing. But again, it is not all of that. Deforestation, the packaging impact, labour conditions, how do we make sure that we are inclusive with our supply base, how do we have supplier diversity part of our road map? These are the ones that as Procurement we are focusing more on, with the way that we are creating categories, with how we engage with our suppliers.

Uwe Schulte

Let us put it to the crunch, Thomas. When a Procurement guy is measured, he has his targets and anybody who has worked in procurement knows that cost saving is always a given target. Does he have other targets that relate to these sustainability ambitions and how is it measured?

Thomas Udesen

The code of conduct and the minimum expectations is a way of avoiding that you have too many of those trade-offs that you are describing. We have truly clear guidance as far as minimum expectation. That is part of the assessments, even before you get invited to a tender, how we assess our suppliers. But then you get into the actual crunch, the sourcing event. And of course, sustainability has a big rating in many of those matrixes towards the decision. In that way you are also able to swing a product that may cost a little bit more but provides a favourable status when it comes to sustainability, and with that we make better decisions. Of course, you can make that even more concrete by also introducing internal carbon prices. We are doing that, for example, for all our CapEx where we are really assessing whether this is now a configuration that brings us the best long-term environmental footprint or not. You can put those externalities into your decision-making and we have done that for many parts of the organisation. Of course, we will continue to look at where else it makes sense to do that. When our Procurement colleagues are making those decisions, they are convinced that they are also making a better decision.

Uwe Schulte

You are tempting me here, but you do not have to answer the question what internal carbon price you are using. That might be confidential.

Thomas Udesen

I do not think so. We use 100 € per tonne and we recognise that this is not the perfect figure. You can have a whole bunch of scientists try to calculate this and we will come back next Christmas and still not be any cleverer. We are looking at it very pragmatically. We are introducing it as a measure right now and we are assessing as time progresses. Do we need to change that, increase, or reduce it?

Uwe Schulte

Thank you for sharing because I think more of us are facing that issue. And if we do not use that, then we invest into the wrong technologies in the future. Whilst the EU is trying to do this with taxonomy, I think being clear about your own business model will help. Now, let us get a little bit more to the crunch. One of the things you do is produce seeds, right?

Thomas Udesen

That is correct. We have tens of thousands of smallholders who are producing seeds for us as well.

Uwe Schulte

That is exactly my point, because a lot of people still believe that these are these huge farms that produce that, but a lot of our agriculture is still smallholder farmers. How do you, as a large conglomerate as you are, engage with them on a decent platform? Can you describe that?

Thomas Udesen

Yes. First, we are managing a lot of those relationships locally because it is typically co-located with our seeds reception centres. And here we are also part of the local economy. We help educate with our agronomists as far as: how do you get the biggest yield? How do you use resources optimally? Whether it is the crop protection or also the water usage, so that again we minimise the environmental impact. And it is certainly one of the topics which in many developing countries is front of mind: how do we make sure that we eliminate child labour into their fields and make sure that the children go to school, and they are not being used as a labour force in the fields? This is not something we do alone. This is something we do in a multi-stakeholder environment where local NGOs, local regulators, educational facilities are educating those farmers to make sure that we eliminate those risks. It is a very community engaged programme that we have. And that goes across multiple geographies where they have specific challenges around this (Fig. 4).

Uwe Schulte

The issue with smallholder farmers, as you no doubt know, is that they must first finance the seeds, the chemicals they need, and it takes them a while to reap the benefits. Therefore, there were initiatives to make sure that sharks do not do loans, but in a decent way. Are you, as a company, engaged in that or how does that work?

Child Labor Incidence in Relation to the Total Number of Laborers Monitored in Seed Production for Bayer Taking India as an Example[1]

	Child labor incidence	Total laborers monitored	Child labor incidence in relation to total laborers monitored	
	2021/22	2021/22	2020/21	2021/22
Rice[2]	0	84,124	0.0025%	0%
Vegetables[3]	0	36,009	0%	0%
Corn[3]	0	57,584	0%	0%

Fig. 4 Example child labour incidence monitoring. Source: Bayer AG, Sustainability Report

Thomas Udesen

Most of these relationships are, if not multi-generational, multi-year, decades long. These are partnerships that are going on for extended periods and we make sure that these commercial aspects, also around access to funding and cash flows, are such that they are attractive for everybody. The abusive behaviour that exists in certain parts of the supply chains is not representing the values we stand for, and those certainly are not practices we believe in. In fact, as part of our sustainability strategy, we are also looking at ways to engage 100 million smallholders and give them access to modern technology in a way that again they can use their land for bigger yields. This is separate. These are different smallholders, but the group of smallholders, and we know they are the biggest producer of food around the world, is a super critical group for humanity, and we understand that and partner with it.

Uwe Schulte

In your vision, you talk about 'hunger for none'. Now that is a huge challenge that we are facing again. How do you see the situation? Are we going to manage that issue? The crop that comes out of Ukraine is slow.

Thomas Udesen

We are concerned about the trajectory on food production and that is also one of the reasons why we continuously argue that we need to have a multi-stakeholder dialogue around how we increase yields without damaging the environmental footprint. We strongly believe it is through a combination of science where we also adopt innovative technologies in this quest that we all have. Because failure to increase yield on reducing arable land will mean that it is not 600 million people who are undernourished as it is today, those figures will increase dramatically. We are deeply concerned that right now things are not going in the right direction. The war in Ukraine/Russia where we have seen limitations on availability, and where the grain coming out of Ukraine is blocked. It does not necessarily mean that Europeans do not get the food that they need and often are able to pay for. This really impacts populations in the Middle East, in East Africa, who are dependent on this food and

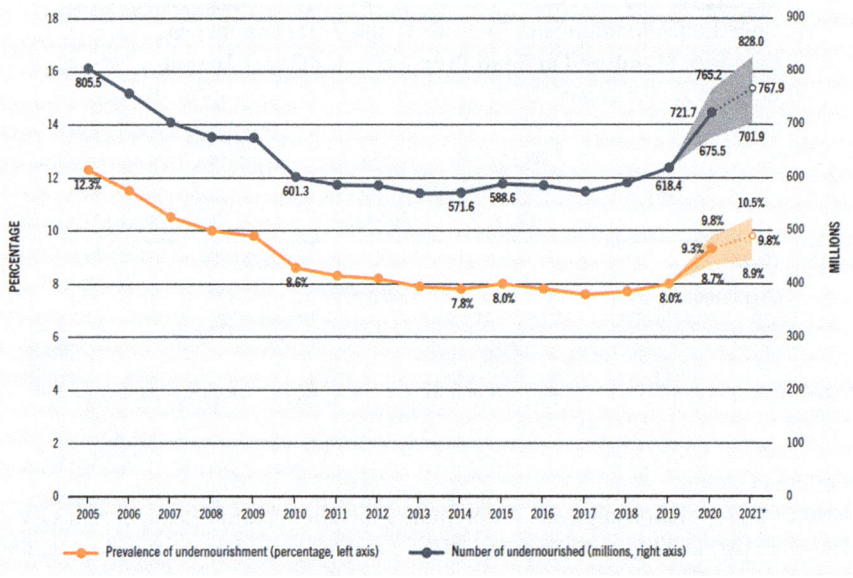

Fig. 5 Development of hunger—FAO Report 2022. Source: Food and Agriculture Organization of the United Nations. Reproduced with permission

have absolutely no way of paying for it. It is a big challenge for us as a world community and we want to have this constructive dialogue with everybody. A lot of it is going on and most of this is not directly impacting Procurement, as you can appreciate, but we certainly see this as our aspiration: 'hunger for none'. It is a bold aspiration, and we are not there (Fig. 5).

Uwe Schulte
No, definitely not. The other part, and you can speak a little bit to that as well, is 'health for all'. How does that relate to Procurement?

Thomas Udesen
Well, it is also making sure that our products, our technologies are available and that we do innovate into new modalities, into new diseases where so far there are no cures available for humanity. We have many areas where we are novel in our solutions. We are having trials in areas such as Parkinson where there is no current cure. We believe that through science and through some of these investments we are also making, whether it is biotech but also through more traditional small molecules, that we will be able to pursue the elimination of diseases where we simply today do not have the solutions.

Uwe Schulte
Let me come back to the Procurement part. In the past I have very often seen it that regarding the knowledge around sustainability in the commercial function as such and not just Procurement, and Procurement is not just a commercial function, it is a

logistical one as well, there are aspects missing. Of course, sustainability is a complex thing. People very often look for black and white, and nothing is black and white in this field as you and I know. Taking greenhouse gas Scope3 and let me explain as a background for the audience. I think most of them will be insulted but let me say it again. If you produce your energy yourself that is Scope1. If you procure your energy directly that is Scope2. The footprint from procured goods or the use of your products that is Scope3. For Procurement of course, the upstream supply chain is the important one and, in my experience, a lot of companies are struggling to even identify the size of the issue. How do you go about that?

Thomas Udesen

Yes, it is true. And just in terms of relative importance, you will know that most manufacturing organisations are having 80% plus of their carbon footprint in Scope3. This is where you win, or you lose the battle. That is why organisations, ours included, focus a lot on Scope3. Getting the baseline is problem number one. And one of the challenges here is also that the world has not necessarily established a standard. How do you really calculate this? This is not a simple task; it is billions of calculations to get the accuracy that we desire. What do we do? Well, we have taken one of the models that exist, and we have assessed our carbon footprint through models, spend-based models. It is step #1 where you look at: this is our spend, these are the averages of spend, and the averages of the averages, and that gets you a baseline with which you can work. We then complemented that with real data that we collected from our suppliers using the carbon disclosure project (CDP)[5] as enabler. But you can build accuracy as you go along and that has helped us quite a bit. What we are intending to do, and you are also familiar with 'Together for Sustainability', is on 15th September we will launch the first ever global standard for product carbon footprint calculations.[6] This is a guide; this is how you do it for the chemical industry. And of course, we know that the chemical industry is the foundation for all industries. And with that, we can positively drive towards a standard that we can start to compare apples with apples. We have not done that on our own. We have worked with NGOs, SBTi, World Economic Forum, and all those entities who, like us, want to create a common methodology. Those are steps that our teams are taking to get the baseline and now go from 80% accuracy to 81% to 82% and move on. That is nice, we have a baseline. More important is, what are we going to do about it and how do we now reduce? This must happen in parallel. As you mentioned, messaging towards suppliers, making sure we change the choice to be more energy efficient, but this is part of our everyday decisions that procurement practitioners do.

Uwe Schulte

This is interesting because I see and I am glad that more companies are asking, for example, their suppliers to use renewable energy. There are two issues with that. It

---

[5] https://www.cdp.net/en/
[6] https://www.tfs-initiative.com/app/uploads/2023/04/TfS_PCF_guidelines_2022_English.pdf

is not only renewable energy because some of their processes produce a lot of CO_2, much more than the energy. And the second thing, if we all go around, there is not enough renewable energy around now. I think large companies like yourself must help create situations and infrastructure that will enable that progress.

Thomas Udesen

I agree. If there is a market, if there is demand, supply will be created. And most of these big PPAs, power purchase agreements,[7] that we are signing up for are multi-year commitments, which gives the energy providers of renewable energy the economic assurance that they need to make the necessary investments. It is moving along nicely. We are certainly on plan, if not ahead of plan. Our commitment is to have 100% renewable energy for what we are buying externally by 2030, and we are at 25–30% right now globally. We also see that innovation is steering us from the gas situation that has been created by Putin and the limitations we see now in Germany.

Uwe Schulte

I agree. It would be great to continue that conversation about what you are doing in these fields, but you have done something personally, which I am extremely impressed by, and I would like to discuss that a little bit more with you. I talked about the fact that in the commercial function the knowledge around sustainability sometimes leaves a little bit to be desired. And you have been one of the founders of the 'Sustainable Procurement Pledge'.[8] What is this? (Fig. 6)

Thomas Udesen

What is the 'Sustainable Procurement Pledge', how did it come about? My co-founder is Bertrand Conquéret, he is the CPO of Henkel. And like yourself, Uwe, we believe strongly that businesses, and Procurement in particular, carry an enormous power in driving business to business, the world trade towards good or not. Often the decision sits with us in the moment when we make deals, we shake hands, we give people contracts to execute. We have seen progress over the last decade, but we also have to say that things are not moving fast enough. Whilst 15,000 organisations have signed the UN Global Compact, we see thousands of organisations having signed the 'Science Based Target initiative'. If you talk to practitioners sitting across the world asking them what exactly they are doing, often the answer is unsatisfactory, unacceptable. When the 'Climate Strike' took place in October 2019,

Fig. 6 Sustainable Procurement Pledge logo.
Source: Sustainable Procurement Pledge, https://spp.earth/

---

[7] https://en.wikipedia.org/wiki/Power_purchase_agreement
[8] https://spp.earth/

we were inspired to say, 'Let us do something about it. Let us make sure we go back to the basics, the principles from the United Nations Global Compact, the ten principles, which are all sound, business principles that all of us would understand. Our parents would have taught us exactly that as children, to not do dreadful things, to be nice, to not overuse resources'. We condensed those principles into five things/ actions that we can do as Procurement practitioners. We launched that and since then I have seen the world of Procurement respond overwhelmingly positive. We believe there are around one million procurement people on the planet, and they control world trade, 8.7 trillion business to business. And our simple plan is to make sure that we give them the tools that they require to equip them to make better decisions. How to calculate Scope3? How do you engage your suppliers? How do you include social procurement, social businesses? And that is what it is. We are capacity building Procurement practitioners. We are now moving a little bit forward, three years or so, as a total volunteer organisation. We have chapters, most parts of the world, 142 countries, have active members. We are eight thousand ambassadors. And now of course, we must grow up, so we are professionalising. We have found organisations who are prepared to donate to our non-profit organisation. And we are days away from hiring our first employee, the executive director who will then be helping the world of Procurement with the answers that they need. And you are familiar with Khan University[9] in the academia. There is also the guy who wanted to make everything available for free, and that is what we want to do. We want to help the people who sit in an organisation in a remote place, which do not have a boss who takes this seriously, so that they can start a positive change from within their organisations.

Uwe Schulte
Your objective is capacity building. Is that what this is about?

Thomas Udesen
Capacity building, and the fallout consequence is that we will all make sure that the United Nations SDGs that you have as your background picture, that those targets are delivered by 2030. We see this as a task until 2030 to make sure that the SDGs are delivered, and we all can look back with pride when future generations ask us, 'What did you do when things looked a bit dark? Were you part of the solution or did you contribute to the problem'? We want to make sure that Procurement contributes to the solution.

Uwe Schulte
Indeed, I am a critical supporter of the SDGs. We are not making enough progress and certain things are not covered, but they are a common denominator. Everybody can talk about them. And if people are not box-ticking them but trying to make an impact on one or two of them, that is sufficient. Thomas, I must congratulate you, because there are two guys, they take the initiative and 2 years later 8000 people have engaged, they call themselves ambassadors or you call them ambassadors.

---

[9] https://www.khanacademy.org/

That is a nice word, and I would like to also use this podcast to advertise this. Please tell us the name of your website and if people then go there, they can sign up and commit themselves.

Thomas Udesen

The content, so what we are crowdsourcing from our global community of practitioners and academics, is www.spp.earth. Our actual counting of the number of ambassadors is the LinkedIn group, so if you check the 'Sustainable Procurement Ambassadors' on LinkedIn,[10] you will see there is a group. Please join, it is highly active, we are 8000.[11] Some of you may be familiar, but we realised that everybody has a 'day' and we do not have one as Sustainable Procurement. So, this year we launched the first 'World Sustainable Procurement Day'. It is on equinox, it is 21st March, and it is going to be 21st March until 2030. We will come together, and we will have 24 hours. We follow the sun around the equator and make sure that we have discussions and content. We try to have something for everybody as the sun turns around the equator. And through this we capacity build and we create this community. It is not just knowledge; it is also courage. It is building a vocabulary, it is seeing role models who have done it, who fell on their nose and got up and in a way made a lesson and moved on. We need that courage to also drive positive change, and that is what the communities are doing. We are launching chapters in most countries, we are launching chapters in industries, we are having chapters and topics like you mentioned Scope3 and many others. We are creating this three-dimensional community platform for Procurement, by Procurement, a safe space where we can share our knowledge and help each other in a way to drive progress.

Uwe Schulte

What I like about it as well is the positive outlook. A lot of people who look around now see all these issues, the crisis, the climate crisis, the war, the increased block building that is going on, the issues about the impact of severe weather events, the pandemic. We are facing lots of crises at the same time, and you can start to despair. But what you are doing is you say, 'We are active, we can influence things and we will do our part'. And nobody must do a huge lift, but if everybody lifts a little bit in the right direction, that I think is your idea, and I can just applaud you for that.

Thomas Udesen

A million Procurement practitioners that are lifting together will make a difference. And with 8000 we are there. There are only 992,000 missing. We are on a good path, and it is tempting at times to despair, it is. We are all clear, we read the same news. But then you must be reminded of the gravity. What are we talking about? We are talking about securing a great life for future generations. Many of us have children. It is their life we are talking about, so you cannot give up. We cannot give up. We will fight, hopefully not to the end.

---

[10] https://www.linkedin.com/groups/8845732/
[11] In August 2023: 13.000.

Uwe Schulte
Absolutely. And that is a nice last word here on this podcast. I thank you very much for that, Thomas. Thank you for sharing and thank you for pushing the procurement pledge, and I wish you all success with that.

Sustainable Mining and the Biodiversity Challenge

Recorded July 2022

Uwe Schulte

Today I will be talking to Cyril Giraud, Senior Vice President Performance Minerals APAC at Imerys. Please let me introduce our guest for today. Cyril joined Imerys in 1998 and held several positions in strategy, finance, project management, or general management. He has been based in different countries in Asia and Europe where he was leading the carbonates business until 2018. Since then, Cyril has been a member of the Imerys Executive Committee, and he is based in Shanghai. Welcome, Cyril. Please tell us a little bit about yourself and how sustainability has entered your professional life.

Cyril Giraud

Hello Uwe. First, I am happy to be with you today and to share about sustainability, which is an important topic for me. You said it in the introduction, I had the opportunity in my career with Imerys to work in a number of different geographies and that opened my eyes to quite a number of different things and maybe I should start by telling a couple of stories that triggered my interest in sustainability in the past. You know that in our business we have some mining activities, or I should say some quarrying activity, because most of our mines are in fact open pits or quarries, this means they are very visible for outside people coming close to them. Usually, it is a sensitive topic, and in the beginning when I joined Imerys I did not realise how sensitive it could be, because we have ambitious standards, we have good practices and benchmarks on how to rehabilitate a mine which is out of use, for instance.

I was assuming it was the standard across the industry. Then along the years I discovered a few different situations. I remember one time in Turkey, for instance, there was a huge area of quarries in use since the Roman times, and over the centuries several small or big pits were open all over the place, a lot of unused blocks covering the full landscape. Really a kind of situation that you think is out of control and will never be restored, never. Then in Vietnam, I discovered some situations where you had what we call monkey mining, which is basically people going to the top of a cliff, putting a rope around a tree, and going down the face of the quarry, and then just starting with their hammer to break some rocks and people below just getting the rocks. That it is not safe, and you have a lot of accidents with that. And on top of it, when you start to exploit a quarry like that it is extremely difficult to rehabilitate properly and to do something nice with it after you have finished to exploit it. In our case, what we try to do is to have some clear benches, well-established, which are much safer, and on top of it when you have finished you can rebuild some slopes, put some vegetation onto it, create some small lakes or ponds at the bottom, a much nicer structure.

The second thing that alerted me more than 15 years ago, was a conference that I attended in China. It was one of my first visits to China at the time, and the topic of sustainability came up, and I realised how big the gap was between my own meaning of sustainability and the meaning of the Chinese attendants. For them, the only thing that mattered at the time was 'sustainability is for me: how can I secure more reserves of whatever raw materials I need to sustain economic growth in the future'. Nothing else. And that made me think that behind the same word you can have quite different meanings. Today, I am living in China, as you mentioned in the beginning, and I am pleased to see that it has evolved. Now, you have a kind of cohabitation of both securing long-term resources but also taking care of the environment and how you do it. That is a good evolution over time.

Uwe Schulte
That is quite a journey of bad examples. That is not nice, but the good news is, of course, that there are better practices, and we will talk about the practices of Imerys you already mentioned a little bit more. But before we do so, could you describe a little bit more your business? Not all of our audience will be familiar with your company.

Cyril Giraud
Yes, sure. Imerys is a global leader in industrial minerals. It is a multinational company based in France generating 4.4 billion € revenue. It is a listed company on the stock exchange, and we have 17,000 employees. We are selling in 140 countries. Our business is organised in two main categories: performance minerals, which is

the business I am active in, and high temperature solution. Overall, what we are really targeting is to create through our solutions some value for our customers and overall, for a better tomorrow.

Uwe Schulte

Everybody has heard the word minerals, but you could you please describe a little bit more what types of products you provide because not everybody knows where minerals go.

Cyril Giraud

That is a particularly good point. And this is what is in fact unique and fascinating with our business—our products are everywhere, but almost no one knows about them. In fact, the applications, and you have a limitless number of them, are all around you in your daily life. For instance, you have some calcium carbonate in your toothpaste, you have some kaolin in your bathroom floor tiles, you have some talc in your cars, in the plastic parts of your car, you have some diatomite which is used to filter the beer you are drinking, or the oil you are using for cooking, and many others. I could also mention cosmetics, I could mention some components for electrical batteries. Minerals are really a key component participating in many, many things which contribute to our lives, our homes, and our economies in general.

Uwe Schulte

You just surprised me, I have to say. Talc in cars? Talc for me is something that people use to powder themselves to avoid sweating.

Cyril Giraud

It is also used for that, but it has many other applications. For this specific example when you add the proper talc to the polymer in your plastic compound, you manage to get the same mechanical properties while having a lighter plastic part. Thanks to that you can save some energy when running the car, and therefore you can consume less fuel for internal combustion engine cars, or you can have longer battery range for electrical vehicles.

Uwe Schulte

That is a broad product portfolio, but I guess that means that you have a vast variety of customers because these applications are so different. Or does that go through a trader in between?

Cyril Giraud

No, you are right. The fact is that we have thousands of customers—small ones, medium sized, and large companies. We have a lot of different customers in different industries.

Uwe Schulte

I understand. You already mentioned in your story how sustainability and the understanding of it developed for yourself and that you have seen practices that are not very conducive to the community and the wildlife of mining and quarrying. And there is also, as I learned recently, a significant greenhouse gas footprint of some of these operations. How do you, you already mentioned it a little bit, but how do you approach these challenges?

Cyril Giraud

The way we approach it is to try to be as organised and as comprehensive as possible. We have always been quite proud of behaving as a responsible company. But I would say that a few years ago we have gone to the next step, and now we have really a comprehensive scheme defining clear objectives and communicating about it. Communicating for reasons first internally to reinforce awareness because it is such an important topic. And secondly, externally, because we are taking official commitments, and we want people to be aware about it and we want to be bound to these commitments as well. Yes, we consider that one of our core values is about enabling a better future, and due to our specific position in the value chain, we really have a strong role to play in that. And it is towards our employees, towards the communities in which we work, towards the environment in more general. To come back to your initial question, we can really do something about how we approach this challenge. We can do it in a direct way by taking action to reduce our own footprint, the CO2 emissions, how we manage our mines, how we manage the consumption of water or the energy consumption. But also, indirectly. Our solutions can help our customers in turn to be more efficient. The example I mentioned about talc in plastic is a good one for instance. But we try to do that across the full value chain. We also try to do it upstream by pushing our suppliers to enter the same kind of process.

Uwe Schulte

Let us spend a second on that carbon footprint, because I was surprised to learn that if you take the whole mining industry around the world, it has as big a footprint as the cement industry.[1] That surprised me. Where does that happen? Where does that large footprint come from?

Cyril Giraud

Well, I must say I have not seen these statistics, and the cement industry being so large I am a bit surprised that it is as big as cement. Surely, we have some CO_2 emissions from the mines themselves, but it is usually limited because you have some trucks, dumpers, but that is about it. And then you have the process of refining the minerals, grinding them, and purifying them. Depending on which end material we talk about, it could generate CO_2. The cement industry, in a way, is part of it because cement starts with calcium carbonate quarries, so that is a significant part of it as well.

Uwe Schulte

I was not implying that your operations, which are open quarries, have a large contribution there. But I guess, it is when iron ore and copper mining and similar

---

[1] https://www.csrm.uq.edu.au/publications/transparency-on-greenhouse-gas-emissions-from-mining-to-enable-climate-change-mitigation

materials require a lot of energy, not only to do the mining but also the transporting and refining. It is always good to look at these things, but then it is also not especially useful if you generalise it around just one industry in principle. Every company must do their own footprint, and we will talk about this a little bit more. In Imerys you are talking about SustainAgility. I saw that on your website. Can you explain what that is?

Cyril Giraud
Yes, SustainAgility[2] is the name of our ESG programme that we have developed within Imerys. Obviously, it is a combination of sustainability and agility. It is built around three pillars which are: empowering our people, caring for the planet, and building for the future. If I take the three of them, empowering our people is really to make sure our employees can operate in safe conditions, stay healthy, but also to promote their development, the diversity and inclusion and fostering social dialogue. That is really something where we want these values to be embedded in the behaviour and the way of workings of all our employees. The second pillar which is caring for the planet is about protecting the environment, taking measures to reduce our consumption of non-energetic resources, preserving the biodiversity, and acting on climate change as well. And the last one, building for the future, is ready to operate in an ethical, fair manner and to really engage through the supply chain. I mentioned the suppliers—we want to engage them in sustainability as well, but also with the communities where we operate and promote in general sustainable products and technologies.

Uwe Schulte
The one thing that always comes to mind for me when we are talking about quarrying and mining, is that we make an impact on the immediate ecosystem there. It is unavoidable, of course. And the question is how one can do that in a manner that avoids biodiversity loss. You are highly active in that field. Can you explain a little bit how you do that?

Cyril Giraud
Yes, that is a good point. It all starts for me by being humble about it. I think, we have good programmes, but you can always improve, and this is what we are trying to do. And wh0en I say humble about it, it means that alone we cannot achieve so much. What we are doing is to build partnerships and to request some assistance from experts who can guide us in improving. When we do that, we also communicate. I come back to communication because it is so important. Every year we have one full day where we communicate to our employees. We stop all the plants at the same time in the world to communicate with employees about critical topics, and we always talk about safety. Last year, 2021, we also dedicated a workshop to biodiversity, so massive impact, and by doing that, we insist on the actions we take. For instance, we have developed partnerships with the French National Museum of

---

[2] https://www.imerys.com/imerys-group/sustainability/pioneering-sustainable-approach-minerals

Fig. 1 French National Museum of Natural History. Source: Wikipedia, Creative Commons Attribution-Share Alike 3.0 Unported, 2.5 Generic, 2.0 Generic and 1.0 Generic, Author: Spiridon MANOLIU, Source: own work

Natural History,[3] which has renowned experts in that field. We also internally promote awareness and actions to reduce our biodiversity impact. For instance, when you are in the mining industry one of the most obvious or visible impacts you can have, is the loss of habitat for animals living in the area. It is fairly obvious to say, but by doing progressive restoration, meaning you rehabilitate the area, you plant trees again, etc., when you have finished to exploit one area while exploiting the next one, your impact is much reduced, compared to the situation where you just exploit the big quarry over the years and only after tens of years when it is finished you start the rehabilitation process. That are the kind of things we are trying to promote (Fig. 1).

Uwe Schulte
Can I just briefly interrupt you there because I want to make sure that I understood it correctly. What you are saying is, when you do a quarry, you will open part of the landscape and before you go to the next part of the same quarry you will start restoring the first part. Is that what you described?

Cyril Giraud
That is exactly the point. It is not always possible. It depends on the configuration of the site, but there are many cases where it is possible. You can work in different areas, and once you have finished with one area, you can start to rehabilitate.

Uwe Schulte
Interesting, and that way the recuperation of the ecosystem is easier because the disruption does not last that long. Is that the idea?

---

[3] https://biodiv.mnhn.fr/organizations/museum-national-dhistoire-naturelle

Cyril Giraud

It is faster, you are right, it is easier, and it is less impactful because the net area that is used for our operations in average is much reduced in that configuration. The other point I want to mention is the possible impact that we may have on pollution. We are really taking a lot of care to reduce our impact on the environment by having monitoring programmes to check what our impact could be, and to take actions to avoid negative things that could happen, as much as possible. We have tools for that. We have what we call, for instance, an environment maturity matrix,[4] which is assessing for each site whether we have good practices (if not, what can we improve?), if people running the site are really committed to these actions. Overall, the important thing to keep in mind is that there are really three distinct phases where we can have a significant impact. The first one is during the preparation. When we think about opening a new quarry or expanding a quarry, we make studies to assess the impact on the ecosystem and to find remediation. It is also obviously especially important as well for reassuring and explaining to the local community what we will do, but also what we will not do. Then you have the phase when we are running the operations. Here, we continue to be careful about what we could find, and I can give you an example which happened last year. In one of my operations in New Zealand, we discovered a kiwi nest in one of our sites. The Kiwi,[5] as you know, is a protected species, and this bird is the emblem of New Zealand. Obviously, we took it very seriously, and we mandated an expert to come and assess the situation so that we could take the right action to protect the Kiwi. We took this opportunity to initiate a wider programme to identify the Kiwi habitat in the region, and make sure we can minimise the impact. That is also a good example of the fact that we continue to take care when we operate. And finally, the last step is the rehabilitation or restoration. I mentioned a little bit about it already, but this is obviously particularly important because this is what is left afterwards. And there can be a significant difference between restoration, which is done according to good practice and the rules, where you end up having something quite good or even very good according to the expert in many cases in terms of biodiversity with vegetation, with ponds, with new soil, trees, etc. And overall, we have evidence that a restored habitat is in fact very often favourable to biodiversity, so for us that is a big point of attention as well (Fig. 2).

Uwe Schulte

That is a crucial point you make, because in theory it could be possible that you restore this to a way of being more amenable to the circumstances of the existing ecosystem, so that actually the gene pool and the variety of species increases compared to before you even started.

---

[4] https://www.imerys.com/public/2023-04/Imerys-Annual-Sustainability-Report-2022.pdf
[5] https://en.wikipedia.org/wiki/Kiwi_(bird)

Fig. 2 NZ North Island brown kiwi. Source: Wikipedia, public domain worldwide, Author: Maungatautari Ecological Island Trust, Source: https://www.sanctuarymountain.co.nz/

Cyril Giraud

Yes, indeed. And the fact is that we will not be able to restore it in the exact same condition as before. But what we can do is in some cases bring even more value, as I mentioned already. Very often when you have a used quarry it leaves a hole in the ground and a safe way is to feed it with water to have a pond or lake. This in turn can attract more species of birds, and other animals. This is the kind of thing which in fact ends up having a positive impact on biodiversity.

Uwe Schulte

And sometimes even for the community, of course. But we will focus on biodiversity for the time being. The interesting point for me is that I learned that you are doing something that we at The Conference Board believe is a particularly important part of the sustainability approach corporations should take to reach out and be a leader and bring others in. Can you explain how you do that?

Cyril Giraud

Yes. In fact, we have concluded two key partnerships in that respect. I already mentioned the first one which is with the French Museum of Natural History. It is a partnership that we initiated in 2018 and which brings a lot of knowledge and experts and outside guidance for all our actions. On top of it, we are also a member of Act4nature.[6] This is a forum of companies and different public actors, scientists, etc. The goal is to make biodiversity a bigger priority overall, as big as climate

---

[6] https://www.act4nature.com/

Fig. 3 Act4nature partners. Source: act4nature international, https://www.act4nature.com/

change. And for us, it is a strong commitment, being part of it helps us to also get some feedback and to be part of global dynamics of actions and to make some official commitment to improve the situation. For instance, we had work on combating invasive alien species or these kinds of things. The other benefit is that we can in turn bring these experts into our quarries and they find it to be a particularly good kind of 'open-air laboratory', if I may say so, to study biodiversity in different conditions. We are enriching each other by providing different situations, different information, benchmarks, guidance, recommendations, and that is helpful to us (Fig. 3).

Uwe Schulte
You sparked my curiosity when you talked about that you are helping your customers to come to a more sustainable solution, and you mentioned talc in car interiors which surprised me a lot. Can you give us another example how your minerals can do that?

Cyril Giraud
Sure, we have quite a few good examples. There is one that I like a lot, which is a solution that we call Barrikote. Here, we are talking about the paper and board

industry. I did not mention it before, but we also have a lot of business in this industry. This solution is about providing what we call barrier properties to paper or board, which means protecting it from water or grease. Briefly, it is helping to be able to, for instance, put some content into a cardboard coffee cup, which is a typical example. You want to protect the inside of the coffee cup so that you can pour water or coffee inside it without completely soaking the cardboard. You have solutions on the market to do that, very efficient solutions. And the dominant solution today is to apply a polyethylene film onto the cardboard so that you have perfect impermeability of the cardboard, and you can pour your coffee inside the cup. The problem with that solution is that it makes the cup non-recyclable or difficult to recycle, because you cannot really remove the layer of polyethylene easily. What we have developed is a solution where we managed to get similar barrier properties but without polyethylene, meaning that after use the cup is fully recyclable. The solution is working, it is on the market today, and in fact, we are the supplier of one of the leaders in Europe producing this kind of cup. In turn, it helps them a lot to propose the solution of these coffee cups, which are now recyclable, to the market. That is also one example of ourselves helping our customers (Fig. 4 and 5).

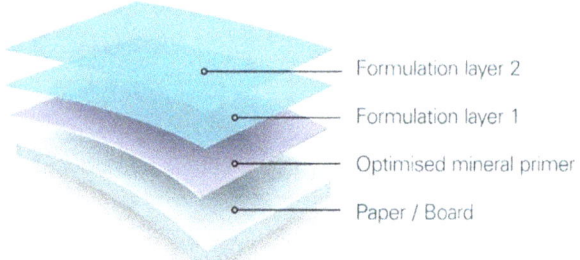

Fig. 4 Barrikote waterproofing paperboard. Source: Imerys S. A., https://www.imerys.com/product-ranges/barrikote-systems

Fig. 5 Barrikote food tray. Source: Imerys S. A., https://www.imerys.com/product-ranges/barrikote-systems

Uwe Schulte

This is interesting because I think if we can get away from polyethylene lamination of paper in certain applications, which would be very promising. And the way I understand it happens is that whilst the polyethylene is glued onto the paper, and then when you want to recycle it, you cannot easily separate the two, with your mineral it can just be flushed out by water. Is that what we are talking about?

Cyril Giraud

Yes, this is how it works.

Uwe Schulte

I have to say, I must be a bit critical on this one. I would rather have no single-use coffee cups and people using different solutions, like using porcelain cups. But your product is of course not limited to coffee cups and can make a great contribution. What also sparked my curiosity, and you only mentioned it in a half sentence, that you are heavily into batteries, for example, for electric vehicles. What do minerals have to do with that?

Cyril Giraud

Indeed, minerals have a lot to do with batteries. As you know, they contain electrodes. You have the anode on one side and the cathode on the other one, and in between you have an electrolyte and a separator. And the goal is to make the electrons travel from one side to the other when you charge and discharge the batteries.[7] Here you have a few properties which are important when you design and operate a battery, and one of them is about conductivity. The more conductive your battery is, the more you facilitate the flow of electrons, the higher the performance of your battery can be. You can achieve an excellent level of conductivity by adding what we call conductive additives to your battery. The most efficient ones are either graphite or carbon black. We are leading this market, we are producing and commercialising extremely high standard products which are in a lot of the high performing batteries today that you see on the market. This is a vital component on the overall performance of the batteries, and therefore it is helping the transition towards electrical vehicles. The good thing is that you need this good conductivity properties, irrespective of the technology. We are talking about the lithium-ion batteries, but it is also valid for fuel cells, it is also valid for solid-state batteries and so on. For us, really the key is to follow the market demand. Because as you know, there is a lot of interest for batteries so far, so we are investing a lot into capacity to follow market demand, but also into innovation to always increase the performance of our solutions and help the battery makers to develop even more performing batteries (Fig. 6).

Uwe Schulte

Yes, let us get to the material again, because let us understand this a little bit more. It is impressive that this is so key to the performance of these components of the electric vehicles. But graphite and carbon black are chemically the same. It is just

---

[7] https://storagewiki.epri.com/index.php/Lithium_Ion_Batteries

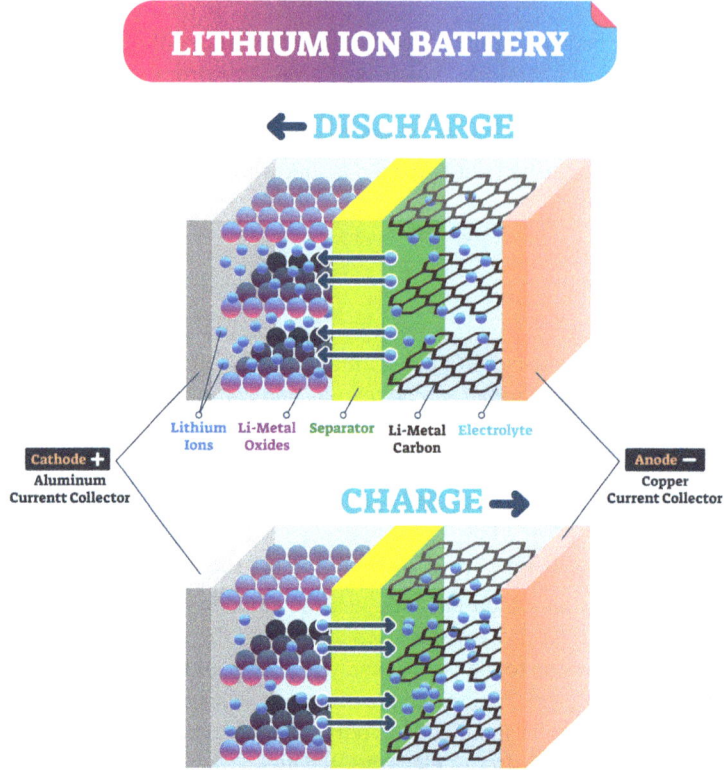

Fig. 6 Lithium-ion battery. Source: VectorMine, https://vectormine.com/

carbon. If I pull out coal from the ground and take the carbon out of that, is that the raw material you are using?

Cyril Giraud
Yes, but then you have all the mineralogy, all the shapes of the particles, which give different properties. In our case, we use synthetic graphite. We produce it ourselves through a process that lets us control the final product extremely well, and this consistency of the product allows us to have this extremely reliable performance and the same goes with carbon black.

Uwe Schulte
As normal consumers we would know graphite from pencils, that is where we get to know graphite, is that correct? (Fig. 7)

Cyril Giraud
You get it in pencils, you get it as well in friction materials like in braking pads, for instance, you get them in refractory materials for the heat conductivity properties, you get it in quite a few applications.

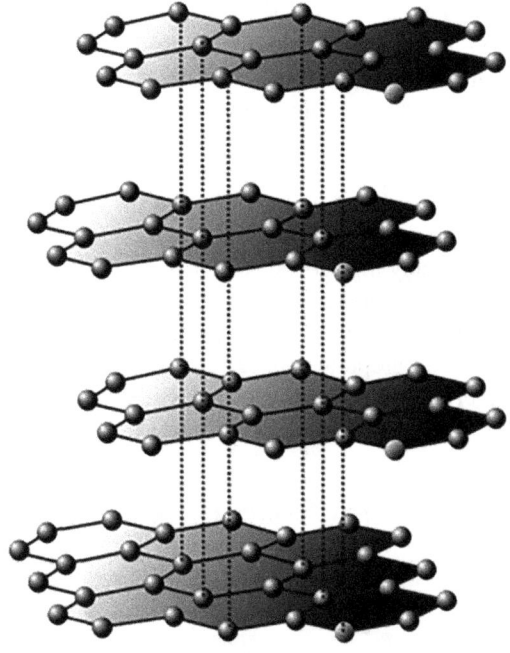

Fig. 7 Graphite. Source: Wikipedia, CC BY-SA 2.5 DEED, Attribution-ShareAlike 2.5 Generic, Author: Intercalactionrp.png: Anton, derivative work: Mattman723 (talk), Source: Intercalactionrp.png

Uwe Schulte

I just heard you say that you make it synthetically. That means you do this to be able to control the properties better, because there are also graphite mines, I understand.

Cyril Giraud

There is natural graphite as well, you are right. But here we are at such an elevated level of standard in terms of consistency of the product for the high-performance batteries that for some applications we get better performance by producing synthetic graphite.

Uwe Schulte

I understand. We are talking about how you are supporting a sustainable solution, and electric vehicles is of course an obvious one. But the way to look at these things is always, of course, to look at the entirety of the lifecycle of such a product. How do your products perform under that scrutiny of a life-cycle analysis?

Cyril Giraud

Yes, you are right. It is indeed important. And for me there are really two key points here. The first one is, as you say, to take the full cycle, and the second one is to get support from third parties to be as robust as possible in our analysis. Through our SustainAgility programmes that I mentioned already, we have defined a strong methodology, which is organised in five steps. But the main goal is really for us to be able to quantify both, on one side the impact and on the other side the benefits of each of the key products that we are making in their main applications from the extraction to the end of the life. This allows us to rate our products in terms of sustainability. In practices, we do that by following a framework which is called the

World Business Council for Sustainable Development. We are not inventing our own thing. And we developed a scientifically based, robust, and most importantly fully auditable approach to make sure that we do it in a transparent way, and we base our analysis on input from our own teams, but also from researchers and other experts. We really want to have a view as complete as possible on all these impacts from mining to manufacturing, but also during the usage phase of our minerals in our customer solutions, as well as the end of life. Based on that we have defined a pioneer label that we grant to products which in each application are providing remarkably high social and environmental contribution to the entire value chain, so low environmental impact during production compared to the economic value and downstream contribution. To come back to the example we just mentioned, our synthetic graphite and our carbon black for automotive battery applications have received this pioneer label, but it is also the case if I continue with, for instance, the graphite used in the alkaline batteries and several other (Figs. 8 and 9).

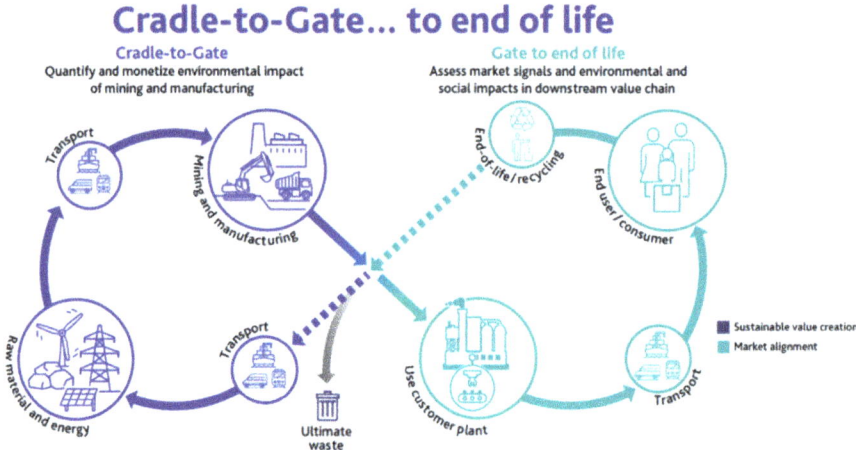

Fig. 8 Imerys life-cycle analysis method. Source: Imerys S. A., https://www.imerys.com/sustainability

Fig. 9 Imerys Pioneer label. Source: Imerys S. A., https://www.imerys.com/sustainability

Uwe Schulte

Yes, this is an impressive process and I hope that more companies take that approach. But you mentioned an important proviso in here and that is something that we must bear in mind in each application because you can only do this for one of your applications. You already mentioned how many different customers and applications you have. Each of those applications needs to be looked at separately, of course.

Cyril Giraud

Yes, you are right and that is a difficulty when you have so many products and so many applications. We are focusing on priorities, on the most important products and the most important applications to conduct this analysis.

Uwe Schulte

That is clear. It cannot be done everywhere. But that is something that we all must learn, to set priorities. Sometimes people try to do too many things at the same time. It is much appreciated, and it is also important what you mentioned that this is externally audited. That is important in this context, because credibility and trust is so important. You talked about graphite and all of that for electric vehicles. We are now experiencing a significant growth of these units. Will supply be able to keep up because we have lots of supply issues these days?

Cyril Giraud

Yes, you are right. It is a big challenge overall. It will be difficult in the coming years. It will be difficult to continue to get all the supplies that everybody would want when we look at all the projects or the new factories for electrical batteries. On our side, we try to anticipate by having plans over several years to plan for new production capacities for our carbon black and our graphite. But of course, we are not the only critical component in batteries. These days, we talk a lot about lithium, for instance, and there will need to be a good balance overall of all these critical resources to make sure that the industry can develop as needed in the future.

Uwe Schulte

You are giving me some sense of optimism here. That is good. Let us get to another point. It might be a bit facetious to ask a mining company about recycling, and I know you are not a mining company, you are a minerals company. But nevertheless, how do you see it going for batteries, for example?

Cyril Giraud

Recycling is indeed an especially crucial point, and it is a difficulty. From time to time, we hear about urban mining, for instance, which is trying to reduce the number of resources that we take from the ground, to take them from the waste from products which have been already in operation. In practice, it is often difficult. In batteries, for instance, separating the graphite and the carbon black is extremely difficult with the current technologies. But there are some other applications where it is easier, and I am quite optimistic that over the coming years we will start to see more opportunities to use recycled materials. If I can give you one example, we have a product called ImerLoop which is in fact a product for the paper and board industry made from waste from the process of the paper mills. We are helping them to recycle their own waste to become a raw material again. That is the kind of thing we can do. It is not possible in all applications, but I am sure that the trend will develop in the future, and we are supporting it obviously.

Uwe Schulte
Let us just get back to urban mining that you mentioned. Surely, for these batteries, we do not need urban mining, because my understanding is that urban mining would mean that it goes onto a waste disposal, a landfill or something like that and we pull it out again. But for batteries and similar products, we can have a full loop, correct? Or was I misunderstanding something?

Cyril Giraud
You can have several lives to a battery. Typically, what happens is that you start with the first usage of the battery in electrical vehicles, because this is where you need power, where you need longevity. But then overtime the battery performance is decreasing and a second usage for these batteries is to use what we call energy storage solutions. Typically, the batteries that you can use in your home to store solar energy. That is the kind of recycling solution, if we may say, re-use solution for the batteries. And indeed, when I refer to urban mining it was more to break down used products to recover the raw materials which contributed to make them in the first place.

Uwe Schulte
Urban mining for me is that you go to one of these big dumps and you dig up the dumped materials there. But what you are talking about is after re-using breaking the battery into parts, and that still has some challenges. But I understand there are now large-scale facilities being built as we speak, for example, in Norway.

Cyril Giraud
Indeed, yes.

Uwe Schulte
Last time we touched a little bit on greenhouse gas, we focused very much on biodiversity before and this is a very important part, and it was very gratifying to hear that you are collaborating with others. Still, carbon footprint is something that is important. How do you approach that in your operations?

Cyril Giraud
Yes, we consider this to be a particularly important topic as well. The good thing is that there are lots of things we can do about it. However, it takes time and effort, and for me the key is first to be aware about it, and secondly to have plans over several years to launch the right action. For ourselves we have set up a strong target, an ambitious target to reduce our emissions of CO_2 overtime. We are working on several different options, all in parallel, I should say. The first one is obviously to use more renewable energy, but the second important one is to recover energy from our processes. Very often we generate some heat that we can then recover to re-use later. We can improve our process efficiency to consume less energy in the first place. We

can also, I mentioned already, engage our suppliers to have science-based targets for themselves to reduce their own carbon footprint. And finally, we are now systematically including an assessment of the CO_2 emissions in our key business decisions, important investment projects, and acquisitions of other companies. We look at the CO_2 footprint impact on the group as part of the decision process.

Uwe Schulte
I do not want to spy on your business decision, but this is very encouraging, and I would love to understand a little bit better. This means that you assume a price of carbon, and you introduce that into your CapEx decision. Is that what you are saying?

Cyril Giraud
Indeed, we put a price per tonne of CO_2 that is impacting the financial return positively or negatively depending on the project. And at the same time, we also look at the mix of energies in the country where we operate. We know very well that depending on the country where you operate, the energy can be carbon intensive. We take that into account together with the opportunity or possibilities to improve the situation over time. Our focus is to be able to make progress in that respect. For instance, if we have a project which has a good perspective of being improved thanks to a future biomass project, then it is something that we see very positively.

Uwe Schulte
Okay, that is also a key point, that you make certain assumptions of technology becoming available for you. I think in these fast-moving times that is a key step.

Cyril Giraud
Yes, it is an important one. And to be clear, we are more in the early stages on that one. We are looking at the options available, we are progressively including that in our decision process, but we still have some way to go.

Uwe Schulte
No, of course we all must get started on these things and it is important. And on the other hand, a difficult one to judge, because the price of carbon might even vary from region to region over a longer period. But hopefully that gets everybody into the right direction. You sparked another question in my mind. You talked about engaging suppliers and encouraged them to go for science-based targets—the initiative that tries to have sector-specific targets for companies to reduce the carbon footprint of the operation to achieve the 1.5 degree based on science target. What is your experience there? Because when we talk to other companies, a lot of suppliers, especially smaller scale suppliers, have not got visibility of their carbon footprint yet.

Cyril Giraud
Yes, that is exactly the main difficulty that we are facing as well. We have some success, but it takes time and effort. For large suppliers, multinational ones, it is a discussion that is easy to have, because they understand. And even if some of them are sometimes a bit late—this is a direction in which they want to go. For smaller ones, especially in certain countries, it is something much more difficult to achieve. So,

we are not targeting 100% of our suppliers to be a part of that, but we are pushing to get more of them involved. Betting on the fact that the more we do it, the more it will have a positive impact on the overall chain, and that in turn will also push them to request the same from their own suppliers.

Uwe Schulte

Excellent. Thank you for clarifying that. Unfortunately, we are running out of time. This was extremely interesting. I saw how you personally learned from bad examples, how not to do quarrying, from your journeys around the world, how your company Imerys is trying to have a restorative approach to biodiversity, and we spent some time on understanding a bit more about these fascinating minerals you are dealing with from toothpaste to talc in cars, to carbon in batteries. That was fascinating, thank you for sharing that with us and giving us some background on sustainability aspects of mining.

Cyril Giraud

You are welcome. It was a pleasure to share this time with you. I hope I could convince you that minerals have really a vital role to play in contributing to the solutions of tomorrow. And in fact, this is what we are continuously trying to do at Imerys, and to find ways to operate more efficiently to reduce our impact for ourselves, but also with our partners, customers, and suppliers.

Uwe Schulte

Thank you so much, and I wish you continued success with that.

Decarbonising Container Shipping

Recorded September 2022

Today I will be talking to Jacob Sterling, Senior Director and Head of Ocean Decarbonisation and Innovation at Maersk. Please let me now introduce our guest for today. Jacob joined Maersk in 2009, having worked prior as a Conservation Director at the World Wildlife Fund. He has held several positions at A. P. Moller-Maersk, and he has a master's in biology. Welcome, Jacob. Please tell us a bit about yourself and how sustainability has entered your professional life.

Jacob A. Sterling

Thank you and thank you for the invitation. I think that sustainability has entered my life early on. When I think back, I can recall that when I was around 13 years old, I wrote a piece in Danish class, in Denmark of course, and used that as a reader's letter for the local newspaper, which got published in the newspaper around that time. I do not know if that is where it started, but that is my earliest record of having that interest. And yes, that naturally led to studying biology. I am very much focused on biodiversity conservation, I spent quite some time on Borneo, and then that naturally led to WWF, where I was for 7 years. At some point during that period, I thought it could be interesting to work for a big corporate and see if I could help them change in a more sustainable direction.

Uwe Schulte

Now you made me curious, what was this letter to the editor about?

Jacob A. Sterling

It was about environmental issues, and I cannot recall it word for word, but it was something around that we should be better at cleaning up after ourselves and we should not leave waste in nature and things like that. A bit more down-to-earth than the topics we talk about today. It was about that we cannot use nature as a trash can, and we should behave better as human beings.

Uwe Schulte

I am really impressed, because boys entering puberty normally have other things on their mind, but that is amazing, great. Look, our audience will, at some point in time, have seen a container going around somewhere on the streets with a Maersk logo on. But Maersk is a bit more. Can you describe Maersk a little bit to our audience?

Jacob A. Sterling

Sure. Maersk has been in business for over one hundred years, and our core business has always been shipping in various shapes and forms. In recent years, we have decided to focus very much on container shipping and integrated logistics. Whereas if you go back 5–10 years, it was the norm that we would typically transport containers from port to port. Now, to a much greater extent, we take care of the full transportation of our customers' goods from end to end. From where it is produced at a factory or wherever, to a distribution centre or even to a store or where it is going to be consumed.

Uwe Schulte

But it normally involves a container somewhere.

Jacob A. Sterling

It certainly does, because it has shown since the 50s to be a very practical and very efficient way of storing and transporting goods long distances. The invention of the container is the single most important invention to bring down the cost of global trade. So yes, it usually involves a container (Fig. 1).

Uwe Schulte

Maersk is really a truly multinational company, and that makes it interesting to hear that you are coming from WWF, joined a company like that. Was that a big shock to your system?

Jacob A. Sterling

To be honest, I expected it to be a bigger shock than it turned out to be. I cannot really explain why, perhaps it was just the specific department I joined at Maersk, but I think that the mindset of wanting to make positive change was very much the same as where I came from. The substantial difference was that it was a lot shorter taking a decision to action at Maersk than when working at WWF, for obvious

Fig. 1 Allen, Cecil J. (1928), The Steel Highway. Source: Wikipedia, public domain, Author: Andy Dingley (scanner), Source: Scan from Allen, Cecil J. (1928), The Steel Highway, London: Longmans, Green & Co., pp. facing page. (II) 108

reasons. As an NGO you decide on what you want to focus on in terms of changing the world, and then you go out and try to convince others to help do that through lobby work or projects or other means. Whereas in an organisation like Maersk, if we decide to do something, most of the time we can just decide to do it and that just makes an enormous difference. That was very empowering and very motivating.

Uwe Schulte

When I talk to people in non-governmental organisations, for some of them multinational companies are the enemy, so for them you have changed sides. But what I hear you say is that it does not feel like that for you. Could you explain that a little bit?

Jacob A. Sterling

I understand where they are coming from because there are examples of big companies that are doing less than what you would think they could do, but I certainly do not think that there is an antagonistic relationship or should be between NGOs and companies. I would say, as I also mentioned before, companies actually have the ability to act, and we as corporates can take inspiration, and we still do, from NGOs which are very often much more at the forefront of the thinking in this space, and therefore can give a lot of important insights on what is going on, and what the trends are, and maybe what the topics are that we have not really thought about so much yet in big corporations, where we maybe tend to focus more on certain big topics like climate change, for example, and then go really deep on that. There can be a healthy tension between NGOs and corporates, and there can certainly also be a super valuable collaboration.

Uwe Schulte

You are making a key point. I just said that on the NGO side, some see multinationals as the enemy, but it is the other way around very often as well, and that hinders of course communication and joint progress. What you just said is important, that when you are a large company, it is worth your while, even if it is difficult to try to communicate with at least some of the NGOs. Now, you already mentioned how important containers are and containerisation of ship freight was a huge efficiency booster after the Second World War. But today, there is a concern now about the environmental impact. It would be nice if you could tell us a little bit about how you are approaching all the sustainability challenges at Maersk that relate to your business.

Jacob A. Sterling

Sure. Shipping is a multinational industry that by nature that has significant impacts, positive and negative around the world. On the positive side of it, as we talked about, we enable trade, and we make it possible for very remote parts of the world to trade quite efficiently with the rest of the world. Those are some of the positive impacts. On the negative side, of course, I know we are going to talk more about climate change later but that is just the one big issue, because we use fossil fuels and because of the size of the industry, it really has a huge impact, 2–3% of the global CO_2 emissions.[1] But at Maersk, and I also think others in the industry, we are of course also looking at other issues that are not related to climate change such as anti-corruption. In the past, corruption or facilitation payment was notoriously something that the industry was facing and had big problems with. We are beginning to be able to seriously do something about that. Things like responsible procurement, human rights, the broad sustainability agenda are of course also important for shipping. When we look at our impacts and try to assess the materiality, it is really our use of fossil fuels that is the biggest challenge to us and to the societies that we serve. The fuel that a company like Maersk alone uses, which is around 11 million tonnes of fuel per year, emits 0.1% of the global CO_2 emissions. While we are at times being portrayed as an environmental leader for some of the steps that we are taking to do something about that, it is important to bear in mind that this is the beginning of the journey, and we are not there yet. There is so much more to do, and as I said, shipping as a total is around 3% of the global CO_2 emissions, so a massive impact, a massive responsibility that we need to take on us.

Uwe Schulte

Of course, this is the key point, but before we enter the discussion about greenhouse gas there is another one that always comes up when we talk about shipping vessels and especially container vessels. I live close to Hamburg, and I can see them going up and down the Elbe River and it is quite amazing. And the industry has been challenged. The shipping industry is challenged about malpractices on scrapping retired vessels. Can you say something about that?

Jacob A. Sterling

Yes, it is rightly as you said, also an issue for the industry that the practices around ship recycling or ship scrapping, however you turn it, are not always up to the standards that they should be. At Maersk, for more than the last five years, we have invested in upgrading facilities in India to the standards of the Hong Kong

---

[1] https://www.iea.org/energy-system/transport/international-shipping

Convention,[2] which is the international regulation in this space to make sure that it is done in a proper way.[3,4] Because of course, when we operate ships for their entire lifetime then it is also our responsibility to make sure that they are dismantled in the right way, and by the way, that the materials from the ship recycling are also used in a good way, because steel that is being re-used is much more sustainable than steel that is being made directly from iron ore. There is a lot of focus on ship recycling—both from the social impacts, as you mentioned, where we need to make sure that the workers involved in this can do this in a proper way where it is safe for them, but also the environmental impacts both on the direct pollution in the areas that should be prevented, but also the resource use around ship recycling, making sure that the steel is recycled and re-used to the extent possible.

Uwe Schulte

I recall that a couple of years ago, I saw a project mentioned that you were trying to start at the design phase of new vessels to make them more easily recyclable. Is that correct?

Jacob A. Sterling

Yes. When we did the Triple-E ships some years back, we had a project where we investigated how we could potentially design and map the materials that are used to build the ship. In such a way, that when you get to the recycling phase, you can both recycle it better because you know what materials are where on the ship, so to say, thereby enabling that you get a higher price for the ship when you send it for recycling, because you can better document the value of the ship that you bring to recycling. That project is still something we are finding our way to do because it is hard to do as one company alone. There is a whole issue around steel use in container shipping, and we use a lot of steel both to build ships, to build containers, to build cranes in the terminals, and so forth. Steel is a big issue, and it is an issue around circularity where we need to make sure that we, to the extent possible, really design, use, and re-use the steel in the smartest viable way.[5]

Uwe Schulte

And you also must do that jointly with steel manufacturers to form collaborations there.

Jacob A. Sterling

Exactly, we need to join with the shipbuilding industry, with the steel manufacturers and the whole value chain. When you look at the ships in Hamburg, you would think that building ships that size must make you important for the steel industry, but the

---

[2] https://www.imo.org/en/About/Conventions/Pages/The-Hong-Kong-International-Convention--for-the-Safe-and-Environmentally-Sound-Recycling-of-Ships.aspx

[3] https://circulareconomy.europa.eu/platform/en/good-practices/maersk-designing-ships-can-be-dismantled-and-reused

[4] https://www.shiprecyclingtransparency.org/srti-signatories/

[5] https://www.oecd.org/en/publications/environmental-policy-and-technological-innovation-in-shipbuilding_5jm25wg57svj-en.html

fact of the matter is that we are quite small. We also need to link up with a lot of other industries that use a lot of steel because it is only when we all join forces that we can make the case for turning towards green steel in a bigger way.

Uwe Schulte

Yes, absolutely. I am encouraged that there now is a large-scale pilot plant for hydrogen-based steel in Sweden. And I know that other steel manufacturers are working on at least starting with grey hydrogen. That is a starting point. That is great and I am glad that you mentioned the human rights issues around the recycling of ships there because we have seen horrific pictures of children working there. But even if there is no child labour involved, the work safety had not been considered. I understand that you are really taking the Hong Kong agreement seriously.

Jacob A. Sterling

Yes. We believe that the facilities we use are, and we have external verification of that, live up to the Hong Kong standards and in fact go beyond that, as we have set our own Responsible Ship Recycling Standards which add additional requirements on anti-corruption and labour rights to align with ILO standards and the Maersk Code of Conduct.[6]

Uwe Schulte

That is admirable and obviously there is progress, but we all agree that the industry still has a long way to go there. Let us come back to what you already talked about. One thing we always say when we have discussions with companies: 'What is the key point? Where is your significant impact on the sustainability agenda'? And it is no use ticking off the box of 17 United Nations Sustainable Development Codes. It is important that you do something about where you really matter, and as you said, you really matter on carbon footprint. Can you talk about what your ambition is there? (Fig. 2)

Jacob A. Sterling

Sure. We set our first net zero target in 2018, and back then it was a result of a thought process where we said that we needed to become much more ambitious on climate change, and we could also see that setting a net zero target would be the only right thing to do. So, we set a net zero target where we said that we wanted to go to zero in 2050 for our shipping operation. After that, we started looking into how we do that? Because up until that point, we had primarily focused our efforts regarding climate change on energy efficiency, making the ships more efficient, using less fuel when moving the cargo. But we could see that this would not help us reduce our absolute carbon footprint, because while we were becoming increasingly efficient, we were also growing. We could see that even though we became much more efficient, and we were around 40% more efficient compared to our baseline, our absolute emissions were the same. We could see that this was an issue of changing fuels. We started looking into that and we investigated that for a couple of years

---

[6] https://www.imo.org/en/ourwork/environment/pages/ship-recycling.aspx

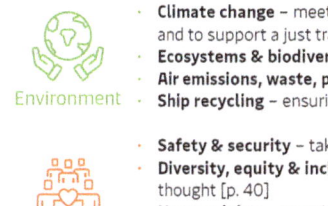

- **Climate change** – meeting our obligation to decarbonise our end-to-end operations and to support a just transition [p. 18]
- **Ecosystems & biodiversity** – protecting the ecosystem in which we operate [p. 29]
- **Air emissions, waste, pollution** – minimising impacts of our activities [p. 31]
- **Ship recycling** – ensuring safe and responsible ship recycling globally [p. 33]

Environment

- **Safety & security** – taking care of our people [p. 36]
- **Diversity, equity & inclusion** – creating an inclusive workplace with diversity of thought [p. 40]
- **Human rights** – ensuring respect for human rights across our value chain [p. 43]
- **Labour rights** – ensuring decent working conditions [p. 42]
- **Sustainable/Inclusive trade** – contributing to an inclusive trade environment [p. 8]

Social

- **Sustainable procurement** – ensuring responsible practices in our supply chain [p. 46]
- **Responsible tax** – being a responsible and transparent taxpayer [p. 49]
- **Citizenship** – contributing to communities and societies where we operate [p. 50]

Governance

Fig. 2 Maersk assessment of social and environmental materiality. Source: A.P. Moller—Maersk, 2021 Sustainability Report, https://www.maersk.com/

and concluded that it was realistic for us, not easy but realistic and achievable, if we went all in to go for net zero in 2040.[7,8] So earlier this year, we cut 10 years off our deadline. And when we did that, we also expanded the scope to not only cover our ocean business, our shipping business, but actually to cover the entire business, including all the scopes—Scope 1, 2, and 3, so both our own direct emissions, which are the biggest because that is the fuel we burn, but also the electricity consumption and the whole supply chain of our business. That is our scope and that is our ambition now.

Uwe Schulte

It is interesting to understand how that process internally worked. I remember the days when Maersk offered customers a journey, to and from China, for example. Going more slowly and that way consuming a lot less fuel per tonne of cargo delivered, but you would lose 2 or 3 days in the journey and see whether people would accept that. That, of course, is nice, but it cannot be the solution, you already mentioned that. What made the change inside Maersk to go from this approach to a much more radical approach? We will talk a little bit more about going from 2050 to 2040, but the main point is that for a company like yours to say 'we can actually do net zero' is an amazing step and needs a lot of visionary risk taking from some senior executives. How did that happen?

Jacob A. Sterling

It is a good question and something that I also actually reflect on quite a lot. I think that to really understand what makes a company do something like that, put upon themselves a voluntary target in that magnitude, you need to look at company

---

[7] https://www.maersk.com/news/articles/2022/01/12/apmm-accelerates-net-zero-emission-targets-to-2040-and-sets-milestone-2030-targets

[8] https://www.maersk.com/~/media_sc9/maersk/corporate/sustainability/files/our-approach/policies-and-positions/responsible-ship-recycling-position-paper.pdf

culture. Maersk is a company that has been in business for more than one hundred years, and it is our clearly stated ambition to also be around for the next one hundred years.

We are essentially a family-owned company which also enables long-term thinking in a way that is different from some others. And then we have always had a tradition of really innovating in the space of energy efficiency, trying to see how much we can really squeeze the energy efficiency, either by going slower, designing better ships, or installing new gadgets on the ship. Whatever it might be, we have always investigated that a lot, so it is in our blood, if you will, to push the boundaries on that. But you are right, it is a massive shift to go from that to set a net zero target. Back in 2018, what led up to it was that we could see that both among our customers, our investors, our employees, and society, that climate change was becoming an important topic. The net zero target was about: 'This is something we must do'. And it was the first time where we set an environmental target where we did not really know the pathway yet. We also knew that we were taking a lot of risk, but we also felt that it is only if you jump into the deep end, so to say, that you find your way.

We cannot stay on the safe side and just set targets that we know we can achieve. We need to lean in here. On the one hand, it is about something we must do, it is an obligation, but we can also see that expectations are changing rapidly in the society around us. And if we want to continue to facilitate a model where goods are produced in one end of the world where it is more efficient to do so, and consumed in some other part of the world, and that is connected by global trade where we are a very important part, for that model to continue to be socially acceptable, basically we would have to decarbonise trade. We would have to decarbonise the way global trade works; the way globalisation works. I do not know if that answers your question fully, but those are some of the thoughts that went into it.

Uwe Schulte

You made several points that I noted for myself. A particularly important one was that family-owned long-term thinking. And what I am hearing you say, and correct me if I am wrong, if we want to stay in that business, if we do not want this to be shut down because it is causing too much carbon, we have to take another type of risk to develop something which we are not quite sure what it is going to be, but we know what our ambition is.

Jacob A. Sterling

Yes, and we get to a point where we say that it is a much bigger risk if we do not act. We might take wrong decisions and it might cost us money to move into this space, but if we do not do it, we are at a much greater risk as a company. And that changed the conversation.

Uwe Schulte

That does change the conversation. That is a crucial point you are making here. For me it is interesting, repeatedly a lot of people have made net zero commitments without even knowing how to get there. That is fine as we see with you, but then you must sit down and define the steps and that is something you and I should explore a little bit more when we discuss what you are going to do. How will you achieve your commitments, because the challenge is of course, if you make a net zero commitment and have no clue and then let things go by, then it is green washing. I hope you are not greenwashing.

Jacob A. Sterling
I certainly hope so as well, and I know we are not. You are right. You can set a target and you can be bold, and you can lean out, but when you have set a target then you are also obliged to then follow it up with a fairly specific road map, and to figure out for all of your emission carriers how you are actually going to do it. Those were our next steps. And it was building those road maps that led to cutting 10 years of the deadline, because if we believe this is a climate emergency we should act accordingly and we should push ourselves to the max (Fig. 3).

Uwe Schulte
You started ordering vessels that can run on alternative fuel. What is the challenge there? When I was living in Brazil, we could run a car on petrol or on ethanol, which was always a strange experience—when you filled up your tank it smelled as if you were drunk. That technology has been around, has it not?

Jacob A. Sterling
The challenge for shipping, just to take one step back if you will, is that we are today using almost 100% fossil fuels, 100% oil. The first thing you do when you get into this journey is you ask what the energy source is going to be for the future? And we have two main sources of energy from which we can choose. One is renewable electricity, either in its raw form or turned into hydrogen or fuel. Or you could use biomass somehow converted into a fuel. Those are the two main energy sources. We have looked deeply into that to see what the options are there. And there are a lot of

Fig. 3 Maersk roadmap to net zero. Source: A.P. Moller—Maersk, https://www.maersk.com/news/articles/2022/01/12/apmm-accelerates-net-zero-emission-targets-to-2040-and-sets-milestone-2030-targets

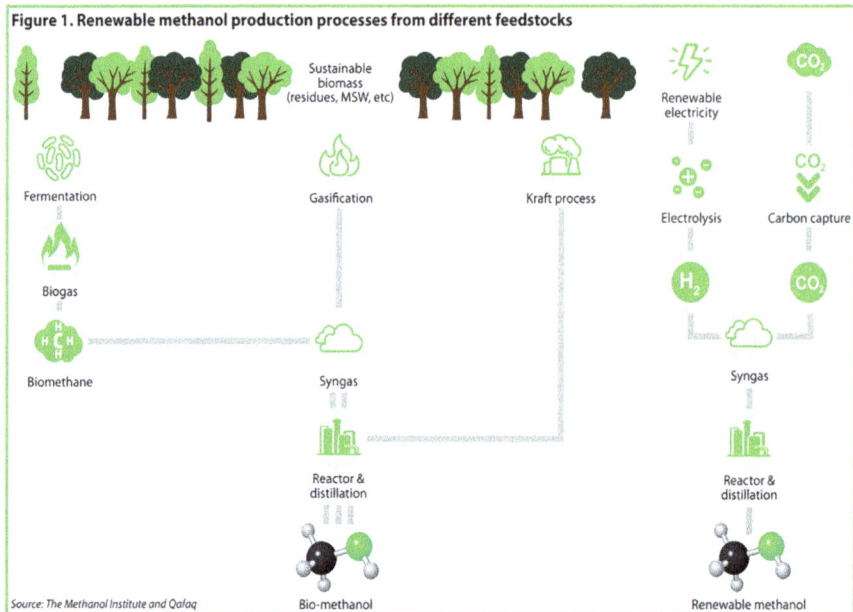

Fig. 4 Green methanol production process from different renewable feedstocks. Source: The Methanol Institute, https://www.methanol.org/wp-content/uploads/2020/01/Methanol-Emerging-Global-Energy-Markets-energy-industry-forum.pdf

diverse ways that you can convert biomass into fuel. We have biodiesel today that is made from rapeseed oil or palm oil or even used cooking oil or food waste. And we also have other technologies that can make methanol or ethanol, for example, or other products. The issue for shipping is that none of this has the sufficient scale. Also, if you talk about, for example, ethanol or a different alcohol methanol which we are focusing on quite a lot, then you cannot use those in an existing ship engine, whereas you can put it in a normal combustion engine (Fig. 4).

You just mentioned the example regarding the car. You do need to modify your engine and you do need to modify your tank system to be able to use it on a ship safely. We were really in a situation where we could say that the types of fuels such as biodiesel that you could use in a ship engine as of today, are not able to scale to the extent we need, because shipping is using around 300,000,000 tonnes of fuel oil today. And if you just said 'Okay, well, let's just scale up biodiesel to cover that', then we would have other issues that we would not want to deal with such as land use changes around the world. Biodiesel, which is the fuel we can use in existing engines, is not scalable and cost effective eventually. We started looking into alcohols, i.e. ethanol and methanol and others.

Uwe Schulte
Before you go on, it was naughty of me, of course, to say that in Brazil I could use alcohol or fuel. You are using diesel engines, and you cannot, even in Brazil, put

alcohol into a diesel engine because the way the explosion is managed is significantly different. I was being too much of a challenger.

Jacob A. Sterling

No, it was a good point you were making, because if you want to change a two-stroke diesel engine on a container ship to one that can run on diesel and methanol it is not that big of a change and the engine exists today. The thing is just that none of the ships that we have are, of course, fitted for that because they were designed for something else. But one of the things we found out in this process, this looking into the details, building a road map process that I talked about, was exactly that, that you do have ships running on methanol. There is a small fleet, a fleet of methanol tankers that have a methanol engine and run on part of the cargo that they carry around. We looked at methanol and we could see that. Before, I talked about that we could either get our energy from a bio source or from a renewable electricity source. And we could see that methanol was one of the fuels that could be made from both pathways.

Methanol can be made from renewable electricity, which you turn into green hydrogen, and then you add CO_2 molecules, and you have methanol, but you can also do it via various chemical processes where you convert biomass into methanol. And that made it a very flexible fuel. You could say that many different pathways get you to the same molecule, if you will, which makes the scaling channels a little bit easier, or you have more options. As I already mentioned, we got to a point in our journey where we decided to order a ship that could run on methanol.[9] The reason for doing that was really that we could see that it could scale now, the technology is ready now. And since we want to have impact in this decade, this is a fuel that is good for us now.

Uwe Schulte

For me, we are getting into too much detail, and sometimes my prior profession gets through. The energy density is, of course, lower in methanol than when you have diesel. You certainly have a storage problem on your vessels, do you not?

Jacob A. Sterling

Well, that is something you can design your way out of, but you are right, your fuel tank needs to be twice the size for methanol.

Uwe Schulte

Twice?

Jacob A. Sterling

Twice, yes. And then on top of that, you also want to have a diesel tank because you want to be able to switch to diesel, you must for safety reasons. Because methanol is such a new fuel and diesel is such a well-known fuel you need to be able to switch back to diesel, if necessary. That is why you need some more tank space on the ship. But we cannot expect that everything can go on as usual, just with a slightly

---

[9] https://www.euractiv.com/section/alternative-renewable-fuels/news/maersk-orders-eight-large-container-ships-to-run-on-carbon-neutral-e-methanol/

different fuel. We will also need to make tweaks to the designs of these ships, and it is not a massive change. We just need a bigger fuel tank.

Uwe Schulte

The need to have two tanks and run on both, that is because of the transition, because you are not sure that everything works, but eventually you would expect that you completely switch over, would you not?

Jacob A. Sterling

Probably. I would not speculate on that, but we will always also need, I think at least for the near future, a diesel tank because we need diesel for the ignition of the fuel. Whereas diesel self-ignites in a two-stroke engine, methanol does not, so you need a little bit of diesel just to get the combustion going—back to your point on the ethanol car.

Uwe Schulte

That is how it works, I see. You start it with diesel.

Jacob A. Sterling

Yes, exactly. So that is another reason, yes.

Uwe Schulte

Oh, interesting. Okay, let us just spend a little bit more time on methanol. This is interesting because you explained, and I do not think we can go into the details of the different path routes but let us just take the renewable energy for a second. What I hear you say is that there is a wind farm, for example, that creates the energy. You electrolyse water, and you create hydrogen. That is the starting point. What happens then?

Jacob A. Sterling

Then you take the green hydrogen and put it through a chemical process where you combine it with a CO_2 molecule to create the methanol. One point that is important to make here, without getting too technical, is that if you have renewable electricity, if you can, you would always want to use that directly as you do in electric vehicles, because then there is limited energy loss. If you then choose to convert it into hydrogen, which is the first step away from direct electrification, then you lose energy, but you get something that you can more easily transport, or at least you get a different molecule. If you then can use the hydrogen directly because that can also be used as an energy source, that is fine, but hydrogen takes up so much space that it would be—we talked about doubling the fuel tank for methanol—it would be more for hydrogen. In some instances, you need to convert it further and take the energy loss that comes with it and convert it into methanol or ammonia, for example. That is the basic pathway, and it is all about having the renewable electricity source, and then making sure that in that process you lose as little energy as possible, because you want to, of course, preserve as much energy as possible to not have to put up too many wind farms and so forth.

Uwe Schulte

I understand. When I listen to this, then you will have a competitor as customer of methanol and that is the airline industry. But one could turn that argument the other way around and say that you could collaborate with them to build that infrastructure.

Jacob A. Sterling

Yes, aviation is one that very quickly springs to mind. But, if you just look at the decarbonisation overall, there are a lot of sectors that depend on electrification. And really, this is a type of electrification, also for shipping. Even though we do not use electricity directly, we use something produced from electricity. You are right, there will be a massive need from so many sectors in electrifying their businesses with renewable electricity, and we are one of them. There will be competition and, as you say, preferably also a lot of collaboration, because it is a common challenge, we all have.

Uwe Schulte

The interesting thing about what you also said is that your choice of methanol also explains why in private cars and even lorries, methanol is not the option, and hydrogen is not the option. The direct use of electricity is the option because of the intermediate. That debate to keep all these different fuels open is fine when we talk about all mobility, but not for normal passenger cars. Tell me, obviously you must have investigated the supply of this and that must have helped you to cut 10 years off your time scale. That is fascinating.

Jacob A. Sterling

You would think that. And in a way we did, but just to be completely open and honest with you, the global market for green methanol today is non-existent. I believe that globally there are around 30,000 tonnes of green methanol being produced, and we do not know what it is being used for, but it is certainly not being used as fuel for shipping. For the first container vessel that we ordered, we need around 10,000 tonnes of fuel. And for the next 12 that we also ordered, we need close to half a million tonnes of methanol fuel. Yes, we had engaged in a lot of dialogue with potential suppliers prior to ordering the first ship, but we could also see that we were stuck in a chicken or egg dilemma. Could we order a vessel when there was no fuel to put in the tank? And on the other side, could we expect someone to build a green methanol factory when there was no customer? And we decided that we wanted to take a step forward and break that dilemma by ordering the first ship and committing to only ordering dual fuel ships as of now. Dual fuel is the key here because it is like an insurance premium in a way, because we did not know whether we could get the green fuel, the green methanol. But we knew that if we did not get it, then at least we could sail the ship on regular diesel until it became available. That is also the beauty of the dual fuel engine that we use for these ships. But it did trigger a lot of attention when we then made this commitment and ordered this ship, and we managed later in the same year, so last year, to make an agreement with a company in Denmark, that would then produce the

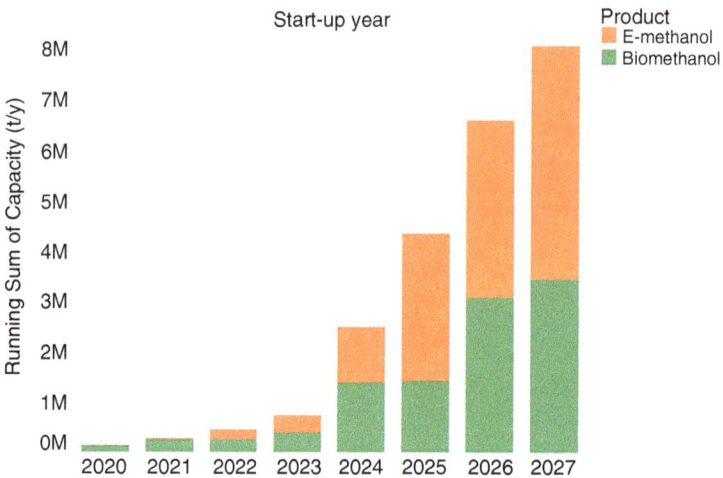

Fig. 5 Projected renewable methanol production capacity. Source: The Methanol Institute, https://www.methanol.org/renewable/

10,000 tonnes of fuel for the first ship. The ship is being built, the facility is being built as we speak, and in a year from now, it should be ready.[10] And we are also deep into dialogue, and we have made several so far non-binding agreements with various companies on producing green methanol that will take us much beyond what we need for the first 12 ships. Realistically, within the next 3–5 years, we will count the global production of green methanol in the millions of tonnes, not in the thousands of tonnes (Fig. 5).

Uwe Schulte
Wow, I praised you already, and I must repeat it because the ordering of those ships has precipitated something in the market. Having been a procurement guy myself, of course, you need to know where you get your stuff from, and to go this way without being sure is bold, but also it then actually drives the suppliers to say: 'There is a new market, and I can do something and then investment will follow'. And it already followed. That is great. That is the vessel going across the ocean. But we also spoke about that, that you are now providing end-to-end service to your customers. What do you do about decarbonising that?

Jacob A. Sterling
It is an interesting one, because you can say that most of our emissions from transporting goods comes from shipping. That is where we are biggest, and we have a lot of ships. There are 700 ships, 750 ships, and they are all controlled from the headquarter in Copenhagen. We have a large degree of control on what happens with those ships, what fuels get into the tank and so forth. Whereas if you look at trucking, for example, we have thousands and thousands of suppliers of trucks. None of them, or very few of

---

[10] https://www.ieabioenergy.com/wp-content/uploads/2020/12/Case-Story-DK_-Green-Methanol_web-1.pdf

them, will be owned by us. Some of these suppliers will own one truck, or five trucks. Some of them are in places like Germany, where EV trucks might be coming first, but some others are in Africa or elsewhere where it will be a lot harder. We have committed to also decarbonising the rest, the whole land side, and the air business that we have, and the terminals that we have, and we are building road maps for that as we speak. Talking about trucks, we have ordered around 400 electric trucks, which I believe was one of the biggest single orders of electric trucks to get started on this. The trucks are not with a battery capacity yet, where they can go wherever you need them to go and so forth. But you can use electric trucks to go on more fixed routings between, say, a terminal and a specific warehouse. So that is where we start. You can say the emissions are less on the land side, but the complications are greater.

Uwe Schulte
Because the complexity is so much higher, and the number of players involved.

Jacob A. Sterling
Exactly, yes. And we do not have all the answers to that yet, definitely not. But we know we need to do it, and we are building our road maps and beginning to take these actions, investing in EV trucks and so forth.

Uwe Schulte
That is many EV trucks. Is that in Europe or is that elsewhere as well?

Jacob A. Sterling
It is in the USA.

Uwe Schulte
We talked about that you are big, and you have a fair share on all of that. Your market share is around 15% of sea freight, correct me if I am wrong. That is impressive, but on the other hand, there are 85% that are not Maersk, and if we want to decarbonise sea freight it is great you go ahead, but the others must do something similar, do they not?

Jacob A. Sterling
Sure. Our market share is closer to 20%, but that does not really change the question, whether it is 80% or 85% that is left, you are completely right. But we are all part of the same industry, and we share many of the same customers, and our regulators are the same. And for many, some of the mindsets are also the same. I think in container shipping there is a good group of companies that are willing and able to do something in this space to take real action. And that is also necessary that we all move in this direction, but I am quite confident that we all will, and I would love to see this become something that we really compete on, who can be the greenest, who can become green faster than the rest, and have the best green products for our customers and so forth. That is what we need, that we really can work together on making sure that the standards are right, and that the regulation is pushing for the right thing. But we should really compete on this like everything else, so that we can get even smarter in a faster way.

Uwe Schulte

That is a good intention. I hope every other player sees it the same way, because this is a huge challenge ahead of us. I am just wondering, when you look back on your journey now, that basically started in 2018 when you got very serious about that net zero target, what would you say are the main insights, learnings you have taken as an outsider coming into Maersk that you could tell other companies when they look at their net zero commitment? What should they look out for, and what is good insight, and what should be avoided?

Jacob A. Sterling

That is a particularly good question. The main point for me is really to get to tangible action as fast as possible. Because it is only when you get into the real action that you will learn stuff. You can spend so much time analysing, calculating, strategising on what to do and where to start and how to de-risk all of that, but you only really learn when you do something. The first vessel that we ordered is one small container ship. It is going to trade in Northern Europe between Germany and Finland. How hard can it be? And we learned that it is super hard to get off the ground with this. There are so many questions that we need to answer that we did not even realise to be questions before. But we only get to understand these questions and then get to the answers when we get into the action. We had not thought so much about where to store the fuel, how to move it from a storage to the ship, and all the regulatory things that might be in this. To do these projects where you act and get learnings, I think is valuable and something that we at least get a lot of value out of.

Uwe Schulte

It sounds like the good old saying 'think big, starts small'. But your emphasis is on 'start', 'do something', rather than just have wonderful PowerPoint slides.

Jacob A. Sterling

Exactly. And it is also a lot easier to change the course if you are moving, at least on a ship. You cannot change the course unless you have some speed in the ship. And this is the same, we need to start going towards the target in a tangible way and then we can learn, and we will learn along the way: this was a wrong choice, this was a wrong decision, this does not work out, and so forth. But if we do not move and take those learnings, then it will be much harder when we then eventually start.

Uwe Schulte

One of the really encouraging things from your action that I heard you say is that we will be in the millions of tonnes of green methanol in the not-so-distant future. And that is something that is extremely encouraging. Do you think that there might be major obstacles on the way that are worth mentioning and that, for example, governments must play a more significant role to speed this up?

Jacob A. Sterling

Yes, and just to stay with the millions, just for our vessels we expect to need 6 million tonnes of fuel by the end of this decade. That is the figure we go for. And hopefully there will be much more by that time because others would use it as well. But you are right, governments can play a crucial role in this. Because as it is today and will be for the near future, green fuels will be much more expensive than fossil fuels. Because there is no carbon tax on shipping, for example, and that does not really make sense. You have cheap fuels that pollute the planet, and you have green fuels, so you are going to have green fuels that are much more expensive. We are calling on governments to develop a global carbon tax on shipping. We have proposed a level of around $150.00 per tonne of CO_2 which would be the equivalent of around $500.00 per tonne of fuel oil, so a significant increase. That is what we think is needed to at least level the playing field between the fossil fuels and the green fuels that we are going to have, and that is very necessary. And I believe that can drive things forward. On top of that, of course, we need governments to be open to the new green fuels, to allow them into their ports and to allow that it is being used as flag states for ship owners. The carbon tax is crucial. And we are happy to see the EU's work on inclusion of shipping in the EU Emission Trading System (ETS).[11,12] We are deeply engaged in that and supporting that. But we would, of course, much prefer that it happened at the global level in the International Maritime Organisation,[13] because that is the global regulating body for shipping, and they have been dragging their feet, or rather the member states of the IMO have been dragging their feet for too long. That is something we need to change, because we need a carbon tax that will make it very painful not to go green.

Uwe Schulte
On that critical note, I would say that is an even bigger challenge than getting the supply for green methanol, I guess. But it is something that is worthwhile engaging in, and I do not think that the number 150 is exorbitant. We all know that the cost of using fossil fuel is much higher, the environmental and social cost of that. Thank you so much for giving us some hope and a perspective on net zero for container freight. That is something we will cherish.

Jacob A. Sterling
Well, thank you. It was a pleasure speaking to you.

Uwe Schulte
Thank you. And we wish you all the success that you need. It is for us as well.

---

[11] https://climate.ec.europa.eu/eu-action/eu-emissions-trading-system-eu-ets_en

[12] https://climate.ec.europa.eu/eu-action/transport-emissions/reducing-emissions-shipping-sector_en

[13] https://www.imo.org/en/MediaCentre/PressBriefings/pages/ISWGHGMay2022.aspx

Just Transition

Recorded November 2022

Uwe Schulte

Today I will be talking to Shamini Harrington, Vice President Climate Change at Sasol and Presidential Climate Change Commissioner for South Africa. Please let me introduce our guest for today. Shamini joined Sasol 18 years ago. She held several positions in the line of sustainability and environment. She holds a Master of Science and Climate Change from the KwaZulu-Natal University. Welcome Shamini.

Shamini Harrington

Thank you, Uwe. Great to be here.

Uwe Schulte

Please tell us a bit about yourself and how sustainability has entered your life.

Shamini Harrington

That is quite a long story. It is strange how things work. You start doing a degree in a particular way and life draws you into something where you were meant to be. I started out focusing on medicine in the early years and did a filler in environmental science and sustainability, and just absolutely loved what we were trying to achieve and the impact that it was going to have on the world. Climate change and particularly climate change and sustainability, food security and energy security really became something that I held a whole lot of passion for, given the fact that this was an area that is very much needed in terms of South Africa and where we were going. That is how I got into this area. I then worked for an organisation called the Centre for Scientific and Industrial Research and really honed my skills on sustainability and climate change science and got taken up into Sasol and absolutely loved this company, what it stands for and the focus on safety, health, and environment at the time that morphed into a sustainability function that I have been part and parcel of growing in the company. So, very much part of the sustainability journey for the company.

Uwe Schulte
That is interesting that you say that you love the company. You should tell us a little bit about Sasol because I think quite a few of our listeners might have heard the name but are not aware of what you are up to.

Shamini Harrington
Sasol is an integrated energy and chemicals company. We are about 70 years old and one of the companies in South Africa that is the largest contributor to the GDP in the country. Also, we are a large employment provider. We provide about close on 28,000 jobs in the country. We operate in about 22 different countries. So, despite being a South African-born company, we are a global company operating across the world—in Europe, in the USA, in the Middle East. And we do an interesting process. We process coal and gas and run it through a process called Fischer-Tropsch,[1] which is a German process. It produces products like liquid fuels and various chemicals. The same thinking and unique chemistry are then replicated throughout the world in various other regions. Of course, not always using coal because that is most dominant in South Africa, but really using gas and other feedstocks globally. In South Africa, we produce liquid fuels primarily from one of our facilities, our Secunda facility. It is a 160,000-barrel-per-day facility, a huge facility. It is also a large producer of CO_2 and greenhouse gases because of the large amount of coal we use. We have another facility in South Africa, Sasolburg facility, where we produce a lot of chemicals. And in fact, many of our products are used as primary feedstocks into other chemical manufacturing downstream. So, very much integrated into the fabric of the South African economy, but very much a global player in terms of the products we produce (Fig. 1).

Uwe Schulte
I have to say that I have been to that plant in South Africa in my old life which is a long time ago. I took a little bit of objection to say it is funny that Fischer-Tropsch is German, me being a German chemist of course. We were leading the field in those days, but enough of German pride which is inappropriate anyway. Let us get back to the point. That means you are really a fossil fuel-based company and at the same

---

[1] https://pubs.acs.org/doi/10.1021/acscatal.2c03404

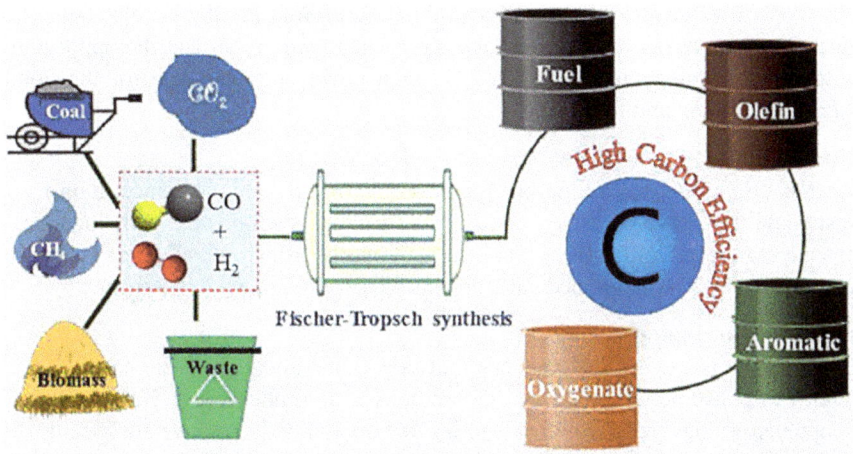

Fig. 1 Fischer–Tropsch synthesis—ACS Publications. Source: Reprinted with permission from ACS Catal. 2022, 12, 19, 12092–12112 Publication Date: September 21, 2022, https://doi.org/10.1021/acscatal.2c03404, Copyright © 2022 American Chemical Society

time you are supporting the Paris Agreement to achieve the global net zero greenhouse gas economy. How do these two things go together, I wonder?

Shamini Harrington
That is an interesting question. And if you spoke to us 10–15 years ago, some of what we are talking about today, we did not even think possible. We are a large consumer of coal; South Africa has a lot of coal. But the strange thing is, the same technology as Fischer-Tropsch can be used in a manner that produces sustainable fuels and chemicals very much needed in the low-carbon future. Our technology, the Fischer–Tropsch technology and gasification is agnostic to feedstock. If you change out the feedstock and supply this process with sustainable feedstocks like sustainable carbon, renewable energy, or green hydrogen, you have a process that can decarbonise other sectors, hard to abate sectors in the economy and continue creating value into the future. We ran through a very lengthy process, it took us about 5 years, where we evaluated all the options around where the world was going. The climate challenge is real. We see it, we are experiencing it. And we are a large producer of greenhouse gases. We must change that. We are very alive to that. In our evaluation process, we came to realise that if we get the right feedstocks we can contribute to our own decarbonisation, meet the net zero requirements, and continue contributing to an economy like South Africa that needs jobs, needs energy security, and needs continuous economic growth. These were the opportunities for us. Last year we came out with our future Sasol strategy, which really put forward a fossil fuel free vision, and put forward a view on a 30% reduction on greenhouse gases by 2030, and net zero emissions ambition by 2050. We are aiming to reduce emissions in scope 1 and 2. Then for net zero, we are also looking to have part of

our scope three emissions, our category 11 (Use of Sold Products),[2] also being net zero. It is an extremely ambitious ask given where we are at. But the opportunity with our technology really represents a huge pivot and transition for the South African economy and for Sasol.

Uwe Schulte
We must dive into this a little bit. We have a knowledgeable audience in terms of sustainability. Net zero, scope 1 and 2 is the stuff that is within your own boundaries of your own physical facilities. Scope 3 is of course from your suppliers and using your products. You mentioned category 11, please explain what that means.

Shamini Harrington
Category 11 is exactly the category that you spoke about. It is the category that relates to consumers purchasing our products and combusting it. Now, regarding Scope3 emissions there are 15 categories that are defined.[3] And we are specifically honing in on the largest, most significant category for our profile, and that is related to our consumers buying our liquid fuel products. And those products are petrol, diesel, paraffin, fuel gas, gas, coal. We want to be able through this process to demonstrate and through our strategy, our commitment for sustainability by saying, given our Fischer–Tropsch process we want to produce various sustainable products for the consumer. We want to produce sustainable products that do not have or have less emissions and are compatible with the low-carbon future; for example, sustainable aviation fuels. They are needed to decarbonise the transport sector, the aviation sector. We are looking at fuel cell batteries. We are looking at sustainable chemicals, green methanol, green ammonia. All these are very much possible if you have the right feedstock, if you have green hydrogen and you can push it through a Fischer–Tropsch process. And this is what we are looking to unlock. Scope 3 and category 11 demonstrate our commitment and our belief in the ability of this process to transform our product slate.

Uwe Schulte
I admire this ambition, I must say. But we recently talked with another company about their ambition and the uncertainties that are in the plan, of course. Some of these technologies have worked on small scale, but they need to be scaled-up. How do you deal with these uncertainties? This is important for many of our listeners because they are facing the same challenge. And I think what we should be looking for is having ambitious plans, but also pointing out to the public what the uncertainties are, so that this is not something that is just an ambition, but it is something real and the uncertainties are being addressed.

Shamini Harrington
That is an excellent question. And this is a challenge, like you said, all industries are facing. We have a significant percentage of the technologies required to

---

[2] https://ghgprotocol.org/sites/default/files/2022-12/Chapter11.pdf
[3] https://ghgprotocol.org/scope-3-calculation-guidance-2

achieve net zero not being mature today. You sit with, 'We must get to net zero, the climate science is clear on that. We must be able to limit temperatures to well below 2 degrees and pushing for efforts to 1.5 and more 1.5 given what the implications are at 2 degrees'. We sat back and we said that we can sit here, and we can just wait for the technology landscape to change, or we can be an active contributor to unlock the space. And this is what we are doing. What we need in this space is to firstly understand what the challenges are to transition, electrolyser costs, to be able to split water with renewable energy to get green hydrogen. How do we play in the space of looking at bringing down those costs? We need renewable energy at scale in a country where it is difficult to get renewable energy going right now. We are facing an energy security issue right now. There is a reliability issue. We are going through load shedding in the country. There is an opportunity here. How do we play in the space of activating the market? By saying that we need demand, that we want renewable energy of 600 megawatts. That stimulates the market, causes this catalytic reaction where then IPPs, Independent Power Producers, come to the market to supply that. That then has the effect of stimulating the market, getting the renewable players to start playing in this space and then regulatory approvals. We have been doing these things actively. We have also been looking at proof-of-concept projects. We are saying that we need to repurpose our facilities. We have electrolysers that can be repurposed already. We are doing that. We have got our first project to produce green hydrogen, 3.5 tonnes per day by end of 2023. We are not saying that we have got this all bedded down, and we know exactly what we are going to do, but we must start somewhere. We must start in the value chain, stimulating the ecosystem, putting proof-of-concept projects down, crowding-in capital, getting more investment, getting an ecosystem of partners going. That is so critically important. I am sure you have heard several industry players saying to you how important it is to have partners. We do not have all the answers, but someone has an answer to some of the problems we are facing. How do we put this together and unlock a value chain, a supply chain, a momentum that effects change in the country? That is what we are starting with. We are doing all those partnerships. SDG 17[4] is critically important, but how do you see it in practice? We want to see that happen. We have signed up several partners; we have proof-of-concept projects. We are rolling out renewable energy to make this happen, and we are seeing a need for policy incentives as well. You need this to stimulate new sectors, something as expensive as green hydrogen. I do want to spend a minute on this. The EU has been really a front runner. They put out the 'Fit for 55' policy package. And it has opportunities to unlock these expensive technology options today, and that is the challenge. You need policy to stimulate this, so you can get business to play a role. Recently we saw the U.S. government coming out with the 'Inflation Reduction Act'. Within it are several incentives that are pushing business to adopt low-carbon alternative energy sources and mechanisms, and to play in the space of saying, 'Here, we will help incentivise

---

[4] https://sdgs.un.org/goals/goal17

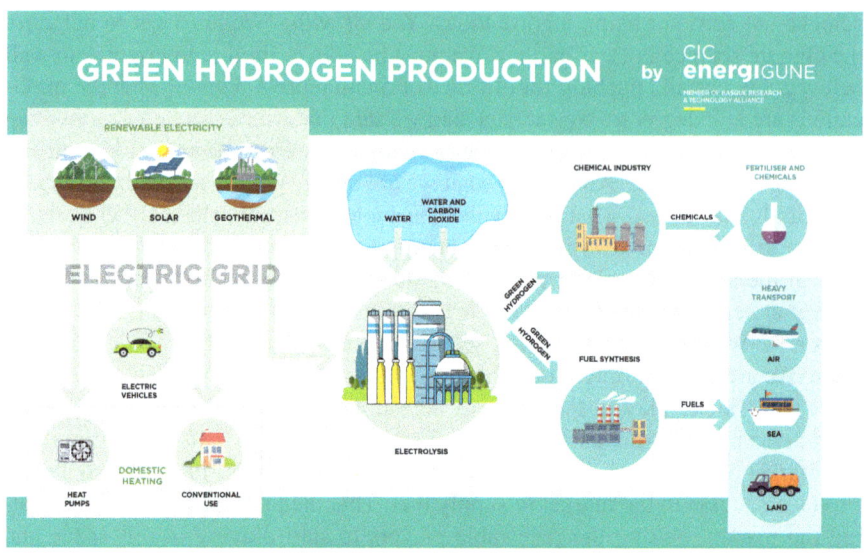

Fig. 2 Green hydrogen production. Source: CIC energiGUNE, https://cicenergigune.com/en/blog/electrolysis-water-sustainable-produce-green-hydrogen

very expensive technologies, but which are needed in a low-carbon future'. And we are looking to then play in these markets. Look at affordability, South Africa does not have it. Let us play in the spaces that do, and then stimulate the markets here and local demand. That is how we are playing a role. There are several risks in this space, regulatory approvals, it is uncertain. The grid in South Africa—how do we get that balanced and how do we get it strengthened? But again, these are not challenges we are only facing as a country, these are challenges that are being faced globally. Look at what is happening in the EU right now, energy prices, gas prices. How do we look at how we change these mechanisms? We need to start somewhere. That is the most important thing (Figs. 2 and 3).

Uwe Schulte

Our listeners recognise what you are saying, which are three important things, as far as I get it. One is that as a sustainability leader, you must put notice out there in the market that others are safe to invest, because you will uptake things that are required. The second one is that you cannot do this alone, you must build partnerships. Repeatedly, this has been mentioned in this podcast. And the third one is an especially key point you just made: policymakers must create conditions which enable businesses to go ahead and do the right thing. Thank you for pointing out how you are doing it. I read a little bit in your sustainability report, and you are looking at different scenarios as we all do. Your pessimistic one says that we are going to overshoot 1.5. It might not actually be the pessimistic, but the realistic one, unfortunately. And you are having an ambition to not overshoot, so that is great. But you also prepare for a potential future where we are reaching 2 to 3 degrees. What are you doing?

Fig. 3 UN Sustainable Development Goal 17. Source: https://www.un.org/sustainabledevelopment/. The content of this publication has not been approved by the United Nations and does not reflect the views of the United Nations or its officials or Member States

Shamini Harrington

That is just our scenario process.[5] What we are trying to do is be realistic and say that across all the scenarios we want to be robust. That is the important thing. You want to be able to plot all of it down and identify the no-regret opportunities. It does not matter whichever scenario is playing out. We need to still do things to change where we are today. And some of the no-regret opportunities that we have found from the scenarios that we have plotted are renewables. It is an easy decision; it must be done. It lays the foundation for all the other opportunities that we need to unlock in the space. Batteries, I spoke about green hydrogen, green steel. We are always going to need steel, but we need it to be greener than the process we have today. And these are the things that come with renewable energy, and this is what we are trying to identify. What we have done further is, we have taken that, and we have plotted scenarios related to our reduction to get to net zero. What are the levers that we can pull and what are the signposts that we need to monitor to pivot when something becomes viable? We have built these into our road maps and our decarbonisation flexibility. You do not want to lock yourself in and then suddenly you are locked into gas. But gas is not sustainable into the future and green hydrogen becomes cheaper, quicker than you thought. You want to be able to have flexibility (Fig. 4).

---

[5] https://www.sasol.com/sites/default/files/2022-11/SASOL_CC%20Report%202022%20%202_2.pdf

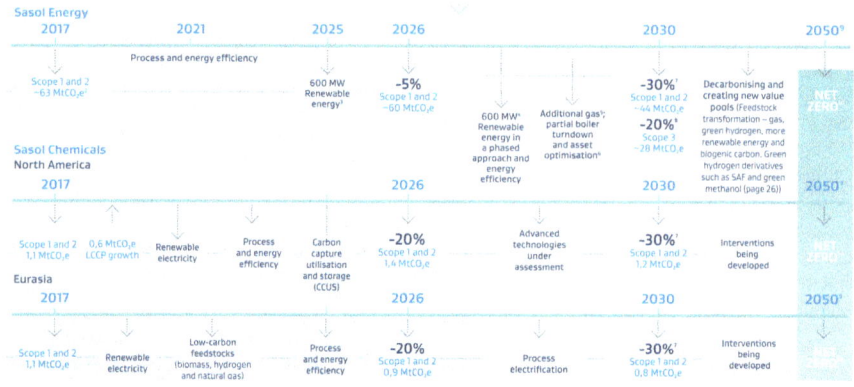

Fig. 4 Sasol GHG reduction roadmap. Source: Sasol—used with permission, https://www.sasol.com/sites/default/files/2022-11/SASOL_CC%20Report%202022%20%202_2.pdf

To give you an example what Sasol did: I told you about coal, we have coal in the country. We have little gas, but we see gas as a transition fuel in the interim to be able to watch and see the market and see what happens around green hydrogen. We do not want to now be spending copious amounts of money on pipeline infrastructure when we know we might not need that into the future, because green hydrogen costs are likely to come down. We are looking at our gas sources to introduce gas as a transition fuel. That is the kind of thinking. We need to be able to put all the information down and choose the pathway with the least resistance that gives you maximum flexibility to be able to pivot, and you need to know what you are monitoring in the market and that is what the scenarios have given us—a mechanism against which to do this. As a big company, you do not want to shock the company. You have people that you employ, you have shareholders to answer to. You have stakeholders, communities that depend on you, but at the same time you do not want to shock the economies where you operate. This is why we do what we do, and we are doing it in a very measured and orderly way, and we are monitoring all the right variables so that we can make the right decisions at the right time.

Uwe Schulte

I might be too much of a chemist now, so I am worried to ask the question. I will ask it anyway. I get it that you say we need renewable energy, and it is a lot of solar where you are, but there will be some wind as well and that will then drive the electrolysis of water so that you can create hydrogen. You are runing Fischer-Tropsch now using coal. You take carbon and out of the carbon you make a carbon chain. You want to create a carbon chain where you do not dig coal out of the ground. Where is your carbon coming from?

Shamini Harrington

We have a lot of CO_2 ourselves. We want to be able to recycle, but we know that that has some time frames on it. We cannot use a fossil fuel carbon source for too long, but we can certainly use it in the interim. The EU 'Fit for 55' clearly recognises this up to

2035, and potentially in a developing country, there might be opportunity to use it for longer. We are also looking at other industrial carbon streams. For example, I mentioned iron and steel. They are not going to be able to decarbonise quick and fast, given heat. Green hydrogen is the mechanism against which to do that. That is a hard to evade sector, but they have CO_2, they have carbon. We can use that and cannibalise that within our process and still have a benefit to the overall inventory for the country. We can do the same for cement. We can do the same for the electricity sector. These are opportunities. And of course, the other one is biomass or biogenic sources of carbon. We are looking at that. And into the future there is obviously the CCUS (Carbon Capture Use and Storage)[6] type opportunity. Direct air capture is an opportunity for us, to be able to do that. But there are obviously challenges. That is a technology that is far into the future. The likelihood of it really being used to the maximum is not fully understood right now. But all these other options are being used and trying to be cultivated and nurtured to be able to do that in our process.

Uwe Schulte

Let me repeat what I heard you say. For your process to work, you need CO_2 and now what you would do is re-use all the CO_2 that is released into the atmosphere now still coming from fossil sources, and therefore giving it a second life span. And you could then re-use that again, so that already is a huge benefit because per production unit or per calorie provided in warmth you produce a lot less CO_2, but that is not for the long run. You then need sources of CO_2 like bio-based CO_2 sources that can help you still run the process, rather than it is coming directly from coal. That makes the next point interesting. Your business in South Africa, for example, but not only there, depends on coal mining and then the production around it. And I have seen the formidable and the huge facilities you have with many people employed. How do we do the change that is required without worsening human rights and increasing already existing inequalities? It is called 'Just Transition'.[7] Can you tell us what the concept entails.

Shamini Harrington

Yes, no problem. That is such a critical issue. It is surfacing now within the negotiations. It is part of the Paris Agreement. And what that means in South Africa's case or Sasol's case is that we cannot exacerbate the issues that are currently faced in the country through the transition and decarbonisation that we are undergoing. We have to make sure that whatever we do, we do it in a measured and orderly way, that as we are transitioning and moving out of the facilities that we know today, we are cultivating and growing sectors where people that are impacted, communities that are impacted can be redeployed, reskilled, upskilled into these new areas of work.

The economy is struggling. We have the highest levels of poverty now, of unemployment. We are one of the highest in the Gini-coefficient[8] and the Gini-coefficient

---

[6] https://www.iea.org/energy-system/carbon-capture-utilisation-and-storage

[7] https://climatepromise.undp.org/news-and-stories/what-just-transition-and-why-it-important

[8] https://en.wikipedia.org/wiki/Gini_coefficient

demonstrating that unequalness of our society. It is an absolute imperative that whatever we do, we need to do it in a careful way. To give you another example of what we are doing: regarding our 30% reduction on our greenhouse gas emissions by 2030 on scope 1 and 2, we are looking to pull levers that do not have an impact on the social dimensions that I was speaking about. We are looking at a cutback on 25% of coal and we are looking to keep the job implications at the lowest levels possible. And in fact, we do not have an impact in that period. Many stakeholders have asked us, why we do not move quicker and faster with reducing our emissions. But if we do, we are going to have those impacts.

It is critically important that we do this in a way that creates opportunities and harnesses opportunities rather than exacerbating the risks and the challenges we face in the country. That is what we are doing. We are bringing in a small amount of gas without impacting. But post 2030, we will see implications as we reduce our coal consumption more heavily. But at the same time, we have these proof-of-concept projects, we have got the ones repurposing our current assets to start using green hydrogen, produce green ammonia, green methanol. We also have green hydrogen Greenfield studies in the Northern Cape. We have opportunities around renewable energy I was speaking about. What does that mean for manufacturing hubs? And we are playing in this space, trying to understand as the fossil fuel sectors are getting pulled back what are growing sectors, low-carbon sectors, more sustainable sectors that create jobs and socioeconomic development for the country. And that is what we are trying to do. You need to make sure that there is a balance, there is order and that we are not causing further issues to how we transition.

Uwe Schulte
That is a formidable approach that has several challenges built in, of course, and uncertainties as well. Before we do so, let me ask the following. What are the main aspects of 'Just Transition'? I get it that you are talking about employment. Are there others? We should look beyond Africa because this is an issue that arises everywhere, does it not?

Shamini Harrington
Correct. And it would be specific to the national circumstances within which the countries are transitioning. Germany is going through the same thing. Many of the states in the USA are also going through the same thing. You must make sure that the supply chains, that the communities that are dependent on fossil fuel activities, activities that are no longer going to take place as you transition, have other sustainable forms of livelihoods, that the economies can thrive. If you look at what is going on in the Middle East, economies are built on the oil industry. What does that mean in terms of how you deal with that transition as the world moves away from oil? It is beyond just one area. But it really has different implications, and some can be more pronounced than others, particularly if you do not have the resources, or the capacity, or the technology to deal with the change and the pace of the change. Those are real determinants for how it is going to vary within the countries where you operate, or the regions where you operate.

Uwe Schulte

Let us now dive a little bit deeper into 'Just Transition'. You have developed several principles for 'Just Transition'. Could you explain what they are, and you have a couple of examples?

Shamini Harrington

'Just Transition' is something new in terms of every country and every company. In different places it will be different in how you think about the 'Just Transition', what the nuances are, what the impacts are. But what it really means is that you need to inform or encompass a few key principles. I would like to say that these are our principles, that we have really made it our own, but it really is adapted from existing literature around what a 'Just Transition' should entail, and from engagements with communities where we operate.[9,10] Some of the key things that really underpin our 'Just Transition' is inclusivity. I cannot emphasise that one enough. It really focuses on making sure that we are engaging through the process right from the get-go in trying to understand stakeholder needs and wants. No one wants to be told how to live their lives, or where to live for that matter, what their livelihoods would be. People should be empowered to be the owners of the transition, and what they are going through and really refocusing on that. We are trying to bring into the discussion stakeholder wants and needs right from the get-go. Another key one is that the 'Just Transition' is not divorced from the national 'Just Transition'. Ours certainly is not. In the South African context, it needs to be done in tandem with how different companies are operating and moving towards a low-carbon future. In this way, you can get economies of scale. One of the key things we are looking at is ensuring alignment with national approaches and national policies. Another key one we are looking at is of course, alignment to future Sasol. We are looking at skills development in alignment with green hydrogen, renewable energy, because those are key components of our future Sasol strategy. When we think about rescaling, redeployment, it is obviously with the bias to how we are looking at future Sasol. And of course, some of the other ones is to prioritise impacted communities, stakeholders, employees. That is our key priority, but that is not to exclude anyone else. We want to really stop there, because you must take this in small bites, nice chunks. Otherwise, you are not going to be able to give the attention where the attention is required. And then of course, a key one that we are looking at is partnerships.

I mentioned a little bit about the policy alignment, national government, other companies, but what we really want is to get economies of scale. And to be able to scale that, we need more people to be part of an ecosystem of change. If you are looking at agricultural projects to absorb jobs, or to create new opportunities, you want to get more parties involved. We have partnered with various people to be able to achieve this. One of the key platforms is 'Impact Catalyst'[11] with other companies

---

[9] https://pccommissionflow.imgix.net/uploads/images/A-Just-Transition-Framework-for-South-Africa-2022.pdf

[10] https://www.iej.org.za/wp-content/uploads/2022/08/IEJ-JustTransition-PP-Aug2022.pdf

[11] https://www.impactcatalyst.co.za/

in South Africa. But we can talk a little bit more about that. That is briefly, some of the key principles we are focusing on.

Uwe Schulte
And that is something that we should explore in a second. But I would like to understand a little bit better the elements that you are actively pursuing now. You talked about capability building. What I understand is, someone in your remit, one of your employees or even a supplier were very much engaged in a process based on coal. And what you are now saying is we want to go to various sources of carbon, and we want renewable sources of carbon and renewable energy which requires a different skill set. I do not know whether it needs more jobs, less jobs. How do you in practice approach that?

Shamini Harrington
For us, it starts with looking at existing initiatives. For example, we have bursary schemes, we have one of the largest bursary schemes in Southern Africa.[12,13] And what we are looking to do is redirect that to these new areas that are contained within future Sasol. Green hydrogen—what skill sets would be required there? How do you tailor the university programmes, the team, their colleges, which are the technical colleges, to these new skills and these new requirements? A key component of green hydrogen is renewables. But let us think about construction type jobs to put the renewable farms up. But also, how to assemble these things in the country? How do you ensure that you set up these plants in the country? A lot of the supply chains do not exist in Africa or South Africa for that matter. It exists elsewhere in the world. These opportunities, bringing that here.

We are also looking at entrepreneurship. How do you look at the programmes we have today, which we do, focused on entrepreneurship in farming to see if that can become a new opportunity area for the areas where we operate? How do we train people that used to be in mining into farming, farming for food security. Could we, from an angle where we are operating today which is coal-based, become the new food capital that supplies food globally? These are challenges that we are trying to address through opportunities. Climate change presents both opportunities and risks. As seasons are changing, as weather patterns are changing, certain areas that were not farming activities are becoming. How do you use that knowledge to then look at the 'Just Transition' in a better way? That is what we are talking about. It is not always directly in alignment with future Sasol, but certainly also in alignment with the strategies that the government is putting in place, as well as what the local communities are saying can be done.

Uwe Schulte
I understand that. That requires of course, additional investment in people from your side. How can you convince your CFO that this is something that needs doing?

---

[12] https://allbursaries.co.za/

[13] https://www.sasolbursaries.com/welcome/

Shamini Harrington

It is not necessarily about convincing the CFO. This is a commitment that the company has put in place. It is part of future Sasol. There is a little bit of a nuance in terms of how we operate in certain countries. I might have mentioned this already. For corporates, in a lot of developing countries, it is about the social licence to operate, not that it is not important anyway, but in South Africa particularly, our corporate reach extends beyond just getting shareholder returns. It is also about service delivery, about maintaining the areas we operate, looking at infrastructure development, because you need to partner with the public and private sector to be able to come together to grow the economy. These are things that we already must build in in terms of how we think about our future world and our future operations. The 'Just Transition' is very clearly not supposed to exacerbate the issues we face in South Africa. And South Africa faces very pronounced issues around poverty and unemployment. It is incumbent, it is also our responsibility how we are going to operate in the future to think broadly about people, planet, and profit. This is really underscored in all the future Sasol strategy. It is how we think about things. We have even chosen opportunities around decarbonisation that were not as profitable, because it had a strong people's element to it. And that is what we must do in terms of where we operate. It requires us to do so.

Uwe Schulte

Are you going to use certain performance indicators to measure whether these efforts you are making are fruitful?

Shamini Harrington

Yes, that is a key component of our 'Just Transition'. We disclosed about it this year in our Climate Change Report 2022, where we clearly indicated that we would have this entire process needing to be driven by data, number one, and then number 2 performance and tracking, which would have to be defined through KPIs. How many jobs you create, what are the opportunities, how many people have been skilled. In fact, Sasol has been tracking a number of these metrics already. It is part of our people focus within broadly the company and how we operate on sustainability. It is now about thinking about the metrics that make sense for future Sasol and make sense to track our progress around the 'Just Transition'. Are we there yet in terms of defining these? No, not yet. We are at the phase of still developing the road map and then we will put in place some of the key metrics we want to track.

Uwe Schulte

It is important, of course. Only what you measure you can improve. That is obviously an underlying principle you apply. And I completely get it that you cannot do this on your own. This is a changing environment, certainly emphasis is on hugely different businesses. You already started talking about the partnerships that you are aiming for, and you call them partnerships for impact which I find positive, because that is what it is about. It is about impact. Can you explain how you approach that? How do you convince others to join in?

Shamini Harrington

The key thing is transparency and communication. We are in constant discussions with our supply chain partners and with other industry in South Africa. You will notice that 'The Impact Catalyst' has other members like Exxaro and Anglo. They are the founding members. And every one of these companies is also undergoing a 'Just Transition' in one shape, way, form, or the other. That is happening. We have a common goal. I must say, in South Africa's transition and putting forward to target for COP 26 last year, business came together in a way that probably we have not seen before with this very clear support for the new NDC (Nationally Determined Contributions),[14,15] which made the discussions about how we are going to transition, where the opportunities for scale and pace to be achieved, a little bit easier to get going. Sasol took on the role last year already where our CEO made our announcements around 'Future Sasol'.[16] We said we want to be an energy champion and through that we pulled together something called the 'Energy Council',[17] which now has a wide membership base across the different companies, some big in matters, some mining companies, some smaller focus low-carbon technology providers, which offers a platform for us to have those conversations about where we can come together for scale to be achieved. It is progressing well, and we are providing a lot of views around where that can happen. And the Homeland has been prioritised, so a lot of focus is going there, and the partnerships are focusing there. But just in terms of our internal process, we have put in place a partnership framework and we have various criteria that we are looking to ensure we meet, around who we partner with, why we partner with them, and what we want to achieve from the partnership. There is a 'Just Transition' lens to all these things, and we evaluate these partnerships very vigorously with this framework being used as the basis.

Uwe Schulte

One of the issues that a lot of people are not realising is that it is easy to paint the picture when everything is lovely, and one day we will be fully in renewable energies, and cost will come down once we have done that. But in the meantime, costs will go up and that is something that a lot of people currently are struggling with. And then we have crises going on at the same time, at least in parts of the world and that exploding inflation is not helping. I can visualise that you have a good case for partnerships, but then I see some companies having an automatic reaction saying, 'But now is not the time. I must deal with the crisis'. Is that something that you are facing?

---

[14] https://unfccc.int/process-and-meetings/the-paris-agreement/nationally-determined-contributions-ndcs

[15] https://unfccc.int/sites/default/files/NDC/2022-06/South%20Africa%20updated%20first%20NDC%20September%202021.pdf

[16] https://www.youtube.com/watch?v=BFGEwx6iLzQ

[17] https://society.sasol.com/sasol-and-key-energy-stakeholders-establish-the-energy-council-of-south-africa/

Shamini Harrington

COVID has taught us that there are opportunities in crises. And what we are seeing is very clearly an awareness of the long term. A lot of what we are facing right now—energy prices going up, inflation you spoke about—it is short term. We must not lose sight of the long-term goal. Many companies are on that page. Why? They are doing themselves scenario analysis of how things are changing. We are feeling the impacts of climate change today. I am not saying in the case of how we have been operating that many of the companies we are engaging with and who we have partnered with are still very much on the course to see change in the long term. There might be challenges around how capital is allocated in the short term where priorities might have changed, but the long-term partnerships remain, and they still focus on the key opportunities in the space. And costs come down on your partner. Each one brings something else to the partnership. We are not trying to do everything; we do not claim to be experts in absolutely everything. But if you bring more partners together, you will then look at the value chain differently. You are not trying to achieve everything in one goal, and you can then compartmentalise and say, 'This is what I can deliver now, with a view in 2- or 3-years' time coming with more'. But at least it keeps the partnership going, it keeps the projects on the go, it allows business cases to be developed. And this is what many corporates are seeing. The benefit of partnerships really does reduce costs as well as then allows you to spread risk.

Uwe Schulte

That is encouraging. When I introduced you, I mentioned that you are the Commissioner for the Government on 'Just Transition' as well. What do you tell the South African President, what needs doing?

Shamini Harrington

That is an interesting question, Uwe. I should give some context before I answer that question. I am *one* of the commissioners in South Africa. We have a setup which is called the Presidential Climate Commission.[18] It was set up by the President. It is going to be enacted formally in terms of a climate change bill that is currently going through Parliament, and the Presidential Climate Commission is within that bill going to be formalised as part of the government of South Africa. Right now, we have about 20, give or take, commissioners[19] that have been appointed across various constituencies within the country. I form part of the business constituency, but there are NGOs, there is government, there are some ministers that are set as commissioners. And the idea is to bring different perspectives and diverse views around the table to find and forge a way forward around a complex, difficult challenge. Climate change being really at the centre of that because it really talks to economies, the fabric of how we are going to operate going forward as business, as well as what the policy landscape is going to look like. So, it really allows us to have those tough conversations in a safe environment, and really to find a way that we can

---

[18] https://www.climatecommission.org.za/

[19] https://www.climatecommission.org.za/commissioners

build a social compact. That is what we are aiming to do. And this has been innovative in my view because few developing countries have done this. But the President is leading us, we have a co-chair that he has delegated, and we have the President coming in quite regularly into our meetings to provide steer. If I were speaking to him directly, one of the key things that I would put forward is that we need to start accelerating the opportunities we see. And we need to now unlock the blockages we see. Policy is so critically important to be able to get renewable energy off the ground, which is so important to unlock further opportunities. I would ask to rush with urgency to uplift those. Look at how we look at the IRP (International Resource Panel)[20] ensuring that we get as many renewables on the ground as fast as possible. There is also an urgent issue we are facing as South Africans which is energy security. We do not have power 24/7. We have loadshedding, what we call it. We cut the load during peak periods so that the grid is still stable. We are facing this every day. We must cook during certain periods. You do not have access to power and a lot of people are going off the grid, which is not helpful in a situation where you need people on the grid. I would say, 'Look to unlock the urgencies right now to get the policy going, to crowd in finance to get private sector and public sector to move with urgency around renewable energy. And in doing that you can also start working towards the long-term vision of net zero by 2050'.

Uwe Schulte
When we look at that, that is the specific South African situation. And there are lots of challenges there and we did not even touch on water which is another big issue as we all know. Let us step back a little bit. Does what you just said also apply for the other countries in Africa, and does it also apply for Europe or the USA, for example?

Shamini Harrington
The energy security issue is a global one we are facing right now. I was in Europe just a few weeks ago and I was told that also there is likely to be blackout, during winter particularly, which is not something that most Europeans are used to at all. I do think this is something we are facing with the high energy prices. There is a need to look for opportunities. We should not just see this as risk. There are opportunities here to move to low-carbon solutions. Renewables should be deployed faster. But I would also say that one of the key things we must be aware of is exactly what I said regarding partnerships. Short-term needs and national security needs must still have a long-term view in how we think about it. The North Star on what we are trying to deal with should not change because there are blips that we are seeing. We need to address the immediate whilst recognising that we should not lose sight of the future in the long term. In terms of South Africa, in terms of Africa, there is a real need for support. And because of what is going on globally, there are challenges around that support being forthcoming. We need to still be real with the fact that if Europe and the other developed countries are facing energy security needs, this is also going to

---
[20] https://www.resourcepanel.org/

be very pronounced in developing countries. We need to be aware of the support that is still required and should still be forthcoming. We should not forego those for the short-term needs to be met. We should be thinking about long term, medium term, and how we are going to achieve this together, because collectively this can be done. Each one of us needs the other and that is so pronouncing, and it came through during Covid. We all are a global community, and we need to recognise that if one fails, all fail in what we are trying to achieve.

Uwe Schulte
I am wondering, in South Africa you are very much focused on coal. If I look at Nigeria, for example, very much focused on oil, but they will have to go through a similar process and that is even more aggravated than it is in South Africa.

Shamini Harrington
All the African countries are also going through similar issues, different energy sources, different dynamics, playing out of national circumstances. But it just speaks to the special needs of Africa. We are as a continent highly vulnerable to climate change. We do not have the resources to adapt to these quick and fast, or to respond in a quick way, and we have limited resources to transition. Some of the key discussions with stakeholders are around how we use the resources we have while still meeting the climate change ambitions, whilst ensuring that support is forthcoming. These are the key things that are being discussed and you are quite right—all these countries that we are speaking about need support and there are also going to be 'Just Transition' implications pronounced that need to be addressed with urgency. When we think about COP 28 this year, we should be thinking about financing the special needs of Africa. We should be thinking about how we ensure a 'Just Transition' and what kind of multilateral relationships or arrangements are needed to support this. Do we replicate the JET process, which is the 'Just Energy Transition Partnership'[21] process? Something that has been put forward for South Africa but is now being replicated. How do we do this at scale to support other countries in need?

Uwe Schulte
Thank you so much for sharing these things. Time flies and before we wrap up, I would like to hear from you personally how optimistic you are that we at least achieve two degrees?

Shamini Harrington
Where we are at, obviously there are days where I am despondent about what we are seeing, especially when we have the weather impacts hitting us so hard. But there are other days where you see the partnerships and you see the effort that is being put by governments as well as private sector that I am optimistic and I do believe that it is going to require more of us coming together, speaking, talking about the difficult things to unlock this phase. Am I hopeful? We must be, we really must be. Otherwise,

---

[21] https://ec.europa.eu/commission/presscorner/detail/cs/ip_21_5768

we are going to really feel the wrath of what it means to have climate change hit us with weather events impacting us. The ability to then adapt is going to be exceedingly difficult. I am very hopeful. I do think it is going to take us a long time to be able to unlock the technologies needed, to see that massive step change and realisation of what the Paris Agreement is asking for. And it needs every one of us to really say, 'What is my fair share and how do I play a role in this'? We are seeing more of this, just not fast enough.

Uwe Schulte
And if you could give a piece of advice to other companies around the world, from what you learned about your interaction on 'Just Transition', what should they be focusing on?

Shamini Harrington
From a decarbonisation perspective, as well as the 'Just Transition' perspective: know your operations. Really go out there and understand your emissions. There are so many companies that really have not even developed inventories. It is so critically important that we need to know what our impact is to be able to set KPIs, to be able to set targets, to understand where the opportunities are. You are never going to understand the opportunity landscape until you know what the impacts and the risks are. That is so critically important. And that is the first step. And then trying to think about what your role is in the bigger scheme of the area where you operate, what that impact is, what your sphere of influences is, and how you work with the governments where you impact and broadly in the global communities. It starts with the first step: know your operations. And know what you are emitting and what your targets are going to be, to be able to then extend it beyond.

Uwe Schulte
And expose that to a couple of scenarios that are facing you in the future, I guess.

Shamini Harrington
100%, that is a key component. You start with your understanding first, and then you start looking at strategy. You start looking at governance, you start mainstreaming these issues. Some companies will have small emissions but huge opportunity for change in terms of facilitating the change for other sectors. But you need to start with yourself first and then expand that into scenarios and strategy and governance.

Uwe Schulte
Excellent. Thank you so much Shamini, for providing the background on the sustainability road map of Sasol and the challenges of 'Just Transition' and giving advice on how to go forward and giving us an optimistic perspective. Thank you so much.

Shamini Harrington
Thank you, Uwe. Thank you for having me.

Epilogue: Net Positive

A Book Conversation Recorded December 2021

Uwe Schulte

Hello, I am Uwe Schulte, the Leader of 'The Conference Board Global Sustainability Centre' and it is my pleasure to welcome you to 'Off the Shelf', a book discussion series brought to you by 'The Conference Board'. Today I will be speaking with Andrew Winston about the book he co-authored with Paul Polman: 'Net Positive—How Courageous Companies Thrive by Giving More Than They Take' (Paul Polman, 2021). Andrew is a writer, speaker, and consultant on corporate strategy. His work focuses on megatrends and how to build companies that serve many stakeholders, not just shareholders. Andrew has written hundreds of articles for the 'Harvard Business Review', 'MIT Sloan Management Review', and other outlets. His perspective on business is rooted in his earlier career, with experience in consulting at 'Boston Consulting Group' and media like 'Time Inc.', 'Viacom', and dotcoms. Andrew holds a master on environmental management from Yale. Welcome, Andrew.

Andrew Winston

Glad to be here. Thank you so much for having me.

Uwe Schulte

Andrew, business books often have clickbait type of long-winded titles and Paul Polman and you have been very succinct: 'Net Positive'. Your subtitle then explains what you mean by that?

Andrew Winston

Somewhat, yes. You are right, in book titles it is hard to get everything in there and 'Net Positive' is not as simple an idea probably as it sounds, but we tried to find some language that was simple, but the subtitle is about being courageous. It says how courageous companies thrive by giving more than they take, and that gives you a hint as to what we mean by a net positive business, one that is fundamentally creating a positive impact on society. And we have a couple of different ways of describing that; it means a company that makes money by solving the world's problems, not causing them, and by improving the well-being of everybody that they touch (And that includes a full range of stakeholders which we can discuss further). And at every scale, every product and service, every interaction with the community, every factory, every country you operate in, and so on—this is the North Star. This is something that I do not think any company could claim to have reached yet, but we hope we have laid out what it looks like or how to build a company that really is heading down this path (Fig. 1).

Uwe Schulte

Before we get into the substance of your book, you must satisfy my curiosity a little bit. It must have been an interesting experience to co-author with a well-known businessperson like Paul Polman. How actually did the two of you decide to embark on this project together?

Andrew Winston

It was interesting. I have written two books alone and co-authored two books, and co-authoring is much more difficult. It is exponentially more difficult because you

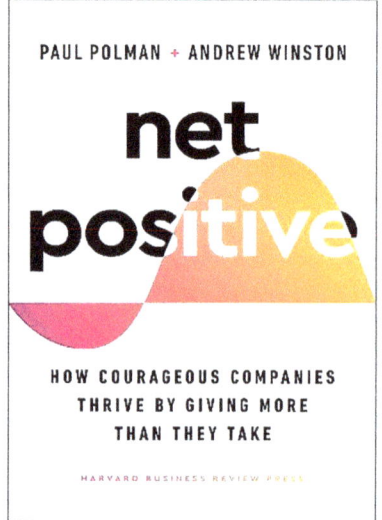

Fig. 1 Polman/Winston, Net Positive. Source: Paul Polman, Andrew Winston, https://netpositive.world/book/

have different voices. Someone must lay pen to paper philosophically and start the process. We started working together a little over two years ago now. Paul approached me during climate week in New York and said that he had been asked about authoring a book many times over the years and had never really had a strong desire to do it. He fears—and he talks about this in the preface—that CEOs just try to rewrite history and that his work had spoken for itself. But enough publishers, including the publisher of Harvard Business Press, had said to him, 'You should get your story out there. You are trying to create change; you need more people to hear it'. And then he decided he needed a writing partner and someone who knew what they were talking about. That is how we got together. And he could have found a ghost writer. There are plenty of people who could write. But what I brought was having written books in this space and collaborating with companies for 20 years, so some sense of strategy and structure and synthesis of what is going on in the world. And I could really listen to him and talk about Unilever but also bring in other examples and other stories from him and from me.

About half the book ends up being really about Unilever and half is others. But the framework was developed by Paul and I sitting down for a two-hour conversation every week for a year. We did around 50 of them. It was a lot of time. Then a lot of back and forth on actual writing once we started putting it down on paper. It was a fascinating process for me. I learned a lot about Unilever, even though I had collaborated with them and already knew them well. I also learned a lot about his thinking. As a CEO, how do you think about these issues when you are running a €50 billion revenue business across 180 countries? And it was fascinating because for all the speeches and talks that Paul has given for years, he had not really been able to sit down and say, 'What were the eight or nine things that need to be in place to do the things I did'? That is in part because he is a great leader and was a great CEO. So, he just knew what the answer was often, where he had a gut feeling about what he thought was the right thing to do. And that is different than writing that down. Getting it down was a tough, fascinating process. I had an enjoyable time, but it was hard. It was the hardest thing I have ever done workwise, to take a systems-thinking approach, a circular approach, and make it make sense in a book. All the things we want business to be is the way he thinks and the way I try to think. But to try to make that a linear story is difficult.

Uwe Schulte
If you want my pennies worth, that was worth the effort. Having read it, I would say it is a nice constructive collaboration about the wealth of things you have seen and the very concrete activities that Paul had done. That is coming together very nicely.

Andrew Winston
Thank you, I appreciate that. That is the goal.

Uwe Schulte
Let me try to see whether I got it. Let me feedback to you some of the things I hear you both say and then see whether that makes any sense to you. First, companies must understand the impact on all stakeholders. Then companies must thrive to make a positive contribution to society with a suitable business model. They need to

be open, honest, and transparent about what they do, and that is quite a key thing, I think. And something that a lot of people have not realised as much and you are making that point very well, is companies' boundaries need to be open for collaboration as no one company can achieve all this necessary positive impact on their own. Have I got some of your key messages, right?

Andrew Winston
You downplay your understanding of this space, to ask whether you got it. I am sure you did. Yes, those are a lot of the main ideas. You started with a version of what we say is the first principle which is ownership, taking responsibility. 'Responsibility' has been used in many ways, corporate or social responsibility, so I prefer the word ownership. We talk about the old line 'if you break it, you own it'. Taking ownership of impacts on all stakeholders along the whole value chain, and really taking a much broader view of what those impacts are. We have seen real progress on that. In recent years, as companies start to talk about their Scope 3 carbon emissions, and thinking about suppliers and customers, which is a big extension from previous views of the world, which were, 'If we are in compliance with the law, we are fine'. But there are broader impacts, especially for multinationals, but really any company, even SMEs that affect the communities that they are in, and the lives of the people they work with. It is an extended view of the role of a company in society. The last thing you mentioned was collaboration, and that you need to collaborate to solve these larger systemic problems. You captured that the core need for honest and transparency is certainly a big topic throughout the book and that gets you buy-in to start into these partnerships. The core of the book really is building to these partnerships within your supply chain with suppliers, with peers, and then these bigger systemic ones where you need civil society and NGOs that know what they are doing and are critical but have knowledge. You need the business community and government, to work together to solve big problems for all, not just see companies pursue narrow aims like asking for a tax break. They need to step back and say, 'How do we solve these shared problems and make business across our entire sector, work better and work more in service of the world'? Those are the key messages. There is a lot of nuances and, as you said, courage. Part of it must be at core about leaders who are willing to take some risks and put themselves out there.

Uwe Schulte
There are a lot of people who are willing to take risks, but they must be in the context here. Let us get a grip on that aspect of yours. Can you give an example how sustainability can create business opportunities? We had the old way of looking at things: 'risk, risk, risk and avoid risk to reputation', but we have now seen companies that really have grasped the opportunity.

Andrew Winston
In some sense, I will step back to my first book, 'Green to Gold' (Andrew Winston, 2009). We had a simple two-by-two that said that there are four big buckets of value creation and business just in general, aside from sustainability. You are reducing costs and slashing risk—that is, trying to control the

downsides—or you are building the upside (which people find more exciting), driving revenues through innovation, and building hard-to-measure brand value. That intangible value is now most of the market value of companies, this hard-to-measure thing of employee loyalty or attraction of talent, customer loyalty, licence to operate, etc. These are the main buckets of value creation. We are still frankly making that business case in business far more than I thought we would still be doing when I got into this 20 years ago. I still get asked a lot about, 'Well, doesn't sustainability always cost more'? I find that an increasingly strange assumption. It is like asking, 'Does marketing, or does R&D always cost more'? Things take investment. Some things pay off very quickly and some things do not, but we make investments. There are many examples. The easy stuff is obviously cutting energy, cutting waste, and just saving a bunch of money. When you get into a larger view of purpose-driven products and brands and trying to be net positive, then you get into deeper engagements. There are many stories in the book. To give one example: one of the longest standing brand and purpose plays that Unilever is undertaking is their Lifebuoy soap brand which is big in India and South America. It is a soap brand they have had since founding in the 1870s. It was quite stagnant as a product, but they started a campaign under the brand, not as a cause-related marketing, but just as the brands' marketing, to teach kids health and hygiene around the world. If you tutor kids and new parents to wash their hands more, you will save millions of lives because they are dying of diseases that are easily avoidable. And that brand has made this mission the way they approached the world. The brand started growing fast in the decade that Paul was there as CEO, and it became a billion-euro brand. It is a win–win which some people do not like to say, but it is something that shows that you can grow through values. It can sound like philanthropy to go teach kids hand washing but if it is deeply embedded in what the product is about then it is part of the business. The people working on that brand know that they are not just selling more soap, they are trying to solve hygiene issues. And that led to innovation. Since there is not enough water in many places, and kids cannot always focus for 30 seconds on handwashing, they developed a version of Lifebuoy that could kill germs in 10 seconds. And the product would change colours, so the kids knew when they had done enough washing. Things like that have created interesting innovation opportunities. That is one of my favourite stories because it is partly well-known and partly not as much in terms of how much it helped grow the business. Sometimes companies are afraid to say, 'This was good for the business'. That is something Paul is extremely comfortable with, and Unilever has been growing increasingly comfortable with to say, 'We can sell more of this thing that we find to be helpful to the world'. And that is fine. It is a good thing. It is what we need (Fig. 2).

Uwe Schulte
In a funny way, if something must be sustainable, it must be sustainable. It is as easy as that. If you build a business on philanthropy, that is not sustainable. If you have some spare cash, fine. But what happens if you run out of cash? You must generate things that make sense and make business sense.

Fig. 2 Lifebuoy soap brand. Source: Reproduced with kind permission of Unilever PLC and group companies

Andrew Winston

True, but there have always been loss leaders; companies do that because it is strategic. You could do that for many reasons. It could be to get into new markets, it could be for sustainability reasons. They have products like water purifying products, like P&G and others have, and some of those are not meant to make a lot of money. They want them to break even, but they are part of a suite of things to improve water quality because so many of their products rely on water. If you want an area and people to have enough clean water to do things like use your shampoos and soaps, you are justified in trying to help purify water at cost or some small loss. You must take a complete, systemic view like any company would. Some things they do take a loss on, or some things they just spend a lot on marketing, because it is part of the brand, it is part of pushing the product. But yes, eventually a company must make money, or it does not exist. And that is okay. A more philosophical debate that I get into later at night is, 'How much profit'? I do not think we go into that too much in the book. We talk about growth and consumption and the big challenges in the world. But I constantly think about that the problem we are in is that companies believe they are supposed to maximise profit in the short run, no matter what. And that is what is killing us. We must rethink what we mean by profit and ask, at least in the short run, 'Is maximising really the best path'? Some of it may be worth investing in a brighter future for all. I could sound anti-business, but I am a business guy, I have my MBA, I have my check mark on my business passport. I think I can say it.

Uwe Schulte

What you have done, and you have done it before and you have done it in this book, is make people more comfortable in saying that if you run a business and you make profit, and that is done through sustainable products or sustainable services, there is nothing wrong with it. Some people have the view that if you do not make huge losses there, then it cannot be sustainable.

Andrew Winston

Right, exactly.

Uwe Schulte

And that is nonsense on both sides. There are these conservative businesspeople who believe that and then do nothing. And there are the NGOs who believe if people are making profit and it is sustainable then it must be a fraud.

Andrew Winston

That is right. You worked in big companies, Uwe, I am sure you have seen this where someone will say, 'Well, we do that energy efficiency stuff'. Of course, we do that, that is good business. And they do not count that as sustainability anymore. Once it becomes clearly profitable then, in their mind, that is not sustainability. And I would reply, 'No, that all is sustainability work. If you keep taking out the profitable ones and say that sustainability is just the things that cost more, then of course it is not going to look like it is good business'. I have seen that so many times. Over time it should become more like, 'Well, that is just how we do business'. Right, exactly, that is what sustainability is supposed to be.

Uwe Schulte

I remember 10 years ago, we were starting an initiative with many FMCG[1] companies of looking at suppliers together to get to map compliance and a large drinks company said to me, 'We have reduced a lot of our packaging over the last few years. Can I count that as a step forward'? And I said, 'Of course you can, it makes sense!' And they would reply, 'But this saves cost'. So be it, that is great. Let us get back to the book. You have seen companies in the past trying to make sustainability efforts, but they get stuck in exceedingly small, incremental steps. You are now asking for more courage. How can that happen?

Andrew Winston

There are a lot of ways. Part of it is that some courage is forced upon us. There is just too much pressure and too much logic in going forward, so you get more courageous. It is hard for companies at this point, especially large ones, to avoid pressure from key stakeholders. It is clearly coming increasingly from investors. That can supply some courage because you know you must do this. It is coming from employees, more than any other group. And if you want to attract and retain talent, you must. But there is also something in what Paul and his new organisation IMAGINE[2] are doing. They gather CEOs from sectors and try to bring together enough for a tipping point for change across apparel or food. What they talk about is collective courage. There is something about working with others as you get to a tipping point in a sector or on a particular challenge. And we are getting there fast on sustainability in business, where it becomes easier because everybody is doing it, and you start to see the benefits of thinking big and being the leader rather than just waiting for others to set the stage. It is always a funny conversation about courage and leaders because CEO pay has gone up dramatically over the last 30 years. And I part jokingly say, 'What are we paying them for'? If you are getting that kind of money, you think courage would be an expectation from the board. But there is a weird thing where the more money people get, the safer they seem to be and that just seems like a big mistake. It is such an opportunity to be courageous.

---

[1] FMCG: Fast Moving Consumer Goods (e.g., Food, Drinks, Cosmetics).
[2] https://imagine.one/

Uwe Schulte

A particularly key point in your book is that you talk about that not everybody is ready for net positive, yet. But you can give some help there. Can you explain a little bit what you are trying to do there?

Andrew Winston

Look, we are thinking big, we must. Part of this is driven not just by some desire for two guys named Paul and Andrew that companies do more. We are basing this on thresholds, scientific thresholds, on things like climate, water, biodiversity, and moral humanity-based thresholds on sufficiency and people having enough in life to thrive. It is that doughnut economics, middle ground that we need to live in the safe operating space. That really shapes all of what we are talking about. But given the story that business has been operating in for so long, where they must maximise short-term shareholder value, it feels like a big leap. They do not feel ready. There are some things you need to do to get ready for the scale of thinking and effort that we are proposing. On the book website,[3] we posted a readiness assessment that a bunch of people have downloaded. It is just twenty-five questions. Some people have told me it gave them anxiety, which was not the purpose. But it is a big enough agenda that it makes people think, 'Oh wow, we have not really looked at that and maybe that is a problem'. The first few four or five questions are really the base of information and mindset that you need. For example, 'Do you know your footprint across environmental and social issues across your value chain'? Not every company does. A lot do, but many do not have a good sense of that. 'Do you know how the big mega trends and the big environmental and social issues affect your business and vice versa? Where do you contribute? Where do you get affected by them? Do you know what your stakeholders want? Have you asked employees what they expect of you, or your customers? What do these groups expect of you today and in the future'? It is those grounding exercises and information that some companies have a lot of in place. They have done sustainability reports for years, they have a good sense, and they are ready to say, 'Okay, what is next'? The next set of questions is harder. For example, 'What are the big, shared issues that your peers and you face on which you can partner? Do you know much about your human rights and your supply chain'? These are the tougher things that you start to ask. You can stage this in levels of getting your base information and then getting increasingly courageous with the things you take on (Fig. 3).

Uwe Schulte

Let us spend some time on your title again. We started that way, and we end our conversation on this one. A lot of people have now made commitments to net zero. And that, of course, only relates to carbon reduction. Your ambition is much wider than carbon, of course. And it is net positive and that is quite a leap. Let us first talk about what we mean by impact, and then talk about how we get to 'positive' there. What do you mean by impact?

---

[3] https://netpositive.world/what-is-net-positive/

Fig. 3 Doughnut Economics. Source: Wikipedia, CC BY-SA 4.0 DEED, Attribution-ShareAlike 4.0 International, Author: DoughnutEconomics, Source: own work

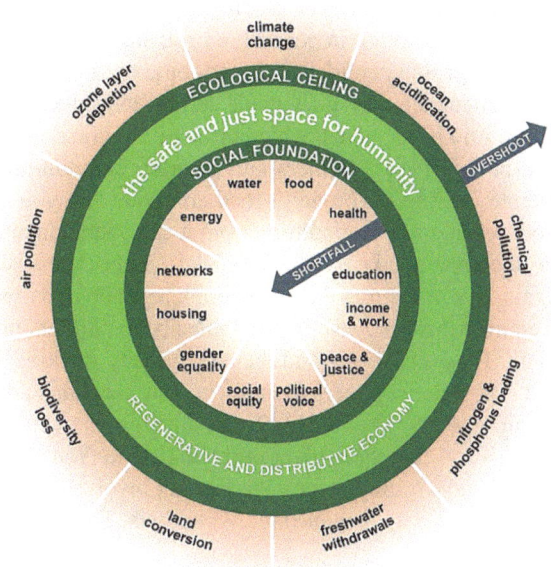

Andrew Winston

It is a good question and there have been a lot of people working on this from a metric perspective for a long time. Environmental is easier on some level. 'What is your carbon footprint? How much water do you use? How much waste do you produce'? The social site is harder, but there are lots of people getting better and better at putting metrics on it. But your impacts on people are quite broad. We start from: if you take this model of scope 1, 2, and 3 on carbon, we take that towards the end of the book and we say that it is not just carbon. There are other attributes. And there are several people who have proposed or suggested that there really is scope 4 or 5, 6. And we borrow from that, and build on it and say, you can go past your own supply chain and customers and look at the impacts of your whole sector and measure them. If you are food and agriculture, there is a piece of the world's carbon, and a piece of the world's land use and labour that is used for this set of products, and a huge portion of the human rights issues and supply chains with child labour and indentured servitude. You start to think broader about your sector. Bigger than even that sector view is your policy impact, your advocacy. This to me, the biggest, most important thing for the big companies to be thinking about, because they are being drawn into big discussions now. Not just 'should we have a carbon price', but 'how do we defend democracy', 'how do we defend truth and fact' and all these tough issues. And they must be part of the right side of policy, not just advocating for no policy. Most companies just look to reduce regulation to zero. That is what they think their purpose is. And we must shift that dramatically. If you start to think about, 'Okay, we have an impact on the policies that we embrace or, through our silence, allow trade associations to set the agenda on—we have an impact on the much larger picture of something like carbon or wages'. And then at the largest level there are impacts, for example, if you are a consumer products company, it could be on just consumption in general, on self-image. Unilever has addressed women and body image and confidence. It has come out that Facebook and some of its subsidiaries affect the way girls think about themselves. These are real impacts on the world. And if you take the human side of it, you do get more into thinking about the well-being of, say, farmers and farming communities and the communities they operate in. And if you are a food company, are you supporting policies that drive more regenerative agriculture? And it can sound daunting, I know, to say, 'How can I as a company take on hunger'? Well, part of the answer is that you are not alone. Again, in some sense, the whole book leads up to partnership, and that this is doable to address these big issues, but it must be in partnership. And that means you are not alone. There are others and they are already working on this if you have just come to it. There are suppliers, customers, and peers that are starting to work on it. There certainly are NGOs all over it and government agencies. You do not have to come into this to solve these giant problems alone. You cannot possibly. And that is both freeing and exciting to say, We can get involved in the larger story without saying that we are solely responsible'. Nobody is. That is not how it works.

Uwe Schulte

You are making two important points, and they are elaborated in the book but let us just focus for a second on them. To make positive impact, not just have an impact and live with it, but be restorative in tourism, for example, so rather than just not doing any harm on where you build a place, resort, or whatever, but restoring some of the nature and the cultural heritage. Doing that on your own will be extremely difficult and people must overcome that. And I believe what you are asking for is that if you can take leadership in your sector and drive it through advocacy, but also by putting your money where your mouth is, right?

Andrew Winston

Tourism is a good example. Right before the pandemic started, I spoke at a leadership meeting at one of the big cruise companies and they were flying high. They were building the biggest ships in the world; they were growing at exponential rates and their biggest sustainability issue was not health and pandemics. It was overtourism. It was killing these places like Dubrovnik and Venice. It is a fitting example, because you could see how a given tour company, a given cruise ship, or a given hotel chain could say, 'Well, we cannot just cut back because then we are disadvantaged'. Because you cannot solve the problem alone anyway. You would need to have some kind of agreement across all the cruise companies, across all the hotel companies with the local people. It must be sitting down with civil society and municipalities to do things like, 'This centre zone of this city is not open for these X hours, or we coordinate how many people come in'. That is what a net positive action starts to look like, where you think, 'How do we make it better for the people living there? This is their home. How do we bring them the economy of tourism and all of that, but not destroy what makes the place special'? These are tough issues. It is certainly not always easy to do this, but there are ways. And having these broader conversations can end up being great for everybody involved.

Uwe Schulte

You are quoting some good examples in the book. I can only recommend everybody to have a go. Maybe go to the website first, answer the questions and I hope it does not frighten you when you do that. That is great. Andrew, I would like to thank you very much for sharing these insights, and 'Net Positive' is something that will make its mark. And I know that anybody who is interested in it can buy it online or go to any good bookstore. Thank you, Andrew, for joining us today.

Andrew Winston

Thank you for inviting me. It was a pleasure.